Environmental Decision Making

Environmental Decision Making: A Multidisciplinary Perspective

Edited by
Richard A. Chechile and Susan Carlisle

Tufts University
Center for the Study of Decision Making
Medford, Massachusetts

VNR VAN NOSTRAND REINHOLD
New York

Library of Congress Catalog Card Number 91-19849
ISBN 0-442-00659-4

Printed in the United States of America.

Van Nostrand Reinhold
115 Fifth Avenue
New York, New York 10003

Chapman and Hall
2-6 Boundary Row
London, SE1 8HN, England

Thomas Nelson Australia
102 Dodds Street
South Melbourne 3205
Victoria, Australia

Nelson Canada
1120 Birchmount Road
Scarborough, Ontario MIK 5G4, Canada

16 15 14 13 12 11 10 9 8 7 6 5 4 3 2

Library of Congress Cataloging-in-Publication Data
Environmental decision making: a multidisciplinary perspective /
    edited by Richard A. Chechile and Susan Carlisle.
        p.   cm.
    Includes index.
    ISBN 0-442-00659-4
    1. Environmental protection—Decision making.   I. Chechile,
Richard A.   II. Carlisle, Susan.
TD171.8.E58   1991
333.7'068'4—cd20

91-19849
CIP

Contents

Foreword

The environment is the physical world in which humans and all other living things exist. The air, water, and land inextricably linked with all living things constitute the biosphere, which both affects the survival of living organisms and is affected by the actions of living things. In the last century and a half, we have seen the combination of rapid population growth and the industrial revolution cause significant environmental changes that affect the health and well-being of humans in both positive and negative ways, and affect the viability of thousands of species of plants and animals. Environmental science, policy, and management is indeed complex. We believe that understanding how to analyze and solve complex problems involving our natural environment will be one of the most important tasks for society in the twenty-first century.

Environmental Decision Making: A Multidisciplinary Perspective makes an important contribution to the art and science of decision making on environmental issues. The book is also an important contribution to an ambitious program at Tufts University designed to develop the intellectual capital necessary to have a future that will meet human needs and wants in an environmentally sustainable manner.

Moreover, the book is the result of two major thrusts of Tufts University. One is to have our students understand that no complex problem can be solved by paying attention to only one facet of the problem, no matter how important it is. The study of any complex problem must be multidisciplinary, and solutions must weigh a number of factors. Furthermore, most complex decisions must be made with incomplete, uncertain, and often conflicting information.

The second thrust of the University is to make an important contribution to environmental management by educating Tufts students to be environmentally literate and responsible citizens, and also to appreciate multidisciplinary research. An important component of this thrust is teaching environmental decision making that often involves sophisticated evaluation of data and the consideration of a number of fields of study which include science, social sciences, engineering, law, ethics, and aesthetics.

Tufts has pioneered in both these areas through two multidisciplinary units of the University: the Center for the Study of Decision Making, and the Center for Environmental Management. It is our hope that this book will be a useful tool in educating students to deal with a matter on which our world and that of future generations depend.

Jean Mayer
President of Tufts University

Anthony D. Cortese
Dean of Tufts Environmental Programs

Preface

This book is the result of a concerted effort of the Tufts University Center for the Study of Decision Making working with support from the Tufts University Center for Environmental Management. We at the Decision Center realized that there was no existing book on environmental decision making, and we realized that decision making was at the core of environmental problems as well as at the core of solutions to those problems. To meet this challenge, an Environmental Decision Making (EDM) group was formed by bringing together interested researchers from a wide spectrum of disciplines. The EDM group included individuals from 12 different disciplines each of whom has part of the story to tell in regard to environmental decision making. The EDM group met frequently in order to explore the problems, tools, discoveries, and challenges of environmental decision making. The EDM seminar series went on for more than a year and has lead directly to the present work. The resulting book is quite unlike most edited books, since all the chapters have been reviewed and debated by all the other members of the EDM group. We have found this project to be exciting and hope that this book will stimulate further developments in the environmental decision-making area.

This book is intended to be read at several different levels. For the interested nonprofessional and introductory university student, it represents an introduction to the problems and challenges of decision making and management in relation to the environment. For environmental professionals, the book provides a concise series of introductions to disciplinary approaches other than their own. For decision scientists, the book presents the new challenges that are posed in decision making in the environmental arena. For the advanced university student, end-of-chapter suggestions for additional reading, suggested projects, and questions are provided in order to stimulate further research. For everyone, special efforts have been made to present clearly technical and mathematical concepts without assuming advanced training in mathematics and science. Disciplinary jargon has been avoided or explained in order that the general reader can understand the issues without being a disciplinary specialist.

Finally, we wish to acknowledge the valuable contributions provided by members of the Tufts University Center for the Study of Decision making and the Tufts Center for Environmental Management. We appreciate the partial support provided by Corporate Affiliates Program of the Center for Environmental Management to the Decision Center for this project. We also appreciate the suggestions and stimulating discussion provided by Louis Rossman, William Gutowski, Thomas Kelly, and Norton Nickerson. We are deeply indebted to Jean Intoppa for her secretarial and organizatonal skills, Constance Putnam for her sharp mind and editorial pencil, and Judy Feldmann for her enormous contributions in helping to pull together many of the separate pieces of this project.

List of Contributors

Richard A. Chechile, Editor, is Director of the Center for the Study of Decision Making and Professor of Psychology at Tufts University. Professor Chechile received his B.S. and M.S. in physics from Case-Western Reserve University and his M.S. and Ph.D. in psychology from the University of Pittsburgh. He has worked in research and development for the General Electric Company, Rockwell International, and Philco Ford. The author of many publications in physics and psychology, he is also a member of the American Statistical Association, the Society of Mathematical Psychology, the Psychonomics Society, and the Judgment and Decision Making Society. Professor Chechile is one of the founding members of the Tufts Center for the Study of Decision Making. Currently, he is doing research in the areas of decision theory, mathematical psychology, cognitive psychology, and human factors.

Susan Carlisle, Editor, has been Curriculum Coordinator at the Center for the Study of Decision Making at Tufts University since 1981. A graduate of Cornell University with an M.A. from Boston University, she has taught English in the State University of New York and at Tufts. Since receiving a grant from the National Endowment for the Humanities to study French Civilization at Harvard, she has been writing on cultural differences in the handling of space. Publications include poetry and articles on the connection between French behavior and the built environment.

Hugo Adam Bedau is Austin Fletcher Professor of Philosophy at Tufts. Professor Bedau received his B.A. from the University of Redlands, M.A. degrees from Boston University and Harvard University, and his Ph.D. from Harvard University. Prior to joining the Tufts faculty in 1966, he taught at Dartmouth,

Princeton, and Reed. He is the author, coauthor, editor, or coeditor of 36 books and a 150 articles and reviews in philosophical, legal, and other journals and magazines. His research has been supported by grants from the Social Science Research Council, Russell Sage Foundation, American Council of Learned Societies, and he has held fellowships from the Danforth Foundation, Harvard Law School, and the National Endowment for the Humanities.

Patricia Dillon is a Senior Environmental Research Analyst at the Tufts University Center for Environmental Management. She has a B.S. in biology and an M.S. in environmental engineering from Tufts University. She specializes in corporate-environmental management, community management of chemical risks, and the Emergency Planning and Community Right-to-Know Act of SARA Title III. In addition to her research activaties, she has developed educational workshops on management of chemical risks for community leaders.

Dominic Golding is a Research Associate in the Department of Urban and Environmental Policy at Tufts University, and a Senior Research Associate at the Center for Technology, Environment, and Development at Clark University. He received his B.A. from Oxford University and his M.A. and Ph.D. in geography from Clark University. His research focuses on the social aspects of risk assessment and risk management. He has recently published a book entitled *The Different Susceptibility of Workers to Occupational Hazards*.

David Gute is a Assistant Professor at Tufts University with appointments in both the department of Civil Engineering and the department of Community Health at the medical school. Prior to joining the Tufts faculty in 1988, Dr. Gute served as an assistant commissioner responsible for personal and environmental risk-factor reductions with the Massachusetts Department of Public Health and as an epidemiologist with the Rhode Island Department of Health. While in these posts, he oversaw major environmental health-research studies including the ongoing investigation of childhood leukemia and adverse reproductive outcome in Woburn, Massachusetts and the investigation of food-chain exposure to PCBs in New Bedford, Massachusetts. Dr. Gute's research interests concentrate on the use of available data to delineate groups of people at excess risk due to either occupational or environmental exposure and in the planning of intervention activities. As a consequence of these activities he has dealt extensively with many different constituencies surrounding environmental problems including citizens, the media, public officials, and the private sector. Mr. Gute is an epidemiologist who received a Master of Public Health (M.P.H.) and a Ph.D. from Yale University.

Judith T. Kildow has a doctorate in Science Policy and International Relations from the Fletcher School of Law and Diplomacy, Tufts University. She has been on the faculty of the Department Ocean Engineering at M.I.T. since 1971, where she has taught and done research in the field of coastal and ocean policy and international-technology policies, with emphasis on environmental and common-property issues. She is currently on leave at the Fletcher School of Law and Diplomacy in order to build a new program in International Environmental Policy. Professor Kildow currently serves on the Marine Board of the National Academy of Sciences and has participated in numerous national commissions and committees.

Sheldon Krimsky is Professor of Urban and Environmental Policy at Tufts University. He received his bachelors and masters degrees from Brooklyn College, CUNY, and Purdue University, respectively, and a masters and doctorate in philosophy from Boston University. Professor Krimsky's research has focused on the social and ethical impacts of science and technology. He is the author of more than 70 papers and *Genetic Alchemy: The Social History of the Recombinant DNA Controversy;* and the coauthor of *Environmental Hazards: Communication Risks as a Social Process.* His latest book is *Biothechnics and Society: The Rise of Industrial Genetics.*

Stephen H. Levine received an Sc.B. and A.B. in engineering from Brown University in 1963 and an M.S. in electrical engineering from the University of Pennsylvania in 1964. From 1964 to 1970 he was employed primarily as a digital system-design engineer. He received his Ph.D. in electrical engineering from the University of Massachusetts in 1973 and then spent one year as a postdoctoral research associate in the Biological Sciences Department at SUNY/Albany. He was an assistant professor in the Department of Electrical Engineering at Merrimack College, North Andover, Massachusetts from 1974 to 1979 before coming to Tufts. At present he is an Associate Professor in the Department of Engineering Design at Tufts University. His interests include dynamic system and structural models, mathematical and computer models, adaptive systems, and optimization. Included in a wide range of applications are population biology and environmental systems, input-output–based models in both economics and ecology, the use of simulated evolution algorithms in interface design, and pattern representation.

William Moomaw is Director of the Tufts Center for Environmental Management. Dr. Moomaw earned his B.S. in chemistry from Williams College and his Ph.D. in physical chemistry from M.I.T. He joined the Tufts community after being Director of the Climate, Energy, and Pollution Program at the World Resources Institute (WRI). Prior to WRI, he was the Fitch Professor of Chemistry and Director of the Center for Environmental Studies at Williams College. Currently he serves as member of the Global Climate Change Subcommittee of the EPS's Science Advisory Board. He is also chairman of the steering com-

mittees of the Office of Interdisciplinary Earth Sciences at the University Center
for Atmospheric Research in Boulder, Colorado, and the American Chemical
Society's Task Force on Biotechnology and Toxic Substances. He is a member
of the American Chemical Society's Subcommittee on Regulatory Practices and
the World Resources Panel on Climate Change. He also serves on the editorial
boards of *The Global Climate Change Digest* and *The International Environmental Affairs Journal*. In the mid-1970s, he served as a legislative assistant on
environmental, scientific, and energy issues for the U.S. Senate after being
awarded a Congressional Science Fellowship by the American Association for
the Advancement of Science.

Kent E. Portney is Associate Professor of Political Science at Tufts University.
He received his A.B. degree from Rutgers, his M.A. from the University of
Connecticut, and his Ph.D. from Florida State. Professor Portney teaches
courses in methodology, public-policy analysis, judical politics, and survey
research. He is the author of *Approaching Public Policy Analysis, Current
Controversies in Environmental Policy,* and coeditor of *The Distributional Impacts of Public Policies.* He is also the director of the citizen-survey program at
Tufts' Lincoln Filene Center.

Ann B. Rappaport has been on the staff of the Tufts Center for Environmental
Management since 1984. She received her bachelors degree from Wellesley
College in environmental studies and Asian studies and she received her M.S.
from M.I.T. in civil engineering. She is currently conducting research on
environmental, health, and safety programs of multinational companies, with an
emphasis on how corporations respond to differing regulatory, social, economic,
and political climates in the various countries in which they have operations. She
is also working toward a doctorate in environmental engineering. Earlier she held
a variety of positions in the Massachusetts Department of Environmental Protection. As Deputy Director of the Division of Hazardous Wastes, she represented
the Division in efforts to site hazardous waste–handling facilities, and provide
staff assistance in legislative-commission efforts to draft Massachusetts' facility
siting law.

Peter P. Rogers is the Gordon McKay Professor of Environmental Engineering
and Professor of City and Regional Planning at Harvard University. He received
his bachelors degree from Liverpool University, his M.S. from Northwestern
University, and his Ph.D. from Harvard University. Professor Rogers is interested in developing plans for the environment and natural resources. Much of
his efforts are devoted to assessing methods of analysis. He is currently incorporating the technology of energy and water systems into macroeconomic
models and testing the models in actual settings where decisions are made. He is

also developing formal models for treating conflicts involving resources and the environment that cross political boundaries as well as models for financing and planning urban infrastructure. During 1989 he headed a panel for the U.S. Department of State to study the causes, effects, and remediation of the catastrophic 1988 floods in Bangladesh. He recently participated on an international panel to review the Aral Sea crisis for the Soviet Academy of Sciences. He is a Member of the Center for Population Studies at Harvard, and is currently writing a book on federal water policy.

Richard M. Vogel is an Associate Professor of Civil Engineering at Tufts University. He holds a Ph.D. in water-resource systems from Cornell University and B.S. and M.S. degrees from the University of Virginia. His primary expertise is in the application of systems methodologies and statistics to water-resource engineering problems. His research interests include the design, operation, and management of water-supply systems and the development of regional hydrologic models for flood-flow and low-flow investigations. He teaches courses in the area of hydrology, hydraulics, water-resource systems, statistics, engineering economics, and engineering management.

Walter Swap is Dean of Undergraduate Education at Tufts University, where is is also Professor of Psychology, a department he chaired for six years. He received his bachelors degree from Harvard University and his Ph.D. in social psychology from the University of Michigan. He is the general editor and a contributor to *Group Decision Making* and is the author of numerous articles on altruism, aggression, personality and attitude measurement, and terrorism. In 1983 he was awarded the Lillian Leibner Award for outstanding teaching.

Environmental Decision Making

Environmental Engineering

1

Introduction to Environmental Decision Making

Richard A. Chechile

1 ENVIRONMENTAL PROBLEMS AND DECISION MAKING

Our survival as a species on planet Earth has become an open question because of human-produced environmental degradation. We have stressed our environmental quality in many ways: by uncontrolled population growth and consumption rates, by industrial activity, and by careless waste disposal. Why have we done this?

In part, the answer to this question is that we have been ignorant of the complex interdependencies that occur in nature and only slowly have come to identify and appreciate these dependencies. We are beginning to understand that complex subsystems of the planet   such as oceans, land masses, and the atmo sphere—are not isolated from one another. But our ignorance is only partly to blame for our environmental problems. There are also cases where we have damaged our environment despite detailed knowledge of the complex ecological interdependency. We have made too many faulty decisions.

Human decisions are at the core of most actions affecting the environment. Consider for a moment the following questions:

- What are the environmental impacts of a planned action? Does human action or inaction pose worrisome risks to health and safety?
- What risks must be accepted by society and what is a fair policy for distributing those risks?
- What rights does the next generation have and how can we balance present needs with the needs of the future?
- What psychological factors contribute to exploitation of the environment? What psychological factors contribute to conserving environmental resources?

1

- What is a sensible and stable policy for harvesting a natural-food resource without undermining other natural resources?
- How can the aesthetic value of nature be balanced against the economic forces of development?
- How can a plan for providing society with an adequate supply of a natural resource (e.g., water) be developed?
- How can organized citizen participation affect the course of an environmental problem?
- What actions ought state or federal agencies take to protect environmental quality?
- How can international disputes over environmental policy be resolved?
- How can a company's long-term environmental policy be implemented in practice?
- How can we protect the environment while maintaining economic and technological development?

The need to make decisions on environmental questions of this sort is increasingly vital, yet few people have the tools or knowledge to understand or appreciate them in all their complexity. Individuals, policymakers, and corporations have influenced our environmental quality without fully considering the ecological system, often through the dynamics of existing incentives rather than the actions or inactions of "mean spirited" individuals.

For example, automotive engineers do not design automobiles in order to pollute the air. They design cars to satisfy many criteria; the final product reflects many trade-offs. A vehicle that pollutes the air could be the result of a series of decisions in which the impact on environmental quality was either unknown, ignored, or trivialized. While early automotive engineers were ignorant of the scope of pollution effects, why was the industry still slow to develop research directed toward pollution-reduced and pollution-free vehicles even after the problem of pollution became apparent? In part, the answer to this question is found in the industry response to regulatory standards. The imposed standard becomes a mere design constraint for the engineers. As long as the standard was satisfied, the car was not causing a pollution problem from the engineer's point of view. Without incentives for doing better in the elimination of polluting emissions, there is no reason to expect such improvements to occur. There are too many other design constraints. Consequently, the decision-making processes and the system of incentives used by the automotive industry determine, to a large extent, the degree to which its products remain a source of pollution.

Decisions are important not only because they are at the origin of environmental problems, but also because they are at the core of solutions to those problems. In fact, the solution to a given environmental problem often requires a host of decisions. Consider, for example, the question of what technology best produces transportation that is both affordable and environmentally safe. This one problem leads to the need to make other decisions, such as how much to spend on research and development (R&D), which R&D projects to support, and what the best available technology is. Thus, in general, the decision-making framework is essential for both understanding and dealing with environmental issues.

2 THE MULTIDISCIPLINARY FRAMEWORK FOR DECISION MAKING

While decision making is a vital human activity, only recently have decision sciences emerged as an academic field of inquiry. Formal decision-analytic tools have been applied in a number of different problem areas such as business, medicine, and military planning. While most decisions require a wide range of knowledge, the complexities of environmental problems are especially noteworthy for the extraordinary range of inputs required to produce an informed decision. For example, environmental problems often involve physical, chemical, biological, technological, economic, psychological, ethical, legal, and political factors. Omission of any of these factors is likely to oversimplify the problem and render the decision process incomplete and unrealistic. No academic discipline has a monopoly on environmental decision making; rather, the examination of environmental decisions requires an integrated effort from many disciplines. In fact, the National Environmental Policy Act of 1975 specifically states that "all agencies of the Federal Government shall (A) utilize a systematic, interdisciplinary approach which will ensure the integrated use of the natural and social sciences and the environmental design acts in planning and in decision making which may have an impact on man's environment" (p. 71:0101). Of course, it is more difficult in practice to examine a problem from multiple perspectives than it is to use the concepts of a single discipline, which perhaps accounts for the scarcity of multidisciplinary approaches.

The major premise of this book is that environmental decisions require a multidisciplinary understanding. To that end, this volume contains introductions to a number of quite different aspects of environmental decisions. Each chapter was designed to address the major issues, methods, premises, tools, shortcomings, and accomplishments that arise from a particular disciplinary viewpoint. In addition, we have included at the end of each chapter a set of additional readings and exercises for the reader to explore. While the chapters reflect different disciplinary frameworks and different aspects of the general problem of environmental decision making, the chapters have not been created in isolation from each other. The book is a product of the Tufts University Center for the Study of Decision Making. For nearly two years the Center held frequent meetings in which the contributors to this volume explored the subject area and developed the interdisciplinary perspective that these chapters contain. We believe the resulting volume is unique in its breadth, depth, and integration of varying disciplinary perspectives.

In the remainder of this chapter, a set of key concepts and distinctions in the decision sciences is provided in order to establish a common foundation for the rest of the book.

3 PROBLEM SOLVING, DECISION MAKING, AND ENVIRONMENTAL DECISION MAKING

Both problem solving and decision making take place in the context of some problem. The problem context includes all the constraints that define our current situation, including factors such as the rules we are required to follow, the budget and other resources available to us, and the cast of characters with which we must deal. It is important to remember that problem solving and decision making are always relative to the problem context. Given the problem context, some action might be required in order to achieve our desired objectives or goals. If there is only one way to achieve the objectives, then we have engaged in *problem solving*. Problem solving is important; however, most realistic problems do not have single solutions. When there is more than one possible alternative for attempting to obtain our objectives, then *decision making* is involved since we must select a course of action from a set of possible actions.

Environmental decision making occurs whenever a decision must be made that affects the present or future quality of the environment. Clearly, deciding how to dispose of hazardous waste is, foremost, an environmental decision. However, there are many other decisions where the environment is not the primary concern, yet the environment is affected by the decision. For example, when individuals decide whether to have another child or what type of diaper to use for their infants, they have made environmental decisions. Corporations and governmental bodies also make numerous environmental decisions. If it were easy to make good decisions on all issues affecting the environment, then there would be no need for this book; however, that is not the case.

4 DECISION PROCESS VERSUS DECISION PRODUCT

After a decision has been made, there is a chance (we hope a good chance) that our original problem will, in fact, be solved. There is also a chance that we will not have solved our problem. While everyone wants the result of their decision to be a good outcome, there are no guarantees at the time the decision is made. It is natural for people outside the decision sciences to focus on the *product* or result of a decision as a way to evaluate the quality of the decision; however, decision scientists realize that this is misleading. We could reason flawlessly, only to have a very rare and unfortunate event occur and undermine us. We might be victims of bad luck; decision scientists know not to question the wisdom of the reasoning or the decision-making *process* in such a case. Another time we could again reason flawlessly and exercise care in the decision process on a similar problem, and we might have better luck. Consequently, decision analysts emphasize the decision process and not the decision product: The best chance for a good decision product lies with a good decision process. Even when the outcome of the decision is good, decision scientists worry if the decision process is flawed. Luck may have been the key; next time a flawed process could cost dearly.

5 WHAT IS A GOOD DECISION?

If the alternative selected is from a *thorough set of alternatives and is efficacious, implementable, ethical, and "optimal,"* then we have done well. By efficacious we mean that the alternative must, in fact, be effective as a solution to the original decision problem. Moreover, the alternative must be capable of implementation and it should not violate any norms of ethical conduct. An ethical alternative would not only consider the rights and best interests of the party making the decision, but also give consideration to the rights and interests of those affected by the decision but not directly involved with the decision process.

Even if the selected alternative is efficacious, implementable, and ethical, it still may not be the best choice. If there is another alternative that is also efficacious, implementable, and ethical, and that alternative is preferable to the first alternative, then we have not selected the best available alternative. Consequently, the selected alternative must be an optimal choice (according to some set of criteria) from among the efficacious, implementable, and ethical alternatives. (The concept of optimal is discussed further in Section 8 of this chapter.) However, even if we select the optimal alternative that is efficacious, implementable, and ethical, we still may fall short of achieving a good decision. This can occur if we did not have a thorough set of alternatives and a better alternative than the one selected failed even to be considered. Clearly, it is a challenging and difficult task to decide wisely, and it is not surprising that so many poor decisions are made.

Another way to understand a good decision process, environmental or otherwise, is to look at the ideal processing steps involved in decision making and management. The ideal process is illustrated in Figure 1–1 as a sequence of six steps. If any of these six steps is poorly executed, then we have a flawed decision process. The six-step process is a prescription for a good decision.

Step 1 is problem identification and goal definition. This step starts the whole processing chain. Too often, people rush ahead to consider alternatives when they do not know what the problem is. The problem formulation should make clear what the current difficulty is and what the goals are. Obstacles should be

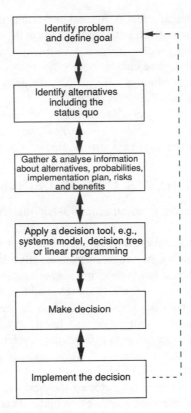

FIGURE 1–1.   The Six-Step Decision-Making Process.

spotted quickly or even anticipated. In the environmental area this step is particularly difficult because of scientific uncertainty and incertitude. The scientific community may be slow to detect problems or it may be slow to understand the issues. For example, the Antarctic ozone hole surprised the scientific community. While some scientists predicted a problem of ozone depletion from the widespread use of chlorofluorocarbons in refrigerants and aerosols, the Antarctic ozone hole, which began forming in 1975, was not detected until 1985. Problem identification is one of the most important steps in a decision analysis. We need to ignore nonproblems, but we need to recognize and clearly understand real problems.

Step 2 is to identify the alternatives that are candidate solutions. The failure frequently encountered here is lack of thoroughness in considering alternatives. Settling for the first good idea may save time, effort, and worry, but it can also lead to a disaster. Sometimes the status quo—no new action—is a reasonable alternative, particularly if there is reason to believe the problem will disappear of its own accord. In fact, in the National Environmental Policy Act of 1975, an alternative to any proposed action is required; usually that means the status quo is included in the set of alternatives.

In Step 3 we need to understand more deeply what each decision alternative really involves. How would an alternative be implemented? What outcomes might occur if a particular alternative is chosen? How acceptable are these various outcomes? What are the short-term and long-term considerations? What risks are involved and how acceptable are those risks? What probabilities are involved? What laws, ethical norms, and government regulations are applicable? Are there any good policies that apply to the case? Who are the people who understand the issues? What groups are affected by the decision? What political factors need to be taken into account? What benefits and costs are involved? What is unknown, but knowable? How can we come to know the missing information? What will remain unknown and unknowable at the time we must decide? These are the types of questions the decision maker should ask. Step 3 requires gathering information first and then thinking critically about each of the alternatives; it may require quantification. Most people fail to complete this step because it is so demanding.

Step 3 usually leaves the decision maker with an overwhelming number of facts, judgments, and opinions. Without a decision tool like a systems model (Chapter 3), or a decision tree (Chapter 4), or a linear programming model (Chapter 7), it is difficult to use all the available information consistently and coherently. Factors need to be traded off. That is, the decision maker may need to settle for less on one aspect of the case in order to gain more on another aspect.

Such trade-offs are difficult for the human mind to process completely; there is generally too much to remember. Consequently, in Step 4, a decision tool is applied (preferably one that permits some form of quantification). The result of Step 4 is usually a set of score values for the various alternatives. Based on these values and the decision objectives, a decision needs to be made. This is Step 5. Most importantly, after the decision is made, the plan still needs to be implemented. Thus step 6 is implementation and management of the decision. Without good management, even a good decision can be undermined. If we find that the decision is impossible to implement (e.g., it would require violating a law, or there is not enough money to procure the space and services needed), then that is an indication of an incomplete or poorly executed analysis in Step 3. Even if we understand how to put our decision into practice, actual implementation still requires skillful management if the desired outcome is to be achieved.

The arrows in Figure 1–1 illustrate the interconnections between steps, with the double-headed arrows indicating that we may return to a prior step (depending on what is discovered at a given step). For example, on examining the alternatives (Step 2), we may discover that we have not formulated the decision problem correctly. Thus, we will need to redefine the problem (Step 1). Finally, there is a dashed arrow from Step 6 back to Step 1, indicating that, in the process of managing a plan, we might encounter a new problem necessitating a new decision.

6 PRESCRIPTION VERSUS DESCRIPTION

Decision scientists frequently label their activity as being either a *descriptive* analysis or a *prescriptive* analysis. For example, Chapters 2 (psychological issues), 9 (political factors), 10 (governmental regulations), 11 (corporate framework), and 12 (international issues) provide largely descriptive analyses, whereas Chapters 3 (systems analysis), 4 (decision trees), 7 (resource allocation), and 8 (ethics) present mainly prescriptive points of view. Chapters 5 (risks) and 6 (economics) are a mixture of description and prescription. Generally, both descriptive and prescriptive analyses are important, and each framework is present to some degree in each chapter.

Descriptive decision analysis refers to the ways decisions are actually arrived at by real people and groups, regardless of the merits of the process. Researchers in psychology, sociology, and political science often observe irrational behavior in decision makers (Kahneman, Slovic, & Tversky, 1982). Researchers in descriptive decision making assume that an understanding of actual decision behavior is required to prescribe how decisions ought to be made.

Prescriptive decision making deals with how a good decision ought to be made. The six-step procedure shown in Figure 1-1, for example, is a prescription for the decision process. Prescriptive decision analysis emphasizes rationally consistent behavior in an effort to achieve the best solution to a decision problem. Researchers in this area acknowledge that people do not actually behave according to prescriptive norms. Nevertheless, the prescriptive analysis persists in recommending these norms for decision making, precisely because if followed they lead to demonstrably superior results. The prescriptive decision maker points out that the best solution is often not obvious and that special tools are needed in order to see the problem clearly. The tools are based on some assumptions and rely on human judgments. For example, scarcely anyone seriously believes that the six-step process for making a decision (Figure 1-1) is a bad idea or a flawed process. It is a general norm for how a decision ought to be made. However, one may argue with the results of a specific decision analysis, especially if one does not like the resulting decision. If your backyard is going to be adversely affected when a certain public-policy decision is implemented, then your reaction to the decision is likely to be very different from that of groups not directly affected by the decision. In Chapter 9 we address this issue in exploring the political processes that arise when citizens participate in environmental decisions.

7 UNCERTAINTY AND INCERTITUDE

Sometimes in decision making the outcome of an action is certain. For other actions, however, there is uncertainty. Uncertainty complicates the decision-making process. Chapter 4 deals with these issues in greater detail, but in anticipation it is useful to distinguish between two different types of uncertainty: *ordinary uncertainty* and *incertitude*.

Ordinary uncertainty is uncertainty about what will occur in the future even though one understands all the processes involved. For example, it is uncertain which card will be selected from a well-shuffled deck of 52 ordinary playing cards. Nevertheless, we understand what is involved in shuffling the deck, we know the backs of the cards all look alike, we know there are 52 cards in the deck, and we know each card in the deck is unique. Predicting the selected card involves ordinary uncertainty.

Incertitude differs from ordinary uncertainty; it arises when we do not have all the information. We may not know all the factors that are involved. For example, suppose a special deck of playing cards were made up by someone else who keeps from us a number of vital facts. This deck could have all aces or any combination of cards. We do not even know how many cards there are in the deck. Predicting which card will be selected in such a situation involves incertitude. One of the familiar 52 cards will still be selected, but now there is more vagueness regarding what the selected card will be.

Prescriptive models of decision making treat these two different cases as both involving uncertainty; however, psychological studies of how people form judgments find differences in these two cases. People prefer gambles with ordinary uncertainty to situations with incertitude (Curley & Yates, 1989). In decision making, we often must deal with both types of uncertainty. Even though the calculation of probabilities is complex, especially when incertitude is involved to any degree, there are methods that are tools for probability measurement.

8 WHAT IS OPTIMAL DECISION MAKING?

The whole point of decision making is to select the best alternative available. But what is the best alternative? One answer is to select the alternative that maximally satisfies some criterion against which all alternatives are judged. Decisions made on this basis are clearly optimal with respect to that particular criterion or dimension. However, rarely are *thoughtful* decisions based on any single dimension (such as affordability). Usually several different dimensions are important, for example, safety, profitability, and aesthetics. The best alternative with respect to one dimension might not be the best alternative in regard to another. If the same alternative is selected on each relevant dimension, then that alternative is called a *dominant* solution to the decision problem . Most problems, however, do not have dominant solutions. In Chapter 4, a measurement procedure is discussed that weighs all the individual dimensions of value so as to create a single, aggregated dimension of *utility* or perceived worth. Maximizing on the basis of an aggregated utility scale should result in the choice of an alternative that is adequate on each dimension and optimal in regard to overall utility, though it will not necessarily be optimal on any of the individual dimensions.

Determining utility is one of the more difficult problems in decision making, and it involves a number of judgments. However, the judgments of one individual often are not shared by others. When a group is deciding, it is difficult to say what the optimal utility alternative is. Where judgments are involved, we are not surprised that one person's best alternative is another person's worst. If there are only two alternatives and a group of equally powerful individuals, then the optimal utility alternative is the alternative with the majority of first-place votes. If, however, there are more than two alternatives, then we know there is no way to guarantee that the group utility satisfies all the requirements of a fair and rational voting system (see Chechile, 1984). There are many different voting methods possible, and the various methods can result in selecting different alternatives. Consequently, when groups decide, there may be no optimal utility alternative independent of the method for voting.

9 INDIVIDUAL AND ORGANIZATIONAL FACTORS THAT INFLUENCE THE DECISION OUTCOME

A decision can be made either by an individual or by a group. In both cases, we expect that the decision outcome is dependent to some degree on the characteristics of the decision makers. The decision process requires numerous judgments, and individuals can be expected to differ with respect to their perceptions, knowledge, and values. For example, individuals often vary in their willingness to accept risks and in their perception of those risks and of the potential benefits. Consequently, the best individual decision alternative should be expected to vary with characteristics of the decision maker.

For group decisions, the characteristics of the group members and leader, the group size, and the nature of the group task can all influence the outcome of the decision. While there is no universal formula for an ideal group, the descriptive analysis of group decision making does provide some general prescriptions that increase the chances of good environmental decisions. First, the group size ought to be large enough to contain the knowledge and opinions relevant to the decision problem. Second, since large groups result in less member satisfaction and more time to make a decision, the group size should not be any larger than it has to be in order to satisfy the first point. Third, the group leader should not be overly directive in the effort to reach agreement on a solution, since that could reduce the group's effectiveness in thinking critically about the decision problem. Fourth, since group pressure for conformity and cohesiveness can impair the group's critical thinking, divergent positions ought to be thoroughly examined. (Swap, 1984, discusses these and other issues at length.)

10 HOW ARE ENVIRONMENTAL DECISIONS DIFFERENT?

To some degree environmental decisions are simply a special class of decisions—those about or affecting the environment. Instead of the problem being environment-neutral, like "What colleges should one apply to," the decision problem is one that has an impact on the environment. The six-step procedure and other tools can be used in both environment-neutral and environment-relevant cases. Common human failings to behave prescriptively without proper training or tools tend to occur in both kinds of cases. Both can be serious and life-threatening; both are often complex and require a multidisciplinary analysis. In fact, the need for a multidisciplinary approach has been emphasized in the previous books produced through the Tufts Center for the Study of Decision Making (Hill, 1978, 1986; Swap, 1984). However, environmental decisions also have at least seven aspects not common in other decision-making applications.

First, while many decision problems in business, education, or medicine are complex, environmental decisions are generally far more so. The decision sciences typically prescribe simplifying a problem to its essential elements. Environmental problems are less easily simplified than others. As mentioned earlier, the elements in an ecological system are highly interconnected; the consequences of an action are difficult to determine and more difficult to evaluate. Bad environmental decisions can occur when the decision maker oversimplifies the problem. For example, Moomaw (1989) points out that narrowing the focus too sharply in regard to reducing atmospheric carbon dioxide can possibly make a greenhouse warming effect worse. This could occur (1) if we were to increase oceanic photosynthetic rates through ocean fertilization, and (2) if microorganisms were to convert dead plants to methane in the oxygen-deficient water. The remedy is to use a systems model, and Chapter 3 examines, in more detail, issues associated with this type of approach.

Second, in addition to greater scope, environmental decisions frequently have a greater degree of incertitude. In many cases we simply do not have a thorough scientific understanding; we are unable to predict or envisage all the possible outcomes and consequences. In other cases we do not know what the courts will award in damage settlements if a catastrophe occurs. As mentioned above, techniques for dealing with decisions involving incertitude are discussed in Chapter 4.

Third, since the ecological system is a system with inertia, decision actions today may not immediately produce the desired results. The system is a dynamic system requiring an examination of the changes over time. This point is explored further in Chapter 3.

Fourth, environmental risks and hazards stimulate citizen involvement. In many decision-making areas, such as deciding on a computer system or an investment, the public does not generally mobilize into a visible citizen-action group the way it does on environmental decisions that may affect the health of people and the value of their back yards. Citizen involvement results in political pressures that are not typical of other decision problems. The consequences of this active role by citizens are explored directly in Chapter 9 and indirectly in Chapter 10.

Fifth, environmental decisions challenge orthodox notions concerning utility in economic models. Economists typically estimate the worth of a recreational area, such as a river, by evaluating only the actual usage of the area. However, there are many others who value the opportunity to vacation someday on that river. Traditional economic analysis has ignored utility of this second type, but thoughtful and responsible environmental decision analysis requires dealing with utility in its fullest sense. Such considerations are discussed in Chapter 6.

Sixth, classic Western ethical thought is challenged when individual and corporate conduct is evaluated from the environmental perspective. This problem is explored at length in Chapter 8, and a reformulation of ethical decision making is proposed that is more appropriate for dealing with environmental decisions.

Seventh, technological development has been so rapid that international environmental decision-making disputes need to be resolved in nonstandard ways. For example, normal diplomacy among nations is too slow to be effective in dealing with global warming issues. This topic is addressed in Chapter 12.

Undoubtedly, there are many other ways environmental decisions are different, but these seven aspects illustrate the claim that environmental decision making is not just the application of traditional decision-theoretic concepts to environmental problems. Environmental decisions pose some new challenges for the decision sciences.

Finally, the authors of this book are concerned about both technological development and preserving our environmental quality. We believe that it is not acceptable to optimize development regardless of environmental cost, and we cannot expect to reduce environmental risks to zero. Since neither extreme can be achieved, tough trade-off decisions are required. Our belief is that such trade-offs should be made only with a rich appreciation of all dimensions of the problem.

REFERENCES

Chechile, R. 1984. Logical foundations for a fair and rational method of voting. In *Group Decision Making*, ed. W. C. Swap. (pp. 97–114). Beverly Hills, CA.: Sage Publications.

Curley, S. P., and J. F. Yates. 1989. An empirical evaluation of descriptive models of ambiguity reactions in choice situations. *Journal of Mathematical Psychology* 33:397–427.

Hill, P. H., ed. 1978. *Making Decisions: A Multidisciplinary Introduction*. Reading, MA.: Addison-Wesley.

Hill, P. H., ed. 1986. *Making Decisions: A Multidisciplinary Introduction*. Lanham, MD.: University Press of America, Inc.

Kahneman, D., P. Slovic, and A. Tversky, eds. 1982. *Judgment Under Uncertainty: Heuristics and Biases*. Cambridge: Cambridge University Press.

Moomaw, W. R. 1989. Our record with the environmental crystal ball. *EPA Journal*, May/June: 37–39.

Swap, W., ed. 1984. *Group Decision Making*. Beverly Hills, CA.: Sage Publications.

2

Psychological Factors in Environmental Decision Making: Social Dilemmas

Walter C. Swap

1 INTRODUCTION

Should an upper-middle class German couple decide to limit the size of their family? Should nomads on the edge of subsistence in the African Sahel do the same? Should I trade in my gas guzzler for a more fuel-efficient, cleaner-burning car? Should a farmer bordering the Amazon rain forest decide to clear-cut another acre of jungle? All these questions deal with decisions concerning the use, or misuse, of the resources—food, air, energy—to which most people have ready access. The systems containing such resources are called *commons*.

Such questions all involve trade-offs between short-term needs, economy, or comfort and the long-term effects of satisfying them. The sub-Saharan family's additional child will add incremental pressures on available food, fuel, and water in an already stressed environment. Yet the immediately felt need for the security of having children may override those future considerations. Can the same be said of the German couple, whose child will undoubtedly draw more than the Sudanese from world food and fuel supplies? My Chevy wagon is big and comfortable, and I can afford to support its gasoline habit. Have I the right to criticize the Brazilian farmer's behavior as shortsighted, contributing to the accumulation of carbon dioxide in the atmosphere and possibly to global warming?

Of course, uncertainty adds to the complexity of decisions like these. Former Administrator of the Environmental Protection Agency, William Ruckleshaus, recently commented on the difficulties of "trying to get a substantial proportion of the world's people to change their behavior in order to (possibly) avert threats that will otherwise (probably) affect a world most of them will not be alive to see."*

Source: From Ruckleshaus, W. D. 1989. Toward a sustainable world. *Scientific American* 261:166.

14

Such social dilemmas present a challenge to those whose faith in human rationality and technological innovation has led to a "don't worry, things will work out" attitude. The particular social dilemma that is the subject of this chapter may well have no technological solution. As we shall see, rationality may actually intensify the dilemma. It is the thesis of this chapter that we must look beyond technology and pure rationality for solutions to environmental dilemmas; that the social sciences, particularly psychology, may offer insights into these solutions.

2 THE TRAGEDY OF THE COMMONS
AS A MODEL SOCIAL DILEMMA

Biologist Garrett Hardin's "The Tragedy of the Commons" (1968) has long since become a citation classic, an honor bestowed on those works that have been referred to in print more than 100 times, as tallied in the *Scientific Citation Index*. Political scientists, demographers, philosophers, psychologists, economists, historians, and biologists have been much taken by Hardin's cold logic in charting the rush to ruin for those who exploit common resources. Consider his basic argument: A field of sweet grass is freely available to all herdsmen or farmers who wish to pasture their cattle there; the animals are then brought back to private property for milking or slaughter. So long as the number of beasts is sufficiently low that the grass can grow back quickly enough to satisfy their hunger fully, all goes well. In the fall, when a rational Farmer Jones must decide whether to take his heifer to be courted by Farmer Brown's bull, he will certainly decide to do so, since the family's well-being is measured in part by how much milk or beef is produced. But after a few years, a point is reached when the commons can no longer fully support all the animals that utilize it. Weeds begin to spread through the closely cropped grass, and all the cows are a little less plump. Now fall has once again arrived. What is Farmer Jones to do?

Consider Jones's decision-making process as he pursues a rational course. Jones knows that the *carrying capacity* of the land has been reached, that an additional cow will incrementally stress the environment, resulting in a slightly smaller yield per cow for all who use the commons. However, if Jones adds that additional cow, while the costs will be diffused among all who use the commons, his family alone will derive the full benefit of its pasturage. Self-interest, therefore, dictates he should decide to breed his cow. Ah, but Jones is not alone in his ability to pursue this remorseless logic. Brown, Smith, and Johnson each make identical decisions, and the following year the commons is severely overgrazed.

Suppose Jones is fully aware of the situation, however, including the inclinations of his neighbors. Should he not, therefore, voluntarily refrain from breeding his stock? Not at all. He should add another cow *even so,* since to decline to do so would merely reward his neighbors for their rapacity. He would, in fact, have been exploited, with a smaller number of undernourished cows compared to his neighbors. Understandably refusing to be thus abused, Jones increases his herd and the "Tragedy of the Commons" unfolds. In the oft-quoted words of Hardin, "freedom in the commons brings ruin to all" (1968, p. 1244).

In Figure 2–1, the tragedy of the commons is demonstrated with a concrete example. This commons has a carrying capacity of 40 cattle. Farmer Jones has ten cows, as does each of three other farmers, thus reaching the carrying capacity of the commons. Each cow gets its fill of sweet grass and attains its maximum weight of 1000 pounds. For purposes of this example, we shall assume that additional cows will deplete the commons at an accelerating rate. Thus, if one cow beyond 40 is added, each of the 41 will attain a weight of 970 pounds; if two are added, each of the 42 will weigh 930 pounds; if three are added, the 43 cows will each eventually weigh 880 pounds; and, if each farmer adds one additional beast, each of the 44 resulting cows will weigh 820 pounds. Figure 2–1 illustrates the outcomes for Farmer Jones and for the *average* of the other three farmers in the four cases in which Jones either adds or does not add an additional cow, and the other three all either add or do not add another. If we assume that Jones wishes to maximize the weight of his herd, then he might engage in the following line of reasoning: "Suppose I knew for a fact that my neighbors each plan simply to maintain the present size of their herds. Then clearly I should add to mine, since my 11 cows will each be a little thinner, but together they will give me 10,670 pounds of meat rather than 10,000. Suppose instead that I know positively that my neighbors will each add to their herds. Then, obviously, I should do the same; if I do not, I will be left with only 8800 pounds of beef, while if I do, my 11 cows will weigh a total of 9020 pounds." Thus, *regardless* of what Jones's neighbors do, it is in Jones's self-interest to add another cow. But the real tragedy occurs when each of the others, employing the same line of reasoning, does exactly the same thing. The result is, from the perspective of maintaining the commons, the worst possible joint decision, that in the lower-right box. *No matter what the other farmers do, Jones's rational choice is to add that other cow.*

In this example, rationality has clearly failed, as each farmer, pursuing his own self-interest, dooms the common good by reaching the *least*-rational joint decision. But suppose one of the farmers altruistically sows a new super-hybrid grass that grows twice as fast as the native variety. This technological advance allows the herd to be doubled, but merely delays the day of reckoning; when the tragedy of the commons is fully played out, the result is that twice as many beasts (and their owners) suffer.

Hardin's metaphor of the village commons may be applied to other

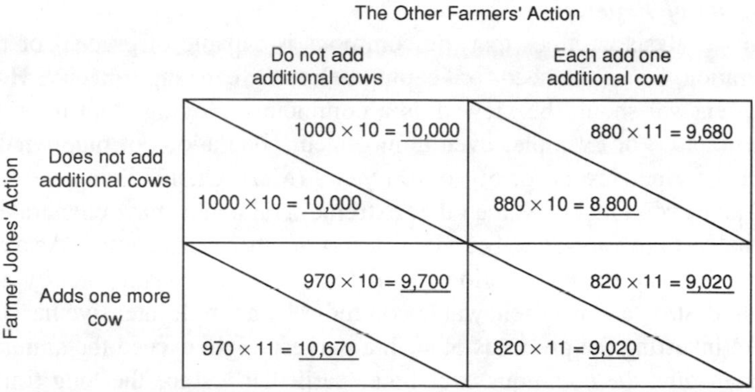

The Other Farmers' Action

FIGURE 2–1.   Payoff Matrix Representing the "Tragedy of the Commons." *Note:* The total weight of Jones's herd is represented *below* the diagonal; the average weight of each of the other farmers' herd is represented *above* the diagonal.

resources.[1] A special issue of *Scientific American* (September 1989) on managing the environment featured articles on such commons as air, soil, groundwater, timber, and the biosphere (e.g., fish, whales, denizens of rain forests, or elephants), and the effects of rapidly increasing human populations (particularly in developing countries) on these commons. Under pioneering conditions, free and unlimited use of these commons exerts little or no destructive pressure, and future generations are assured of a continuing, bountiful supply of the common resource. However, under pressures of increasing population, technological advances in harvesting, and the absence of external controls, carrying capacities may be quickly exceeded. If rationality and technology are useless or, far worse, counterproductive, where are the solutions?

2.1 A Typology of Commons

It would be a serious error to assume that all environmental commons have identical dynamic elements. The likelihood of exploitation, or the ease of management of a common resource, will surely be determined by a number of probably varying factors or dimensions. In some commons, solutions must be sought in economics or the political process, whereas in others, psychological findings may be most directly useful or applicable. The following typology is meant to suggest the complexity of an often oversimplified concept, as well as to point to those commons dilemmas where psychology is likely to be most useful.

---

[1]In reality, the European grazing commons was a successful management system for a millennium (Cox, 1985; Levine, 1986), succumbing at last to privatization (enclosure) in the last century. As Levine writes, "Hardin . . . presented the scientific community with a parable—not a history lesson" (1986, p. 82). This does not in the least, however, diminish the usefulness of Hardin's analysis for understanding the essential nature of environmental commons dilemmas.

2.1.1 Rate of Renewal

Hardin's analysis assumes that the commons is capable of gradual or periodic regeneration, hence the need for keeping below the carrying capacity. However, rate of renewal should be viewed as a continuum, ranging from unobservably slow to rapid. For example, even unmolested, populations of blue whales may not reach former levels for 50 to 100 years (McHugh, 1977); redwood forests would take even longer. At the other extreme, grasslands may regenerate almost continually if not allowed to become a desert or otherwise degrade. As a result of this variable rate of regeneration, it may sometimes be *economically* advantageous to destroy a slowly renewable commons by a rapid, intensive harvest. The value of investing the proceeds of such a harvest might exceed the annual return from managing the commons over time, particularly since the long time frame precludes people currently utilizing the resource from benefiting in the future (Fife, 1971).

2.1.2 Reversible Versus Irreversible

Other factors being equal, one would expect that if a commons cannot be "brought back" after its carrying capacity is exceeded, users of the commons might be more cautious than if the consequences were no more severe than the necessity of a replanting. Much of the worldwide outrage at the rape of the Amazon rain forest stems from the belief that the damage—both to biological diversity and to the atmosphere—cannot be reversed, that "extinction is forever." The problem, of course, is that we seldom know whether a commons can come back, or how long it might take. Can global warming be reversed? Depletion of the ozone layer? Damage to Prince William Sound? Making credible, accurate information available is an essential first step in averting irreversible damage.

2.1.3 Subjective Resource Value

Certain commons (e.g., breathable air, potable water, fertile soil) have immediate or near-term human-survival value. Clear threats to these commons will normally arouse concern. Other commons are imbued with high emotional value. Thus, threats to whales, elephants, condors, or bald eagles, none of which is strongly linked to human survival or widespread economic benefit, have taken on great symbolic and psychological significance and, consequently, have aroused heroic efforts to maintain them. Yet the species of fungus or mite that is quietly and anonymously extinguished in the wake of rain-forest clearing, having no advocates, passes without our giving it much or any thought, even though the genetic diversity that is sacrificed might someday be of great practical value. One would expect psychological processes of public-opinion formation to be particularly important in raising the subjective value of commons with minimal current economic value. Consider the case of the snail darter, a rather unprepossessing fish that once held up construction of a major dam that threatened its existence, thanks to the persuasiveness of its vocal advocates.

What may seem to be profligate waste from one group's perspective may appear quite different from another's. Even tropical deforestation, which most people in the North consider an unmitigated evil, is viewed by many in tropical countries as far less of a sin than either the economic alternative of *not* farming the land (particularly given the uncertain effects of deforestation on global warming), or the prodigal release of greenhouse gases by their cousins in the North (Radulovich, 1990).

2.1.4 Uncertainty

Without changes in policy, some commons are sure to be extinguished. E. D. Wilson (1989) has estimated that, in the Amazon basin, between 4000 and 6000 species are being extinguished *annually*. On the other hand, the prospect of substantial global warming is far from assured, even at projected increased levels of carbon dioxide and other flux in the atmosphere (Beardsley, 1989). The imminent certain destruction of a commons will arouse greater concern than one whose demise is doubtful (Brann & Foddy, 1987). Clearly, however, the subjective *value* of the threatened commons will interact with the likelihood of its destruction to determine concern and action. While significant global warming may be uncertain, because of the high subjective value of the atmosphere, considerably more concern is generated (e.g., McKibben, 1989) than for the assured extinction of a Brazilian mite or fungus. One way around this problem of uncertainty is to plan interventions that, even if the disaster fails to materialize, will provide "tie-in benefits" (Schneider, 1989). Thus, reducing pollutants by increasing energy efficiency and developing alternative sources of energy will provide benefits regardless of whether global warming becomes a reality.

2.1.5 Scale of Utilization

The tragedy of the commons is often viewed as a variant of the "free-rider" problem in economics. If an individual can conveniently refuse to contribute to the common good, he or she may nonetheless enjoy all the benefits of that good. While often discussed in the context of labor-union membership, the farmer who adds to his herd while his fellow farmers restrain themselves or the suburbanite who sprinkles the lawn during a water emergency are also free riders. As the size of the group utilizing the commons increases and the chance of being observed decreases, free riding should become more likely (Stroebe & Frey, 1982). On the other hand, social psychological research on the closely related "social loafing" phenomenon (Latané, Williams, & Harkins, 1979) reveals that the diffusion of responsibility resulting from participation in large groups can be reduced either through surveillance (e.g., checking water meters during a drought emergency) or by helping people feel their contributions are unique or significant (e.g., providing feedback on progress toward a conservation goal).

2.1.6 Dominion (Jurisdiction): Global to Local

The high seas, Antarctica, and outer space characterize the "global" end of this continuum; small lakes are typically controlled more locally. The atmosphere is an example of a commons that is considered local by most users, but may have global effects (e.g., through the production of acid rain). "In the absence of clear property rights to the resource and of a coordinating arrangement based on some rule other than that of willing consent, the resource will be unnecessarily depleted" (Baden, 1977, p. 139). The economic solution frequently proposed is "privatization" of the commons, forcing users to pay the price of irresponsible management directly (see Section 3.1 in this chapter and Chapter 6).

2.1.7 Stationary and Fugitive Commons

Some commons "stay put," and are much more likely to fall under local dominion than are "fugitive" commons, which cross areas of jurisdiction. Thus, people might dump waste into a lake that lies wholly within a town's boundaries or into a river that flows through several other towns. If both the lake and the river are treated as commons by the people who live alongside them, the people along the lake will become more motivated to restrict their polluting than those along the river, whose despoliation is visited only upon those living downstream. Similarly, industries responsible for acid rain have little immediate motivation to limit their behavior, since effects are felt only downwind, in other states or countries. Political solutions are often the only recourse for those downwind or downstream.

2.1.8 Ubiquitous Versus Scarce

Godwin and Shepard (1979) have argued that the emergence of institutions to allocate ubiquitous resources such as air is rare. As clean air becomes scarce, it is more likely that institutions will be created to manage it. Problems develop when a currently ubiquitous resource (e.g., petroleum) is projected to become scarce in the future, but consumers at present see little reason to restrict their use.

2.1.9 Iterated Versus One-shot

Typically, users of a commons interact with one another over time. They extract resources, they may monitor others' behavior and the status of the commons, and they may decide to moderate their future behavior. Some researchers have studied different type of commons, where all users make a single simultaneous decision as to whether they will exploit or conserve the commons (as in sealed bids for oil leases in Alaska). In the absence of any feedback or possibility of influencing the behavior of other users, this "one-shot" utilization tends strongly to encourage exploitation (Dawes, van de Kragt, & Orbell, 1988).

2.1.10 Framing: Taking from or Giving to the Commons

Maintenance of a commons may take two forms: restraining use of resources (e.g., limiting electricity usage to prevent a brownout) and contributing resources (e.g., donating food for famine relief). While the tragedy of the commons generally refers to the former, and the latter is usually labeled the "public goods" problem, the two are functionally, if not psychologically, equivalent. As Kahneman and Tversky (1984) have demonstrated, people are more likely to risk incurring large, uncertain, future losses than to accept a smaller, immediate certain loss. Conversely, when contemplating a gain, people tend to prefer an assured small gain to a larger, but uncertain, future gain. Social psychologists have extended this reasoning to commons situations, demonstrating that people respond differently to a declining common resource depending on whether the dilemma is framed as a matter of taking or giving. When the commons is to be maintained through contributions, users tend to be less supportive of the commons than when maintenance occurs through restraint in taking (Brewer & Kramer, 1986). Fleishman (1988) has found that users will look to others to determine how much to take from a declining commons, taking little when others show restraint and taking much when others are greedy. Just the opposite occurs when the commons depends on users' contributions: A person tends to donate more if others are stingy, and donate less if others are generous. As Fleishman (1988) has concluded, "Framing a social dilemma in terms of giving may facilitate diffusion of responsibility."

Table 2-1 summarizes the preceding analysis. This is not meant to be an

TABLE 2-1   Variables Affecting Exploitation of Commons

	Exploitation of Common Resources Is	
	More Likely	Less Likely
1. When resources are:	slowly renewable	rapidly renewable
2. When effects of exploitation are:	reversible	irreversible
3. When resources have:	low subjective value	high subjective value
4. When resources are:	not certain to be depleted	certain to be depleted
5. When resources are:	utilized by many	utilized by few
6. When the commons has:	unclear property rights	clear property rights
7. When the commons is:	fugitive	stationary
8. When resources are:	ubiquitous	scarce
9. When use occurs:	once only	repeatedly
10. When the commons is maintained by taking:	and other users are greedy	and other users show restraint
11. When the commons is maintained by giving:	and other users are generous	and other users are selfish

exhaustive list of how commons may differ from one another, but it probably contains the most significant factors.

No attempt has been made to order these factors in terms of their importance. One could infer, however, that a commons characterized by conditions under the column headed "More Likely" would slide effortlessly into overuse and tragedy. As conditions shift to those under the column headed "Less Likely," the likelihood increases that decisions will be made that avoid a tragedy of the commons. The remainder of this chapter will deal with ways in which this shift might be accomplished. I will first look briefly at economic and political solutions that have been suggested, and then examine in more detail the contributions of psychology to averting the tragedy of the commons.

3 FACTORS THAT PROMOTE
CONSERVATION OF THE COMMONS

An unwillingness to forego short-term gains in the interest of continued future benefit when others may not be trusted to behave similarly is the essence of the tragedy of the commons. Despite the self-evident nature of the desired goal, ways to accomplish it are elusive. Most proposed solutions have focused on factors that either induce people to change their current behavior (e.g., limit their use of the commons) or change their relationships with others sharing the commons (e.g., develop trust that others will limit their use). Most nonbehavioral scientists tend to emphasize the former, often openly scorning proposals that depend upon building trust or cooperation among users of a commons. Psychologists seem more willing to entertain both types of solutions.

3.1 Nonpsychological Solutions to the Commons
Dilemma

Many proposals to solve commons dilemmas tend to be variants of a common economic theme, nicely expressed by Ruckelshaus (1989): "The central lesson of realistic policymaking is that most individuals and organizations change when it is in their interest to change, either because they derive some benefit from changing or because they incur sanctions when they do not . . ."* This view of human nature is echoed in psychological behavioral analysis approaches to the problem (see Section 3.2.1).

Despairing of a "technical" solution to the tragedy of the commons, Hardin (1968) originally proposed that "mutual coercion, mutually agreed upon" is the best hope. Essentially, people must freely choose to be punished by one another

---

*Source: From Ruckleshaus, W. D. 1989. Toward a sustainable world. *Scientific American* 261:168.

for exploitative behavior (and, presumably, be rewarded for conserving behavior). Ruckelshaus (1989) seems to be arguing for this position when he asserts that the tragedy of the commons can be avoided if consumers are required to pay the *full* cost of a resource, including environmental costs. He refers to this as "closing the loops in economic systems."*

Hardin's proposal differs from a Hobbesian Leviathan, in which a coercive central state is accepted by the people because, however hateful, it creates a social order out of anarchy and destructive competition. Hardin's vision is far more benign, relying on an enlightened populace to recognize its own inability to avoid the tragedy of the commons and to guard against it by freely choosing a central authority to monitor and punish inappropriate behavior. (One is reminded of the dieter instructing a friend to "Hit me if I reach for another cookie!")

Yamagishi's (1988) research clarifies the conditions under which people caught in a commons dilemma are likely to opt for a system of sanctions to compel conservation. In a laboratory analog of a commons dilemma, Yamagishi demonstrated that as the dilemma becomes more serious (i.e., the gains to be achieved by cooperating increase in tandem with incentives for defecting), group members are more willing to institute a system of punishing noncooperators. In his analysis, the original commons dilemma (whether to forego individual outcomes for the general good) has been replaced by a secondary dilemma (whether to cooperate in changing the system). Thus, as the commons deteriorates and utilizers of the commons find themselves unable to cooperate in conserving resources, they become more willing to cooperate in *forcing* conservation.

A variant of this system is socialism. Exploitation of natural gas fields offers a useful illustration (Pierce, 1987). In an open (commons) system, each person whose land lies above part of the gas dome is motivated to tap into it and draw off the gas as quickly as possible, to maximize short term personal profit. However, this reduces the pressure needed to pump underlying oil. Under a system called "unitization," landowners organize and designate a committee to manage the resource, distributing profits equitably.

A second solution to the tragedy of the commons is essentially to change the entire management system. Generally this means privatizing the commons. Historical examples abound: extending the territorial fishing limits to 200 miles, fencing the American prairies, the enclosure movement in England. Maine lobstermen enjoy greater harvests from waters with controlled access than from common, open areas (J. A. Wilson, 1977). If the users of a resource must now personally suffer the consequences of overexploitation, they will be motivated to manage it effectively. There are difficulties with this proposal, however. One is

---

Source: From Ruckleshaus, W. D. 1989. Toward a sustainable world. *Scientific American* 261:169.

that inequities frequently develop: Who is to be disenfranchised from the commons and included in the privatization? (The enclosure movement in England increased inequities by enriching the nobility at the expense of small farmers and herders.) Furthermore (as pointed out in Section 2.1.1), it might be economically advantageous under certain circumstances to exploit a commons totally rather than to manage it over time. Finally, privatization is often simply impractical (as in the case with fugitive resources).

3.2 Psychological Solutions

Purely economic or political solutions to the tragedy of the commons, those that fail to take individual and group psychology into account, cannot possibly deal effectively with what is, after all, the ultimate goal of an effective environmental strategy: to change people's motivations, attitudes, and behaviors toward the commons. If people *want* to be environmentally responsible, the need for political or economic sanctions to compel behavior will be less.

Proposals by psychologists to influence the decisions of commons users include those that aim to modify existing attitudes and behaviors concerning resource use, and those whose goal is to create among users a fundamentally different way of viewing one another. The following sections deal with these two major themes.

3.2.1 Incentives and Punishments: Behavior Analysis

One psychological approach most nearly approximates the thinking of many economists, in that people are assumed to behave predominantly in their own self-interest. Concern is far less with changing people's awareness of the commons or their conceptions of one another than with changing the offensive behavior itself, primarily through the use of sanctions. For example, Platt (1973) views the tragedy of the commons as a "social trap," caused when short-term rewards reinforce immediate behaviors and lead to long-term adverse consequences for all. His proposed solutions are directly derivable from basic principles of learning theory: changing the time interval to make the long-range negative consequences more immediate; adding counterreinforcers (e.g., punitive laws) for exploitative behaviors; and positively reinforcing more appropriate short-term behaviors.

One particularly effective application of behavioral principles to the area of home energy conservation utilized a variety of interventions: daily feedback to participants of their electricity use, a tape providing information about the energy crisis, and a "modeling" tape that included specific techniques of thermostat control (Winett et al., 1982). The greatest savings (25%) in energy use were obtained when these interventions were used in combination. Furthermore, people who had demonstrated conservation during the experiment continued to show savings during a follow-up period.

The importance placed on feedback in the Winett et al. (1982) experiment is shared by most behaviorists. Discrepancies between the feedback and the target behavior provide information essential to modifying behavior. Such feedback must be credible (e.g., must come from a reliable, unbiased source) and frequent. Monthly or bimonthly electricity or gas meter readings are virtually worthless as mechanisms for altering behavior, since they summarize energy use over long intervals. But a device that beeps when outside temperatures are low enough to turn off the air conditioner can be very useful. Such feedback is particularly likely to be effective if the consumer is already motivated to conserve and if the likely personal savings are substantial (Stern & Oskamp, 1987).

Critiques of behaviorist approaches have ranged from economic (some of the reward systems have cost more than the energy savings) to humanistic (the approach evokes a "brave new world" dehumanized view of people incapable of responding to environmental crises for other than selfish reasons). The most telling criticism, however, is that the effectiveness of behaviorist approaches has generally been limited to small-scale interventions. Attempts to modify behaviors in large institutional settings, or where overall savings would be substantial, have had little success. Nonetheless, behavior analysis gives researchers reason to be optimistic in that it is generally far easier to change the situations that affect human behavior than it is to change inner motivations or personalities.

3.2.2 Attitudes: Public Opinion and Persuasion

A second approach to modifying people's use of commons comes from social psychology. Social influence forms the core of this discipline, so it is not surprising that social psychologists have studied ways in which attitudes toward conservation, and subsequent behavior, can be altered to avoid the tragedy of the commons. Consider, for example, Indonesia's successful effort to encourage family planning. "Educational programs promote the notion that a family should be 'small, happy and prosperous.' The barrage of public messages about family planning is relentless: The national family-planning jingle plays when a train passes a railway crossing, religious leaders give lectures on contraception at the local mosque . . . , and at five o'clock every afternoon sirens wail to remind women to take their pill."* Such an approach incorporates a number of well-honed persuasion principles, including education, repetition, and credibility of the communicator.

Since 1981, *New York Times*/CBS polls have asked respondents whether they agree or disagree with the following statement: "Protecting the environment is so important that requirements and standards cannot be too high, and continuing environmental improvements must be made regardless of cost." Agreement has soared from 45% in 1981 to 80% in 1989 (Ruckelshaus, 1989). Public opinion, particularly in a democracy, assumes considerable importance. Not only does

---

Source: From Keyfitz, N. 1989. The growing human population. *Scientific American* 261:124.

knowledge of people's environmental attitudes frequently permit prediction of how those people will actually treat the environment (Weigel & Newman, 1976), but elected officials must seriously consider prevailing attitudes when they enact legislation. Furthermore, shared attitudes often form the basis for well-organized groups of citizens whose combined voices may exert considerable influence through lobbying and public-information campaigns (Bish, 1977). The resulting outcry may be "so widespread and demanding that it generates enough political force to bring about the establishment of a regulatory agency to insure the equitable, just, and rational distribution of the advantages among all holders of interest in the commons" (Crowe, 1969, p. 1106). While Crowe is skeptical about the long-term effectiveness of such agencies, the crucial point is that public attitudes, if strongly and widely held, can translate into both private behavior and public policy. How those attitudes form and change is the province of the social psychologist. What follows are some of the specific recommendations that follow from social psychological research on persuasion and attitude change.

1. *Tailor conservation messages to people's attitudes.* Seligman (1986) surveyed families in New Jersey and related their attitudes toward energy use and conservation to actual energy consumption. The most consistent finding was that the more people were concerned with their personal comfort and health, the more home energy they consumed. Seligman concluded: "Rather than being exhorted to make sacrifices to energy conservation, people should be told of the ways they can save energy and be comfortable at the same time" (p. 169). Francis (1983) found that once people felt that the environment was in worse condition than the economy, they were open to a variety of steps (e.g., social action, increased taxes) to restore environmental quality.

2. *Dramatize clear and present dangers.* People are reluctant to modify their energy consumption or other forms of commons exploitation if they feel the crisis is chronic or will become acute only in the future. There seems to be an abiding belief that human ingenuity will solve all future problems before they become present crises. Yet wartime experiences of conservation and rationing, and peacetime experiences with crises such as the 1976–77 water shortage in California, show that people will dramatically alter their behavior when the crisis is perceived as a real and present danger (Seligman, 1986). Thus, while *certainty* of the crisis encourages sacrifices, there are many instances (such as global warming) where such a claim cannot yet legitimately be made. In that case, information campaigns could focus on other factors in Table 2–1, such as value, irreversibility, or scarcity, to create the level of concern necessary to instigate constructive action.

Social psychological research on emotional appeals is particularly relevant in this context. Research has repeatedly demonstrated that a persuasive communication that dramatically emphasizes the negative consequences of persisting in an undesirable behavior will have greater impact than a less emotional appeal (Leventhal, 1970). Such messages, often designed to evoke a certain amount of fear in the audience, are particularly effective when combined with specific instructions on how to alleviate the fear-producing situation. For example, showing how depletion of a commons such as breathable air can have powerful and dramatic effects on health must be combined with a set of steps that citizens and industries can take to reduce the threat.

3. *Present information as personally and vividly as possible.* Although statistics and "talking heads" might present more information, people tend to be more swayed by vivid examples, even when those examples might not be representative of the facts. Nisbett, Borgida, Crandall, and Reed (1976) give the example of the person contemplating the purchase of a Volvo. Having consulted *Consumer Reports* and discovered the Volvo's outstanding repair record, he announces his choice to a friend, who regales him with the story of a brother-in-law who had nothing but trouble with his Volvo. While, rationally considered, this story should add only one datum to the thousand or so cases in *CR*, it is likely to take on greater value because of its vividness and immediacy.

Similarly, Yates and Aronson (1983) recommend that, to encourage home energy conservation, one could point out local families who are "super conservers," indicating what they have done to conserve and how much money they have saved. On a wider scale, these findings suggest that simply informing people of the square mileage of the *Exxon Valdez* disaster or the annual percentage of the Amazon rain forest being razed will be insufficient to galvanize public opinion and action. Vivid photographs and descriptions of oil-soaked seals and vanished species, particularly if related personally by actual observers, will add substantially to the impact.

4. *Use visible and credible models.* As just suggested, personal experiences, vividly presented, can powerfully influence behavior. The mass media, television included, have a rather limited effect when it comes to persuading people on issues more important than deodorant choices. Much of their impact seems to be limited to setting agendas of what the important issues are, without actually persuading people what their attitudes should be (Iyengar & Kinder, 1987). Real people, on the other hand, can be far more influential. Direct modeling of energy-conserving behavior has been shown effective by Aronson and O'Leary (1982–83). Recall also that, in the study by Winett et al. (1982) of energy conservation, a modeling videotape proved effective in inducing appropriate behavior in viewers. If these people then serve as models for their friends and neighbors, the behavior can gradually "diffuse" through the population.

Yates and Aronson (1983) suggest that the normal social-diffusion effect can be accelerated by "cultivating visible and credible models." These models would persuade other opinion leaders who would in turn serve as models for larger numbers. The recent emergence of high-visibility rock music and motion-picture stars as spokespeople for an endangered Earth typifies this approach. A benefit concert, "Don't Bungle the Jungle," was organized by Madonna in New York City; Robert Redford was prominently featured in the Prince William Sound cleanup.

5. *Create opportunities for behavioral commitments.* Consider a chap named Ralph, who is not particularly bothered by the threat of overpopulation in developing countries. However, Edna induces Ralph to donate $5 to a group favoring increased aid for population control, and to solicit contributions from several of his friends. When asked why he is doing these things, Ralph responds that he now thinks overpopulation is one of the most serious issues affecting world commons. The theory of cognitive dissonance (Festinger, 1957) attempts to explain this sort of change in attitudes. When an individual believes or behaves in ways that are psychologically inconsistent (dissonant), he or she will feel uncomfortable and will be motivated to restore consonance. This is normally accomplished by changing either the attitude or that behavior that is in dissonance. In Ralph's case, the attitude "I am not bothered by overpopulation" is dissonant with "I have donated $5 for population control; also, I have persuaded three of my friends to contribute." To restore consonance, he brings his attitude in line with the behaviors and becomes a population-control advocate.

Sometimes dissonance can be induced directly, by simply reminding people that their behavior and attitudes seem inconsistent. Kantola, Syme, and Campbell (1984) reminded high consumers of electricity that they had earlier expressed attitudes favorable toward conservation. When provided with feedback about their energy use and given a booklet explaining specific ways to conserve, these people conserved more energy than did controls, both during the two weeks of the study and two weeks later.

Usually the key to creating high levels of environmental concern and subsequent constructive action is to induce people to make an initial verbal or behavioral commitment to the cause. For example, Pardini and Katzev (1983–84) found that simply asking people to commit orally or in writing to recycle newspapers was effective. Pallak and Cummings (1976) induced homeowners to agree to conserve energy. Those who were told their names would be mentioned in a public report on the results were more likely to conserve than were those told their names would not be used. One year later, the public-commitment group was still using less energy. In a study by Arbuthnot et al. (1976–77) interviewers made from zero to three requests of people related to recycling. These requests included asking them to answer a survey, save cans for a week, and send a postcard supporting recycling to a government official. The greater the number of behavioral commitments requested by the experimenters, the more people began recycling, both during the study itself and in a follow-up 18 months later.

The results derived from cognitive-dissonance theory indicate the importance of people's need to view themselves as consistent. However, for dissonance to be an effective motivator, people must feel that their behavior has real consequences. "Thus, to the extent that people act in the absence of coercion; publicly commit themselves to act in front of others; or invest time, money, or personal prestige in an activity, they come to see themselves as believers in that sort of activity and develop a personal interest in it" (Yates & Aronson, 1983, p. 441). Particularly noteworthy in the studies cited above is the repeated finding that the behavioral results endure over time. This suggests that the effects of dissonance reduction have been internalized and may serve as guides to behavior long after the original dissonance was created.

3.2.3 Group Communication, Discussion, and Negotiation

The tragedy of the commons dilemma arises when users of a commons are unwilling to forego short-term individual benefits for long-term group benefits. Even when people realize that the best solution would be to restrict one's usage, trusting others is a risky business (see Figure 2–1). Behavior analysis and attitude research have addressed the first component of the dilemma—how to induce users to change their short-term behavior. However, in the absence of some system for ensuring trust in the other users' willingness to conserve, such solutions are likely to be only temporary, to disintegrate at the first signs that one is being exploited.

To examine ways to change relations among users of a commons, psychologists have developed laboratory analogs of commons dilemmas. While there are a number of these analogs, they share certain essential features. Consider the one I have used with some success as a demonstration in college classes and management seminars. Three participants are told that the goal of the "game" is to "earn as many points for yourself as you can, where points should be considered a valuable resource." People are told specifically that they need not try to "beat" the other participants. The "commons" in this demonstration is a pool of 100 points, from which the three "users" may draw during a series of rounds. Each user decides privately how many points he or she will harvest, up to a maximum of 25 on each round. To make the commons renewable, they are told that after every third round, any remaining points will be doubled, up to the maximum of 100 (the "carrying capacity"). No communication is allowed. The game typically begins with one or two users asking for 25 points, and the third user taking 10 or 15. Thus, after only one round, over half the points have been extracted. The game often ends after the second round, when the third user tries to make up for lost points by extracting 25 and the other two users take 10 or 15. Very seldom does the game ever reach the point where any points are left to be doubled. In other words, the "tragedy of the commons" is almost always played out. When I then ask who "won" the game, participants usually rather sheepishly admit that nobody won, given that the game could theoretically have continued forever had they each limited their harvest to about five or six points per round (the maximum harvest that would leave 50 points to be doubled after three rounds).

Sometimes, however, I have a second trio play the game, but with one additional rule: The three may discuss strategy with one another prior to making their (still private) choices. When this is done, most groups arrive at a coordinated strategy that succeeds in preserving the commons. The group discussion seems to have several different effects. First, it enables the participants to clarify the rather complex game. For example, it is far from obvious at the start that users should restrict their choices to five or six points on each round; most people intuitively feel that about twice that number will work. The result is, therefore, to shift the focus from immediate gratification to long-term consequences. Second, discussion provides a forum within which participants can make promises about future behavior, even though the rules of the game permit defection. The importance of *commitments* (see Section 3.2.2) is clearly relevant here. In two related experiments, Orbell, van de Kragt, and Dawes (1988) demonstrate how potent promise-making is in maintaining the commons—but only when *everyone* promised. [These studies are particularly noteworthy, since a one-shot design was used (see Section 2.1.10), thus strongly encouraging exploitation. Despite this, more than 80% cooperated when all had promised to do so.] Third, discussion may serve the function of establishing a group identity, thereby enabling members to consider the overall welfare of the group (see Section 3.2.4); typically this will result in shifting the game from an individualistic to a more cooperative one.

The implications of this research are clear: Even when exploitation of a commons is obviously the rational individual decision, the opportunity to discuss strategy with all other users of the commons can lead to wise group decision making.

3.2.4 Group Identity, Trust, and Community
Group identity can result from a variety of other processes besides group discussion. Similarity to other commons users (Smith, Beli, & Fusco, 1988) and shared group membership (Kramer & Brewer, 1984) both relate to cooperative, nonexploitative use of commons in laboratory analogs. Appeals to kinship ("saving the planet for our grandchildren") also reflect an attempt to foster conservation through group identity, in this case with future generations. There is a seductive appeal to the sense of community to be enjoyed by fellow passengers on Spaceship Earth as the ultimate solution to the tragedy of the

commons. In dismissing purely economic solutions, Boulding (1977) has elegantly queried, "What, then, is the answer [to the tragedy of the commons] if it is not property, primogeniture, and class? The only answer to the tragedy of the commons is the comedy of community" (1977, p. 286).

In his careful analysis of proposed solutions to the commons dilemma, Edney (1980) proposed two alternatives, one of which is essentially a variant on privatization (see Section 3.1); the second is the need to develop greater trust and community. Although such a solution may lie outside traditional scientific logic, Edney argues that the inherent intractability of the tragedy of the commons compels nontraditional solutions. We know, for example, that individuals who are intrinsically trusting (Brann & Foddy, 1987), cooperative, or altruistic (Liebrand & van Run, 1985) are less exploitative in simulated commons with diminishing resources. To the extent that such motives can be induced in people, Edney's "illogical" goal could be realized. There is some irony in the fact that some of the strongest historical support for the importance of community in maintaining the commons is found in the traditional medieval European grazing commons. Levine (1986) argues that it was just this ethic of group solidarity that prevented the tragedy from actually occurring. The community set limits on the number of animals allowed per person, and these "stints" were "backed by the intense norm of solidarity" as well as by more formal sanctions.

More recently, Berkes et al. (1989) have argued that Hardin confuses *open access* systems, in which there are no well-defined property rights, with *communal property*, where a group of users manage the resource (including limiting access to the resource). They give numerous examples, such as beaver hunting in Canada and woodcutting in Nepal, where loss of control over resources by local communities resulted in near destruction, whereas restoration of that communal control has returned the resources to sustainability. Indeed, one should not underestimate the ability of groups to exert self-regulation of resources over which they have communal ownership.

3.2.5 Personal Norms of Responsibility
for the Commons

One danger when there is a high degree of group solidarity is a tendency to develop feelings of exclusiveness and superiority that can actually have a devastating effect on a commons shared with an equally cohesive "out-group." In the absence of some superordinate regulatory agency, for example, whalers or fishers might strongly distrust their counterparts from other nations and attempt to exploit the commons "before the other guy gets there first."

Therefore, an even more powerful restraint on exploitation is the expansion of these "we-boundaries" to encompass all users, accompanied by the activation of personal moral norms supporting the commons. The focus of action thereby shifts from "What is in it for me?" to "What is right?" Fleishman (1988) has demonstrated a strong relationship between feelings of personal responsibility and willingness to contribute resources to a diminishing commons. In Schwartz's (1977) formulation, once individuals become aware of the negative consequences caused by some event and then take some responsibility for averting these consequences, the result is a moral obligation to act. As Stern and Oskamp (1987) have suggested, when polluters downplay the health risks of their effluents, they are attempting to prevent the activation of moral norms in the public. "It is possible to examine public pronouncements about pollution and toxic wastes as a struggle over the moral norms of the citizenry. At stake are corporate profits, political power, environmental quality, and public health" (Stern & Oskamp, 1987, p. 1055).

Although it is easy to discard notions of creating widespread moral norms as unrealistic, the increasing concern with maintaining the global commons for future generations has much of the flavor of a moral norm. As William C. Clark recently wrote, "Building a capacity for adaptive management of planet Earth will require a desire and an ability to reflect continually on the values and objectives that guide our efforts."*

4 CONCLUSIONS

This has of necessity been a suggestive, rather than an exhaustive, review of the contributions of psychology toward helping us avert the numerous potential tragedies that lurk about most environmental commons. Perhaps the most serious omission from the discussion is a consideration of world population trends. In virtually every example of a commons dilemma, carrying capacity is exceeded not because of a natural reduction in the ability to produce the resource (indeed, world food harvests continue to grow), but because of pressures on the resource brought on by the increasing number of users. It naturally follows that efforts to stabilize or reduce population will alleviate many commons crises (Ehrlich & Ehrlich, 1990). Social scientists, including demographers, sociologists, and psychologists, have been in the vanguard of educational, persuasive, and political campaigns to help nations bring their populations into balance with their resources.

Understandably, some people are skeptical about acknowledging the potential contributions of psychology to solving environmental dilemmas. Laboratory analogs are often criticized as artificial and unrepresentative of real-world dilemmas. For example, only about one third of total U.S. energy use is residential, but little psychological research has been done on energy consumption in the industrial sector—and government support for such costly and difficult research is inadequate (Freudenberg, 1989). Psychologists, burdened with stereotypes of

---

*Source: From Clark, W. C. 1989. Managing planet Earth. *Scientific American* 261:54.

inkblots and phallic symbols, are often not taken seriously by policymakers, who feel that economic, political, and engineering solutions need not take human behavior centrally into account. Finally, part of the blame for failing to translate psychological research into policy decision making rests with psychologists themselves. Failure to take the perspective of policymakers, reluctance to make clear recommendations, and an unwillingness to take political realities seriously are among the shortcomings that have been mentioned (Freudenberg, 1989, p. 139).

Why, then, should we take seriously the contributions of psychology detailed in this chapter? In the first place, psychological research findings demonstrate how exploitative behavior toward the commons may be moderated. Behavior analysis indicates quite precisely how, for example, to go about modifying consumers' home energy or water usage. Social psychologists inform us how best to persuade people to make personal decisions of the sort that must be made if the commons are to be managed effectively. The importance of group discussion in arriving at coordinated decisions has been demonstrated. Perhaps more important than pointing toward these modest but demonstrably effective tactics, psychology alerts us to strategies that are far more difficult to realize, but that lie at the heart of the tragedy of the commons: shifting our perspective from short-term, personal benefits of environmental exploitation to the long-term welfare of future generations; engendering a sense of community and trust with other users; and making norms of individual responsibility for the commons salient. The challenge is to extend these findings from the commons created in the psychologist's laboratory to the behavior of all of us who share in the responsibility for managing Earth's commons.

EXERCISES

1. Consider the example of the "Tragedy of the Commons" used at the beginning of this chapter—that of a farmer deciding whether to increase the size of his herd. Assume that the carrying capacity of the commons is reached with the present number of 40 cows. Assume further that increases beyond 40 will result in decreased weight of each cow according to the formula suggested in the chapter, that is, 41 cows will each weigh $1000 - 30 = 970$ pounds, 42 will each weigh $970 - 40 = 930$, 43 will each weigh $930 - 50 = 880$, and so on until with 48 cows the average weight will be so low (480 pounds) due to energy expenditure in foraging for scarce grass that all will die if dependent exclusively on the commons for sustenance. Construct a payoff matrix corresponding to the following situation:

Each farmer (including Farmer Jones) may add 0, 1, or 2 cows to their herds. (Hint: Set up the matrix as a 3×7 table, with Jones's choices as adding 0, 1, or 2 and the other farmers' choices ranging from 0 to 6.) With this situation, is it possible that the commons will "crash," leading to extinction of the herd? What is the most rational behavior for Farmer Jones from a self-interest point of view? Is there anything inherent in the system to prevent extinction? What other factors would likely enter in if this were a real-world problem? How might these lead to a solution that would preserve the commons?

2. Suppose the three farmers other than Jones formed a corporation so the commons is now grazed by two parties, Farmer Jones and the corporation of the three farmers. Re-analyze the project 1 matrix, using the total of the three farmers versus Jones. Determine the optimal solution for each party. Try carrying out the analysis a second year. Discuss these results in terms of long-range versus short-range planning and social pressures to achieve a negotiated solution so that the behavior of the farmers results in stabilization of the commons at or below the carrying capacity.

3. For the case below, analyze the situation *without* a matrix—that is, discuss the case in the general sense that people might perceive the case without using mathematical analyses. In particular, consider three commons similar to the one described in Exercise 1, but this time build in the reasonable factor of mortality (including death by disease, predators, and slaughtering) in the herd. Specifically, suppose that in Commons #1, average annual mortality has always been low (10–20% lost per year); in Commons #2 the rate has been high (40–50% lost per year); and in Commons #3 the rate has historically been high but, due to new inoculations, last year only 10% of the herd was lost. What do you think the behavior of farmers in each of the three commons is likely to be? What effect is that behavior likely to have on each commons?

Relate your answer to the reproductive behavior of people in developing countries, where advances in medical science have drastically reduced infant mortality rates.

ADDITIONAL READINGS

For further reading on the stabilization and management of the commons see Berkes, Feeny, McCay, and Acheson (1989) and Cox (1985). For a review of the psychological factors involved in environmental management, see Stern and Oskamp (1987). For further reading on social influence in inducing behavior change regarding the commons see Edney (1980), Kramer and Brewer (1984), and Seligman (1986).

REFERENCES

Arbuthnot, J., R. Tedeschi, M. Wayner, J. Turner, S. Kressel, and R. Rush. 1976–77. The induction of sustained recycling behavior through the foot-in-the-door technique. *Journal of Environmental Systems* 6:353–366.

Aronson, E. and M. O'Leary. 1982-83. The relative effectiveness of models and prompts on energy conservation: A field experiment in a shower room. *Journal of Environmental Systems* 12:219–224.

Baden. 1977. A primer for the management of common pool resources. In *Managing the Commons*, eds. G. Hardin & J. Baden. pp. 137–146. San Francisco: Freeman.

Beardsley, T. 1989. Not so hot. *Scientific American* 261, (5):17–18.

Berkes, F., D. Feeny, B. J. McCay, and J. M. Acheson. 1989. The benefits of the commons. *Nature* 340:91–93.

Bish, R. L. 1977. Environmental resource management: Public or private? In *Managing the Commons*, G. Hardin and J. Baden, pp. 217–228. San Francisco: Freeman.

Boulding, K. E. 1977. Commons and community: The idea of a public. In *Managing the Commons*, eds. G. Hardin and J. Baden pp. 280–294. San Francisco: Freeman.

Brann, P. and M. Foddy. 1987. Trust and the consumption of a deteriorating resource. *Journal of Conflict Resolution* 31:615–630.

Brewer, M. B. and R. M. Kramer. 1986. Choice behavior in social dilemmas: Effects of social identity, group size, and decision framing. *Journal of Personality and Social Psychology* 50:543–549.

Clark, W. C. 1989. Managing planet Earth. *Scientific American* 261:46–54.

Cox, S. J. B. 1985. No tragedy on the commons. *Environmental Ethics* 7:49–61.

Crowe, B. 1969. The tragedy of the commons revisited. *Science* 166:1103–1107.

Dawes, R. M., A. J. C. van de Kragt, and J. M. Orbell. 1988. Not me or thee but we: The importance of group identity in eliciting cooperation in dilemma situations: Experimental manipulations. *Acta Psychologica* 68:83–97.

Edney, J. J. 1980. The commons problem: Alternative perspectives. *American Psychologist* 35:131–150.

Ehrlich, P. and A. Ehrlich. 1990. *The Population Explosion*. New York: Simon & Schuster.

Festinger, L. 1957. *A Theory of Cognitive Dissonance*. Evanston, Ill.: Row, Peterson.

Fife, D. 1971. Killing the goose. In *Managing the Commons*, eds. G. Hardin and J. Baden. pp. 76 81. San Francisco: Freeman.

Fleishman, J. A. 1988. The effects of decision framing and others' behavior on cooperation in a social dilemma. *Journal of Conflict Resolution* 32:162–180.

Francis, R. S. 1983. Attitudes toward industrial pollution, strategies for protecting the environment, and environmental-economic trade-offs. *Journal of Applied Social Psychology* 13:310–327.

Freudenberg, W. R. 1989. Social scientists' contributions to environmental management. *Journal of Social Issues* 45:133–152.

Godwin, R. K. and W. B. Shepard. 1979. Forcing squares, triangles and ellipses into a circular paradigm: The use of the commons dilemma in examining the allocation of common resources. *The Western Political Quarterly* 32:265–277.

Hardin, G. 1968. The tragedy of the commons. *Science* 168:1243–1248.

Iyengar, S. and D. R. Kinder. 1987. *News That Matters*. Chicago: University of Chicago Press.

Kahneman, D. and A. Tversky. 1984. Choices, values, and frames. *American Psychologist* 39:341–350.

Kantola, S. J., G. J. Syme, and N. A. Campbell. 1984. Cognitive dissonance and energy conservation. *Journal of Applied Psychology* 69:416–421.

Keyfitz, N. 1989. The growing human population. *Scientific American* 261:118–126.

Kramer, R. M. and M. B. Brewer. 1984. Effects of group identity on resource use in a simulated commons dilemma. *Journal of Personality and Social Psychology* 46:1044–1057.

Latané, B., K. Williams, and S. Harkins. 1979. Many hands make light the work: The causes and consequences of social loafing. *Journal of Personality and Social Psychology* 37:822–832.

Leventhal, H. 1970. Findings and theory in the study of fear communications. In *Advances in Experimental Social Psychology,* ed. L. Berkowitz. Vol. 5, pp. 119–186. New York: Academic Press.

Levine, B. L. 1986. The tragedy of the commons and the comedy of community: The commons in history. *Journal of Community Psychology* 14:81–99.

Liebrand, W. B. G. and G. J. van Run. 1985. The effects of social motives on behavior in social dilemmas in two cultures. *Journal of Experimental Social Psychology* 21:86–102.

McHugh, J. C. 1977. The rise and fall of whaling: The tragedy of the commons illustrated. *Journal of International Affairs* 31:23–33.

McKibben, B. 1989. *The End of Nature.* New York: Random House.

Nisbett, R. E., E. Borgida, R. Crandall, and H. Reed. 1976. Popular induction: Information is not always informative. In *Cognition and Social Behavior,* eds. J. S. Carroll & J. W. Payne. pp. 113–134. Hillsdale, NJ: Erlbaum.

Orbell, J. M., A. J. C. van de Kragt, and R. M. Dawes. 1988. Explaining discussion-induced cooperation. *Journal of Personality and Social Psychology* 54:811–819.

Pallak, M. S. and W. Cummings. 1976. Commitment and voluntary energy conservation. *Personal and Social Psychology Bulletin* 2:27–30.

Pardini, A. U., and R. A. Katzev. 1983–84. The effect of strength of commitment on newspaper recycling. *Journal of Environmental Systems* 8:471–481.

Pierce, R. J. 1987. State regulation of natural gas in a federally deregulated market: The tragedy of the commons revisited. *Cornell Law Review* 73:15–53.

Platt, J. 1973. Social traps. *American Psychologist* 28:641–651.

Radulovich, R. 1990. A view on tropical deforestation. *Nature* 346:214.

Ruckleshaus, W. D. 1989. Toward a sustainable world. *Scientific American* 261:166–175.

Schneider, S. H. 1989. The changing climate. *Scientific American* 261:70–79.

Schwartz, S. H. 1977. Normative influences on altruism. In *Advances in Experimental Social Psychology,* ed. L. Berkowitz. Vol. 10, pp. 221–279. New York: Academic Press.

Seligman, C. 1986. Energy consumption, attitudes, and behavior. In *Advances in Applied Social Psychology,* eds. M. J. Saks and L. Saxe. Vol. 3 , pp. 153–180. Hillsdale, NJ: Erlbaum.

Smith, J. M., P. A. Beli, and M. E. Fusco. 1988. The influence of attraction on a simulated commons dilemma. *Journal of General Psychology* 115:277–283.

Stern, P. C. and S. Oskamp. 1987. Managing scarce environmental resources. In *Handbook of Environmental Psychology,* eds. D. Stokols and I. Altman. Vol. 2, pp. 1043–1088. New York: Wiley.

Stroebe, W. and B. S. Frey. 1982. Self-interest and collective action: The economics and psychology of public goods. *British Journal of Social Psychology* 21:121–137.

Weigel, R. H. and L. S. Newman. 1976. Increasing attitude-behavior correspondence by broadening the scope of the behavioral measure. *Journal of Personality and Social Psychology* 33:793–802.

Wilson, E. O. 1989. Threats to biodiversity. *Scientific American* 261:108–116.

Wilson, J. A. 1977. A test of the tragedy of the commons. In *Managing the Commons,* eds. G. Hardin and J. Baden. pp. 96–111. San Francisco: Freeman.

Winett, R. A., J. W. Hatcher, T. R. Fort, E. N. Leckliter, S. Q. Love, A. W. Riley, and J. F. Fishback. 1982. The effects of videotape modeling and daily feedback on residential electricity conservation, home temperature and humidity, perceived comfort, and clothing worn: winter and summer. *Journal of Applied Behavior Analysis* 15:381–402.

Yamagishi, T. 1988. Seriousness of social dilemmas and the provision of a sanctioning system. *Social Psychology Quarterly* 51:32–42.

Yates, S. M. and E. Aronson. 1983. A social psychological perspective on energy conservation in residential buildings. *American Psychologist* 38:435–444.

3

Ecosystem Perspectives in Environmental Decision Making

Stephen H. Levine

1 INTRODUCTION

Ecosystems are important components of environmental systems. Ecology, therefore, plays a significant role in environmental decision making. Information that is often inadequate, poorly understood, and controversial makes ecological considerations particularly troublesome to decision makers. Should forest fires be prevented? allowed? encouraged? Will introduction of a new species help control an existing outbreak of pests or merely compound the problem? To what degree is the present rate of species extinctions due to human activities? Or is it just another cycle in the history of life on earth? Typically, even the experts exhibit great uncertainty in answering questions of this sort. The wrong answers to these questions can lead and have led to decisions that are both economically costly and environmentally disasterous.

Several characteristics of ecosystems are particularly important in establishing successful environmental-management policies. Ecosystems are unusually diverse systems; they typically contain a great number of species, individual organisms, and numerous abiotic components. The organic constituents exhibit a wide array of behaviors, with the result that interactions are varied and often subtle. The system components, living and nonliving, are linked together by numerous ever-changing flows of matter and energy. Ecosystems are dynamic. While ecosystem dynamics involve repetitive or cyclic phenomena, decision making is often centered around unique or irregularly occurring events, such as the impact of a dam or a drought. Ecosystem dynamics can lead to major, unpredicted, and often irreversible changes in system composition.

Human activity disturbs ecosystems in several ways. The exploitation of naturally available biotic and abiotic resources is a major disruption; food

38

gathering, hunting, fishing, foresting, and mining are examples. Fishing may alter the mix of species (Scudo & Ziegler, 1978); excessive hunting may lead to species extinction; foresting may destroy the natural habitats of species. Removal or substantial modification of natural ecosystems to make land available for alternative uses plays a major role. Agriculture replaces one ecosystem with another and usually replaces the natural ecosystem with a less diverse artificial one. Urban growth is even more dramatic; New York City presents a very different ecosystem from that found on Manhattan Island 400 years ago. Even building a house in the woods alters the local ecosystem.

Direct exploitation is not the only way humans disturb ecosystems. Pollution of the air, the water, or the land is a common indirect effect of human activity. Urban smog is a fairly localized example, whereas acid rain is more widely distributed. Global warming represents disturbance at the biosphere level. The mere presence of human activity may have a profound impact. Many animals do not reproduce near human settlements. The construction of roads, rails, and pipelines restricts the free movement of many species, especially large herbivores and carnivores. The introduction, often accidental, of plant and animal species to regions where they were not previously found has substantially altered ecosystems and human history as well (Crosby, 1972, 1986).

Finally, many major ecological disturbances result from the combination of two or more effects. The concern over the greenhouse effect is a dramatic and worldwide example that involves the production of several air pollutants and the destruction of extensive tropical forests for alternative uses (Graedel & Crutzen, 1989; Schneider, 1989). The potential interactions of these different phenomena, possibly in ways not yet understood, further complicate critical environmental decisions.

2 ECOLOGY AS A SYSTEM SCIENCE

A system is a set of elements or components related to each other through interaction or interdependence (Beachley & Harrison, 1978). The pattern of interactions or linkages within a system, along with characteristics of the system components, represent its structure.

Man-made systems are common in our lives. The automobile—with components such as engine, transmission, and suspension—is a familiar physical example. The importance of structure to such a system is clear; not until these components are correctly joined together do they constitute an automobile. Complicated as an automobile may seem, it is, in fact, far simpler than an ecosystem. The forces by which the parts interact are fewer in number and better understood. The effects of design decisions can usually be accurately predicted.

Ecology, the study of the interrelationships between organisms and their surroundings (Ricklefs, 1973), clearly fits this systems mold. The great number of species, each with its characteristic behaviors, and the variety of competitive, mutualistic, parasitic, and exploitative interactions, gives ecosystems unusual complexity. A basic ecosystem interaction such as predation represents not a single, universal phenomenon such as gravity, but rather a spectrum of predator strategies, ranging from high-speed pursuit to web spinning and filter feeding.

Systems are subject to external influences; these constitute their "environment" (Halfon, 1979). The behavior of systems is determined by the interplay of external influences and internal structure. Thus, the smoothness of a car's ride depends in part on the road surface and in part on the car's suspension. Similarly, the number of fish in a pond depends in part on the nutrients and pollutants that enter it and in part on the different plant and animal species that coexist within it. Abiotic influences such as the daily and yearly cycles of solar energy, temperature, and rainfall drive corresponding biotic cycles of growth and decline, but the exact nature of these biotic cycles depends also on numerous interactions within the ecosystem. Failure to differentiate between external influences and internal structure has plagued decision makers in ecology as well as other disciplines (Forrester, 1968).

Because system structure determines how external influences and internal changes are felt throughout the system, structure plays two major roles in decision making. First, the effects of decisions on systems cannot be predicted unless the structure of the system is understood. Often the structure of a system can work to thwart the objectives of decision makers. Fertilizing a lawn to encourage the growth of grass may be counterproductive if weeds are able to outcompete the grass for this new source of nutrients. Physically removing the weeds may do no better; the resulting disturbed area is ideal for recolonization by weeds. The inertia inherent in system behavior is a major theme of social-system analysis (Forrester, 1968) equally important in the management of ecological systems. Second, indirect effects in systems are often as important as direct effects and generally are less well understood (Levine, 1977; Higashi & Patten, 1986). The results are often seen as unanticipated, undesirable reactions to policies. Spraying pesticides to reduce insect populations resulted in significant damage to predator bird populations because their position at the top of the food chain tended to concentrate the pesticide poisons and resulted in weakened egg-shell strengths.

3 ECOSYSTEMS IN ENVIRONMENTAL DECISION MAKING: AN EXAMPLE

In order to illuminate the role of ecological phenomena within the framework of environmental decision making we will consider a hypothetical, simplified, yet still representative, situation. Consider a large section of land that in its natural state consists of a mix of woodlands and grassy plains. The woodlands contain several varieties of deer as well as numerous small mammals. The deer browse on the variety of trees, consuming leaves, twigs, and bark. The plains are home to several varieties of antelope that graze on the prevalent grasses. In both woods and plains, wolves are present and prey on the deer and antelope. In addition, several lakes and streams contain numerous species of fish.

The owners of this land recognize that it potentially contains a number of resources. These include:

1. trees, for lumber
2. grasslands, for cattle raising or for farming
3. fish and game, for fishing and hunting
4. woodland scenery, for recreation and tourism
5. water, for irrigation
6. mineral deposits, for mining

They are faced with the problem of deciding which, if any, of these resources to use. Any decision the owners make will have ecological and environmental impacts. Some of these will be indirect results of the decisions; they may be unintended—and detrimental. The complex nature of ecosystems increases the chance of poorly understood, unpredicted results, and thus presents a significant problem in environmental decision making.

4 A BASIC ECOLOGICAL DECISION: REMOVAL OF THE WOLVES

The owners of the section of land feel that many of their options first require the significant reduction, if not the removal, of the wolf population. Wolves will be a threat to cattle, to casual tourists, and even to lumberjacks and miners. Elimination of this threat is the owners' direct goal. They may well be aware of at least some of the possible pitfalls of such a decision that could occur due to the highly interactive nature of the species comprising an ecosystem (Clapham, 1973; Ricklefs, 1973; Senge, 1981). Before discussing the possible outcomes of such a decision, let us consider these ecosystem interactions in some detail.

4.1 Species and Interactions: Population Ecology

Modern theoretical ecology has developed in two major directions: *population ecology* and *systems ecology* (Gould, 1987; Cohen, 1989). The natural history approach, which emphasizes the struggle of populations within a species and within a community to maximize reproductive success, is central to population ecology (May, 1976). The flows of energy and matter through an ecosystem are the subject of systems ecology. We will first consider population ecology and then address systems ecology.

Ecosystems contain biotic and abiotic components. The biotic (or organic) component includes all living forms, plants, animals, bacteria, and viruses, and all by-products of those forms. The abiotic component includes air, water, earth, and so on, and represents resources required by the biotic component. The great number of organisms, and their division into numerous species, contributes to the complex nature of ecosystems. This complexity is further enhanced by the behavioral differences among the different species, and—in many cases—among members of the same species. Two species of antelope are not separate components merely because they breed separately, but also because they exploit their environment differently; they may, in turn, be exploited differently.

In addition to numerous components, ecosystems display a large number of interactions among these components. This contrasts dramatically with, for example, the solar system, which can be understood—in terms of planetary orbits—with reference to only two component descriptors (mass and velocity) and one interactive force (gravity). The existence of these numerous, qualitatively different components and interactions greatly increases the difficulty of describing and predicting ecosystem behavior, and thereby complicates ecological decision making.

For example, numerous ecological interactions directly involve the way in which species obtain their energy and other nutrients; these interactions define the structure of the food web. Plants are, of course, capable of obtaining energy directly from the sun, and abiotic nutrients from water and soil. Herbivores utilize a wide range of exploitative stategies: grazing and browsing have already been noted; consumption of fruit and sucking of nectar are two more. Predation, in which one animal consumes another, almost always results in death of the prey. Parasitism involves one species living on, or within, another, and may be beneficial only to one. Saprophytism involves organisms that obtain food directly from nonliving organic matter, and is responsible for a significant amount of biotic recycling (Ricklefs, 1973).

Other interactions govern the flow of energy and nutrients, though they are not directly responsible for that flow. Exploitation competition arises when resources are in limited availability and consumption of a resource by one individual or one species reduces its use by another. Interference competition occurs when one species or individual prevents another access to resources, often by territorial behavior including direct attack (Pianka, 1976; Hutchinson, 1978).

Agricultural endeavors by human beings represent a major commitment to a stategy of interference competition; land is enclosed, only specific plants are allowed to grow, and other animals are refused access to the crops being grown. Competing species, whether plants or animals, are considered pests. The control of pests is an important ecological aspect of environmental management (Conway, 1976; Rabb, DeFoliart, & Kennedy, 1984; Hassell & May, 1989).

Mutualism is a term that covers a range of interactions between species (or individuals) that are beneficial to both. The large, multispecies herds of Africa are believed to provide mutual protection from predators. Symbiosis, the particularly close association of two species, may be mutualistic or parasitic. Bacteria in the digestive systems of cattle (which make possible the digestion of grasses by these herbivores) is a mutualistic interaction of particular importance to humans. The recent controversy over the killing of marine mammals by fishermen catching yellowfin tuna arose because of a mutualistic relationship between the mammals and the tuna allowing each to benefit from the others' sensory skills to the overall advantage of both (Chandler, 1990).

The term "community" is often used in ecology to refer to species that occur in a group (Ricklefs, 1973). Thus, we might refer to a tropical lowland forest community or a temperate zone grasslands community. In this sense of the word, the section of land we are considering contains two different communities—the woodlands and the grasslands. The wolves (as well as other species) may belong to both communities.

4.2 The Initial Effects of Wolf Removal

Removal of the wolves by hunting, trapping, or poisoning is an example of interference competition. The widespread use of interference competition as an ecological policy has played a major role in shaping modern ecosystems. The goal may sometimes be safety, as presumed in our example, but, as in the case of agricultural practices, is more often the redirecting of a greater fraction of the Earth's resources to human consumption.

Wolves are the chief predators of antelope in the plains and deer in the woodlands. If wolves are numerous enough, they will limit the antelope and deer populations to levels where the food resources for grazing and browsing are more than adequate. Competition among the various individuals and species of antelope and deer will therefore be at a low level. The removal of the wolves will initially reduce the death rate of the herbivores, allowing their populations to grow. After some time, this growth will reach a level where grass for the antelope and browse for the deer become limiting resources, that is, the availability of these resources will dictate future population growth. Whereas prior to the removal of the wolves, competition might have been of minor importance, it now becomes the dominant interaction.

When wolves were critical in controlling the antelope and deer populations, the relative abilities of different individuals and species to avoid predation played an important role in determining the herbivore populations. The subsequent control by competition means reproductive success is largely based on a new criterion, namely, the ability to obtain increasingly scarce food. The result is often a change in both the genetic makeup of each species and the representation of each species in the herbivore population. In certain cases, the removal of a predator can result in the near or complete extinction of one or more of its prey species (Paine, 1966). The combined result of eliminating the wolf population and decreasing many plant populations can be a substantial decrease in biodiversity.

4.3 Ecosystem Diversity and Stability

The decline in biodiversity is the subject of increasing worldwide concern (Wilson, 1989). Ecosystems exhibit a considerable range of species diversity, from the extremely high amounts typical of tropical rain forests to the contrasting fewer numbers of species in more abiotically stressed environments, such as polar or desert regions. Although earlier periods of decline have certainly occurred, human activity is contributing significantly to the present decline, both directly (through the killing and harvesting of plants and animals) and indirectly (through modification and sometimes elimination of their habitats). Previously, this impact of human activity was felt primarily at the local level in isolated ecosystems, and was due to causes and policies at that level. More recently, the impact is becoming evident at broader levels.

Decreased biodiversity is of concern for several reasons. Along with moral and scientific concerns centered around humanity's role in destroying species whose evolution required millions of years, the loss of species carries a possible economic cost as well, since the destruction of a species entails the loss of materials with potential medical and commercial usefulness. In addition to the loss of specific species, there is a concern—frequently observed though poorly understood—that ecosystem diversity and ecosystem stability are somehow linked. The direction of causality is in question (May, 1973), but certainly major human interventions represent potentially destabilizing events. Both the number of species and the number of individuals within a species are of concern. Population explosions and crashes present dramatic evidence that ecosystems are, at times, highly unstable. Outbreaks of well-known pests, such as locusts, or previously benign creatures, such as rabbits (in Australia), can have disastrous effects.

Ultimately, other global events such as global warming may prove central to the problem of maintaining species diversity. Given that the biosphere is an integrated system, this is hardly surprising. Climate determines the ranges of species, and climate changes—especially in the extremes—will mean local extinctions. It is often the extremes of climate, and not the averages, that are critical. One hard freeze is all that is required to destroy many tropical species.

4.4 Further Effects of Wolf Removal

If the populations of antelope and deer are allowed to grow to high densities, the increased levels of grazing and browsing can lead to significant, long-term damage to the plant life. Grasslands may become overgrazed, in some cases leading to the loss of soil through wind and water erosion. Widespread starvation of the antelope may result as well. The situation involving the woodlands is even more complicated. Excessive browsing will first remove all accessible leaves and twigs; these can, of course, be renewed on a fairly short-term basis. The renewal of trees is a much slower process, however, and the starving deer may destroy a great number of trees through their increased dependence on bark. Once again, the ultimate result will be mass starvation and a great decrease in the deer population. A situation very much like this occurred on the Kaibab Plateau in Arizona earlier in this century (Clapham, 1973).

One might imagine that the collapse of the herbivore populations through starvation would signal the return of the ecosystems to their original states. For several reasons, this is not necessarily so. The woodland situation is particularly illuminating. First, the remaining deer are likely to feed on the emerging saplings, greatly slowing the process of reforestation. Second, large numbers of dead trees increase the chances of further devastation through fire. More generally, when ecosystems are significantly disturbed they typically undergo a process known as "succession" rather than return immediately to their final, or climax, state (Ricklefs, 1973). Initially, faster-growing species that specialize in disturbed habitats appear, and only later—if ever—do the original species regain their dominance.

4.5 Dynamic Systems and Decision Making

The results of the wolf-removal policy emphasize the dynamic nature of ecosystems. In part, dynamic systems are those that undergo change over time, that is, those in which the "state" of the system changes. Much as the position and velocity of a car change, so do the numbers of deer in the woods and the concentrations of pesticides in a lake. But "dynamic" implies more than a simple change of state over time; it also implies that the state of the system at one moment is influenced by its state at other times (Luenberger, 1979). Car velocities and deer populations generally do not change abruptly. In particular, both the present state and future state of a dynamic system depend on past as well as present influences. For example, to explain the present deer populations one must know, among other things, the history of predation by wolves and hunting by men. The number of deer killed not only this year, but also in previous years, will influence the present population. Similarly, pesticides take time to pass through or accumulate within an ecosystem, and their present levels of concentration depend on their history of application.

In a general sense, a dynamic system can be said to have a "memory," in that its present behavior is influenced by its past. The nature of this memory, that is, how a system weighs its past in determining its present state, is in turn determined by the structure of the system. In the simplest systems—those exhibiting a linear relation between their input and their response—this nature, though not the "memories" stored, is independent of the inputs (DeRusso, Roy, & Close, 1967). In nonlinear descriptions, which reflect reality more accurately, the system structure—and therefore the nature of its memory—is influenced by the system inputs.

The structure of a system not only determines the effects of external influences but may be responsible for internally generated periodic occurrences such as the outbreak of pest populations and predator–prey cycles. These characteristic behaviors are not necessarily associated with yearly climate cycles; they may rather arise directly from interactions among the ecosystem's components (Maynard Smith, 1974). Determining whether the dynamic behavior of an ecosystem is exogenous (generated from without) or endogenous (generated from within) is often difficult, yet doing so is central to ecosystem management. As an example, the owners of the section of land we have been reviewing have records indicating fluctuations in the deer population prior to implementation of their wolf-reduction policy. If this is due to exogeneous effects such as variations in the severity of winter weather, the variations may be little affected by the policy. If, on the other hand, they result from wolf–deer, predator–prey interactions, the fluctuations should be substantially modified.

The causal relationship of the past to the present and the future, characteristic of dynamic systems in general and ecosystems in particular, is critical to the nature of environmental decision making. Specifically, if we are to estimate the future impact of past and present decisions, we must have adequate knowledge of the dynamics of the system under discussion. The nature of interspecies and intraspecies interactions, as well as the life cycles of many species and many abiotic influences, is such that the outcomes of many decisions will be significantly delayed. Furthermore, the actions dictated by such decisions must be appropriately timed if they are to be effective. The predominance of indirect effects and the resultant possibility of counterintuitive outcomes mean that the counterproductive nature of decisions may not be evident for substantial periods of time (Forrester, 1971). In our example, tree damage is certainly not the goal of wolf removal, but instead results from indirect and unanticipated ecological interactions. Moreover, this damage, and the accompanying weakening of the deer herd through starvation, are delayed effects of the wolf-removal policy; the short-term effects of this policy—an increase in the deer population and a decrease in the wolf population—seemed positive.

The concern today over global warming also illustrates unanticipated ecological interactions. The emission of large amounts of carbon dioxide into the atmosphere and the detrimental effects of the emissions are the unforseen results of decisions that greatly improved transportation and energy production, undeniably improving the living standards of millions. Now, the possibility exists that the long-term costs of those decisions may outweigh even these major short-term benefits.

As many experts have noted, the effects of many past policies that influence global warming have not yet been felt. Conversely, even if new policies were implemented immediately, they would require time before present trends could be changed. Moreover, since our knowledge of global temperature balance—a very complex dynamic system of which the world ecosystem is but one component—is rather poor, our predictions of future changes are unreliable. Gaining knowledge about most complex systems is ideally a "laboratory" experience. In the case of global warming, concerned theorists have pointed out that humanity is using nothing less than the planet Earth as its laboratory (Schneider, 1989).

5 EXPLOITATION OF RESOURCES

We began discussion of our hypothetical situation by noting that the owners of the section of land recognized it contained a number of potentially valuable resources. Value arises from a combination of usefulness and limited availability. The need to make environmental decisions arises from the desire to exploit these resources. All living organisms exploit resources found in their environment; human activity is unique first in the scale of utilization, second in the broad range of resources used, and third in the use of conscious (often long-range) planning.

Resources can be divided into two broad categories. First, there are natural resources, those natural conditions and raw materials that man uses to meet his needs (Isard, 1972). Natural resources may be biotic or abiotic. Ecosystem components are, of course, a subset of natural resources. In addition to natural resources, human resources such as capital, manpower, and time play major roles in environmental decision making. The importance of these three reflects the strong economic component of most environmentally related decisions. The implementation of any policy, such as construction of a wastewater treatment plant or the reduction of a wolf population, is going to be in competition with other alternatives for available human resources. In this chapter we will concentrate on natural resources; economics is the subject of Chapter 6.

The availability and importance of any given natural resource is not constant, but rather changes with technology and taste (Fisher, Krutilla, & Cicchetti, 1972; Smith, 1972). Uranium ore became an important resource only with the development of atomic fission. Whale oil ceased to be important for lighting after the development of gas and then electric lights. Birds with colorful feathers have at times faced extinction due to fashions in hats. The increased price of lobsters reflects the increased demand for (and diminishing supply of) what was once, at most, a regional food.

5.1 Natural Resources
in an Environmental-Decision Problem

Nature provides numerous resources. A traditional method of classifying these natural resources is based on renewability (Isard, 1972). *Nonrenewable* resources are those available only in fixed quantities, or for which the rate of renewal is so slow as to be negligible; once exhausted they cannot be replaced. *Renewable* resources, in contrast, can be replenished. Traditionally, living organisms have been classified as renewable resources (Clark, 1976) because of their ability to reproduce and thus replenish themselves. Inorganic resources, along with certain organic products such as coal, have been generally considered nonrenewable; they exist in fixed amounts and once exhausted are forever gone. However, these traditional classifications must be somewhat reinterpreted when considered within the systems framework required for decision making.

The renewability of a natural resource is an important parameter in decisions that determine its use. Long-term strategies of the United States for the utilization of its existing domestic oil reserves will differ from those for its domestic timber reserves in part because the first is presumed fixed in quantity, whereas the second can regenerate. But classification of a resource as renewable, within the framework of decision making, is not so simple as its ability to regenerate. Decisions are made for specific problems, and problem definition ultimately puts bounds, in space and time, on what is of interest to decision makers (Richardson & Pugh, 1980). In our example, we have noted the possibility of destruction of the woodland environment due to excessive browsing by deer. Such an environment might require as much as 100 years to renew itself. Managers making decisions for use of these woodlands as a source of timber within a much shorter time frame cannot treat them as renewable under these conditions (though individual trees removed by cutting from an intact forest are replaceable within a shorter time frame and may well be viewed as renewable).

In contrast to most organic resources, inorganic resources are often considered nonrenewable since they are only available in fixed quantity. Again, this is subject to the boundaries provided by the problem. In our example the land owners envisioned the sale of water, possibly from several lakes, for irrigation. They may reasonably expect that water levels can be allowed to drop to lower levels in response to certain needs with the expectation that they will be renewed within an acceptably short time span. In contrast, groundwater, widely used in areas such as the American Southwest, often represents a nonrenewable resource due to the long time required for its replenishment (Maurits la Rivière, 1989).

In the Nile delta many inorganic nutrients are deposited yearly by the annual flood. To farmers in this region, these nutrients are naturally renewable. By contrast, if the managers in our example choose to farm the grasslands, nutrient depletion will occur. Natural renewal will be too slow, and sustained farming will require a program of soil replenishment. Even more extreme is the depletion of similar nutrients from tropical rain-forest soils exploited for agriculture. The common result is their long-term impoverishment.

Several distinct mechanisms are available for the renewal of resources. The rate of renewal of biological resources through reproduction has the property that it is dependent on the remaining population. Biological resources may also be renewed, on a local basis, by migration. Elimination of wolves from the section under consideration will be counteracted to some extent by migration from adjacent areas. Certain resources continually flow into a system at rates independent of the rates at which they are used. Rainfall and solar energy are examples, as is soil replenishment in the Nile delta. Recycling is a renewal mechanism where the rate of renewal is often in part dependent on the rate of resource use. For all renewable resources, overexploitation is possible; resource management leads to measures such as maximum sustainable yield (Clark, 1976).

Finally, many natural resources are obtained in exchange for money. From the point of view of the involved parties, these natural resources are renewable if, and only if, their supply of money is renewable. To city dwellers, food is a renewable resource, not because of biological reproduction, but because of their ability to purchase it regularly.

6 ECOSYSTEM MODELS AND DECISION MAKING

Introducing cattle to the grasslands was one of the alternatives for exploiting the resources of the section of land under consideration. Important questions to be decided are the number of cattle that can be maintained and the rate at which they should be marketed, that is, harvested. Mathematical modeling provides a tool of some usefulness in answering questions of this type.

6.1 Ecological Modeling

The use of mathematical models in ecology has a long and rich tradition; many different type models have been used (Scudo & Ziegler, 1978; May, 1973; Pielou, 1969; Maynard Smith, 1974; Halfon, 1979). These include basic deterministic-differential and difference-equation models, stochastic models, flow models, spatial-distribution models, and so on. Applications have covered a wide spectrum as well, from basic understanding of natural ecological phenomena, to management and exploitation of aquatic and terrestrial ecosystems, to the control of pests. Computers have made possible considerable effort in ecosystem simulation, and have facilitated the analysis of large sets of data.

Applications to management, exploitation, and impact analysis involve use of models as decision tools. As an illustration, we will first consider one of the most basic and simple population-ecology models, namely, the logistic equation (Hutchinson, 1978). Simple as this model is, it is still illustrative when applied to the harvesting of renewable, biological resources (Clark, 1976). We will apply it to the problem of harvesting the cattle that are maintained on the grasslands. In order to simplify the problem, we will assume these cattle are free-ranging and that repopulation comes only from reproduction within the herd, though such is not always the case today. For present purposes, we will also ignore the substantial marketing and economic forces that influence decisions of this type.

6.2 The Logistic Equation: A Basic Population-Ecology Model

Two concepts widely used in population ecology, and more recently in other fields as well, are *intrinsic growth rate* and *carrying capacity* (MacArthur, 1972). "Intrinsic growth rate" refers to the growth rate of a species population in the absence of competition, among individuals as well as species, and predation. It is generally the highest growth rate a species can attain in a given environment. The rate at which a newly introduced pest begins to infest an ecosystem is dependent on its intrinsic growth rate. Carrying capacity is a measure of the highest population density a species can sustain in a given environment. Both intrinsic growth rate and carrying capacity are therefore dependent on characteristics of both the species and the environment. Woodland destruction by deer is an example where both intrinsic growth rate and carrying capacity undergo change.

The logistic equation is a model of population change over time based on intrinsic growth rate and carrying capacity alone. Letting

$x(t)$ = population density at time t,

r = intrinsic growth rate,

K = carrying capacity,

$\dot{x}(t)$ = rate of change in population density at time t,

the logistic equation states

$$\dot{x}(t) = rx(t)[1 - x(t)/K]. \tag{3-1}$$

When $x(t)$ is much smaller than the carrying capacity K, the term $x(t)/K$ becomes negligibly small; the rate of change in population density is then approximated by

$$\dot{x}(t) = rx(t); \tag{3-2}$$

the population growth is determined solely by the intrinsic growth rate r. As the population increases, the resources available to each individual decrease. This principle results in both a decrease in the number of offspring each individual can successfully produce and an increase in the death rate of those individuals living, and thus ultimately results in a decrease in the rate of population growth. When population density reaches the carrying capacity K, the population growth rate $\dot{x}(t)$ approaches zero; the birth and death rates become equal. If by some means the population density exceeds the carrying capacity, the death rate will exceed the birth rate, and the population will decrease. This occurred in our example when destruction of trees, with the resultant decrease in carrying capacity, resulted in a collapse of the deer population due to starvation.

Plots of the rate of change in the population density $\dot{x}(t)$ versus population density $x(t)$, and population density $x(t)$ versus time t, are shown in Figures 3–1 and 3–2. Figure 3–1 indicates that the growth rate of the population has a maximum value at a level well below the carrying capacity K and is negative for values above K. This is reflected in the plots of two possible population histories in Figure 3–2. When the population density begins at less than the carrying capacity K, it increases over time; when it begins at greater than K, it decreases. In both cases, it eventually converges to $x(t) = K$.

As noted, this model simplifies reality. It ignores competition, predation, specific behavior of the species being modeled, spatial and temporal variations in the environment, and so on. Inclusion of these would allow far more complex

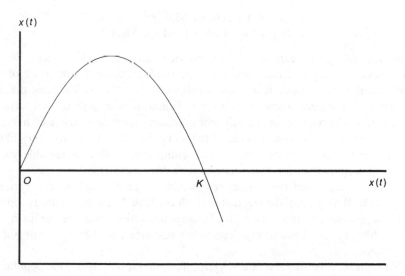

FIGURE 3–1.   Population growth rate as determined by population density for the logistic model.

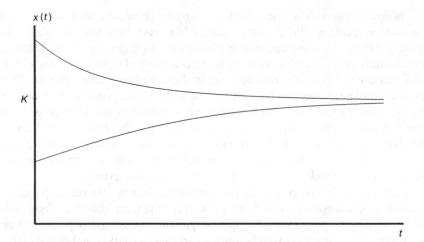

FIGURE 3–2. Two histories of population, $x(t)$, for the logistic model.

population dynamics than predicted by the logistic equation, population oscillations being an important example. Nonetheless, this equation describes some actual populations with surprising accuracy, including human populations (Olinick, 1978); and it is "realistic" in the sense that it does not allow for unlimited growth.

6.3 Decision Making
Using a Population-Ecology Model

If the logistic model, Equation (3–1), provides an acceptable model of cattle population on the grasslands, how can it be used in deciding how much of the cattle population to maintain and how much to harvest? We will assume that the managers of the herd intend a long-term commitment and so do not wish to deplete the cattle population in a way that ultimately leads to a decreased harvest. That is, they wish to pursue a sustainable yield policy (Clark, 1976). Very likely they prefer to harvest at the greatest rate compatible with a sustainable yield. This rate is known as the Maximum Sustainable Yield (Y).

Y is a concept used for abiotic, renewable resources, such as underground water, as well as for populations that reproduce. If underground water is replenished at a constant rate, then clearly any utilization rate greater than the replenishing rate will ultimately deplete the resource and therefore will not be sustainable.

If y represents the harvest rate or yield, then the growth rate of the population is further decreased by y and Equation (3–1) becomes

$$\dot{x}(t) = rx(t)[1 - x(t)/K] - y. \tag{3–3}$$

We can now ask the question: What harvest rate corresponds to the maximun sustainable yield, Y, and what population density, X, results? We note that under sustainable-yield policies the population density will become constant, that is, $x(t)$ will be a constant value x and $\dot{x}(t)$ will be equal to zero. In this case Equation (3–3) can be rewritten as

$$y = rx(1 - x/K). \tag{3–4}$$

Figure 3–3 is a plot of y versus x. Inspection of this plot indicates that Y, the maximum value of y, corresponds to maintaining a population density of $X = K/2$, one-half the carrying capacity, and that the Y is thus given as

$$Y = rK/4. \tag{3–5}$$

Comparison of Figures 3–1 and 3–3 indicates that, not surprisingly, the Y corresponds to the maximum growth rate of the harvested population.

How critical, from a policy-decision point of view, is the omission of a fuller explicit description of ecosystem interactions? As an example, unless we remove the antelope native to the grasslands, they will compete with the cattle we introduce, as all are grazers. Exploitation competition among two or more species has been the subject of numerous mathematical models [MacArthur, 1972; see Scudo & Ziegler, (1978) for historical perspective] and has been extended to the case of harvested populations (Clark, 1976).

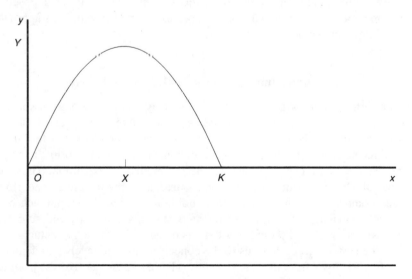

FIGURE 3–3.   Sustainable yield as a function of population density indicating the maximum sustainable yield.

Analysis of this system with competition is far more complex than the previous example and will not be pursued in detail here. [See Clark (1976) for a full description.] Rather, we will consider the question posed above regarding the possibly critical nature of omitting ecosystem interactions within a policymaking model. This competition model indicates that under certain conditions, depending on the relative strengths of the various interspecific interactions, harvesting policies that would work well for a single species in a noncompetitive situation can result in collapse of that harvested population as a result of the combination of harvesting and competitive pressure. Therefore, if interspecific competition is an important contributor to the population dynamics of an exploited species, failure to account for this interaction can lead to erroneous (and possibly disastrous) management decisions. In general, all systems modeling requires that important components and interactions be accounted for if results are to be meaningful. Deciding just which components and interactions are, in fact, important remains the most difficult aspect of modeling.

7 SYSTEM ECOLOGY: AN ALTERNATIVE ECOSYSTEM DESCRIPTION

Modeling the ecosystem in population-ecology terms emphasizes species characteristics such as growth rates, carrying capacities, competition, and predation. An alternative approach pictures the ecosystem as consisting of compartments or components interconnected by flows (Ulanowicz, 1972; Patten, 1982; Baird & Ulanowicz, 1989). The functioning of the ecosystem as an entity, as opposed to the histories of individual populations or species, is emphasized. This approach is termed systems ecology (Halfon, 1979).

7.1 Compartments, Flows, and Trophic Levels

The compartments of a systems-ecology model may represent groups of species, such as all algae or all primary predators; a subset of one species, such as immature robins; or the product of numerous species, such as forest-leaf litter. Compartments need not contain organic components; the sun is a prime example of one that does not. Typical flows are energy, biomass, and carbon. Thus, the contents of all compartments can be measured in common units, and flows between compartments are directly measurable quantities. This approach contrasts with population ecology which—at best—only indirectly measures interactions. The pattern of these flows defines essential ecosystem structures. For energy, the system structure leads to the concept of trophic levels (Lindemann, 1942). Energy flows from the sun to plants to herbivores to carnivores, from the lower to the higher trophic levels.

Systems ecology, therefore, concentrates on properties of the ecosystem as a whole. Different ecosystems may contain different species with their different behaviors, yet they share common structural features such as trophic levels, energy/biomass pathways, and nutrient cycling. Questions such as "How long does a pollutant require to pass through an ecosystem?" can be considered for many ecosystems. Because of its emphasis on broadly defined features, systems ecology is particularly applicable to comparing different ecosystems and to tracking changes in specific ecosystems (such as those that occur as a result of environmental stress). Measures have been developed that describe properties of the entire system, as well as the individual components, in the same way Gross National Product (GNP) does in economic systems or entropy does in thermodynamic systems. Typical are flow measures such as total system throughput and cycling indices (Finn, 1976), and information-theory concepts of structure such as ascendency (Ulanowicz, 1980). System methodologies, like the input-output model (Leontief, 1951) borrowed from economics (Hannon, 1973), have been widely exploited in systems ecology.

7.2 Network Models

Systems-ecology models usually begin with a network or structural model describing the flows between the various compartments into which an ecosystem has been partitioned. The compartments are represented by boxes, and the flows between compartments by directed branches. When the information is available, the branches are labeled to indicate the magnitudes of flows. Figure 3–4 shows hypothetical energy flows for the original, undisturbed grasslands ecosystem, consisting of three trophic levels: (1) grasses, (2) several species of antelope, and (3) wolves (Clapham, 1973). (Note that, once again, we are dealing with a simplification of the actual system, neglecting the many other species—such as small herbivores, small predators, and birds—that inhabit the grasslands.) The energy-flow model includes input from the sun (the ultimate source of energy) as well as output for maintenance (energy dissipated as heat through respiration). Note that respiration involves most of the energy available at each trophic level, with the result that far less is available at the next higher level. Energy-flows between organic compartments involve the energy content of biomass. Decomposition represents a complex set of interactions in which organic matter is broken down and used by earthworms, bacteria, and so on. Some recycling of energy/biomass occurs, as when birds eat earthworms and then are in turn consumed by small predators, but this recycling is not shown in the figure. Similarly, the possibility of energy/biomass inputs and outputs through migration is ignored.

Figure 3–5 indicates nutrient-flows through this same ecosystem. Nutrients are inputted and lost to the ecosystem through a whole array of biochemical

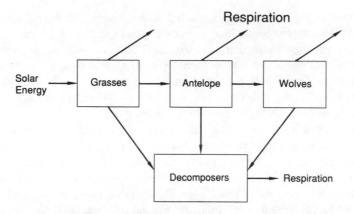

FIGURE 3–4.   Energy-flow in grasslands ecosystem.

processes (Odum, 1989) as well as physical processes such as erosion. Substantial recyling occurs, as indicated by the flow from soil back to grasses.

7.3 Impact Analysis and Decision Making

Systems ecology is particularly well suited for analyzing the impact of management decisions and policies on ecosystems. In the grasslands example, the decision was made first to eliminate wolves and then introduce cattle. Both the

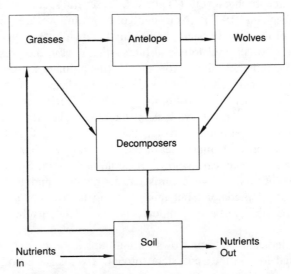

FIGURE 3–5.   Nutrient-flow in grasslands ecosystem.

cattle and the naturally present antelope represent usable resources to the managers—the cattle for beef production and the antelope for hunting. The value of these resources might be enhanced by increasing their populations, the size of individuals, and the rate at which individuals reach their full size. These factors in turn influence the amount of food required by these species. Given that the antelope and cattle represent compartments in the ecosystem, increased food consumption means increased throughput for the corresponding compartments. Throughput is a measure of energy, biomass, or specific nutrients that pass through a compartment.

One method of achieving this goal of ecosystem enrichment is adding nutrients to the soil (Dasmann, 1964). The nutrients—inputs to the ecosystem—will be taken up by the grasses, encouraging their growth, and then passed up to the higher trophic levels. Similar methods can be used in lakes to encourage plant- and fish-population growths. Runoff of agricultural fertilizer often represents uncontrolled enrichment and sometimes produces undesirable growth such as algal blooms. Thus, the change in system input translates into a change in intercompartmental flows and compartment throughputs. The overall system impact can be measured in terms of increased total system throughput and changes in system-cycling indices. Deciding the appropriate levels of enrichment necessary to achieve the desired rates of throughput to the various compartments is a typical impact-analysis problem.

The mathematics of this analysis is beyond the scope of this chapter (see Finn, 1976). Changes in ecosystem structure brought about by these decisions to modify the grasslands ecosystem can be seen, however, by comparing the network models shown in Figures 3–6 and 3–7 to those previously shown. The

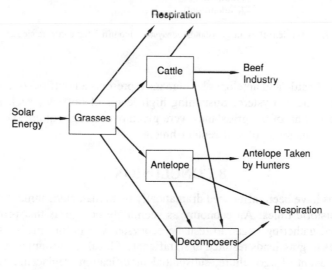

FIGURE 3–6.   Energy-flow in grasslands ecosystem modified for cattle raising.

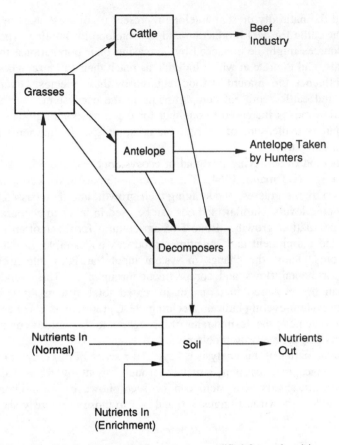

FIGURE 3–7.   Nutrient-flow in grasslands ecosystem modified for cattle raising.

harvesting of cattle and antelopes by humans represents an outflow of energy and nutrients for the ecosystem. Sustaining high levels of outflow, such as would result if part or all of the grasslands were given over to agriculture, necessitates using intense methods of soil replenishment.

8 CONCLUSION

Ecosystems have been influenced dramatically by human environmental policies since prehistoric times. An economy as seemingly benign as that provided by hunting and gathering began to reshape ecosystems. Hunting methods such as setting fires to grasslands resulted in significant, if local, environmental impacts. With the advent of agriculture, substantial modification, replacement, and destruction of the natural environment on a worldwide scale had begun. Whereas agriculture involved a direct modification of the natural environment, the subsequent development of large-scale, energy-intensive production—coupled with an exploding human population—indirectly produced dramatic changes as well. Before now, worldwide complex interactions were not well understood, which is not surprising given that ecology is a systems science that is still in its infancy. Understanding the internal structure and dynamics of ecosystems, and how they in turn form larger environmental systems, presently undergoing changes unprecedented within human recall, will be a major task of the near future.

EXERCISES

1. *Regional Ecosystem Management Study Project.* You are directing a study charged with evaluating the possible utilizations of a region consisting of a lake, bordering wetlands, and surrounding watershed. The lake contains several fish species of recreational value, and the wetlands are home to a number of birds and small mammals. In addition to leaving the region in its natural state, a preliminary study has indicated a number of possible uses:

a. waterfront development for recreational fishing, boating, and swimming
b. waterfront development for private homes
c. dredging part or all of the wetlands to increase the size of the lake and the amount of lakefront property
d. farming in the watershed
e. draining all or part of the wetlands to increase both farming area and home-development area
f. stocking of the lake with native or introduced game fishing species

Clearly, utilization of the region can include some or all of these possibilities. What resources would be used in each case? To what degree are the resources renewable? What are the ecological impacts, both direct and indirect, of each possible utilization?

Let your analysis reflect both the population- and systems-ecology viewpoints.

2. *Basic Computer Simulation Project.* A discrete time version of the logistic equation presented in the chapter is

$$x(k + 1) = x(k) + rx(k)[1 - x(k)/K],$$

where

$$x(k) = \text{population density at interval } k,$$
$$r = \text{intrinsic growth parameter,}$$
$$K = \text{carrying capacity.}$$

Beginning with a value for the population density at interval 0, $x(0)$, the equation above is a simple rule for calculating the population density at all subsequent intervals. Interestingly, this discrete time model displays a wider range of behavior than that of the continuous time model described in the text of the chapter, much of it of ecological and more generally of systems-theory interest. [See, for instance, May (1976).] To explore this we might begin with the values

$$r = 0.5,$$

$$K = 10,$$

$$x(0) = 1.0$$

and simulate the population densities for a large number of intervals. We will need a simple computer program to do this. Next, we can investigate the effects of ecosystem enrichment. Presumably, enrichment would cause increases in both r and K. As an example, we might run a series of simulations allowing r and K to increase by 10% each time with r going from 0.5 up to greater than 3.0. What happens to the long-range behavior of the population density? What does this indicate about possible effects of enrichment?

3. *Biodiversity Project.* The decline in biodiversity is an example of the linkages so characteristic of systemic problems. [For a general discussion, see Wilson (1989).] The present and possible future causes are many (and often on a worldwide scale), such as elimination of natural habitat, increased air and water pollution, and global warming. These in turn are also interlinked. For instance, air pollution and destruction of forests both contribute to the greenhouse effect, with global warming as a possible outcome. Destruction of forests reduces the available habitat for many biological communities as well, and this is a possible cause of extinctions. [See Page, (1988).] The declining biodiversity "problem" can therefore be studied from the systems viewpoint, including many of the possible strategies to alleviate the problem.

You may be aware of some specific regions—possibly the very area where you live—where reduced biodiversity is a problem. Consider this problem. What are the species affected? What are the causes? If there is more than one cause, how do they interact? Can the causes be described in terms of parameters found in population ecology (e.g., carrying capacity, competition, predation)? Can they be described in terms of parameters found in systems ecology (e.g., the flows of energy, water, etc., or on the detrimental side, pollutants, loss of nutrients, etc.)? Carry out such analyses.

ADDITIONAL READINGS

For basic background information on ecology and the environment, see Begon, Harper, & Townsend (1990), Brower, Zar, & von Encle (1990), Odum (1989), and Revelle and Revelle (1988).

For books on ecological modeling, see Halfon (1979), Smith (1972), and Scudo and Ziegler (1978). The Halfon book is mathematically sophisticated, whereas the Smith book is very readable. The Scudo and Ziegler book provides a historical review.

For a description of the values associated with environments left in their natural states, see Krutilla (1972). Sampson and Hair (1990) provide an inventory of natural resources, emphasizing those of the United States, prepared by the American Forestry Association.

MacArthur and Wilson (1967) provide a classic presentation of theoretical ecology, but with major relevance as man creates ecological islands all over the world. See May (1973) for a good discussion of many ideas of population ecology.

Crosby (1972, 1986) describes the worldwide ecological impact that resulted when European exploration of the New World united two largely separated ecological domains. This book gives a description of how such an impact can have consequences disastrous to some and beneficial to others.

Clark (1976) presents a mathematical treatment of the wedding of economic methods to managing ecological resources. This book requires sound mathematical background. Getz and Haight (1989) provide an up-to-date mathematical treatment of a wide range of harvesting and management methods.

REFERENCES

Baird, D. and R. E. Ulanowicz. 1989. The seasonal dynamics of the Chesapeake Bay system. *Ecological Monographs* 59(4):329–364.

Beachley, N. H. and H. L. Harrison. 1978. *Introduction to Dynamic System Analysis.* New York: Harper & Row.

Begon, M., J. L. Harper, and C. R. Townsend. 1990. *Ecology, Individuals, Populations, and Community.* Boston: Blackwell.

Brower, J., G. Zar, and C. von Ende. 1990. *Field and Laboratory Methods for General Ecology.* Dubuque, IO: William C. Brown.

Chandler, D. L. 1990. Rare look at dolphins' world. *Boston Globe,* February 12, p. 33.

Clapham Jr., W. B. 1973. *Natural Ecosystems.* New York: Macmillan.

Clark, C. C. 1976. *Mathematical Bioeconomics: The Optimal Management of Renewable Resources.* New York: John Wiley & Sons.

Cohen, J. E. 1989. Food web and community structure. In *Perspectives in Ecological Theory,* eds. J. Roughgarden, R. M. May, & S. A. Levin. pp. 181–202. Princeton, NJ: Princeton University Press.

Conway, G. 1976. Man versus pests. In *Theoretical Ecology,* ed. R. M. May pp. 257–281. Philadelphia, PA: W. B. Saunders.

Crosby, A. W. 1972. *Biological and Cultural Consequences of 1492.* Westport, CT: Greenwood Press.

Crosby, A. W. 1986. *Ecological Imperialism.* Cambridge: Cambridge University Press.

Dasmann, R. F. 1964. *African Game Ranching.* New York: Pergamon Press.

DeRusso, P. M., R. J. Roy, and C. M. Close. 1967. *State Variables for Engineers*. New York: John Wiley & Sons.

Finn, J. T. 1976. Measures of ecosystem structure and function derived from analysis of flows. *Journal of Theoretical Biology* 56:363–380.

Fisher, A. C., J. V. Krutilla, and C. J. Cicchetti. 1972. Alternate uses of natural environments: The economics of environmental modification. In *Natural Environments*, ed. J. V. Krutilla (pp. 18-53). Baltimore: The Johns Hopkins University Press.

Forrester, J. W. 1968. *Principles of Systems*. Cambridge, MA: Wright-Allen Press.

Forrester, J. W. 1971. Counter-intuitive behavior of social systems. *Technology Review* 73:3.

Getz, W. M. and R. G. Haight. 1989. *Population Harvesting*. Princeton, NJ: Princeton University Press.

Gould, S. J. 1987. *Urchin in the Storm*. New York: W. W. Norton & Company.

Graedel, T. E. and P. J. Crutzen. 1989. The changing atmosphere. *Scientific American* 261(3):58-68.

Halfon, E. 1979. Preview: theory in ecosystems analysis. In *Theoretical Systems Ecology*, ed. E. Halfon. pp. 1–13. New York: Academic Press.

Hannon, B. 1973. The structure of ecosystems. *Journal of Theoretical Ecology* 41:535–546.

Hassell, M. P. and R. M. May. 1989. The population biology of host-parasite and host-parasitoid associations. In *Perspectives in Ecological Theory*, eds. J. Roughgarden, R. M. May, and S. A. Levin. (pp. 319–347). Princeton, NJ: Princeton University Press.

Higashi, M. and B. C. Patten. 1986. Further aspects of the analysis of indirect effects in ecosystems. *Ecological Modelling* 31:69–77.

Hutchinson, G. E. 1978. *An Introduction to Population Ecology*. New Haven: Yale University Press.

Isard, W. 1972. *Ecologic-Economic Analysis for Regional Development*. New York: The Free Press.

Krutilla, J. V., ed. 1972. *Natural Environments*. Baltimore: The Johns Hopkins University Press.

Leontief, W. 1951. *The Structure of the American Economy, 1919–1939* (2nd ed.). New York: Oxford University Press.

Levine, S. H. 1977. Exploitation interactions and the structure of ecosystems. *Journal of Theoretical Biology* 69:345–355.

Lindemann, R. L. 1942. The trophic-dynamic aspect of ecology. *Ecology* 23:399–418.

Luenberger, D. G. 1979. *Introduction to Dynamic Systems*. New York: John Wiley & Sons.

MacArthur, R. 1972. *Geographical Ecology*. New York: Harper & Row.

MacArthur, R. H. and E. O. Wilson. 1967. *The Theory of Island Biogeography*. Princeton, NJ: Princeton University Press.

Maurits la Rivière, J. W. 1989. Threats to the world's water. *Scientific American* 261(3):80–94.

May, R. M. 1973. *Stability and Complexity in Model Ecosystems*. Princeton, NJ: Princeton University Press.

May, R. M., ed. 1976. *Theoretical Ecology*. Philadelphia, PA: W. B. Saunders.

May, R. M. 1976. Simple mathematical models with very complicated dynamics. *Nature* 261:459–467.

Maynard Smith, J. 1974. *Models in Ecology*. Cambridge: Cambridge University Press.

Odum, E. P. 1989. *Ecology*. Sunderland, MA: Sinauer Associates.

Olinick, M. 1978. *An Introduction to Mathematical Models in the Social and Life Sciences*. Reading, MA: Addison-Wesley.

Page, J. 1988. The island 'Arks' of Brazil. *Smithsonian* 19 (April): 106–119.

Paine, R. T. 1966. Food web complexity and species diversity. *The American Naturalist* 100(1):65–75.

Patten, B. 1982. Environs: relativistic elementary particles for ecology. *The American Naturalist* 119(2):179–219.

Pianka, E. R. 1976. Competition and niche theory. In *Theoretical Ecology*, ed. R. M. May. (pp. 114–141). Philadelphia, PA: W. B. Saunders.

Pielou, E. C. 1969. *Introduction to Mathematical Ecology*. New York: Wiley-Interscience.

Rabb, R. L., G. R. DeFoliart, and G. G. Kennedy. 1984. An ecological approach to managing insect populations. In *Ecological Entomology*, eds. C. B. Huffaker and R. L. Rabb. pp. 697–728. New York: John Wiley & Sons.

Revelle, P. and C. Revelle. 1988. *The Environment*. Boston: Jones & Bartlett.

Richardson, G. P. and A. L. Pugh. 1980. *Introduction to Systems Dynamics Modeling with DYNAMO*. Cambridge, MA: Pugh-Roberts Associates.

Ricklefs, R. 1973. *Ecology*. Newton, MA: Chiron Press.

Sampson, R. N. and D. Hair, eds. 1990. *Natural Resources for the 21st Century*. Washington: Island Press.

Schneider, S. H. 1989. The changing climate. *Scientific American* 261(3):70–79.

Scudo, F. and J. Ziegler. 1978. *The Golden Age of Theoretical Ecology: 1923–1940*. Berlin: Springer-Verlag.

Senge, P. 1981. Principles of dynamics systems I. Lecture notes. Massachusetts Institute of Technology.

Smith, V. K. 1972. The effect of technological change on different uses of environmental resources. In *Natural Environments*, ed. J. V. Krutilla. pp. 54–87. Baltimore: The Johns Hopkins University Press.

Ulanowicz, R. E. 1972. Mass and energy flow in closed ecosystems. *Journal of Theoretical Biology* 34:239–254.

Ulanowicz, R. E. 1980. An hypothesis on the development of natural communities. *Journal of Theoretical Biology* 85:223–245.

Wilson, E. O. 1989. Threats to biodiversity. *Scientific American* 261(3):108–116.

4

Probability, Utility, and Decision Trees in Environmental Decision Analysis

Richard A. Chechile

1 INTRODUCTION

Complex decisions are difficult because it is hard for people to maintain a clear picture of all the options available and all the possible outcomes. People also have difficulty dealing with decisions that involve uncertainty. With hindsight, decisions may appear trivial, but unfortunately we must make our decisions without the luxury of hindsight. Additional difficulties arise in determining the worth of all the possible outcomes and in setting criteria for choosing a course of action.

Such complexities often occur in environmental decisions, but they also have a history of occurrence in many other decision frameworks, for example, financial, medical, and military. Fortunately, decision science has developed some powerful tools for handling these factors. In this chapter we will discuss some general tools for decision analysis and apply these tools to an environmental case study. The case described in Section 2 is similar to one discussed by Stokey and Zeckhauser (1978), but the details and analysis are quite different from the earlier study.

2 THE FISH LADDER CASE

The rate of population increase in a metropolitan area has created a need for additional electrical power. The power company is already importing as much power as is available, and still there are frequent power outages and "brown-outs." Given even the lowest estimates of the increase in demand for power, there will be a power crisis in 10 years. The problem is simply that too little power is generated; a new power facility is needed. The power company and city officials agree that a hydroelectric power facility is the best alternative in regard to costs; it is also the best way to minimize negative impact on the environment. While the state EPA highly prefers hydroelectric generation to fuel-fired power generation, for health and safety reasons, there is still concern for the protection of migratory fish. These species are a valued resource for recreation, aesthetics, and food. The local river is known for the migration of several types of fish. To obtain permission to build the facility, the power company agreed to build a fish ladder to enable the migration of the fish. The company is not permitted to build a dam until a ladder is in place and certified as effective by the state EPA.

The construction time for the dam is 2.5 years after the successful certification of the fish ladder. When the hydroelectric facility is fully functioning, a rate increase will be charged to the power users. However, the amount of the rate increase is not known; the utility commission will set it when the plant is functioning, so when construction costs will be recovered is unclear. The whole project now rests on the decision of which type of fish ladder to build.

Three plans for the fish ladder are under consideration by the company. Plan A is for a "sure-fire" design that would take 2.5 years to complete and would cost $14 million. This ladder is known to be effective for migration both up and down stream on comparable rivers. The ladder is attractive and even provides for a scientific test station that can be open to visitors and tourists.

Plan B calls for a different type of ladder. The ladder will cost $10 million and will take 2 years to complete. This ladder has never been used before on a river of this size, although it has been used with some success on smaller rivers. Fewer fish can successfully traverse the Plan B ladder than the Plan A ladder. It may be effective enough for the survival of the fish; independent fish experts give a .85 probability estimate for this. It will certainly diminish the number of upstream game fish. In other words, it is not clear that—on a river of the size in question—the ladder will be effective enough. If the ladder is *not* effective (probability .15), that fact will be known within 2 years. Modifications to the ladder would make the ladder marginally effective, but these modifications would cost an additional $5 million and delay ladder certification one year longer.

Plan C involves a totally new design that will take only 1 year to build at a cost of $7 million. If this ladder is unsuccessful, no modifications can be done to make it effective; the designers estimate that the ladder has a 75% chance of being successful. Fish experts estimate that even if the ladder is successful, it will be less effective than the Plan A ladder but more effective than the Plan B ladder.

However, if after 1 year the Plan C ladder proves unsuccessful (probability .25), then the company would have to go back to deciding between the Plan A and Plan B ladders. Should they choose to build the Plan A ladder, the total cost for adopting first Plan C and then switching to the Plan A ladder would be $19 million and 4 years in time. Should they choose to build the Plan B ladder if it does not require modification, then the total cost of adopting first Plan C and then switching to the Plan B ladder would be $17 million and 3 years in time. If modifications are needed, the total cost would be $22 million and 4 years in time. A further, independent consideration is that although both the Plan B and C ladders appear functional, they are not particularly attractive.

Which fish ladder is the best choice for the company? Which ladder should be preferred by citizens concerned about the beauty of their environment and about the survival of the migrating fish?

This Fish Ladder Case contains a number of the complicating features of interesting but difficult decisions. There are a number of possible outcomes that can occur depending on what course of action is taken. There are a number of different dimensions to consider in evaluating the possible outcomes, for example, time for certification, cost of construction, degree of ladder effectiveness, and the physical appearance of the ladder. Moreover, the trade-offs that must be made among these dimensions and the eventual decision are influenced by the point of view of the decision maker.

Formal decision analysis is a beautiful way to examine the structure of the decision and to integrate all the information consistently. It treats the decision as if it were a gamble and utilizes mathematical concepts that were developed to understand gambles. Before returning to this case, let us first explore some key concepts that are the foundation both of games of chance and of decisions in the face of uncertainty.

3 ELEMENTS OF PROBABILITY THEORY

3.1 Basic Terms

Probabilities are understood in some specific context, which we shall call a "defined situation." A flip of a coin, the roll of the dice, the adoption of Plan B are all defined situations. Now, for any defined situation we can list *all* of the possible outcomes that are mutually exclusive. This complete outcome list is called a "sample space" and is designated by the letter $\mathcal{S}$. For example, for the coin-flip situation, $\mathcal{S}$ = ("heads," "tails"). For the roll of the dice, $\mathcal{S}$ = {(1,1), (1,2), (1,3), ..., (1,6), (2,1), (2,2), ..., (2,6), ..., (6,6)}, where the notation for *(a,b)* means "*a* spots" on the first die and "*b* spots" on the second die. The sample space for a roll of dice contains 36 elementary, mutually exclusive outcomes. For the Fish Ladder Case, the adoption of Plan B results in a sample space associated with whether the ladder will require modification to pass certification, that is, $\mathcal{S}$ = ("no modification," "modification required"). Sometimes it is useful to define a complex event—designated by the letter $\mathcal{E}$—as a grouping of mutually exclusive elementary outcomes. For example, with the defined situation of a roll of dice, the complex event of rolling a total of "5" consists of a list of four elementary outcomes: $\{(1,4), (2,3), (3,2), (4,1)\}$. In general, a complex event, $\mathscr{E}$, is a subset from a sample space, $\mathscr{S}$.

3.2 Probability and Its Measurement

In terms of a sample space, $\mathscr{S}$, with outcomes O_1, O_2, ..., O_n, we can for each outcome associate a probability value, for example, p_1, p_2, ..., p_n. We shall always require that the sum of all the probabilities is equal to 1.0, that is, $p_1 + p_2 + \cdots + p_n = 1$. Furthermore, the probability of some complex event, for example, $\mathscr{E} = \{ O_1, O_3, O_8 \}$ is $P(\mathscr{E}) = p_1 + p_3 + p_8$.

For example, consider the problem of assigning the probabilities for the total number of spots showing for "fair dice" and computing the probability for some complex event. Recall that dice sample space, $\mathscr{S}$, is $\{(1,1), (1,2), (1,3), ..., (1,6), (2,1), (2,2), ..., (2,6) , ..., (6,6)\}$. There are 36 elementary, mutually exclusive, simple outcomes in $\mathscr{S}$. For "fair dice," any of these outcomes is just as likely as any other. Consequently, the first requirement of having the probabilities sum to 1.0 is achieved by having $P[(1,1)] = P[(1,2)] = \cdots = P[(6,6)] = 1/36$. Consider now the complex event of rolling a "7" or an "11" (an immediate win in the game of craps). Since $\mathscr{E} = \{(1,6), (2,5), (3,4), (4,3), (5,2), (6,1), (5,6), (6,5)\}$, it follows that $P(\mathscr{E}) = 1/36 + 1/36 + 1/36 + 1/36 + 1/36 + 1/36 + 1/36 + 1/36 = 2/9$. Most probability calculations are in principle no more difficult than this example.

The question now is "what is probability?" Clearly only a few situations result in a sample space where we will want to assign all elementary outcomes with the same probability. What in general is probability? For many years theorists held that probability for an outcome was a long-run proportion that the outcome occurred. However, today most decision analysts would not accept the long-run proportion notion. A long-run proportion cannot be applied to cases that can occur only once. Usually decision analysts hold that probability assignments are an indication of our *knowledge* or our level of certainty about the defined situation. Probability assignments, rather than measuring an objective property of an outcome, may differ between individuals and situations because they reflect the different degrees of knowledge. Even a case as simple as a coin flip can result in different probability assignments depending on our knowledge. For example, suppose I know nothing about the coin flip other than that the coin is a typical U.S. dime. My lack of knowledge about the *next flip* is represented by assigning $P(\text{"heads"}) = P(\text{"tails"}) = 1/2$. Suppose, however, I knew that the last 1000 flips resulted in 571 "heads" and 429 "tails." Now I might believe that the way I was flipping the coin was slightly biased in favor of heads. Consequently, I could represent that knowledge by assigning $P(\text{"heads"}) = .571$ and $P(\text{"tails"}) = .429$. Suppose further that a group of physicists set up instruments connected to a computer that calculates which side will turn up while the coin is still in the air. Furthermore, suppose that the computer predicts that it is .99 certain that the next flip will result in "tails." Now the detailed physical knowledge of the next flip would be represented by the probability assignment $P(\text{"heads"}) = .01$ and $P(\text{"tails"}) = .99$. Consequently, probability is changeable as our knowledge changes.

The question now arises, how can we go about measuring our knowledge as a probability? To see how we could do this, let us look at another example. Suppose the situation is a young woman's application to three separate jobs which we will call A, B, and C. She believes that C is more difficult to get than either A or B—which she believes are equally probable. There are eight outcomes possible, that is, $\mathscr{S} = \{\sim A \sim B \sim C, \sim A \sim B\ C, \sim A\ B \sim C, \sim A\ B\ C, A \sim B \sim C, A \sim B\ C, A\ B \sim C, A\ B\ C\}$ where the $\sim$ symbol before a letter means that she did *not* receive an offer for that job. The first step in the assignment of probability is for the individual to rank the outcomes from the least probable to the most probable and to denote any outcomes that she judges to be equally probable. For example, suppose the outcome ranking is

$$
\begin{array}{cccccc}
O_1 & O_2 & O_3 & O_4 & O_5 & O_6 \\
\sim A \sim B\ C & < & A \sim B\ C & = & \sim A\ B\ C & < & A\ B\ C & < & \sim A \sim B \sim C & < & A \sim B \sim C \\
r_{12} = 2 & & r_{23} = 1 & & r_{34} = 8/5 & r_{45} = 4 & & r_{56} = 2
\end{array}
$$

$$
\begin{array}{cc}
O_7 & O_8 \\
= \sim A\ B \sim C & < & A\ B \sim C \\
r_{67} = 1 & & r_{78} = 4/3
\end{array}
$$

The individual is also required to estimate *all* adjacent ratios of outcomes. Thus, shown with her ranking of the outcomes are the ratios of all the adjacent outcomes, denoted by subscripts that correspond to the respective outcomes. For example, the ratio $r_{45} = 4$ is her estimate for the value of the ratio between O_5 and O_4, that is, $P(\sim A \sim B \sim C) / P(A\ B\ C)$, reflecting her belief that O_5 is four times as probable as O_4. Note that there is no requirement for judging the value of $P(O_5)$ or $P(O_4)$ directly, but just the ratio of the two. The ratio must be 1 or larger in order to be consistent with the rank ordering. A ratio of 1.0 occurs when adjacent outcomes are judged to be equally probable, such as the case between O_3 and O_2. The ratios uniquely determine the assignment of probability values. The probability values for the outcomes are

$$P(O_i) = t_i/K, \quad \text{for } i=1, 2, \ldots, 8, \tag{4-1}$$

where $\quad t_1 = 1,$ $\hfill (4\text{-}2)$

$$t_2 = 1 \cdot r_{12}, \tag{4-3}$$

$$t_3 = 1 \cdot r_{12}, \cdot r_{23}, \tag{4-4}$$

$$t_8 = 1 \cdot r_{12} \cdot r_{23} \cdot r_{34} \ldots r_{78}, \tag{4-5}$$

and $\quad K = t_1 + t_2 + t_3 + t_4 + t_5 + t_6 + t_7 + t_8.$ $\hfill (4\text{-}6)$

Upon substitution of the values for r_{12}, r_{23}, ..., r_{78} in Equations (4–3)–(4–6), we obtain, $t_2 = 2$, $t_3 = 2$, $t_4 = 3.2$, $t_5 = 12.8$, $t_6 = 25.6$, $t_7 = 25.6$, $t_8 = 34.133$, and $K = 106.333$. Substituting these values into Equation (4–1) yields the following probability assignment:

$$P (\sim A \sim B \ C) = 1 / 106.333 = .0094,$$

$$P (A \sim B \ C) = P (\sim A \ B \ C) = 2 / 106.333 = .0188,$$

$$P (A \ B \ C) = 3.2 / 106.333 = .0301,$$

$$P (\sim A \sim B \sim C) = 12.8 / 106.333 = .1204,$$

$$P (A \sim B \sim C) = P (\sim A \ B \sim C) = 25.6 / 106.333 = .2407,$$

$$P (A \ B \sim C) = 34.133 / 106.333 = .3210.$$

Notice that this assignment of probability results in the sum of all the probabilities being equal to 1.0, and that the ratio of probabilities is consistent with the ratio judgments. Based on these probability values, it is possible to determine that, for example, the probability of obtaining at least one job offer (i.e., all outcomes other than outcome $\sim A \sim B \sim C$) is .8796, whereas the probability of getting a choice of two or more offers (i.e., A B C, A B$\sim$C, A $\sim$B C, and $\sim$A B C) is .3887.

3.3 Expected Value

Expected value was first understood to be the anticipated mean value "in the long run." It is computed by the formula

$$E(v) = p_1 \ v_1 + p_2 \ v_2 + \cdots + p_n \ v_n, \tag{4–7}$$

where the sum of the probabilities $p_1 + p_2 + \cdots + p_n = 1$ and where the values v_1, v_2, ..., v_n are the respective values for outcomes O_1, O_2, ..., O_n.

For an example, let us consider the game of roulette, which—in the United States—has 18 "red" numbers, 18 "black" numbers, and 2 "green" numbers. Consequently, $P(\text{"red"}) = 18/38$ and $P(\text{"not red"}) = 20/38$. If we were to bet \$2 on "red," then we would either win \$2 or lose our \$2 bet. The expected value of the gamble is $(18/38)(\$2) + (20/38)(-\$2)$, or a loss of $10.526¢$.

When we play the game, however, we cannot lose $10.526¢$. What is meant is that the $10.526¢$ loss is representative of the anticipated average in the long term of repeatedly playing this gamble. Suppose after 1140 plays of the gamble we won 540 times and lost 600 times, then we would have lost \$120 over the 1140 turns for an average of a $10.526¢$ loss per turn. Notice that the 540 wins out of

1140 turns is the proportion of 18/38. Of course, if we actually did play 1140 turns there is no guarantee that we would win precisely 540 times. However, since the number 1140 is large, it is reasonable to assume that the actual number of wins would be close to 540. Statistical theory would predict that the number of wins in 1140 turns would be between 507 and 573 for 95% of the time. Of course, with probability theory we must also acknowledge that it is *possible* for us to win on all 1140 turns, even if it is not very likely (that outcome only has a 1-in-10^{370} chance). It is, however, impossible for 10^{370} games of roulette to be played even if the entire known universe were filled with tiny roulette wheels (no bigger than 6 inches on a side) and these wheels were to have been spun once per 20 seconds ever since the beginning of the universe, that is, some 15 billion years ago! A 1-in-10^{370} chance is thus extremely unlikely.

Even though expected value was first defined in terms of the long run, expected value is also the *rationally appropriate value that a person should associate with a single trial*. For the roulette example on a single turn we will either win $2 or lose $2. These are the two possibilities for a single turn, but we are not midway in our belief as to which of the two possibilities will occur. If we were certain of a win (i.e., $P = 1$), then the value of the turn would be $2, which would also be the expected value. If we were certain of a loss the value would be –$2, and *that* would be the expected value. Because we believe that the probability of a win is 18/38, then the value of the gamble before the turn would be 18/38 through the range of value that has –$2 on one side and $2 on the opposite side, that is, –$2+(18/38)($4) = 10.526¢, which is again the expected value. *Consequently, even on a single-trial basis, the expected value is the anticipated value of a gamble prior to playing out the gamble*. This understanding of expected value is critical in the decision sciences. If the expected value of a gamble is negative, then that is not a desirable gamble; if the expected value of a gamble is positive, on the other hand, it is an attractive gamble.

4 UTILITY

Another important task is evaluating the worth of outcomes. Before we tackle complex, multidimensional problems, such as the Fish Ladder Case described earlier, we will first consider single-dimension cases.

4.1 Single-Dimension Utility
and the St. Petersburg Paradox

In 1738 Daniel Bernoulli described a fascinating game in the journal of the St. Petersburg Academy. Because the game was puzzling, the problem exposed by the game has subsequently been referred to as the St. Petersburg paradox. Actually, the game was studied earlier by Daniel's older cousin Nicholas, who conferred with several leading mathematicians, including his cousin, about what he saw as a paradox. The game has two players—Peter and Paul. Peter tosses a fair coin repeatedly until a heads lands. The game ends on the first toss that a heads lands. He agrees in advance that if a heads lands on the first toss then he will pay Paul $1, and if the heads lands on the second toss then he will pay Paul $2, and if the game ends on the third toss he will pay Paul $4, and so on paying Paul at a rate of 2^{n-1} where n is the number for the toss when the first heads appeared. Consequently, if a game were to consist of four tails and then a heads on the fifth toss, the payment would be $16. The question is: What is a fair price for Paul to pay for playing the game? Nicholas and Daniel Bernoulli felt the fair value ought to be the expected value of the game.

This concept is further illustrated by considering a gamble that (with a 5/6 chance) pays $1 and that (with a 1/6 chance) costs $2. The gamble has an expected value of 50¢. Clearly, the gamble is advantageous. However, suppose you have to pay 50¢ to play the game; the new expected value of the game would then be 0, that is, it would be a "fair" game. The problem is that the expected value of the St. Petersburg game is *infinite*, that is, $(1/2)\$1 + (1/2)^2\$2 + (1/2)^3\$4 + (1/2)^4\$8 + \cdots$, which is an infinite number of terms that are 50¢ each. The paradox lies in the fact that Paul would never perceive the game as being infinitely valuable. Thus, he would not be willing to pay the expected value in order to play the game.

Daniel Bernoulli's solution to the paradox was the distinction between the monetary value and the subjective worth of money, which he called the *utility* value. He reasoned that the utility of a small amount of money was inversely proportional to the amount of money the person already had. For example, an individual should value $10 more when they have a total savings of $100 rather than when they have a total savings of $50,000. This assumption led to a mathematical expression that describes the utility as a logarithmic function of the monetary value. Bernoulli then showed that Paul's fair payment should be a natural logarithm of the amount of money that Paul possessed prior to playing the game. Paul should pay less if he had $100 than if he had $10,000.

In the past two and half centuries, many scholars have discussed the St. Petersburg paradox. Although many further complexities continue to fascinate scholars, the distinction between extrinsic monetary value and intrinsic subjective worth or utility is still accepted today. Moreover, we can generalize this distinction to a number of different dimensions of value.

For example, instead of thinking about money, we can conceptualize a difference between the number of years of life and the utility of those years. Moreover, two jobs that have the same salary and job description, but differ in regard to the attractiveness of the office, will have different utility values. In general, for any single dimension of value, we can distinguish between the actual objective value of that dimension and the subjective, internal value held by the individual. Utility is the perceived worth to the individual. Consequently, utility is relative to a context and the experience of the individual; there is no absolute utility value independent of time, individual, and context.

Psychologists have made this point quite clear by means of several experiments with laboratory animals. Premack (1968) showed that when a mouse is deprived of food but has ample opportunity to run in a running wheel, the animal is not particularly attracted to the running wheel but will "work" very hard in order to obtain food; even when a running wheel is not an attraction, the mouse will run all day in order to obtain food reinforcement. Premack also showed the converse, namely, that when the mouse has been deprived of the running wheel but has access to an abundant amount of food, then food has no strong attraction. In such a case, the animal will "work" hard—by eating food even though it is not hungry—to get the running wheel back. In another study, Chechile and Fowler (1973) showed that hungry animals considered 4 food pellets a punitive stimulus when they had had the experience of receiving either 4 or 12 pellets for the same maze-running task, whereas other hungry animals regarded 4 food pellets as a reward when they had received only that amount of food. These experiments clearly demonstrate that utility is defined relative to a specific context. Lobster may be a favorite dinner for many of us, but we can surely tire of lobster dinners if they become too frequent. In the measurement of utility we should be quite clear as to what the context is.

Since there is no absolute utility that is independent of context, the utility scale is scaled without a true zero point. Utility is scaled on a dimension relative to the variation of the alternatives on that dimension. For example, suppose we must determine the relative utility of −$10, $0, $30, and $100, when these are the only possible outcomes in a specific context. Clearly we all would rank order the utility by the dollar value. However, since there is not a true zero for utility and since the utility of any dollar amount can be measured only within the context of the other alternatives, we will define the utility (U) of the lowest, −$10, as being equal to 0, that is, $U(-\$10) = 0$, and—using a 0 to 10 scale—we will define the utility of the largest as being equal to 10, that is, $U(\$100) = 10$. The utility of the two intermediate dollar amounts will be judged to reflect their relative positions on the scale. While $30 is 36% of the full range of the dollar amounts, it might be worth much more than that to us, depending on our circumstances. Our judgment of the utility value of the amount is subjective. For example, suppose we judged $30 to be 4.4 on the utility scale; then we would be thinking of the difference between the utility of −$10 and the utility of $30 as 44% of the distance of the full utility range.

Suppose in another context, we had to scale the utility of $3, $10, $22, and $30, where *these* are the only possible outcomes available. Notice now that $U(\$30) = 10$ and $U(\$3) = 0$. This example illustrates the fact that there is no *absolute* utility for $30. In the first situation, only the four values of −$10, $0, $30, and $100 are available, whereas the context of the second situation is such that values of $3, $10, $22, and $30 are available. If we obtain $30 in the first situation, we have failed to achieve the maximum ($100); however, if we obtain $30 in the second situation, we have done as well as possible. Consequently, as the studies on the relativity of rewards and punishment (Chechile & Fowler, 1973; Premack, 1968) show, the utility of $30 is dependent on the other options available.

In scaling utility on a 10-point scale, a person should judge only the *difference of the intermediate and the endpoints;* that is why in the first case of scaling the utility of $30, we gave the 4.4 value, because $30 was perceived to be 44% of the full range from the lower anchor point. No claim can be made concerning the ratio of utilities, for example, it is *not* true that the utility of $30 is 4.4 times larger than the utility of $0.

The reason utility ratios are not meaningful is that there is no absolute zero for a utility scale. Ratios of a property are meaningful only when we can determine an *absolute* zero value for the property. For example, 0°C is defined as the temperature when water just begins to freeze. However, 0°C is not the absolute zero for the property of temperature; temperature is directly related to the kinetic motion of atoms, and there still is molecular motion at 0°C. As a result it is *not* true that 40°C is twice the temperature of 20°C. Only after considerable research did physicists discover that the absolute zero for temperature occurred at –273°C. On the Kelvin scale for temperature, the freezing point of water is 273°K, and 0°K corresponds to the true temperature where kinetic motion ceases. Thus, ratios of temperatures on the Kelvin scale *are* meaningful. However, with utility we cannot find a true zero because utility is always relative to the options available; utility *ratios* are therefore meaningless.

All we can do is calibrate the intermediate utilities *relative* to the two ends of the scale. Probability, on the other hand, is a scale with a true zero. A zero for probability means that the outcome has no chance of occurring. We insisted (in Section 3.2) on evaluating the perceived ratios of probabilities in the scaling of probability precisely because probability has a true zero.

4.2 Multidimensional or Multiattribute Utility

Decision cases often involve several different dimensions of value. In such cases, we need to generalize the measurement of utility in order to handle more than one dimension. For example, in the Fish Ladder Case there are four attributes, or value dimensions, associated with each alternative:

1. the value of saving time in building the ladder
2. the value of building the ladder for less monetary cost
3. the value of ladder effectiveness
4. the value of an attractive appearance for the ladder

These dimensions are quite different from each other, and they are not equally important. Our recommended method for multiattribute utility measurement is simple, logically sound, and a variation on the Hill (1978) decision matrix and the SMART procedure of Edwards (1971). More complex methods exist, but they are not an improvement on the recommended procedure. This measurement procedure requires six steps, which will be explained in the context of the Fish Ladder Case. We will first examine the multiattribute utility scaling from the power company viewpoint and later address the scaling from an environmental viewpoint. The recommended procedure is the same in either case, though the resulting utility scale will be different.

4.2.1 Step 1: Establishing the Outcomes
In the Fish Ladder Case, a number of different outcomes could occur. Each of these outcomes has a utility score. Consequently, the first step is to *list as row labels* the possible outcomes. The seven possible outcomes for this case are shown in Figure 4–1 and they are also portrayed in a decision tree in Figure 4–3.

Outcome 1 is the result of selecting Plan A, the "sure-fire" design that costs $14 million, takes 2.5 years to implement, and is an effective and attractive ladder. Outcome 2 is the result that occurs (with probability .85) from Plan B; it is a $10-million ladder that takes 2 years to build but has less effectiveness and is not very attractive. (The .85 value represents the belief of several independent fish experts.) Outcome 3 is the result that occurs (with probability .15) from Plan B when modifications to the original Plan B ladder are required, the total cost for the ladder is $15 million, and it takes 3 years for construction. Outcome 4 is the result that occurs (with probability .75) from Plan C—an unattractive ladder of intermediate effectiveness built in 1 year for the cost of $7 million. Outcome 5 is the result that occurs (with probability .25) if the Plan C ladder does not work and the Plan A ladder is then built. Outcome 5 thus is the same ladder as in Outcome 1, but for a total cost of $19 million and a total construction time of 4 years. Outcome 6 results (with probability .25) if the Plan C ladder does not work, the Plan B ladder is built and is successful (with probability .85), not requiring modification. Outcome 6 is thus a $17-million ladder that takes 3 years to construct. Outcome 7 is similar to Outcome 6, except that the Plan B ladder *does* require modification (with probability .15). Consequently, Outcome 7 is a $22-million ladder that takes 4 years to construct.

4.2.2 Step 2: Establishing the Dimensions
With the outcomes determined, we next need to establish the dimensions of value. Our set of attributes should include all the dimensions that are needed in order to describe the differences between the outcomes of the identified options. We want the list to be complete, but if there is a dimension on which all the outcomes are equal, then we should ignore that dimension since it does not differentially impact on utility. *The uncertainty (i.e., the probability) associated*

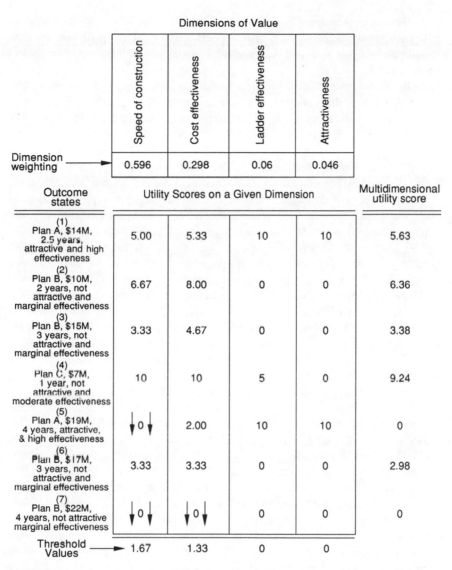

FIGURE 4–1.   Multidimensional utility scaling for the Fish Ladder Case from the utility company's viewpoint.

with an outcome must not be a dimension of value; uncertainty will be taken into account in Section 5 when we discuss decision trees. It is also important to label each dimension of value as a positive characteristic. (For example, instead of the label "construction time," which is negatively associated with value, we should label the dimension as "construction speed.") Without the positive labeling of each dimension, a meaningless mixture of positive and negative attributes in the utility scaling would result. It is also important that each dimension be separate or independent; we will deal with the relative importance of the dimensions in Section 4.2.5.

In the Fish Ladder Case, these guidelines for identifying the dimension lead us to label the dimensions as follows: construction speed, affordability, effectiveness, and attractiveness. These four dimensions are the column labels in Figure 4–1.

4.2.3 Step 3: Rating Outcomes on Each Dimension

Since the various outcomes are not all valued the same, we can scale the alternatives on each dimension in such a way that the most-valued outcome is given the score of 10, the least-valued outcome is given the score of 0, and each outcome that is between the extremes is given an intermediate score between 0 and 10 that reflects the perceived value of the outcome on that dimension. It is by using a 10-point utility score for each dimension that we will eventually form a composite utility value for these very different attributes of value.

The resulting single-dimension utility ratings for each dimension in the Fish Ladder Case are shown in Figure 4–1. For example, on the speed of construction dimension, Outcome 4 takes the least time (1 year), so that outcome receives the score of 10 on this dimension. Furthermore, outcomes 5 and 7 take the longest time (4 years), so these outcomes receive the score of 0. The range in actual construction time from the worst to the best is 3 years. The 3 years of time between the minimum and maximum construction time is the extrinsic value of that dimension; however, the utility or perceived value of the construction speed is its intrinsic value. Although there is no requirement that the intrinsic value or utility be linearly related to the extrinsic scale, there is also no requirement that prohibits a linear relationship between the intrinsic and extrinsic scales. In fact, on this dimension, the intermediate outcomes were given a score value that reflects the proportion of the 3-year range by which the outcome's construction time differed from the minimum time of 1 year. For example, Outcome 2 takes 2 years, which is 1 year more than the minimum time or one-third of the range in construction time. Notice that Outcome 2's score on this dimension is 6.67 which is one-third of the way down the utility scale. Consequently, the utility scores on this dimension, as well as on the affordability dimension, are linearly related to an extrinsic scale of value—that is, time and cost savings, respectively. Notice that even in this case of linear proportionality to an extrinsic scale, we are still better off working with a common scale (i.e., a utility scale) than with two extrinsic scales of quite different units of measurement. Having a common 10-point scale for each dimension makes it possible to combine or weigh the dimensions meaningfully to obtain a single scale for multiattribute utility.

Unlike construction speed and affordability, there is no extrinsic numerical scale for the attractiveness dimension. However, this does not cause us any difficulties in scaling utility on that dimension. The utility ratings of attractiveness, as well as ladder effectiveness, represent the decision maker's perception of the outcomes with respect to those dimensions.

4.2.4 Step 4: Determining Thresholds on Each Dimension

Decision making is always an attempt to solve some problem; it is a matter of selection among alternatives or proposed solutions to the given problem. Consequently, in the scaling of utility we need to examine the acceptability of an outcome with respect to the original problem. Dimensional-utility thresholds— *minimum acceptable utility values on a given dimension*—are important in defining what is an acceptable result.

For example, in the Fish Ladder Case, suppose the decision maker (i.e., the power company) believes that the ladder must be built within 3.5 years. Shorter times are preferable, but anything more than 3.5 years is not an acceptable solution to the problem. Given the proportionality discussed in Section 4.2.3 for the construction speed dimension, 3.5 years corresponds to a utility value of 1.67. Consequently, utility rating on that dimension that is *below* 1.67 would be below the threshold of acceptability.

The thresholds are shown for each dimension at the bottom of Figure 4–1. Moreover, any outcome score that is below threshold has been marked on either side by a ↓ symbol. On the affordability dimension the threshold of 1.33 corresponds to a cost of $20 million as the threshold of acceptability. Because the lowest-ranked alternative is still acceptable to the power company on both the ladder effectiveness dimension and the attractiveness dimensions, the thresholds on these dimensions are both 0.

We should be careful not to set threshold values too high. With high thresholds, we may later discover that the composite utility score is not different for the various outcomes. A dimension threshold should be a value below which the decision maker simply cannot tolerate the outcome.

4.2.5 Step 5: Determining the Relative Weights of the Dimensions

Not all dimensions of value are equally important. Consequently, in forming a composite multiattribute utility score, we need to weight the utility ratings on any given dimension by a measure of the relative importance of that dimension. The weight values are proportions, and the sum of the weights must be 1.0. Moreover, weight scores do have a true zero point; a weight of 0 means the dimension is of no concern to us. Since there is a true zero for weight scores, ratios of weights are meaningful comparisons (remember the discussion in Section 4.1). For example, if a dimension has the weight score of .35 and another dimension has the weight of .2, then the first dimension is 1.75 times as important to the decision maker as the second dimension. Notice that although these properties are similar to probabilities, *weight scores are not the same as probabilities* since they have nothing to do with the concept of chance.

The weight score should reflect the perceived relative importance of the various dimensions of value. It cannot be totally independent of the range of values of the outcome states. For example, suppose—for the sake of simplicity—there were only two dimensions in some cases, and these dimensions were "saving trees" and "affordability." Suppose further that the least-ranked alternative on the first dimension saves 300 trees and the best ranked alternative saves 305 trees. Moreover, on the "affordability" dimension, the lowest-ranked alternative costs $1,025,000, whereas the highest-ranked alternative costs $25,000. For a decision maker, saving trees may be more important than saving money. However, it is possible, by giving a very high relative weight to the "saving trees" dimension, that effectively we would be saying five trees were worth $1,000,000. Clearly that would be an absurd result, because for $1,000,000 we could plant many thousands of trees on protected land. The point of this example is that we need to reduce the weight of any dimension whenever the outcomes on that dimension do not vary widely in order to avoid absurd outcomes.

We will determine the utility dimension weights by a process similar to the one used for measuring probability in Section 3.2. Our goal is to obtain numeric weightings for the different attributes of value. First we will rank the *dimensions* from least important to most important, keeping in mind the range-of-variation issue addressed in the "trees" example above. In the Fish Ladder Case, the power company decision maker's ranking is

$$\text{attractiveness} < \text{ladder effectiveness} < \text{affordability} < \text{construction speed}$$
$$r_1 = 1.3 \qquad\qquad r_2 = 5 \qquad\qquad r_3 = 2$$

Also shown with his ranking is the ratio of adjacent weights, for example, $r_3 = 2$ which reflects the decision maker's perception that construction speed is two times as important as affordability.

The dimension weights are proportions that reflect the relative importance of the dimensions; therefore, the sum of the weights must be 1. This constraint and the evaluation of the perceived ratios of dimension importance completely determines the weight values. The procedure described below specifies the weight values that are consistent with all that is known about the relative importance of the dimensions.

First we need to compute a constant, κ, which is defined as

$$\kappa = 1 + r_1 + r_1 \cdot r_2 + r_1 \cdot r_2 \cdot r_3 + \cdots \qquad (4\text{--}8)$$

The relative dimension weights, ω_j, are computed by the following equations:

$$\omega_1, = 1 / \kappa, \tag{4-9}$$

$$\omega_2, = \omega_1 \cdot r_1, \tag{4-10}$$

$$\omega_3, = \omega_2 \cdot r_2, \tag{4-11}$$

$$\omega_4, = \omega_3 \cdot r_3, \tag{4-12}$$

· · · ·

· ·

· ·

where the subscript on a weight is *not* the column number for the dimension, but rather it is the ranking of relative importance of the dimensions from least to most important. For the Fish Ladder Case, $\kappa = 21.8$, so $\omega_1 = .046$, $\omega_2 = .06$, $\omega_3 = .298$, and $\omega_4 = .596$. These weight scores are shown at the top of each column in Figure 4–1.

4.2.6 Step 6: Determining the Multiattribute Utility Score

There are two computation rules in combining the above information in order to establish a multidimensional utility score for each outcome state. In order to have a positive combined utility the outcome must be perceived as at or above threshold on all value dimensions. Thus, first, the combined utility for an outcome state that has a below-threshold rating on any of the dimensions is assigned a value of 0. Using this first rule on the information in Figure 4–1 results in Outcome 5 and Outcome 7 being assigned a utility value of 0. Notice the concept of threshold and the inclusion of dimensions that are associated with complying to legal requirements or with adhering to ethical norms means it will be possible to develop a utility scale that has all illegal and unethical outcomes scored as a 0.

For the remaining outcomes we compute the composite utility for the ith outcome, U_i, by the equation

$$U_i = \omega_1 \cdot u_{i1} + \omega_2 \cdot u_{i2} + \omega_3 \cdot u_{i3} + \cdots, \tag{4-13}$$

where the score u_{ij} is the single-dimension utility score for the ith outcome and the jth dimension. For example, the first outcome has a combined utility of 5.63, which is $(.596 \cdot 5.00) + (.298 \cdot 5.33) + (.06 \cdot 10) + (.046 \cdot 10)$. In this fashion we can established the multiattribute utility scale for the seven outcomes from the power company's point of view. The resulting values or utility scores are shown in Figure 4–1.

4.3 An Environmental Viewpoint for the Utility
Scaling in the Fish Ladder Case

Since there is no absolute utility that is independent of context and the perception of the decision maker, the multiattribute scaling method need not—and generally will not—result in the same values when considered from different viewpoints. For example, environmentally concerned citizens who live in the town where the fish ladder is to be built would probably disagree with the weighting and threshold values used in the utility calculations of the power company. These citizens are most concerned that Ladder B is not particularly effective as a fish ladder and would result in a noticeable reduction in the stock of fish. They are also concerned that the aesthetics of their town will be impaired by the construction of either Ladder B or Ladder C. Since they prefer not to have the disruptions of normal town life prolonged by construction, these citizens have some regard for the construction speed, but it is a dimension of lesser importance to them. Cost is the least important dimension for them. The ranking of the dimensions and the ratios of importance are

$$\text{affordability} < \text{construction speed} < \text{attractiveness} < \text{ladder effectiveness}$$
$$r_1 = 1.2 \qquad\qquad r_2 = 6 \qquad r_3 = 1.5$$

For these citizens the value for κ is 20.2; thus the weights in ascending order are $\omega_1 = .05$, $\omega_2 = .059$, $\omega_3 = .356$, and $\omega_4 = .535$. These weight scores are shown at the top of the appropriate columns in Figure 4–2.

The dimension-threshold values are also different in the power company's analysis and the environmental analysis. The threshold values for attractiveness and ladder effectiveness are both 5 in the environmental analysis, but the corresponding values for those thresholds in the company's analysis are each 0. The new thresholds are shown in Figure 4–2. The threshold values force the multiattribute utility score for each outcome to be 0 except for Outcomes 1 and 5. Thus it becomes clear that even without a change in the dimension ratings or the dimensions of value, the resulting multiattribute utility score can be dramatically altered by a change in the values for weights and thresholds.

Since all outcomes associated with the building of either the Plan B or Plan C ladder have zero utility in the environmental analysis, the decision is an easy one—build the Plan A ladder. For the environmentally concerned citizens, the probabilities of successfully meeting design specifications associated with the

Plan B or the Plan C ladders are irrelevant because both of those ladders are either unattractive or ineffective. For the power company, however, the decision is far more complex: All three ladders can be acceptable. For the power company, the top choice will be a function of both probability and utility. A decision tree is an ideal tool for this type of problem.

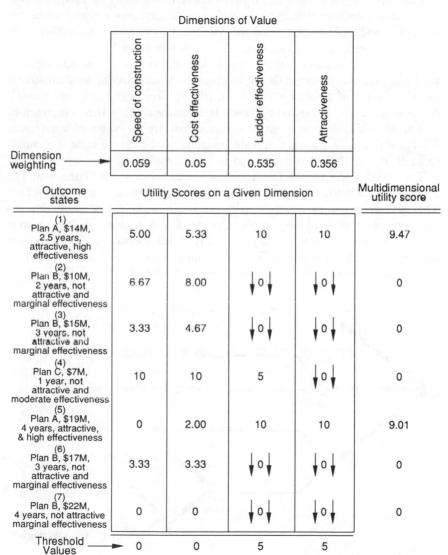

Dimensions of Value

Outcome states	Speed of construction	Cost effectiveness	Ladder effectiveness	Attractiveness	Multidimensional utility score
Dimension weighting	0.059	0.05	0.535	0.356	
	Utility Scores on a Given Dimension				
(1) Plan A, $14M, 2.5 years, attractive, high effectiveness	5.00	5.33	10	10	9.47
(2) Plan B, $10M, 2 years, not attractive and marginal effectiveness	6.67	8.00	0	0	0
(3) Plan B, $15M, 3 years, not attractive and marginal effectiveness	3.33	4.67	0	0	0
(4) Plan C, $7M, 1 year, not attractive and moderate effectiveness	10	10	5	0	0
(5) Plan A, $19M, 4 years, attractive, & high effectiveness	0	2.00	10	10	9.01
(6) Plan B, $17M, 3 years, not attractive and marginal effectiveness	3.33	3.33	0	0	0
(7) Plan B, $22M, 4 years, not attractive marginal effectiveness	0	0	0	0	0
Threshold Values	0	0	5	5	

FIGURE 4–2.   Multidimensional utility scaling for the Fish Ladder Case from an environmental viewpoint.

5 DECISION TREES

A decision tree is a visual portrayal of the entire structure of a decision problem. It shows alternative courses for action; it shows all the possible outcomes that could result along with their associated probability values; it shows the sequence of decisions that could result; and it shows the resulting utility for each outcome.

The entire decision-problem information is displayed as a single figure that consists of nodes of two different types. The first type of node is a *decision node,* which is represented by a small square. Branching out from the decision node are all the possible alternatives we are considering. If "no action" (the status quo) is an alternative, then it, too, is shown as a branch. Since selecting an alternative is the whole point of the decision analysis, *all decision trees begin with a single decision node.* The second type of node is a *chance node,* which is represented by a small circle. Branching out of a chance node are all the possible outcomes that could occur if we are at that node. Essentially, the chance node is a sample space $\mathcal{S}$ and the branches correspond to the potential outcomes.

The decision tree for the Fish Ladder Case is portrayed in Figure 4–3. The outcomes are the same as the outcomes shown in Figures 4–1 and 4–2. In fact, when we analyze a case, it is usually not clear, without first constructing a decision tree, what all of the possible outcomes are. A preliminary decision tree, without the numbers for probability and utility, is still useful as a way to structure the decision problem and identify the relevant outcomes. Notice also in Figure 4–3 that it is possible for a pathway to lead to another decision (such as the

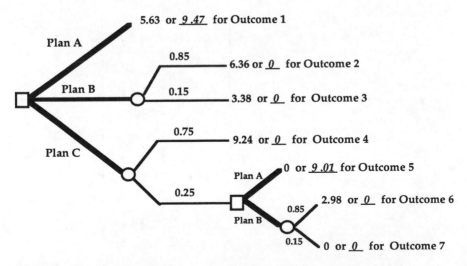

FIGURE 4–3.   Decision tree for the Fish Ladder Case. The first outcome utility score corresponds to those shown in Figure 4–1 (power company's viewpoint) and the italicized and underlined utility scores correspond to those shown in Figure 4–2 (environmental viewpoint).

decision after the first year if Plan C is tried but is determined to be flawed; the decision at that point would be between Plan A and Plan B).

Each chance node is really a gamble, and the worth of a gamble prior to playing out the gamble is the expected utility even when it is a one-time gamble. Expected utility is the counterpart of expected value except that the values in Equation (4–7) are utility values. In order to be consistent and rational, we have to equate the expected utility with the subjective worth of a gamble *prior to it being played*. If we believe that the gamble's worth is different from the expected utility, then it can be demonstrated that we are inconsistent about our belief concerning the probability and utility values. Moreover, whenever we are inconsistent about our probability and utility values, it is possible we can be induced to accept a series of additional wagers that we believe to be all fair individually, but where it is *certain* that we will lose when all the wagers are played out. The guaranteed loss is due directly to the inconsistent set of beliefs concerning the probability and utility values. Decision analysts insist on being rational, so each chance node is represented by its expected utility and thereby avoids paradoxical results. Equating of the gamble with expected utility is an important difference between prescriptive and descriptive decision making (see Chapter 1 for the distinction between prescriptive and descriptive decision making). It has been observed that people undervalue a gamble except when it is a "gamble" with a guaranteed outcome (Kahneman & Tversky, 1979), thereby showing that people generally do not value a gamble as equivalent to its expected value. Prescriptive decision analysts consider such behavior unacceptable and believe decision-making therapy is needed in order to educate people to behave coherently.

Figure 4–4 shows the Fish Ladder tree where all but one of the chance nodes are represented by the expected utility of the node. The operation of replacing the chance nodes with the expected utility of the node is called "folding back" the decision tree. Figure 4–4 is only partially folded back because of the complexity associated with the Plan C branch leading to a possible additional decision node. If we were to select Plan C, but the fish ladder proves to be unsatisfactory (with probability .25), we would have to decide between building the Plan A ladder and the Plan B ladder. From the power company's viewpoint, the expected utility for Plan A after the failure of the Plan C ladder is 0, whereas the expected utility for Plan B is 2.53. Since Plan B has a higher expected utility after the failure of the Plan C ladder, the power company would choose the Plan B option. Consequently, the secondary decision node really has the expected utility value of 2.53 from the power company's viewpoint, which is the expected utility of the action that would be selected. Therefore, we can now compute an expected utility for the chance node for Plan C, that is, $(.75) \cdot (9.25) + (.25) \cdot (2.53) = 7.57$. We can also compute the expected value of this chance node as $(.75) \cdot (9.25) + (.25) \cdot [(.85) \cdot (2.98) + (.15) \cdot (0)] = 7.57$. From the environmental viewpoint, the

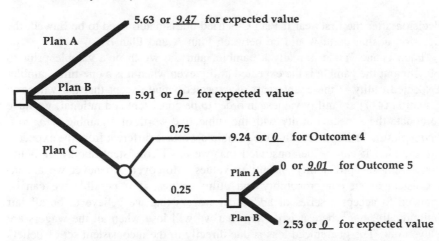

FIGURE 4-4.   Partially folded decision tree for the Fish Ladder Case. Expected utility value is a chance node except for the Plan C chance node. The first values are from the company's viewpoint, whereas the italicized and underlined values are from the environmental viewpoint.

expected utility of the secondary decision node is 9.01, which is the utility of the action that would be selected by the environmentally concerned citizens if Plan C fails to work. Consequently, the expected utility of the Plan C chance node from the environmental viewpoint is (.75)·(0) + (.25)·(9.01) = 2.25. Figure 4-5 shows the fully folded decision tree from the power company's viewpoint as well as from the environmental viewpoint. Based on this information, the power company's decision maker would select the Plan C alternative because it has the highest expected utility, but the environmentally concerned citizens would select Plan A as the option with the maximum expected utility.

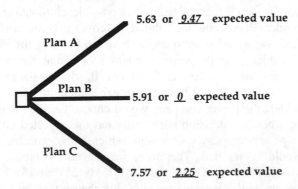

FIGURE 4-5.   Fully folded decision tree for the Fish Ladder Case with the first value from the company's viewpoint and the italicized and underlined value from the environmental viewpoint.

Adopting Plan C is the optimal alternative for the power company, because that alternative is better than any of the other alternatives. It is possible, however, that the decision in favor of Plan C could lead to Outcome 7 [with probability $(.25) \cdot (.15) = .0375$], which has a utility value of 0 for the power company. Consequently, Plan C is optimal in the sense of being the best bet before the company plays the gamble.

Sometimes, however, there is a truly dominant solution where the alternative selected is guaranteed to be better than all others. Such a dominant solution occurs in the analysis from the environmental viewpoint. From this viewpoint, the only reason the expected utility of the Plan C option is 2.25 is because there is a chance the Plan C ladder will fail. However, the environmentally concerned citizens would never choose the Plan C ladder option on the hope that it would fail; rather they would choose Plan A right from the start.

As we have seen, from the power company's viewpoint the Plan C alternative is the optimal choice—given the assumed probabilities values. But if these probabilities were different, either Plan A or Plan B might be optimal. Further analysis—in particular a sensitivity analysis—is needed to understand the relationship between probability values and the optimal choice.

6 SENSITIVITY ANALYSIS

A prudent decision analyst wants to know how much of a change in probability values would result in a different alternative being selected as the maximum expected utility alternative. Such an examination is called a sensitivity analysis. If we define the probability that the Plan B ladder works without modification as $P(B)$, and if we define the probability that Plan C works at all as $P(C)$, then a sensitivity analysis would let these probabilities take on different values and rework the decision tree. Figure 4–6 is a display of the results of a sensitivity analysis from the power company's viewpoint. The best estimates for $P(C)$ and $P(B)$ [i.e., $P(C) = .75$ and $P(B) = .85$] define an operating point; that point is in a region that indicates Plan C is the best course of action. Notice that the operating point is reasonably far from any of the decision boundaries. Consequently, from the power company's viewpoint, its preference for the Plan C ladder is moderately robust with respect to variation in $P(B)$ and $P(C)$ from the operating point. Since there is a dominant solution from the environmental viewpoint, the preference of the Plan A ladder by the environmentally concerned citizens holds for any set of values for $P(B)$ and $P(C)$.

7 A COMPROMISE SOLUTION TO THE FISH LADDER CASE

Despite using the same decision-making tools on the same case, we come up with different recommended actions depending on the viewpoint. While there are

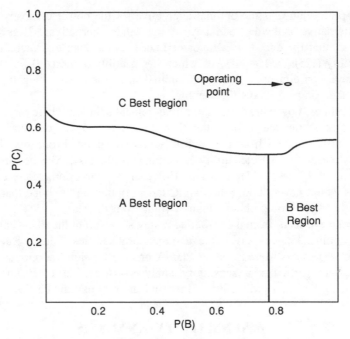

FIGURE 4-6.   A sensitivity analysis for the Fish Ladder Case from the company's viewpoint.

major differences between the two parties, there are also numerous points of agreement. Neither party disputes:

1. the need for greater power generation, which is to be satisfied by a hydroelectric plant
2. what the dimensions of value are
3. the relative rating of the possible outcomes on each value dimension
4. that construction speed is more important than cost
5. that ladder effectiveness is more important than attractiveness
6. the basic decision structure of the case
7. the values for the probabilities involved
8. that the optimal alternative is the one with the greatest expected utility
9. that the Plan B ladder is not the preferred alternative

In fact, the parties agree on all points except the weighting of the dimensions of value and the thresholds of acceptability on those dimensions. Given the different viewpoints for the two groups, the amount of agreement is uncommonly high, but then again, this is a hypothetical case involving hypothetical people who are behaving according to principles of optimally rational decision making.

In reality it might be that neither party believes in those principles; the dispute might have to be resolved by political or legal activities. Descriptive, rather than prescriptive, accounts of environmental disputes will be discussed in detail in Chapters 9 and 12. However, for the Fish Ladder Case let us capitalize on the common interests among the fictionalized parties and imagine that the dispute can be resolved by a compromise analysis.

Since both parties prefer some alternative other than Plan B, let us see if we can reach a consensus by omitting Plan B as an option. The omission of Plan B greatly simplifies the structure of the decision problem; instead of seven potential outcomes there are now only three: Outcomes 1, 4, and 5. These outcomes are shown in Figure 4–7. Furthermore, the probability of success of the Plan B ladder, that is, $P(B)$, is now irrelevant.

A number of dimensional ratings are different in Figure 4–7 from the corresponding ratings in Figures 4–1 and 4–2, due to the omission of Plan B as an

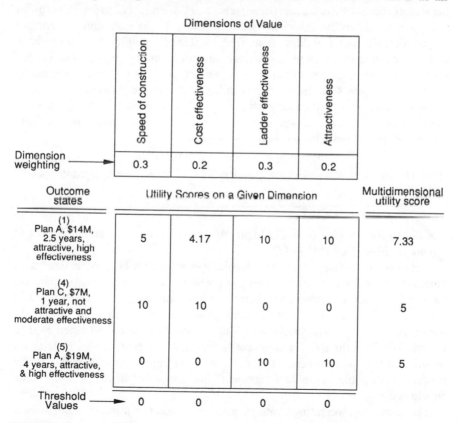

	Dimensions of Value				
	Speed of construction	Cost effectiveness	Ladder effectiveness	Attractiveness	
Dimension weighting	0.3	0.2	0.3	0.2	
Outcome states	Utility Scores on a Given Dimension				Multidimensional utility score
(1) Plan A, $14M, 2.5 years, attractive, high effectiveness	5	4.17	10	10	7.33
(4) Plan C, $7M, 1 year, not attractive and moderate effectiveness	10	10	0	0	5
(5) Plan A, $19M, 4 years, attractive, & high effectiveness	0	0	10	10	5
Threshold Values	0	0	0	0	

FIGURE 4–7.   Multidimensional utility scaling for the Fish Ladder Case from a compromise viewpoint and with Ladder B removed as an option.

option. For example, the rating of Outcome 5 on the cost dimension goes from 2 to 0, because Outcome 5 now represents the lowest outcome on the cost dimension. Moreover, the rating of Outcome 1 is now 4.17 instead of the earlier cost rating of 5.33; $14 million represents 41.7% of the reduced range on the cost dimension, that is, the range between $19 million and $7 million. The rating for Outcome 4 remains equal to 10, since it is still the best outcome in regard to the cost dimension. Moreover, the rating of Outcome 4 on the effectiveness dimension now becomes 0. All the other ratings remain as they were for these outcomes in Figures 4–1 and 4–2.

Two of the dimensions, cost and construction speed, relate to economic concerns, whereas effectiveness and attractiveness relate to environmental concerns. In terms of the weighting for the value dimensions, it is important to recognize that both the company and the environmental group value construction speed more highly than construction cost; they both also value ladder effectiveness more highly than ladder attractiveness. However, the two parties differ widely in regard to how much weight to attribute to the economic dimensions versus the environmental dimensions. The combined economic dimensions have a weight of .895 in the company analysis illustrated in Figure 4–1, whereas the combined economic dimensions have a weight of .109 in the environmental analysis in Figure 4–2. In the compromise analysis, the combined economic dimensions are weighted equally with the combined environmental dimensions of ladder effectiveness and attractiveness. In particular, the compromise ranking and ratios associated with the dimensions are

attractiveness = affordability < ladder effectiveness = construction speed

$$r_1 = 1 \qquad r_2 = 1.5 \qquad r_3 = 1$$

The dimension weights shown in Figure 4–7 follow from the ranking ratios and Equations (4–8) through (4–12).

Definitively stating what a reasonable compromise would be in regard to dimension threshold values is somewhat problematic. Fortunately, for the Fish Ladder Case, several reasonable alternative threshold assignments still result in the same decision action. (In other—real-life—cases, it is frequently difficult to obtain agreement on the thresholds.) The thresholds here are all listed as 0 in Figure 4–7. This threshold assignment is reasonable if both parties have abandoned their veto power in order to achieve a compromise. Later we will consider another "reasonable threshold assignment" and show that it results in the same conclusion.

The dimension weightings, ratings, and thresholds result in the multiattribute utility scale shown in Figure 4–7. These values result in an expected utility of 7.33 for the action of immediately accepting Plan A, and an expected utility of 5 for the action of trying Plan C first. The maximum utility choice is to adopt Plan A as the compromise solution.

In the original company analysis, Outcome 5 was the only outcome of the three possible outcomes in the compromise analysis that was unacceptable, that is, below threshold on the speed-of-construction dimension. In the original analysis by the environmental group, Outcome 4 was the only outcome of the three possible outcomes that was unacceptable, that is, below threshold on the attractiveness dimension. Consequently, as an alternative compromise on the threshold assignments, let us consider some nonzero threshold for the speed-of-construction and attractiveness dimensions. This alternative set of thresholds results in the same expected utility for the Plan A option, but results in an expected utility of 0 for the option of trying Plan C first; thus Plan A is still the top choice. Moreover, this conclusion is upheld for any possible value for $P(C)$, which makes the Plan A ladder a *robust* compromise solution.

8 ADVANTAGES AND LIMITATIONS OF A DECISION TREE ANALYSIS

The major advantage of decision tree analysis is that it is optimal (see Chapter 1 for discussion on optimality in decision making). It consistently integrates all the information known about the case and leads to a prescription for what the "best bet" is before we play out the gamble. This fact alone justifies making the analysis a prescriptive tool we should use whenever possible. It should be stressed, however, that it is the decision-making *process* that is optimal; an optimal process does not guarantee that the course of action selected will be a success. It will be the best that could be done without hindsight.

Despite the advantage of optimality, using a decision tree has some limitations and problems. One practical problem is the difficulty of using a decision tree on a problem where there are an infinite number of possible courses of action. For example, if the decision problem is to find the best recipe for allocating a large area of land with regard to the percentage to be used for recreation, housing, business, and so on, an infinite number of percentage combinations need to be considered. Decision trees can sometimes still be used on problems with an infinite number of possible decision alternatives if the alternatives can be grouped into a finite number of categories. But fortunately there are other mathematical, decision-analytic tools such as linear programming (see Chapter 7) that are well suited for such problems.

Decision trees are underutilized in environmental decision making because the cases usually involve numerous conflicting points of view—as was true in the analysis of the Fish Ladder Case. A decision tree is a way to structure the options, probabilities, decisions, outcomes, and values from a single frame of reference. When conflicting viewpoints must be taken into account, though, the decision process involves politics and political conflicts are rarely resolved by mathematical analyses (see Chapter 9). Nevertheless, decision tree analysis, in conjunction with a careful measurement of utility, serves a valuable function: it is an excellent way to identify potentially hidden features of a case. For example, in the Fish Ladder Case, it is by no means immediately obvious that Plan B is not favored by either group. It is also not obvious, in the compromise analysis, that none of the uncertainties in the case is a factor any longer. In general it is not easy to focus on the most important features of a case; people also have difficulty remembering and integrating all the information in a complex case without the help of a decision tree. The decision tree is well suited for framing a whole decision problem, in particular because it does so visually.

EXERCISES

1. Suppose that the Plan B fish ladder were equal in attractiveness to the Plan A ladder. How would the multiattribute utility change, and how would the decision tree and sensitivity analyses change? What would be the differences between the analyses by the power company and the environmentally concerned citizens? Is a compromise still needed—and if so, what would be a likely compromise?
2. Suppose that the Plan B ladder were equal in effectiveness to the Plan A ladder. As in Exercise 1, address the changes in the various analyses of the case.
3. Conduct an informal study with some friends concerning their perception of gambles. For example, you might ask them to consider two hypothetical gambles. Gamble 1 has a .67 probability for winning $50 and a .33 chance for losing $50. Gamble 2 has a jackpot of $100, while losing would result in a $50 loss. Ask the participants to determine a probability for winning the jackpot, p (and therefore the probability for the loss, $1-p$) so that Gamble 2 is subjectively equal to Gamble 1. Compute the expected values for these two gambles. Are the subjects matching gambles on the basis of expected values? If not, can you persuade them of the wisdom of equating expected value? Also, ask the subjects to compare the two gambles with a guaranteed gain of $17. Comment on these results in terms of the prescriptive-descriptive distinction discussed in Chapter 1.

ADDITIONAL READINGS

For further reading on probability and decision trees, see Chechile (1978), Trueman (1974), and Winkler (1972). See Bontempo and Holtgrave (1989) and Shafer (1988) for additional discussion of the St. Petersburg paradox. For further reading on utility measurement see Edwards (1971), Hill (1978), and Von Winterfeldt and Edwards (1986).

REFERENCES

Bontempo, R. and D. Holtgrave. 1989. Experts, novices, and the St. Petersburg paradox: Is one solution enough? *Journal of Behavioral Decision Making* 2:139–147.

Chechile, R. A. 1978. Decision making under conditions of uncertainty. In *Making Decisions: A Multidisciplinary Introduction*, ed. P. Hill, pp. 128–151. Reading, MA: Addison-Wesley.

Chechile, R. and H. Fowler. 1973. Primary and secondary negative incentive contrast in differential conditioning. *Journal of Experimental Psychology* 97:189–197.

Edwards, W. 1971. Social utilities. *Engineering Economist*, Summer Symposium Series 6:119–129.

Hill, P. 1978. Decision matrix. In *Making Decisions: A Multidisciplinary Introduction*, ed. P. Hill, pp. 120–127. Reading, MA: Addison-Wesley.

Kahneman, D. and A. Tversky. 1979. Prospect theory: An analysis of decision under risk. *Econometrica* 47:263–291.

Premack, D. 1968. Reversibility of the reinforcement relation. In *Contemporary Research in Operant Behavior*, ed. A. Catania. pp. 64–67. Glenview, IL: Scott, Foresman & Co.

Shafer, G. 1988. The St. Petersburg paradox. In *Encyclopedia of Statistical Sciences* eds. S. Kotz, N. Johnson, and C. Read. 8:865–870. New York: Wiley.

Stokey, E. and R. Zeckhauser. 1978. *A Primer for Policy Analysis*. New York: W. W. Norton & Co.

Trueman, R. E. 1974. *An Introduction to Quantitative Methods for Decision Making*. New York: Holt, Rinehart & Winston.

Von Winterfeldt, D. and W. Edwards. 1986. *Decision Analysis and Behavioral Research*. Cambridge: Cambridge University Press.

Winkler, R. I. 1972. *Introduction to Bayesian Inference and Decision*. New York: Holt, Rinehart & Winston.

5

Factoring Risk into Environmental Decision Making

Sheldon Krimsky and Dominic Golding

1 INTRODUCTION

The public is deluged with information about environmental risks. Rarely a day passes when the print or TV media do not report about some environmental hazard. We have been advised to test our homes for radon, quit smoking, eat less meat, and increase our daily exercise. Even when we make life-style changes, we find our lungs are exposed to toxic emissions from automobiles and factories; our drinking water contains alien chemicals with names like trihalomethanes and trichloroethylene; and our food is adulterated with an ever-increasing list of intentional and unintentional additives from ethylene dibromide (EDB) to cyanide. Our communities are besieged by toxic dumps, our beaches are strewn with medical waste, and our lakes and forests are dying from acid rain. Everything we thought we could depend on—air, water, food, even sex—is suspect. Now we learn that global warming threatens the stability of the entire biosphere.

Is our world really becoming more hazardous? How much risk do we face? How should we respond? Why do we worry about some risks and not others? The burgeoning field of risk assessment and risk management attempts to provide some answers to these difficult questions. But is risk assessment a science, an art, or a social process? Who decides how to manage risk—and can we have confidence in their decisions?

These are some of the questions we address in this chapter. We begin with a brief historical introduction to the field of risk analysis, while providing basic definitions of terms and concepts. We then describe the two dominant methods of risk assessment—the engineering and the toxicological approaches. Finally, we discuss the contributions of social theory to our understanding of the selection and management of risks.

Risk assessment is often viewed as an objective, scientific endeavor that is, or should be, isolated from the policy aspects of the decision-making process. Throughout this chapter we use examples to illustrate that science and policy are closely intertwined, and that neither can be isolated from the other. Science and scientists alone cannot determine which risks to worry about (risk selection), what levels of risk should be tolerated (risk acceptability), and how they should be managed (risk management).

In the final section of this chapter, we present a case study that explores the assessment and management of the risks associated with pesticide residues in food.

1.1 Historical Background

People have engaged in risk assessment and management since ancient times (Covello & Mumpower, 1985). By trial and error, they have learned to cope with the vicissitudes of the natural environment, to build structures that collapse only rarely, and to minimize the toll of disease. Each day we all conduct informal risk analyses, for example, when we put on our seat belts or choose where to cross the street (Wilson, 1979).

Not until the early part of this century did engineers, epidemiologists, actuaries, and industrial hygienists—among others—begin conducting analyses of the hazards associated with technology (Kates & Kasperson, 1983). At the same time, geographers, geologists, hydrologists, sociologists, and others were engaged in interdisciplinary research on natural hazards and disaster management (Burton, Kates, & White, 1978; White & Haas, 1975).

Legislation in the early 1970s, beginning with the formation of the Environmental Protection Agency (EPA) and the Occupation Safety and Health Administration (OSHA), elevated the role of risk assessment in the regulatory process and led to the professionalization of risk analysis and decision analysis in conjunction with a newly emerging industry of private consulting firms and academic centers (Kates & Kasperson, 1983; Cumming, 1981; Lind, 1987). This professionalization is illustrated by the formation in 1980 of the Society for Risk Analysis (SRA) with its own journal *(Risk Analysis)*. Since that time, the literature on risk has grown exponentially (Kates & Kasperson, 1983). The field now boasts three additional journals devoted solely to risk *(Risk Abstracts, Journal of Risk and Uncertainty,* and *Risk: Issues in Health and Safety)*. A range of other journals and newsletters regularly deal with related issues (e.g., *International Journal of Mass Emergencies and Disasters, Disasters,* and the *Natural Hazards Observer)*.

2 CONCEPTS AND DEFINITIONS

Terms such as *hazard, risk, risk analysis, risk assessment,* and *risk management* are not consistently used in the growing body of literature (Fischhoff, Watson, & Hope, 1984). For simplicity, hazards may be thought of broadly as "threats to humans and what they value" (Hohenemser, Kates, & Slovic, 1983, p. 378), and risks as "quantitative measures of hazard consequences, usually expressed as conditional probabilities of experiencing harm" (Hohenemser, Kasperson, & Kates, 1985, p. 21). For example, riding a bicycle is a hazard. If you ride a bicycle for two miles a day for the next week, there is a risk of 1 in N that you will break a leg (where N can be determined from actuarial data on bicycle accidents). Risk is therefore a measure of the likelihood and severity of harm, and the hazard is the source of the risk (Cohrssen & Covello, 1989).

When we study the social response to hazards, it is helpful to classify the many different types into a few recognizable categories. A common distinction can be made between natural hazards—such as floods, hurricanes, and earthquakes—and technological hazards—such as automobile accidents, oil spills, and nuclear power plant accidents. Natural hazards may be further classified

TABLE 5–1   Common Natural Hazards by Principal Causal Agent

Geophysical		Biological	
Climatic and Meteorological	Geological and Geomorphic	Floral	Faunal
Blizzards and Snow	Avalanche	Fungal Diseases *For example:*	Bacterial and Viral Diseases *For example:*
Droughts	Earthquakes	Athlete's foot	
Floods	Erosion (including soil erosion and	Dutch elm	Influenza
		Wheat stem rust	Malaria
Fog	shore and beach erosion)	Blister rust	Typhus
			Bubonic Plague
Frost		Infestations	Venereal Disease
	Landslides	*For example:*	Rabies
Hailstorms			Hoof and Mouth
	Shifting Sand	Weeds	Disease
Heat Waves		Phreatophytes	Tobacco Mosaic
	Tsunamis	Water hyacinth	
Hurricanes			Infestations
	Volcanic Eruptions	Hay Fever	*For example:*
Lightning Strokes and Fires		Poison Ivy	Rabbits
			Termites
Tornadoes			Locusts
			Grasshoppers
			Venomous Animal Bites

Source: From Burton and Kates. 1964. "The perception of natural hazards in resource management." *Natural Resources Journal* 3(3):415.

according to causal agent as in Table 5–1 (Burton & Kates, 1964), and by the nature or characteristics of the hazard event, as in Figure 5–1 (Burton, Kates, & White, 1978). Such classifications have important implications for research and managment. Blizzards are quite frequent events in the northern United States, providing a good data base and less uncertainty than for other natural hazards, such as earthquakes. Similarly, the management responses for earthquakes and blizzards are quite distinct because the two hazards differ markedly in terms of frequency, areal extent, speed of onset, and spatial dispersion.

The wide variety of technological hazards may be similarly classified according to a group of characteristics, such as type of consequences (human injury, illness, or death; property damage; ecological and environmental damage), pathways of exposure (air, land, water), and population exposed (workers versus the public; children and other vulnerable groups). Several taxonomies have been developed to simplify this complexity by identifying what appear to be the most pertinent variables for management and response (von Winterfeldt & Edwards,

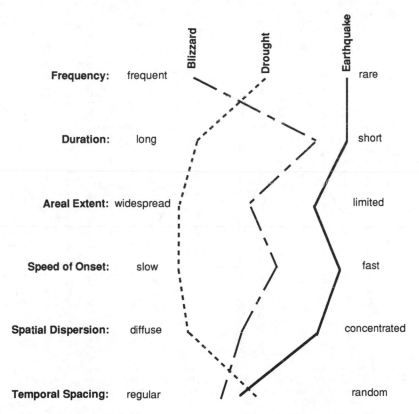

FIGURE 5–1.   Hazard-event profiles. (From Burton, Kates, & White, 1978, p. 29.)

1984). For example, Starr (1969) drew attention to a fundamental distinction between voluntary and involuntary risks, and others have extended the list of dichotomous variables for consideration, as indicated in Figure 5–2 (Fischhoff et al., 1978). Risk profiles, like those in Figure 5–2, are helpful in understanding new technologies. If, for example, a new technology were to have a risk profile that was similar to the nuclear power profile, then one could expect a public response for this technology similar to that of nuclear power.

Another taxonomy (Table 5–2) combines several of the above categories to distinguish between natural and technological hazards (Litai, Lanning, & Rasmussen, 1983). The conceptual distinctions, however, are often "fuzzy" and incomplete. For example, dam failures may be caused by earthquakes, and industrial pollution may be exacerbated under certain meteorological conditions. Some observers also question whether occupational risks should be considered voluntary. These shortcomings aside, taxonomies are useful organizing frameworks that allow us to group hazards with common characteristics of importance in risk assessment and management.

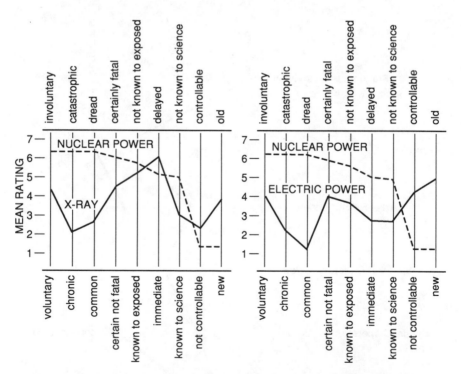

FIGURE 5–2.   Hazard-event profiles. (From Fischhoff et al. 1978, "How Safe Is Safe Enough? A Psychometric Study of Attitudes Towards Technological Benefits," in *Policy Science,* Vol. 9, no. 2, p. 142.)

TABLE 5–2   (Incomplete) Classification of Some Common Risks

	Voluntary		Involuntary	
	Immediate	Delayed	Immediate	Delayed
Man-Made				
Catastrophic	Aviation Passenger liners Railways		Dam failures Chlorine release Sabotage Nuclear energy	Some industrial pollution
Ordinary	Occupational risks Sporting activities Surgery	Smoking Saccharin Occupation risks	Aircraft crashes	Food additives Pesticides, e.g., EDB Nuclear energy (cancer) Coal energy Industrial pollution
Natural				
Catastrophic			Earthquakes Hurricanes Epidemics	
Ordinary			Lightning Animal bites Acute diseases	Various diseases

Source: From Litai, D., D. Lanning, & N. C. Rasmussen, 1983. The public perception of risk. In *The Analysis of Actual vs. Perceived Risks,* eds. V. T. Covello, W. G. Flamm, J. V. Rodricks, and R. G. Tardiff. p. 216. New York: Plenum Press.

Before the technical assessment of a risk is undertaken, it must already have been placed on the public agenda. Ordinarily, however, when risk is the subject of technical study, the starting point is risk assessment. Here we follow disciplinary conventions rather than the chronological sequence of events, and begin with a discussion of risk assessment and conclude by discussing the social and cultural theories of risk selection.

3 RISK ASSESSMENT

Risk analysis involves both risk assessment and management of natural and technological hazards. Risk assessment refers to the technical assessment of the nature and magnitude of risks (Cohrssen & Covello, 1989); risk management is the process of evaluating and selecting appropriate responses to control hazards or mitigate their consequences (Kasperson, Kates, & Hohenemser, 1985; National Academy of Sciences, 1983).

The principal goal of risk assessment is to identify quantitative measures of hazard in terms of probability and magnitude. Methods of risk assessment vary according to disciplinary focus and the nature of the hazard in question, but they all rely on *extrapolation* (Kates & Kasperson, 1983). Actuaries may extrapolate from past to future experience; engineers and experts in natural hazards may extrapolate from computer and simulation models to field conditions; toxicologists extrapolate from animal data to predict effects in humans. All these methods use different assumptions, and the levels of uncertainty will depend on the quality of the data, the level of understanding of the causal linkages, and the use of expert judgment.

While there are different disciplinary approaches to risk assessment, there are two dominant methods derived from engineering and health sciences. As illustrated in Figure 5–3, engineers have been most involved in assessing the probabilities of acute, catastrophic failures of engineered systems, such as airplanes and nuclear power plants, using event- and fault-tree analysis. Engineers have focused on acute events involving rapid releases of energy or toxic materials (such as the involuntary, immediate catastrophic risks shown in Table 5–2). Epidemiology and toxicology have emphasized the relationship between the resulting exposure (dose) and the adverse consequences (effect). Epidemiologists and toxicologists usually focus on chronic exposures and delayed health effects of the delayed voluntary and involuntary risks also shown in Table 5–2.

3.1 The Engineering Approach to Risk Assessment

In Figure 5–3, a loss-of-coolant accident (LOCA) at a nuclear power plant is the initiating event that leads to an eventual release of radioactive materials into the environment. Engineers calculate the probability of such an event using fault- and event-tree analysis (Figures 5–4 and 5–5). In Figure 5–4, the event tree begins with a pipe break, or LOCA, as the initiating event and traces the possible pathways ("branches") that lead to a variety of outcomes ("twigs"). To read the figure, begin at the left. At each node in the tree there is a possibility that the safety system will either be available or will fail. For example, if the pipe breaks, electric power is available, the emergency core cooling system (ECCS) works as intended, fission product removal is accomplished, and containment integrity holds, then only a very small release will result (i.e., the small amount of radioactive water released from the small pipe break). Alternatively, reading across the bottom branch, if electric power is unavailable, the remaining safety systems will necessarily fail and a very large release of radioactivity will result. Engineers calculate the probabilities of each of the safety system's failing to estimate the overall probability that a particular series of events ("accident sequence") might lead to a release. The probabilities of each path are calculated on the basis of previous operating and accident experience with data on human

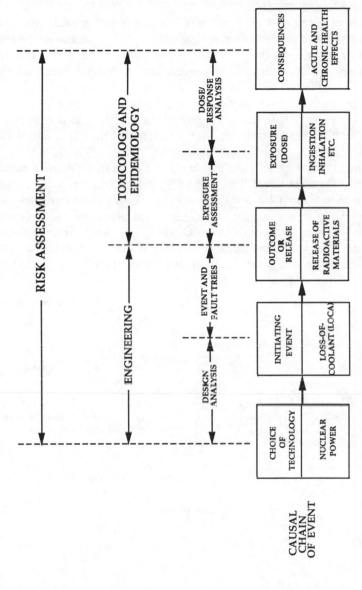

FIGURE 5–3. Methods of risk assessment. (Modified from Hohenemser, Kasperson, & Kates, 1985, p. 40.)

errors, and the failure rates of components such as valves, pipes, and dials. Since data are often missing or inadequate, expert judgment and simulations or models may have to be substituted.

Whereas in Figure 5–4 the event tree has one initiating event and several outcomes ("twigs"), the fault tree in Figure 5–5 has one outcome (the loss of electric power to safety systems) with several initiating events. Using fault trees, engineers begin with an outcome of concern and try to trace backward all the possible events that could lead to that outcome. The logic of a fault tree is therefore the reverse of an event tree. To read Figure 5–5 begin at the bottom. If the reactor loses both off-site ac power *and* on-site ac power, then all ac power is lost. If either all ac power or all dc power is lost, then there will be a total loss of all electric power to the safety systems.

Assuming there is an accident that leads to a release, radioactive materials will be dispersed according to the nature of the release (e.g., particulates versus gases), the local topography, and the prevailing weather conditions. Dose models developed by meteorologists, radiologists, and others are used to estimate how many people might be exposed to radiation and in what amounts. Based on the estimates of exposure, radiological toxicologists and epidemiologists are then able to estimate the likelihood, nature, and severity of the harm. Toxicologists

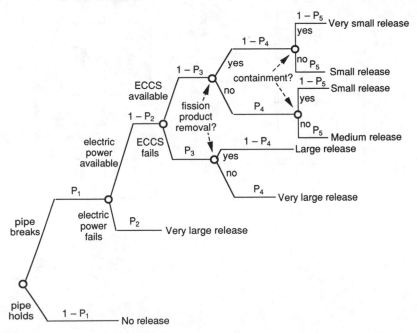

FIGURE 5–4.   Simplified event tree for loss of coolant accident (LOCA) in a typical nuclear power plant. (Modified from Rasmussen, 1981, p. 130.)

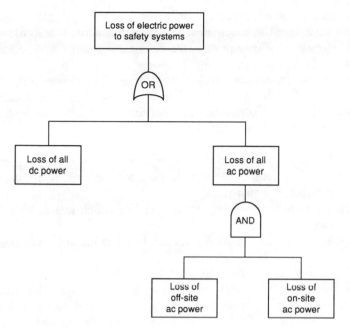

FIGURE 5–5.   Simplified fault tree for loss of electric power in a nuclear power plant. (From Rasmussen, 1981, p. 128.)

extrapolate from experiments on animals to determine the relationship between the dose received and the likely adverse effects (dose–response relationships). Various epidemiological studies may be conducted, but one type looks at adversely affected populations (such as the Japanese exposed to radiation from the U.S. bombing of Hiroshima and Nagasaki) and attempts to correlate observed effects with estimates of exposure.

3.2 The Toxicological Approach to Risk Assessment

One of the outcomes of the professionalization of risk studies has been the development of standardized approaches to risk assessment. The demand for uniform standards came from both public and private interests.

To illustrate this, we will take a closer look at the toxicological model of risk assessment. Often two or more regulatory bodies have the responsibility for evaluating the risks of a single chemical, but different agencies use different approaches to toxicological evaluation. These differences became an obstacle to interagency cooperation and created confusion in the public's mind (National Academy of Sciences, 1983). Moreover, as chemical liability and toxic torts became more prominent aspects of industrial life (Brown & Mikkelsen, 1990), demands were placed on government to promote standard methods of toxicological risk assessment. Consequently, the National Academy of Sciences (1983) pressed for the use of uniform methodologies.

The four-part framework developed by the Academy comprises: (1) hazard identification; (2) dose-response assessment; (3) exposure assessment; (4) risk characterization. Four corresponding questions emerge from this framework (National Academy of Sciences, 1983):

1. Does the agent cause the adverse effect, and if so, what are the pathologies?
2. What is the relationship between the dose received and the incidence of the adverse effect in humans?
3. What exposures are currently experienced or anticipated under different conditions?
4. What is the estimated incidence of the adverse effect in a given population?

3.2.1 Limitations of the Toxicological Approach

The above framework provides guidelines for risk assessment. But each stage in this process involves multiple levels of uncertainty and judgments that are not subject to scientific verification. Yet these are the assumptions that make the risk-assessment process possible.

One of the most refractory problems in toxicological risk assessment is the long-term, cumulative effects of low doses of a toxin. This problem is common to many areas of environmental decision making, including setting air- and water-quality standards, determining safe uses of food additives, regulating toxic chemicals in the workplace, and establishing safe residue levels for pesticides and herbicides in food. The risk-assessment framework is formal; it serves no practical use without data and inferential models. Risk assessors offer decision makers a menu of models that turn data on dose and exposure into risk assessments.

A widely adopted convention assumes that there is a continuity (linearity) between the effects of high and low doses of a toxin. In its extreme form, the assumption implies that even one molecule of a chemical may pose a cancer risk. Increasingly, the linearity assumption has come under attack by those who consider it too stringent a standard for setting public policy. Instead, they believe there are levels of exposure (thresholds) below which there are no significant adverse biological effects. However, the only means available to test the significance of threshold levels in humans involves complex, large-scale, costly, and often impractical epidemiological studies.

The third stage of the standard toxicological risk-assessment framework involves determining exposure. Such a determination can be extraordinarily difficult, however, and it is not unusual to find large error bars in any exposure assessment, particularly when large, diverse populations are at issue. In highly structured situations, such as controlled workplace environments, better exposure estimates can be made; these are nonetheless often still inadequate. The 1989 controversy over the use of daminozide (commonly known as alar), a chemical sprayed on apples to control ripening and improve appearance, illustrates the wide variance among experts on exposure estimates. The EPA indicated that about 5% of apples are treated with alar, whereas the Natural Resources Defense Council (NRDC) presented data that treatment is closer to 20%. EPA calculated a lifetime risk of 3-4 cancers per 100,000 people exposed to alar over the first 6 years of life, whereas the NRDC calculated a risk of 24 per 100,000 (Roberts, 1989).

Science informs risk assessment, yet the determination of risk is not a science. The standard desiderata of science are testability of theories, replicability of results, shared frameworks of analysis, and accumulated knowledge. For any particular risk determination, there are usually important gaps in knowledge; "transcientific ideas" (Weinberg, 1972) often masquerade as science, and hypothesis testing is conducted by analogy. One important difference between science and risk determination is in the standards of validation. In science, results are accepted when the author has met the standards of the discipline. Premature results must wait until there is sufficient evidence. By contrast, the requirements of public policy, and ultimately the market system, drive risk assessment. It is almost unheard of for the release of the results of a risk assessment to be postponed for lack of sufficient information. Technological choices demand publication of risk assessments regardless of the state of scientific knowledge in the field.

Risk determination involves layers of uncertainty. Certain presuppositions of the technical risk analyst are not justified exclusively on scientific grounds. McCray (1983, p. 83) states: "A single risk management decision is often based on an assessment that, itself, comprises many discrete decisions—choices among assumptions, interpretations, relative weighting of conflicting pieces of evidence. . . ." For this reason, risk is sometimes viewed as a social construction and not a property of the real world (Wynne, 1982). Others describe risk analysis as "value-laden." In spite of the theoretical possibility that some uncertainties can be narrowed, once the transition from risk assessment to risk evaluation is made, value considerations are central and irreducible.

4 RISK EVALUATION

According to conventional wisdom, most of the risks people face in daily life cannot be totally eliminated. We can ban a product such as DDT or asbestos and therefore eliminate all the risks associated with it, but then we have to deal with the risks of substitutes. If there are no substitutes, we have to face the risks that the product was designed to eliminate (such as pest infestations and fires).

When it is not practical or politically feasible to reduce risks to zero, how do risk managers decide what level of risk is acceptable? Many factors beyond the hazard outcome itself are relevant to such a decision. Some considerations are the following: Does the activity or product produce widely sought benefits? Are the risks and benefits distributed among the same people? Do people perceive the risks as voluntary or involuntary? Do the risks disproportionately affect vulnerable populations such as children or the elderly? Do the risks affect well-defined groups (such as workers) or are they randomly distributed over the general population? Will setting a lower risk level conflict with individual rights? What are the costs associated with risk reduction? Are the risks new or old?

The technical measure of risk as the conditional probability of experiencing harm [i.e., probability x the magnitude (number affected) and severity (injury, illness, death) of the consequences] is only one of several competing factors relevant to risk evaluation. Let us suppose that the use of a product is expected to result in no more than one fatality per year for a population of N individuals. What value of N makes the risk acceptable or tolerable? In regulating carcinogens, some experts have chosen a one-in-a-million lifetime (70 years) risk as acceptable (Milvy, 1986). Thus, if the population of the United States is 280 million, then at the acceptable level one would expect 280 additional deaths from cancer over a 70-year period, or 4 additional deaths per year. But this one-in-a-million standard has been criticized as being too restrictive when applied to specific occupational exposures. It would result in an infinitesimally small increase in the 450,000 expected cancer deaths per year in the United States.

For several reasons, regulatory bodies sometimes impose more stringent health standards on new chemicals than on chemicals already in use. First, when new environmental laws are passed, chemicals already approved for use are often "grandfathered in," or exempted from the new regulations. In such cases, the regulatory authority must show that the substance is unsafe before it may be banned. There are many examples of substances ranging from aspirin to alar that would not have been approved for use under current standards. Ordinarily, the burden of proof is on the manufacturer to show that the chemical is safe.

Second, most regulatory agencies are obligated to consider benefits in their decision to restrict or ban a product's use. An established product has accrued more benefits by virtue of its position in the economic system. Withdrawing a product is generally more expensive to society overall than preventing one from being introduced.

Third, there are more advocacy groups in support of established products than there are in support of new products. In the case of alar, growers had organized their schedules around the use of a chemical that allowed the apples to remain on the trees longer. The manufacturers of alar, the growers, and their advocates lobbied hard to prevent the prohibition of the chemical.

Several approaches have been advanced for setting acceptable or tolerable levels of risk (e.g., Kasperson, 1983). We shall discuss three of these: *de minimis* risk, comparative-risk, and risk-benefit analysis.

4.1 *De minimis* risk

The term *de minimis* comes from the legal concept *de minimis non curat lex* which means the law does not concern itself with trifles. The idea behind *de minimis* risk is that, below some level of risk, it is not worth the allocation of social or personal resources to address the problem. For example, if the annual expected fatality for a product or an activity is 1 in 500 million, the risk would be considered exceedingly low. Most environmental laws use a term like "significant hazards" when referring to the appropriateness of regulation. Natural hazards sometimes are used as a baseline indicator of *de minimis* risk. If the risk of a particular product or technology (measured as probability x consequence) is less than the risk of some common natural hazards (e.g., floods, background radiation, lightning strikes, earthquakes), then it is sometimes viewed as below the threshold of concern.

Another approach to setting a threshold is based upon the methods of detection. The point at which the risks cannot be detected might be viewed as an acceptable level. This is a much weaker criterion than one based on natural hazards, because methods of detection, particularly in epidemiological studies, are very insensitive instruments and may fail to detect even significant risks. One of the benefits of a generalized *de minimis* risk is that it can be applied across regulatory regimes.

4.2 Comparative-Risk Analysis (CRA)

Comparative-risk analysis (CRA) involves weighing the risks of new products or technologies against other products or technologies that are already "accepted" or "tolerated" by society. Starr (1985, p. 97) maintains that CRA can "provide a basis for the rational distribution of society's resources to improve public health and safety." Wilson (1979) proposes using CRA for setting priorities in risk management and making more sense out of the risks society faces. Wilson (1979) also believes it is better to evaluate the risks quantitatively and then to reduce the largest risks first, rather than to try to eliminate all risks or to spend a lot of time and effort reducing insignificant risks. Comparing risks requires organizing disparate hazard events under a single metric, as illustrated in Table 5–3. This sometimes results in some bizarre comparisons among very dissimilar types of hazards.

TABLE 5–3   A Comparison of Risks

Quantity	Action	Cause of Death
2 (U.K.) 3 (U.S.)	Cigarettes	Cancer, heart disease
2 months	Of living with a cigarette smoker	Cancer, heart disease
½ liter	Wine	Cirrhosis of the liver
40 T.	Peanut butter	Liver and other cancers caused by aflatoxin
1 year	Miami drinking water	Cancer caused by chloroform
30 cans	Diet soda	Cancer caused by saccharin
100	Charcoal-broiled steaks	Cancer caused by benzo(α)pyrene (risks of red meat, fattening, etc., additional)
2 months	Visit to Denver	Cancer caused by cosmic rays
6000 miles	Jet flying at 35,000 ft.	Cancer caused by cosmic rays
1	X-ray in a good hospital	Radiation cancer
20 years	Living within 5 miles of a poly-vinyl chloride plant	Cancer caused by vinyl chloride
2 days	In New York or Boston	Air pollution
3 hours	In coal mine	Accident
1 hour	In coal mine	Black lung disease
150,000 times	Dyeing hair with lead acetate dye	Cancer caused by lead
1000 times	Drinking from banned plastic bottle	Cancer caused by acrylonitrite
6 minutes	In a canoe	Accident
1 year	At site boundary of nuclear power plant	Radioactive accident
3 weeks	Living below a dam	Accident (dam failure)

Note: Actions which can increase the average risk of death by 1 part in 1 million or reduce life expectancy by 9 minutes for cancer or 15 minutes for accident.
Source: From Richard Wilson, 1984. Commentary: risks and their acceptability, in *Science, Technology and Human Values,* Vol. 9, no. 2, p. 19.

The Nuclear Regulatory Commission's classic Reactor Safety Study compared the risks of nuclear accidents with the risks of daily life, of natural hazards, and of other technologies. Its purpose was to show how minuscule the probability of a fatality from a nuclear accident was compared to that of other more commonplace accidents (Nuclear Regulatory Commission, 1975).

Used in conjunction with other methods, CRA provides a basis for determining acceptable levels of risk. The decision logic is as follows: If product A is acceptable to the public and has a risk factor greater than that of product B, everything else being equal, then product B ought to be acceptable. Biochemist Bruce Ames of the University of California at Berkeley is a strong proponent of CRA to evaluate food additives and agricultural chemicals. Ames and Gold (1989) believe the risks of some highly publicized pesticide residues on food (such as EDB and alar) are trivial, based upon their studies comparing the risks of these chemicals to the risks of natural carcinogens in foods, such as aflatoxin in peanut butter.

These types of comparisons often confuse rather than clarify the issues. For example, the comparison between peanut butter and EDB or alar did not make much of an impact on the public. Similarly, the NRC's assertion that the probability of being killed in a reactor accident was equivalent to the probability of someone being killed by a meteorite (National Research Council, 1975) did little to allay public fears about nuclear power. Making such analogies is like trying to compare apples and oranges—there is no common metric.

The risks of nuclear accidents are qualitatively different from the risks of driving, for example. Driving is a voluntary activity over which we believe we have a large measure of personal control—and most of us have *no* sense of control over the way the nuclear industry runs its reactors. Furthermore, comparisons such as those in Table 5–4 are viewed by some critics as disingenuous, plainly intended to influence public opinion and not merely to inform about risk. Although it may be that out of 15 million people we can expect 4200 automobile-related deaths annually, the fear of nuclear accidents is far greater, because it has little to do with the low annual average fatalities (only two) that result from day-to-day operations of nuclear facilities. Rather, people fear the low-probability/high-consequence accidents that may kill thousands of people. This fear is exacerbated by public distrust of the nuclear industry in general (Otway & Wynne, 1989), further blurring the benefits of making comparisons in the first place. Thus, these efforts to make comparisons serve primarily to highlight the differences between the way scientists and the vast majority of nonscientists view risk.

4.3 Risk-Benefit Analysis

A third approach to determining risk acceptability involves the comparison of risks and benefits. As individuals, we face many decisions where risks and

TABLE 5–4   Average Annual Risks from Various Accidents
for 15 Million People Living Near a Reactor Site

Accident Type	Annual Fatalities	Injuries
Automobile	4,200	375,000
Falls	1,500	75,000
Fire	560	22,000
Electrocution	90	—
Lightning	8	—
Reactor (100 plants)	2	20

Source: From Nuclear Regulatory Commission. 1975. Reactor Safety Study Executive Summary. WASH-1400 (NUREG/74/104). Washington, D.C.: Nuclear Regulatory Commission: 9.

benefits are intertwined. An arthritic patient is advised that aspirin may reduce his discomfort, but that the drug may cause side effects like abdominal ulcers. The risks are acceptable or tolerable when the benefits outweigh the risks. For the individual decision maker, this result is tautological. Once advised about the risks and benefits, the individual's choice is an expression of personal risk-benefit balancing. Thus, the notion of setting acceptable risks in this manner is ideally suited to those circumstances where conditions of autonomous choice and best available information are satisfied.

The main problem with risk-benefit balancing is the incommensurability of risks and benefits. This problem is solvable when a single individual is both the decision maker and the recipient of both risks and benefits. Moreover, this method precludes the need to set a fixed acceptable level of risk, since the latter is a function of the benefits, which vary greatly across products and activities.

Problems arise when regulatory agencies are responsible for setting an acceptable risk level and the risks and benefits are not distributed homogeneously throughout the society. In the case of chemical exposures, some individuals—because of their life-style, location, health status, or genetic endowment—may be more vulnerable to harm. Furthermore, those who benefit most from the product usually are not the people who are most at risk. In such situations, the problem of incommensurability of risks and benefits looms large.

While there are no sure-fire methods for drawing comparisons between fatalities and economic savings, the use of risk/benefit or cost/benefit analysis to establish acceptable risks has many adherents (Leonard & Zeckhauser, 1986). One method, often employed, builds on the autonomous-choice model. In following this model, decision makers view society as an aggregate of individuals who separately balance the risks and benefits of products and technologies. The role of the decision maker is to interpret and implement public choice. "Acceptable risk" must be determined for every individual product since there can be no *a priori* comparisons across different benefit regimes. However, implementing such a scheme for the tens of thousands of chemicals, consumer products, and technologies would be prohibitive.

5 CONCLUSION: CULTURAL THEORY AND RISK SELECTION

Decision scientists consider risk assessment an integral tool in environmental decision making. It offers policymakers a rational basis for risk selection and risk comparison. But the public response to many of the risks of industrial society is often at considerable odds with what the experts believe. Recent studies in the social and cultural aspects of risk have brought a fresh perspective to our understanding of the role risk assessment plays in decision making. Instead of viewing risk assessment as a neutral and purely scientific aspect of the policy process, some view it as a social construction subject to the same influences of the political process that befall nontechnical problems. Some cultural theorists maintain that "risk" itself has no objective status and therefore is not fundamental to a decision process. Rather than viewing risk as an ojective phenomenon of the physical world, they consider risk a subjective attribute molded by social processes (Rayner & Cantor, 1987; Schwartz & Thompson, 1990; Thompson, 1980).

A more fundamental question than "What are the risks of a product or technology?" exists, namely: "How did the issue get on the public agenda?" Selecting or rejecting risks is made intelligible by more completely understanding the cultural and social fabric within which the risk is embedded. Different cultures emphasize different risks. Douglas and Wildavsky (1982, p. 8) maintain that: "Each form of social life has its own typical risk portfolio." In the case of the pesticide ethylene dibromide (EDB), the numbers in the risk estimates were largely irrelevant. More important were the powerful messages sent by TV pictures of exposed workers suffering obvious neural disorders, and the fact that people—especially children—would be exposed through the consumption of foods. Any adulteration of food is a social anathema, and adulteration with a potentially carcinogenic pesticide particularly so. The public discourse over EDB is therefore rooted in a more general concern about the use of pesticides, the adulteration of food, and cancer as the scourge of modern civilization.

In contrast to engineers, economists, and decision scientists, cultural theorists reject the idea of a common metric for rating and comparing different hazards. They view risk as a polymorphic concept (Rayner & Cantor, 1987) and advise risk managers not to treat risk as if it were a real property of the world. Rather, they believe that risk managers should focus on the technology and the institutions that control its utilization.

Cultural theorists also distinguish themselves by the way they treat rationality in risk assessment. Wynne (1982) argues that science created an elaborate mythology about risks to legitimate control over technology. Krimsky and Plough (1988) distinguish between technical and cultural rationality of risk, where each mode of analysis is internally consistent and representative of a different set of values and interests. Perrow (1984) cites three forms of rationality: absolute rationality held by economists and engineers, bounded or limited rationality held by risk assessors, and cultural rationality held by the majority of people. Different viewpoints about how risk is factored into decision making can sometimes be explained by reference to the divergent concepts of rationality within microcultures.

The most ardent cultural theorists believe that scientific rationality is reducible to political anthropology and sociology. Weinberg (1981, p. 5) argues that ". . . even when the risks can be quantified, the setting of standards is intrinsically a political act. That is the standards themselves must in the final analysis be arbitrary." This leads to the conclusion that environmental decision making incorporating risk assessment is embedded in a social process that at times yields consensus among members of the scientific community and policymakers, but most often mirrors the ebbs and flows of any political debate.

Perhaps the most significant difference between cultural and technical perspectives on risk bears on the issue of where democratic process enters into decision making. Much of the research in risk studies is grounded on the distinction between a descriptive-scientific component and a normative-policy component in the decision matrix. The scientific component is sought in risk assessment (what are the risks and who is at risk), whereas the normative component is sought in risk management (what risks we should accept and what we should do about the risk levels that are unacceptable). This suggests distinctive roles for the scientific and democratic process. Cultural and sociological theorists reject this division of science and value. Instead, they place risk selection and the public's confidence in scientific and political institutions as primary factors of analysis. Environmental risk itself is derived from a configuration of special interests and selected paradigms of rationality.

To understand fully how and why certain issues are brought to public attention, we must investigate the roles and decision choices of all the actors. This may include nonprofit organizations such as the Environmental Defense Fund (EDF), not necessarily part of the formal process of risk assessment and hazard management.

An excellent example to illustrate the cultural approach to risk selection is the EDB controversy (see the case study in Section 6). First, in the United States, environmental advocacy groups played a key role in highlighting the risks of EDB as a cause for concern. EDB was "selected" and placed on the regulatory and political agenda years before there were conclusive data from animal studies to show that EDB was a potential human carcinogen. The EDF petitioned the EPA to investigate the risks and suspend its use. Organizations like EDF thereby acted in *loco parentis* of society.

Second, EDB has a risk profile similar to other chemicals that have excited major public controversy and concern in the past. Exposure to EDB is widespread: it represents a largely involuntary risk beyond the control of individual citizens. The pesticide is associated with a dread disease—cancer. No safe level of exposure is known to exist, and children may be particularly vulnerable to the toxic and carcinogenic effects.

Third, the media and popular culture respond most effectively to singular, dramatic events, so the disturbing film footage of workers suffering severe neural damage from prolonged exposure to high doses of EDB served as a lens through which to evaluate the long-term effects on consumers of exposure to relatively low doses in food.

Fourth, as a potential human carcinogen, EDB cast a cloud over foods in which people wish to have unqualified trust—foods that are symbolic of sustenence and purity, such as bread, baby cereals, and cake mixes. The selection of concerns is not homogeneous across all food groups. Also, it is a notable cultural irony that, under EPA and FDA regulations, EDB would not have been permitted as a food additive in any amount, but was permitted as a pesticide residue in small amounts.

Finally, while EPA and several states set stricter standards for EDB in 1983, it has not been banned from all uses. Very little public attention will be given to substitute pesticides and their associated risks until the social selection process highlights a new concern.

Risk assessment cannot be ignored as a component of environmental decision making. But the particular role it plays and the influence it exerts in public policy are still very much matters of debate. Two cultures are in stark contrast. The first chooses as its goal the rigorous quantification of risk and the standardization of risk measurements leading toward a unification of the field and a rationalization of public policy. We may call this approach "risk scientism." The other approach sees risk not as a reified property of the natural or technological world subject to objective measurement and quantification, but rather as the outcome of a process of social selection. We may call this approach "risk populism." Environmental decisions generally involve balancing "risk scientism" and "risk populism." The balance point depends on our collective notions of uncertainty and rationality, and on our trust in the institutions that generate and control risks.

6 APPENDIX: A CASE ANALYSIS OF PESTICIDE RESIDUES IN FOOD

To illustrate how risk-analysis and risk-management concepts are applied in a real situation, we present a case in which regulators were faced with assessing the risks of chemical pesticide residues in the food supply. Risk estimation is just one of several factors that are considered in the decision process.

6.1 Background

Certain hazards involving health risks to humans of low doses of chemicals exhibit certain patterns of complexity to decision makers. The following case, which concerns the pesticide ethylene dibromide (EDB), is characteristic of many of the cases where chemicals were brought under regulatory authority. Typically, after the chemical has been in use for many years, information about its potential adverse consequences to human health becomes known. The review process for chemicals that is already part of the industrial system generally requires different considerations of benefits than those chemicals that have not yet been introduced. Additionally, scientific uncertainty preys on the risk-assessment process.

Beginning in the 1930s, ethylene dibromide was widely used in agriculture as a post-harvest fumigant for grains.* EDB protected stored wheat and corn against insects, molds, and fungi. It was first registered as a pesticide in 1948. By 1955, food tolerances had been established for the presence of EDB metabolites. A year later, Dow Chemical Company, one of the principal manufacturers of EDB, petitioned and received from the federal government an exemption from tolerance levels when the chemical was used as a grain fumigant. The justification for the exemption was based on evidence that the compound would not remain active for long. Moreover, it was believed that any residues would be driven off when the grains were cooked.

Advanced technologies for measuring minute quantities (parts per billion) of chemicals became available in the 1960s. Also, animal models were developed to test mutagenicity and carcinogenicity of chemical compounds. Within a decade, laboratory findings linked EDB to cancers in rats and mice.

Regulatory agencies began setting standards for EDB after preliminary risk assessments were completed. In 1977, the EPA concluded that EDB was a potent carcinogen in animals and likely to be carcinogenic in humans. Under what was then the current usage, EPA estimated a cancer risk of 3.3 cancers per 1000 people exposed. Since EDB was used on grains basic to the American diet, practically everyone in the country was exposed to some level of the chemical. Precise estimates of exposure could not be made because several questions remained unanswered: What percentage of EDB remains in processed food? What percentage of EDB is destroyed by cooking? What amount of EDB is found on food that is eaten without cooking? What amount of EDB is consumed on the average by adults and children?

The chemical industry responded to the EPA's risk estimates by funding its own risk assessment. It concluded that EPA greatly exaggerated the risks. A more sober estimate, according to an industry trade association, was 1 cancer per million children exposed and 1 cancer per 12 million adults exposed. Industry spokespersons argued that this would be a miniscule increase in the already significant cancer burden faced by society.

Faced with growing evidence of EDB's potency as an animal carcinogen, EPA began a review of the pesticide permit in 1980. Within three years the issue came to a head. Several states discovered EDB in groundwater. A few issued their own tolerance levels which were more stringent than those set by the federal government. Action by the states and petitions filed by national environmental groups attracted extensive media attention, which eventually led EPA to accelerate its review process.

---

*This case study is adapted from Chapter 2 in Sheldon Krimsky and Alonzo Plough (1989). *Environmental Hazards: Communicating Risks as a Social Process*. Dover, MA: Auburn House.

Throughout its regulatory involvement in EDB, the EPA has been guided by the Federal Insecticide, Fungicide and Rodenticide Act and its 1972 Amendments, which state that pesticides should not present "any unreasonable risk to man or the environment, taking into account the economic, social, and environmental costs and benefits."

By 1983 the EPA was facing a highly charged atmosphere in which health risks were pitted against the economic benefits of a fungicide the grain industry viewed as critical to protecting the grain supply. Public confidence in the EPA was at an all-time low. States were passing their own regulations. Unions were demanding that the government pass an emergency standard to protect workers from occupational exposure. Environmental groups were mobilized. The media dramatized the removal of product lines from supermarket shelves. All these factors contribute to the risk-management decision.

6.2 Agency Options

From our discussion of risk evaluation, we see that the agency decision makers reviewing the health, environmental, and economic impact of EDB were faced with several options.

6.2.1 Delaying Action
Because there were large gaps in the knowledge base, particularly in regard to the potential for cancer in people exposed to relatively small concentrations over a lifetime, one option was for the EPA to delay its decision. The agency could support additional studies on other mammalian species in order to narrow the uncertainty before changing the registration requirements for EDB. This would give EPA time to pursue the availability of substitute products before significantly reducing EBD use.

6.2.2 Setting Stricter Standards
The agency could set stricter standards that would require lower levels of EDB residues on food, thereby reducing the risks of human exposure. Because EDB is destroyed in the cooking process, stricter standards could be set for food products that do not require cooking. The decision on what tolerance levels to adopt would be determined first by what can be measured, second by what can be implemented, and finally by what risk is "acceptable." Determining acceptability would involve a series of comparisons between the risks of EDB and the risks of other pesticides already deemed "safe," between the risks and benefits of using EDB, and between the risks of EDB and the costs of reducing or eliminating them.

The agency could compare the risks of EDB with those of other pesticides it regulates, or with those of other products or activities of daily life. Comparative-risk analysis (CRA) might be used to establish uniform standards of acceptable risk across many different types of products, activities, and environmental media. One of the main problems introduced by CRA is choosing a sample of comparison that will be credible to the general public.

Two prominent toxicologists made the following comparison between EDB and natural substances.

> Eliminating a carcinogen may not always be a good idea. For example, ethylene dibromide (EDB), the main fumigant in the United States before it was banned, was present in trivial amounts in our food: The average daily intake was about one-tenth of the possible carcinogenic hazard of the aflatoxin in the average peanut butter sandwich, a minimal possible hazard in itself.*

The agency could weigh the uncertain risks of cancer incidence from EDB exposure against the risks of removing the pesticide from the agricultural system. A scientist from the American Council on Science and Health (an industry-supported research group) advanced the following argument for the continued use of EDB:

> Just as individuals choose to take voluntary risks, society as a whole takes risks in order to provide the best possible standard of living for its populace . . . [O]ne must evaluate the tradeoff between the risk and the offsetting benefits associated with the product's use. Nowhere does this apply more aptly than to the agricultural and health protection uses of pesticides. Because of the use of EDB and other pesticides, we in America have escaped the negative health consequences of eating uncontrolled amounts of insect fragments and mold toxins in our food.†

Decision makers can look exclusively at the health benefits (i.e., the risks of using EDB versus the health benefits of using EDB, as above) or they can compare the risks with wider benefits (such as reduced spoilage of stored grain due to insects, molds, and fungi). In some cases, chemicals that are proven to cause cancer in animals have been permitted as food additives on the grounds that to remove them would introduce greater risks to the public. One such case is the use of nitrites and nitrates for the preservation of cold meats. If these additives were removed, it has been predicted, there would be a significant rise in food poisonings due to botulism.

Another comparison is that of potential health risks with other costs of reducing or eliminating EDB use. Examples include losses in production, jobs,

---

*From Ames, Bruce and Lois Gold. 1989. *Misconceptions Regarding Environmental Pollution and Cancer Causation*. Washington, D.C.: The Media Institute. p. 33.

†From Krimsky, Sheldon and Alonzo Plough, 1988. *Environmental Hazards*. Dover, MA: Auburn House. p. 16.

international competitiveness, and profits. In this case the decision maker is faced with comparisons of attributes that are not, on the surface, commensurable. Methodologies designed to create a common metric of comparison—such as dollars—exist, but they involve assumptions about which there is no broad consensus. For instance, how can we balance the additional cancers caused by EDB with the savings it yields to the grain industry by protecting grain from pest contamination?

6.2.3 Banning the Use of EDB

The agency's third option would be to withdraw the registration for EDB's use as a pesticide. In doing so, however, the agency would have to take into consideration the economic consequences of such an action on the grain industry. Decisions of this nature have become commonplace in government. The United States regulates thousands of pesticides and tens of thousands of industrial chemicals. The withdrawal of a pesticide from agricultural use is usually restricted to worst cases.

Where there is strong public interest against use of a particular pesticide, the agency may view it as a political liability and defer to public opinion. Arguing against this approach are those who posit scientific risk assessment as a policy instrument that ought to take precedence over the public's perception of risk. The public's views about the risks of technologies are often at odds with experts' views (Fischhoff, Slovic, & Lichtenstein, 1982), as noted above. Moreover, public attitudes toward environmental hazards may be easily influenced by the amount of media attention.

6.3 Agency Decision

In actuality, the EPA followed a combination of options: first, it delayed taking action until its hand was forced by public opinion and the initiatives of individual states. At that point, not acting would have lost the agency significant control over the issue.

The EPA was first petitioned to remove EDB by the Environmental Defense Fund in November 1975, but took no action until September 1983. In the interim the agency reviewed the available scientific data on the risks and benefits of the pesticide while coming under increasing pressure from environmental groups. In July 1983, Florida announced the ban of EDB as a soil fumigant in eight counties of the citrus belt; this forced EPA to announce the emergency suspension of EDB as a soil fumigant in September. Florida again forced the issue in December of that year when it passed a stop-sale order and began to remove grain-based products from grocery shelves. This was a major-risk communication event, providing dramatic film footage that fostered public indignation. Soon thereafter, the EPA banned the use of EDB in fumigating grains and set interim tolerance

BOX 5–1

Chronology of the EDB Case

1948 EDB is registered as a pesticide with USDA.

1949 EDB is registered for use as a soil fumigant.

1956 EDB is registered as a fumigant for stored grains, fruits, and vegetables.

1974 The National Cancer Institute issues an alert on EDB after tests show it caused cancer in animals.

1975 The Environmental Defense Fund petitions EPA to cancel EDB as a pesticide.

1976 EDB is cited by the National Institute for Occupational Safety and Health (NIOSH) as a potential occupational carcinogen.

1977 EPA cites EDB as a carcinogen and begins a review.

1980 EPA issues a position document stating that EDB is a risk to human health and proposes to ban its use on stored grain.

1981 California limits workers' exposures to EDB.

1982 EDB is detected in the groundwater in Georgia.

1983 EDB is detected in California groundwater. Hawaii wells are closed because of EDB contaminaton. Florida finds EDB in wells and sets tolerance levels at 1 ppb.

1984 EPA orders an emergency suspension of EDB's use as a soil fumigant and issues tolerance levels of EDB in the food supply; 900 ppb on raw grain intended for human consumption; 150 ppb on flour mixes and cereal; 30 ppb on ready-to-eat products. Massachusetts sets an EDB tolerance level of 1 ppb on all food products and wins a court challenge on the standard. New York State sets an EDB standard of 6 ppb on ready-to-eat food. Federal interim tolerance standards expire whereupon any detectable levels constitute food adulteration.

levels for residues in food; this was a first step to revoking the tolerance exemptions initially granted in the 1950s. By September 1984, these interim standards had expired, and any food with detectable levels of EDB was considered legally adulterated. Box 5–1 summarizes the chronology of events in the EDB case.

EXERCISES

1. Construct a fault tree for why a car fails to start. What are the major shortcomings of this method? What are some of the ways of overcoming them?

2. Construct a personal "risk diary" for all the risks that you worry about on a daily basis for the period of a week. Indicate the activity or risk, your length of exposure, and the potential adverse outcome. Plot the risk profiles in terms of voluntariness, delay, and so on (see Figure 5–2) for 10 of the biggest risks you face.

3. How would you construct a comparative risk assessment for EDB? What is the appropriate field of comparison? Support a position either for or against comparative risk assessment. What is your response to the argument that there are natural carcinogens in our food that pose equal or greater risk than EDB residues?

4. Select a risk that you think is important in your life. Under what conditions is that risk acceptable or unacceptable? Are you able to quantify the risk? What factors are important in how you view the risk?

ADDITIONAL READINGS

For further general reading on risk, see Glickman and Gough (1990), Hohenemser, Kasperson, and Kates (1985), and Lowrence, W.W. (1976). For more information on the topic of risk assessment, see Cohrssen and Covello (1989), National Academy of Sciences (1983), and Rasmussen (1981). To read more on risk communication studies, see Krimsky and Plough (1988) and NRC (1989).

For more information on the psychometric approach, see Fischoff, et al. (1981), Slovic, Fischhoff, and Lichtenstein (1979), and Slovic, Fischhoff, and Lichtenstein (1980). To read more on the topic of social and cultural theory, see Douglas (1986), Douglas and Wildavsky (1982), and Johnson and Covello (1987). For more information on the issue of public responses to risk, see Brown and Mikkelsen (1990), Nelkin and Brown (1984), Raynor and Cantor (1987), and Schwartz and Thompson, (1990).

REFERENCES

Ames, Bruce and Lois Swirsky Gold. 1989. Misconceptions regarding environmental pollution and cancer causation. In *Health Risks and the Press,* ed. Mike Moore, pp. 19–34. Washington, D.C.: The Media Institute.
Brown, Phil and Edwin J. Mikkelsen. 1990. *No Safe Place.* Berkeley, CA: University of California Press.
Burton, Ian and Robert W. Kates. 1964. The perception of natural hazards in resource management. *Natural Resources Journal* 3(3):412–441.
Burton, Ian, Robert W. Kates, and Gilbert F. White. 1978. The *Environment as Hazard.* New York: Oxford University Press.
Cohrssen, John J. and Vincent T. Covello. 1989. *Risk Analysis: A Guide to Principles and Methods for Analyzing Health and Environmental Risks.* Washington, D.C.: U.S. Council on Environmental Quality.
Covello, Vincent and Jeryl Mumpower. 1985. Risk analysis and risk management: an historical perspective. *Risk Analysis* 5(2):103–120.
Cumming, Robert B. 1981. Is risk assessment a science? *Risk Analysis* 1(1):1-3.

Douglas, M. 1986. *Risk Acceptability According to the Social Sciences*. New York: Russell Sage.

Douglas, Mary and Aaron Wildavsky. 1982. How can we know the risks we face? Why risk selection is a social process. *Risk Analysis* 2(2):49–51.

Douglas, M. and A. Wildavsky. 1982. *Risk and Culture: An Essay on the Selection of Technical and Environmental Dangers*. Berkeley: University of California.

Fischhoff, B., S. Lichtenstein, P. Slovic, S. L. Derby, and R. L. Keeney. 1981. *Acceptable Risk*. Cambridge: Cambridge University Press.

Fischhoff, B., P. Slovic, and S. Lichtenstein. 1982. Lay foibles and expert fables in judgments about risk. *The American Statistician* 36(3):240–255.

Fischhoff, B., P. Slovic, S. Lichtenstein, S. Read, and B. Coombs. 1978. How safe is safe enough? A psychometric study of attitudes towards technological benefits. *Policy Sciences* 9(2):127–152.

Fischhoff, B., S. Watson, and C. Hope. 1984. Defining risk. *Policy Sciences* 17(2): 123–139.

Glickman, T. S. and M. Gough, eds., 1990. *Readings in Risk*. Washington, D.C.: Resources for the Future.

Hohenemser, Christoph, Roger E. Kasperson, and Robert W. Kates. 1985. Causal structure. In *Perilous Progress: Technology as Hazard*, eds. Robert W. Kates, Christoph Hohenemser, and Jeanne X. Kasperson, pp. 25–42. Boulder, CO: Westview Press.

Hohenemser, Christoph, Robert W. Kates, and Paul Slovic. 1983. The nature of technological hazard. *Science* 220:378–384.

Johnson, B. B. and V. T. Covello, eds. 1987. *The Social and Cultural Construction of Risk: Essays on Risk Selection and Perception*. Dordrecht, The Netherlands: D. Reidel.

Kasperson, Roger E. 1983. Acceptability of human risk. *Environmental Health Perspectives* 52:15–20.

Kasperson, Roger E., Robert W. Kates, and Christoph Hohenemser, 1985. Hazard management. In *Perilous Progress: Technology as Hazard*, eds. Robert W. Kates, Christoph Hohenemser, and Jeanne X. Kasperson. pp. 43–66. Boulder, CO: Westview Press.

Kates, Robert W. and Jeanne X. Kasperson. 1983. Comparative risk analysis of technological hazards (a review). *Proceedings of the National Academy of Sciences* 80: 7027–7038.

Krimsky, Sheldon and Alonzo Plough. 1988. *Environmental Hazards: Communicating Risks as a Social Process*. Dover, MA: Auburn House.

Leonard, Herman B. and Richard J. Zeckhauser. 1986. Cost-benefit analysis applied to risks: its philosophy and legitimacy. In *Values at Risk*, ed. Douglas MacLean. pp. 31–48. Totowa, NJ: Rowman & Allangheld.

Lind, Niels C. 1987. Is risk analysis an emerging profession? *Risk Abstracts* 4(4): 176–169.

Litai, D., D. D. Lanning, and N. C. Rasmussen. 1983. The public perception of risk. In *The Analysis of Actual vs. Perceived Risks*, eds. V. T. Covello, W. G. Flamm, J. V. Rodricks, and R. G. Tardiff. pp. 213–224. New York: Plenum Press.

Lowrence, W. W. 1976. *Of Acceptable Risk: Science and the Determination of Safety*. Los Altos, CA: William Kaufmann.

McCray, Lawrence E. 1983. An anatomy of risk assessment: scientific and extra-scientific components in the assessment of scientific data on cancer risks. Working paper prepared for the Committee on the Insititutional Means for Assessment of Risks to Public Health, National Research Council. Washington, D.C.: National Academy Press.

Milvy, Paul. 1986. A general guideline for management of risks from carcinogens. *Risk Analysis* 6(1):69–79.

National Academy of Sciences, National Research Council. 1983. *Risk Assessment in the Federal Government: Managing the Process*. Washington, D.C.: National Academy Press.

NRC (National Research Council, Committee on Risk Perception and Communication). 1989. *Improving Risk Communication*. Washington, DC: National Academy Press.

Nelkin, D. and M. Brown. 1984. *Workers at Risk*. Chicago, IL: University of Chicago.

Nuclear Regulatory Commission. 1975. Reactor safety study. Executive summary. WASH-1400 (NUREG/74/104). Washington, D.C.: Nuclear Regulatory Commission.

Otway, Harry and Brian Wynne. 1989. Risk communication: paradigm and paradox. *Risk Analysis* 9(2):141–145.

Perrow, Charles. 1984. *Normal Accidents*. New York: Basic Books.

Rasmussen, Norman C. 1981. The application of probabilistic risk assessment techniques to energy technologies. *Annual Review of Energy* 6:123–138.

Rayner, Steve and Robin Cantor. 1987. How fair is safe enough? The cultural approach to societal technology choice. *Risk Analysis* 7(1):3–13.

Roberts, Leslie. 1989. Pesticides and kids. *Science* 243:1280–1281.

Schwartz, Michael and Michael Thompson. 1990. *Divided We Stand: Redefining Politics, Technology, and Social Choice*. Philadelphia, PA: University of Pennsylvania Press.

Slovic, Paul, Baruch Fischoff, and Sarah Lichtenstein. 1979. Rating the risks. *Environment* 21(3):14–20; 36–39.

Slovic, Paul, Baruch Fischhoff, and Sarah Lichtenstein. 1980. Facts and fears: understanding perceived risk. In *Societal Risk Assessment: How Safe is Safe Enough?* eds. Richard C. Schwing and Walter A. Albers, pp. 181–214. New York: Plenum Press.

Starr, Chauncey. 1969. Social benefit versus technological risk. *Science* 165:1232–1238.

Starr, Chauncey. 1985. Risk management, assessment, and acceptability. *Risk Analysis* 5(2):97–102.

Thompson, Michael. 1980. An outline of the cultural theory of risk. A working paper for the International Institute for Applied Systems Analysis. Laxenberg, Austria.

von Winterfeldt, Detlof and Ward Edwards. 1984. Patterns of conflict about risky technologies. *Risk Analysis* 4(1):55–68.

Weinberg, Alvin W. 1972. Science and trans-science. *Minerva* 10(2):209–222.

Weinberg, Alvin W. 1981. Reflections on risk assessment. *Risk Analysis* 1(1):5–7.

White, Gilbert F. and Eugene Haas. 1975. *Assessment of Research on Natural Hazards*. Cambridge, MA: MIT Press.

Wilson, Richard. 1979. Analyzing the daily risks of life. *Technology Review* 81: 41–46.

Wilson, Richard. 1984. Commentary: risks and their acceptability. *Science, Technology and Human Values* 9(2):11–22.

Wynne, Brian. 1982. Institutional mythologies and dual societies in the management of risk. In *The Risk Analysis Controversy: An Institutional Perspective*, eds. H. C. Kunreuther and E. V. Ley. pp. 127–143. New York: Springer.

6

The Economic Model

Peter Rogers

1 INTRODUCTION

Since it is not possible to subsist in the environment without causing some change (usually harmful), or without depleting natural resources, the question for humankind would appear to be not "whether to pollute," but "how much to pollute." This does not sound like a question that could be easily answered by economics; it is a political problem and a social choice. Even so, Dorfman and Dorfman (1972) point out that, after several generations of contemplation of this problem, economists have arrived at criteria for judging such policy decisions.

The problem with economics is that the public retains few of the basic concepts, but remembers many of the ideologies. Constant evangelism by disciples of the right or the left, though they may appear unrealistic, results in a widespread rejection of economics as a way to deal with practical problems. In this chapter an attempt is made to strip away assumptions about reality, to look for economic approaches that rely wherever possible on observed behaviors, and to show that rules based on these behaviors—which can be expected of capitalists and socialists alike—can serve as helpful guides for rational environmental policy.

In economics, the term "externalities" refers to those things outside the economic system. Historically, environmental resources have been external to the economic system, but that changed in this century. Economic concepts have played a major role in federal environmental policy since the mid 1930s. For example, the Flood Control Act of 1936 introduced the requirements of a formal benefit-cost analysis in justifying projects for the first time in any federal government activity. This was before the methodology had been developed. In fact, many of the approaches to benefit-measurement in the public sector were

120

developed by economists working on federal water policy. This concern for water-resources projects has been carried over by the same agencies to concerns for water quality. The persons who carried out this work then led the development of economic analysis in other areas of environmental concern. Since water is an interesting and important case in its own right, with a well-developed literature, and since it also is a model for other areas of environmental concern, the examples in this chapter are based mainly on water issues. For example, the economic imperatives of water are embedded in its nature as a fugitve resource that is often treated as a public good. External effects occasioned by water use also invoke important economic imperatives. The nature of property rights and externalities raises financial imperatives that influence the choice of ways to price water to pay for the public supply.

To appreciate fully environmental policy options and how they are evaluated, we must understand how economics is used and misused. One should not, however, therefore conclude that economics is the most important dimension of environmental decision making. As the other chapters in this book demonstrate, at most stages politics controls the outcome, even when the discussion is framed in economic or other terms.

We will start with an example drawn from water-quality management, which helps to characterize an analytic economic approach to environmental decision making. This is followed by a discussion of the fundamental economic theories of environmental and resource management. We will then explore the practical and conceptual issues in benefit-measurement and review empirical studies on estimating the demand for environmental amenities. Finally, we will discuss practical approaches to market-based solutions to environmental problems.

2 ILLUSTRATIVE EXAMPLE

Consider two industries on a river, with industry A upstream of industry B. Industry A takes water from the river, uses it in its processes, contaminates it, and returns it to the river. Industry B now has to treat the river water before it can use the water for its own processes. By its action of polluting the river, in other words, A causes additional costs to B.

Industry B has recourse to several approaches to redressing this situation. The first, and most obvious, is to request A to cease polluting the river. Industry A may agree and immediately resolve the problem by treating its wastes or changing its production processes in such a way that B is not damaged by A's actions. Industry A is then said to have "internalized the externality." But what if A refuses a polite request to stop? Industry A might agree to negotiate with B so that both would share the cost of cleaning up the waste. B might pay A for treating the wastes, or A might reimburse B for cleaning up water it needs for its processes. This might be a lot cheaper than having A treat all of the wastes. In these cases, we internalize the externality by building a "bubble" over the two plants and considering them as one.

Using these types of examples, Coase (1960) showed that externalities do not necessarily lead to economically inefficient solutions, provided the polluters and the people being affected could freely and inexpensively negotiate with each other. Coase claimed that the responsibility for damages is a reciprocal one, where the affected party takes steps to avoid damages as much as the perpetrator avoids producing them. Economic efficiency is achieved by having the costs of avoiding external damages borne by the party that can eliminate them least expensively. Coase skirts the fundamental issue of equity and distribution by saying that the parties "freely negotiate" the agreement. Though this may work quite well in the hypothetical case given between two industrial plants of similar size, it is unlikely to work so easily between one large industry and hundreds of thousands of private citizens. Both the asymmetry of the power to negotiate and the transactions costs of the negotiations themselves argue against achieving a satisfactory solution.

What if plant A refuses to negotiate with plant B? At this point the process has to move beyond the two participants and involve a third party. In the United States, this would typically be a lawsuit brought by B against A; the process would involve the relevant state and local laws as well federal laws. A typical solution would have A being forced to treat its wastes up to the current level of Best Available Technology (BAT) for that particular industry. As a result, B might still be forced to treat its intake water because the residual wastes A is legally allowed to discharge have deteriorated B's water supply. Thus the total costs may be substantially higher than the economically efficient solution. Furthermore, the water-pollution legislation and laws would in effect have created property rights for A to pollute the river up to a certain level.

The current situation in the United States with regard to water quality is almost exactly the situation described in the last paragraph, except that it is more likely to be citizen groups suing the government to enforce the existing regulations against particular industries and—now, increasingly—against municipalities. This is certainly a long way from being economically efficient, but it does have a flavor of being equitable, inasmuch as each industry type and each municipality is more or less forced to use the same kind of treatment and, hence, face similar costs. Because of economies-of-scale, however, small communities may face disproportionate per-capita costs.

Since it is unlikely that the negotiated solutions between the polluters and those affected will come about spontaneously, some form of government regulation is inevitable. Is what we have created in the United States the best possible regulation under the circumstances? The hypothetical two-plant example demonstrates the principles. Figure 6–1 shows the costs for plant A to treat its waste to various levels of purity, ranging from 100% (the water is returned to its

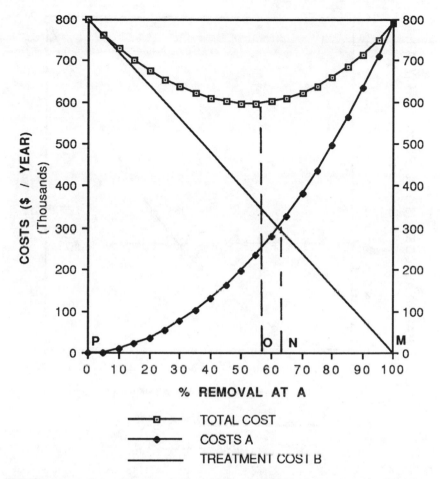

FIGURE 6–1.   Treatment cost curve for industry A and the damage curve to downstream industry B as a function of the percent removal of pollution at A. The top curve shows the sum of these two. Point O represents a 57.5% removal of pollutant at A.

original condition) to 0% (no treatment of the wastes). The figure also shows damages caused to B by A's action, damages measured by the cost to B to treat the water it receives in the river from A. The sums of theses two sets of costs are also plotted and give the total "social costs" of the pollution problem.

Figure 6–2 shows the marginal cost and damages based upon the given data. Although most economic texts explain the functioning of the market system by the use of marginal analysis, the discussion below relies on the total cost and damage functions of Figure 6–1; this is how most noneconomists think about costs.

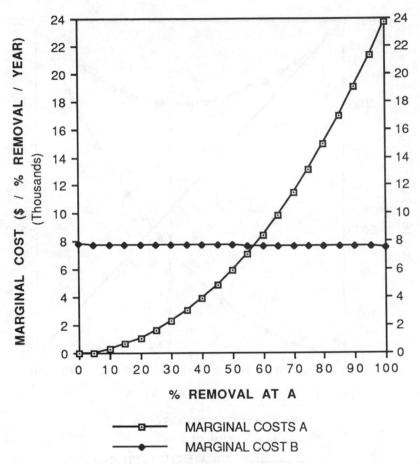

FIGURE 6–2.   Marginal costs at A and marginal damages at B. The total cost is minimized where these curves intersect. This point is equivalent to point O in Figure 6–1.

If there is no negotiated settlement to the conflict between A and B, and the issue is to be resolved by regulatory action of the state, what level of treatment of A's waste should be mandated? Figure 6–1 is informative on this point because it shows the costs to each and also the total cost (to society if these are the only two members). Interestingly, the total cost curve shows a minimum at about 58% removal of A's wastes. This is the same point where, in Figure 6–2, the marginal cost and the marginal damages curves cross. In economic parlance, "where marginal costs equal marginal damages"—labeled O on the axis in Figure 6–1—should be of great interest to the governmental regulators if they are looking for efficient solutions; it is the point of maximum economic efficiency for the problem in question.

Another interesting point in Figure 6–1 occurs at N, where the costs to A equal the damages to B. The gains and losses associated with the various solutions to this problem are as follows:

at level P, A spends $0 and B spends $800,000 per year
at level M, A spends $800,000 and B spends $0
at level N, A spends $280,000 and B spends $280,000
at level O, A spends $180,000 and B spends $320,000

Level M is the strict-liability solution, with A paying for 100% cleanup of its wastes; level P is the laissez-faire solution, with B absorbing all the damages; level N is the "equitable" solution, with the two sides bearing the costs equally. Level O is the economically efficient solution. The economic dictum "of getting the prices right" in the case of regulated externalities now means setting a price on the effluents of A such that the efficient solution, point O, is arrived at without government intervention.

What tax could be levied on A that would lead to this solution? If A produces 100,000 pounds of pollutant per year, treatment at 57.5% (see Figure 6–1) removal would leave 42.5%, or 42,500 pounds in the effluent stream. At this level of pollution, B suffers $340,000 of damages; if A were charged $8 per pound of effluent ($340,000/42,500), B could be fully indemnified for its damages. Also, at this rate of tax, A would treat exactly at this level because at 57.5% removal the marginal cost of treatment is seen in Figure 6–2 to be $8 per pound. Below $8 per pound it would be cheaper for A to treat, and above $8 per pound it would be cheaper for A to pay the tax. Hence, an optimal tax exists, and the problem is solved. All that would be required is for the government agency to set the tax rate and private industry and the market would do the rest.

Or is the problem solved? If it were not practical to reimburse B, B would agitate to move at least to the "equitable" solution at N—which is no longer socially optimal, but at which B suffers fewer damages. Such a resolution has the property that the costs to each would be the same. Therefore, in order to work effectively the tax would have to be used to reimburse the damaged party.

Should the problem be viewed differently if B moved in after A was already polluting the stream, or vice versa, if A moved in after B was already established? What about the entry of a third industry after the others had reached an agreeement? This problem becomes harder to analyze and resolve when the more realistic issues are allowed to intrude; the proposed economic solutions are likely to become less acceptable to society.

So far our discussion has considered only the two industrial polluters, but this is not the whole story. If it were, then we would be tempted to let the polluters fight it out and arrive at any settlement that they could, but two other important interests have been ignored so far: (1) the other actual and potential users of the river, and (2) the fauna and flora and other components of the aquatic environment. How are their interests to be accounted for and protected in this case? This is the crux of any pollution problem. In a typical situation, there are a few major polluters and many thousand individuals who are affected. It is unrealistic to expect them either to negotiate with each other in a meaningful way or to set an optimal effluent tax and then repay each person according to their respective damages. Moreover, in our present hypothetical example it was possible to measure the benefits (or damages) borne by each individual; in a real case this may be impossible. As a result of measurement difficulties and the problems of reimbursing the affected parties, effluent charges have not been used in the United States for pollution control. Instead, effluent levels have been set based upon the expected performance of specific treatment technologies: The current legal requirement [approximately 80% removal of biochemical oxygen demand (BOD) which is an indicator of how much organic pollution still remains in a given waste stream] would force a solution to the right of N in the water-pollution example given above.

All of this still neglects the nonhuman components of the problem. Should the environment be protected for its own sake? If so, by how much? How are we to assess the marginal costs and benefits to the environment itself? These are still largely unresolved issues. Economic theory is, alas, of little help in giving guidelines for resolving them, though Section 5 below suggests some approaches to deal with the problem.

3 ECONOMIC CONCEPTS OF EFFICIENCY

[T]he environment consists of scarce and exhaustible resources. That is where economics enters, for economics is the science of allocating scarce resources among competing ends. (Dorfman & Dorfman, 1972, p.xiv)

Property and ownership rights are fundamental to an economic analysis of environmental policy. The institution of private property and other economic institutions in the United States have evolved together in ways that tend to promote the efficient use of things that are privately owned. A corollary to this phenomenon is that if a resource is not privately owned, then institutions do not work well in promoting its efficient use.

Efficiency is a good place to start, since the economic concept of efficiency differs radically from the corresponding engineering and scientific concepts. For an engineer, efficiency means designing, planning, and using technology in such a way that the amounts of materials handled and used are minimized at the same time that a given task is accomplished. So, for instance, an electrostatic precipitator to remove particles from the smoke stack of a power plant should remove 99% of the particles at the least cost. An ecologist would look at the same problem from the point of view of the impacts upon the ambient environment and define an efficient solution in terms of the ability of the natural systems to process the particulates with minimum damage. An economist, however, would consider all the resource inputs that should be used in concert to achieve the best economic outcome. For the economist, it is not at all obvious that the most important goal is to minimize the cost of prevention because there may be other ways of achieving the goal of improved environmental quality than building the precipitators. By looking at all the resources used, both on the input and the output sides, the economist may see other ways to achieve the desired outcome, for example, a process change induced by taxes on the inputs to the process, or effluent taxes on the particulates. Efficiency, then, for the economist, carries with it some notion of an objective or goal that is broader than the use of one input. Many of the environmental policies promoted by the United States government are guided by engineering and scientific concepts of efficiency, rather than the economic concept.

3.1 Public Goods and Externalities

Dorfman and Dorfman (1972) claim that the resources that make up the environment are unsuitable for private ownership because they lack the "excludability property." In other words, it is not practical to exclude people from using the resource either because it is physically impossible to do so (people just will breathe the air) or because it is very expensive or cumbersome to limit access. Many investments that improve the quality of the environment—such as improved water quality in lakes and rivers, the guidance of navigation lights, public beaches, and security from flood damage—have this feature to a greater or lesser extent at some time or other in the history of the United States and have indeed been considered private property. There is little incentive to provide services or own property from which other people cannot be excluded. Everyone's property is no one's property.

Nonexcludability is not the only thing, however, that makes environmental resources different from classic privately owned resources. Environmental resources also have the property of "mutually interfering usage." Individuals take the valuable commodities of clean air and water from the same environment into which they then dump wastes, which in turn interfere with the use of the no-longer-clean air and water by them and others. In economic parlance, these are referred to as "externalities." Nonexcludability and externality make the environment an inherently difficult resource to manage.

If the demand for public goods cannot be effectively controlled, either by rationing or pricing, then the only relevant public-policy question is how much of the particular public good to provide. This decision has to be a social, not a private, decision, and has to be based on the total "willingness to pay" for the good by all of the potential users. If, however, there are externalities involved, then the criterion for selecting the amount of resource provided should also be limited to the point at which the benefit to an additional user just counterbalances the total cost that he or she imposes upon all the other users. Unfortunately, many natural resources and environmental amenities have some of the features of private property that lead to uses that conflict with their public-good properties and to difficulty in applying these principles.

3.2 Criteria for Assessing Economic Performance

As stated at the outset, the question for humankind would appear to be not whether to pollute or not, but how much to pollute. Following are four criteria economists have arrived at for judging such policy decisions. The first two relate to "welfare" or "satisfaction" in utility terms; the second two relate to the productivity of the economy in monetary terms.

3.2.1 Broad Utility Criterion: Pareto Optimality

Suppose a community consists of two individuals, Mr. A and Ms. B; that the total output of the economy can be divided between them; and that both are affected by whatever public goods or environmental conditions result from the operation of the economy. The level of satisfaction with the current allocation of goods and services of each depends on each one's consumption of private goods and the environmental conditions to which each is exposed. Assume that the economy is operated in such a way that A values his position at 100 units and B values her position at 150 units of a measure of satisfaction called "utility." This may coincide, however, with B dumping her wastewater into A's favorite trout stream. In this case A might be willing to pay B, in the separate medium of exchange called dollars, up to $100 to move her waste to some other location. Let us imagine A offers B $50 to change her dumping practices. B considers the offer and decides that $50 is not enough to compensate for her loss of utility caused by the cost and inconvenience of changing her practices, and she declines the offer—saying, however, that she would be happy to do it for $75. In this case, B's utility is not diminished; although she has to dump her waste some- where else, she has been compensated by $75, which allows her to recoup that lost utility by increasing her consumption of other goods and services. Also, A's utility has been increased by the improvement of the fishing in his trout stream and diminished by the amount of $75 that he paid to B. But since he was willing to pay $100 to B, he is better off than before. In this scenario neither will be worse off, and one will be better off.

However simple and contrived the example, it does exemplify the principles involved very well. The decision by B is a highly personal decision made freely by her and based on all the things she thinks are important to her. The same is true for A; no one forces him to make the offer, and he will do it only if it is in his own perceived best interest. Also note that two measures of value are involved here: utility, which is virtually impossible to measure unequivocally (see Chapter 4 for a discussion of how this may be empirically estimated), and dollars, which are quite easy to measure. The trade-off between dollars and utility is left to each individual to decide. If there are no further possibilities of increasing A's utility without reducing B's utility, then the output is said to be "Pareto optimal" or "Pareto efficient" (after Vilfredo Pareto, the Italian railway-engineer-turned-economist who introduced the concept in 1906).

This example could be expanded to consider all possible modes of operating the economy and all possible trades between these two individuals (and, by extension, all individuals in a society). The points could be plotted on a curve representing all the Pareto-optimal ways of operating the economy. Figure 6–3 shows such a curve schematically. Each point shows the greatest level of utility available to A, given a particular utility level for B. This is called the "utility-possibility" frontier. Any point along the curve cdb is Pareto-optimal. In the absence of any other criterion, production of the economy at any point on this curve is said to be "socially" efficient; hence, the term "broad utility criterion."

In the example given above, both dollars and utility were used. This is

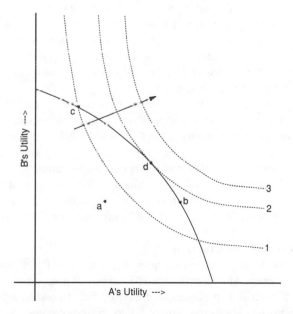

FIGURE 6–3.   Utility-possibility frontier showing the greatest level of utility achievable for A given a particular level for B. Curves 1, 2, and 3 show a social-welfare function with increasing levels of total welfare moving from 1 to 3.

because Pareto optimality does not depend on the ability to measure the utility for individuals but only which outcome he or she prefers in any given choice between a pair. Hence, the monetary transactions described above are perfectly appropriate as measures of utility and satisfaction. This type of analysis could also be applied to groups of individuals if it were possible to assess their group preferences, or they were identical to each other and their preferences could simply be added together. But since these conditions can rarely, if ever, be met, the assessment of Pareto optimality is—realistically speaking—virtually never possible.

3.2.2 Sharp Utility Criterion: Social Welfare

If it were possible to devise a community "welfare function" as some function of the welfare of the community's individual members, then it would be possible to improve upon the broad utility criterion given above. This welfare function would, of course, have to be able to deal with the relative merits of each member in defining the welfare of the whole; equitable distribution of the utility to the various members is a prerequisite of a welfare function. The dotted lines in Figure 6–3 show one such function. Each line represents a constant level of community utility composed of different combinations of A's and B's individual utilities, with higher levels of community utility achieved as one moves out toward the upper right of the figure. Since the curve cdb is the locus of the Pareto efficient solutions, the welfare function will allow us to discriminate between the infinite number of solutions along this line by choosing that one with the highest value of the social-welfare function that is also Pareto optimal. In Figure 6–3 this is at point d, where the social-welfare function is as large as it can be while still intersecting Pareto optimal outcomes.

The elegance of this solution, however, is diminished by the unfortunate fact that no completely satisfactory social-welfare function dependent on individual utilities has ever been constructed [see Chechile (1984) for a review of this problem]. Despite this, the economic literature spends a great deal of time discussing the properties of this hypothetical construct—tending mainly to erode the credibility of economics among policymakers. But, as the next two sections show, when economics comes down from its lofty pedestal it does have something profound to offer in the field of environmental decision making.

3.2.3 Broad Productivity Criterion

In the practical world of goods and services, the concept of Pareto optimality has an analog: the concept of "productivity efficiency." An economy is said to be productively efficient if it produces as much of every good and service as is possible, given the level of the outputs of all goods and services, and the level of resources used as inputs. For example, consider an economy that produces just two commodities: rice grown under irrigation and water-based recreation. For a given amount of resources as input, it would be possible to produce the combination of these two commodities as shown in Figure 6–4. Any combination of output at point a is technically feasible but not efficient, because there are combinations of outputs—at b for example—that produce more of at least one commodity for the same inputs. The line bcd is called the "production-possibility" frontier and is analogous to the Pareto frontier; everywhere along this line the economy is productively efficient.

While an economy cannot be Pareto optimal unless it is productively efficient, it can be productively efficient without being Pareto optimal. In such cases, the wrong combination of commodities is efficiently produced—often true in centrally planned economies. If the production were at point a in Figure 6–4, then it would be possible to produce more of both goods—making at least one person better off without harming anyone else. Hence, productive efficiency is necessary for Pareto optimality. If, however, the economy were producing at point b in Figure 6–4, and if the consumers A and B valued recreation more than irrigated rice production by more than the rate of substitition implied by a straight line joining b and c in Figure 6–4, then a Pareto optimum would imply a shift down the curved line from b toward c. In other words, point b in Figure 6–4 is productively efficient but not Pareto optimal.

The broad productivity criterion is attractive even though it allows an ignoring

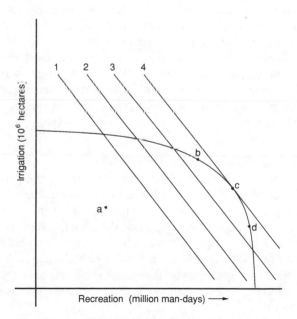

FIGURE 6–4.   Production-possibility frontier. Everywhere along the curve bcd the economy is productively efficient. The lines 1, 2, 3, and 4 represent lines of constant GNP.

of Pareto optimality because it can be used in many more circumstances, for example, where Pareto optimality may be difficult or impossible. The criterion does not, however, help us choose between efficient points (e.g., b, c, and d in Figure 6–4). We can go no further without making major new assumptions about how the economy "ought" to work.

3.2.4 The Sharp Productivity Criterion

Neoclassical economic theory states that the relative desirability of private goods is reflected in their prices. Therefore, the best point to choose on a production-possibility frontier is where the value of goods and services produced is greatest. This is referred to as the gross national product (GNP) criterion; that is the point where GNP is at a maximum. For the example given in Figure 6–4, assume that irrigated rice is worth $1 per pound and recreation is worth $10 per day. The equation for GNP for this two-commodity economy would then be

GNP = $1 multipied by the number of pounds of rice produced + $10 multiplied by the number of days of recreation provided.

This equation can be represented as a straight line on Figure 6–4; the parallel lines are lines of constant GNP according to this formula. The obvious choice, if we wish to maximize the value of the GNP, is the combination of goods produced at point c, where the value of the GNP is as large as possible given the requirement to stay within the production-possibilty frontier.

From a practical point of view, this criterion is the most attractive. It is straightforward to compute and captures the ideas of its predecessors without the drawbacks of being hypothetical. However, despite its attraction and widespread use in benefit-cost analysis, it has some serious flaws in application; they are discussed in Section 6.

3.2.5 Summary of Economic Efficiency Criteria

Even though economic literature emphasizes efficiency and equity as the two goals of economic endeavor, it must be noted that when it comes to operational definitions of equity, economists are no better prepared than others to respond. Of the four criteria discussed above, only the social-welfare criterion deals directly with the issue of equity; it was also the most hypothetical and least operationally useful. Although the social-welfare criterion leaves the policymaker with some useful and quite powerful tools for social analysis, these tools are, nonetheless, deficient in the area most critical to public decision making in democratic societies.

Moreover, the idea of "fairness," which seems to be missing in economists' ideas about equity, raises moral imperatives that are hard to avoid when we deal with externalities in practical cases. For example, it seems to be "unfair" to apply the Coase theorem (recall our discussion in Section 2) to the problem of acid rain between Canada and the United States. From an ethical point of view, it is hard to argue that the damages imposed on Canadian citizens by the behavior of United States citizens are "reciprocal"; rather, the United States should be considered strictly liable for the consequences. Coase is relevant to the discussion on how the United States should meet its liabilities: treatment at source in the United States, paying the Canadians for the damages imposed, or some combination of those strategies. "Fairness" dictates that the United States attempt to arrive at an economically efficient solution to the problem by the least-cost methods, only after acknowledging its liability.

A resource-reallocation decision is said to be Pareto efficient if the decision can improve an individual's well-being without decreasing the well-being of anyone else. Most allocation decisions in the public domain involving environmental resources, however, appear to make some people better off and some worse off; they therefore cannot be evaluated using the simple Pareto concept. In response, economists have developed the "compensation" principle to extend the relevance of Pareto optimality. The Kaldor–Hicks compensation criterion is a widely used version of this principle, under which a reallocation is a "potential" Pareto optimal if the gainers would theoretically be able to fully compensate the losers and still be better off themselves.

For "strict" Pareto optimality, the compensation would actually have to be paid. In real cases, however, there is typically no easy way to make the compensatory payments. For example, the beneficiaries of a large federally financed water project could be charged for the water supplied, and the revenues generated could be used to compensate those who lost access to land and water as a result of the project. However, the beneficiaries are usually a small and clearly defined group receiving substantial amounts of benefits, whereas the losers tend to be a large number of widely scattered people, each suffering small damages. How does one get them together to agree on the levels of compensation to be paid? How does one actually pay the compensation?

The compensation test can be used as an analytical tool even though compensation will not actually be paid. Taking the value of economic goods and services gained or lost, the gains to the gainers are compared to the losses to the losers. *If the gains outweigh losses, it is considered that the overall welfare is increased.* This is the conceptual basis of benefit-cost analysis, which received a boost in Section I of the Flood Control Act of 1936 when it said

> . . . the Federal Government should improve or participate in the improvement of navigable waters or their tributaries including watersheds thereof, for flood control purposes *if the benefits to whomsoever they may accrue are in excess of the estimated costs.* . . . (Holmes, 1972, p.19)

How useful it is to express performance goals in compensation terms, as above, is seen when those goals are contrasted with the vague goals for natural resource development expressed by the Natural Resources Planning Board in 1939:

> That is, in order of (1) the greatest good to the greatest number of people, (2) the emergency necessities of the nation, and (3) the social, economic, and cultural advancement of the people of the United States. (Ex. Order 8248)

Virtually any bureaucrat should be able to justify any decision whatsoever based on such imprecise criteria.

Even though the Pareto discussion is carried on in terms of the preferences of groups, the actual measurements used in applying the compensation principle are based on the GNP criterion. Benefit-cost analysis using the compensation principle also implicitly assumes that a social-welfare function exists in which everyone's welfare is counted equally, and in direct proportion to the goods and services, gained or lost, measured in market prices. Since the demand for goods and services is known to depend on income, this implies that the current distribution of income is an acceptable one and should be used as the basis for further allocation of goods and services. The compensation principle has been widely criticized as a basis for public-policy decisions on this score.

4 DEMAND FOR ENVIRONMENTAL AMENITIES

The "demand" for environmental amenities is an economic term meaning the schedule of quantities of a commodity that consumers are willing to purchase at various prices. In market economies, resource allocation and distribution problems are solved simultaneously by the price mechanism. Demand for a certain resource is brought into balance with available supply at some new price level. As the demand increases the resource becomes more expensive to provide, the price rises, and rationing occurs (in the sense that some consumers consume less than they would have at the lower price); if the demand declines or, if new and cheaper sources of the resource are found, the price drops. In the strictest sense, the concept of a demand schedule applies only to consumer purchases. Purchases of resources and material used as inputs in the production of other commodities that are purchased directly by consumers (for example, irrigation water used for growing food) reflect "derived demand," since call for these materials derives from the final demand of the consumer product that they are used to create.

Unfortunately, in most public discussions of demand for environmental resources and amenities, the word "need" is often mistakenly used for demand. It makes no sense to project the quantities of an amenity needed without specifying how much people would be willing to pay for these quantities. Demand must be specified by the two numbers: quantity and price. For example, in making plans for future water development, current water-use rates are usually put on a per-capita basis and projected by forecasting population increases. This leads to projections of excess quantities of water as "needs." Figure 6–5 shows some of the projections made for various planning studies during the past 15 years for future water needs. The breadth of the range is so wide as to be of no use for practical purposes. For example, there is a threefold difference between the 1965 and the 1975 (which assumed some price effects) Water Resources Council's projection of water demand in the year 2000. The actual 1985 water demand falls outside the entire range of projections into the future, however; so much for our experts' views on the future!

4.1 Demand Curves

The concept of demand curves was first put forward by the French engineer Arsene Jules Etienne Juvénal Dupuit. (Among other things, he invented the concept of consumer surplus and the Laffer curve, all while he was the Inspector General of Roads and Bridges in France during the early nineteenth century.) The concept is very simple: the amount of a commodity that would be consumed over a range of prices is estimated—ideally from empirical observations of the same consumer.

This simple concept immediately becomes complex, however, when applied to environmental amenities such as water quality. First, there are many uses for water, not one. Water, therefore, behaves like several different commodities at the same time; depending on its quality and how it is to be used, it may also belong to one of several markets. While demand curves originally applied to only one market for one good and for one consumer, methods to build demand curves for groups of consumers with similar preferences and market behavior were established early. Demand curves for one commodity used in several markets have been calculated for some time.

Using the example given earlier of the two industries on a river, it is possible to create the demand curve for water quality in the river by user B. The ordinate in Figure 6–6 is the amount user B would be willing to pay for removal per pound of pollutant upstream of her use point, and the abscissa is the amount of pounds of pollutant removed. The total willingness-to-pay is the area under this demand curve, which is seen to be $800,000—the amount of total damages suffered by B in Figure 6–1. Alternatively, this can be viewed as the total benefit accruing to B if the contamination were completely stopped. The question remains, however, as to what B will be really willing to pay for reducing pollution upstream. We cannot answer this question, however, without information about the costs of supplying this reduction.

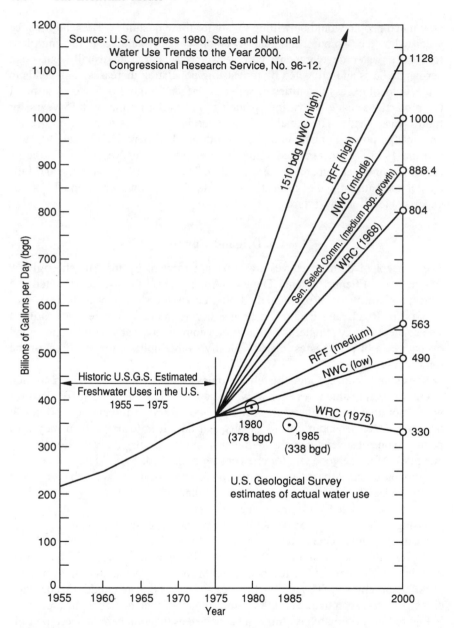

FIGURE 6-5.   Historic and projected freshwater withdrawals, 1955–2000.

4.2 Supply Curves

Another economic concept important to an understanding of environmental economics is that of a "supply curve." The supply curve is created by arranging, in ascending order of cost, the amount of the environmental amenity available to consumers in a given market area.

In Figure 6–2, we already observed two functions dealing with the incremental costs of providing wastewater treatment. These are supply curves. Note that the supply curve for removing wastes at A is an increasing nonlinear function, whereas the supply curve for removing wastes at B is a horizontal line. The supply function at B is then said to have "constant marginal costs," whereas the supply function at A has "increasing marginal costs." The supply curve at A is a typical shape of supply functions.

4.3 Market Clearing

One of the great conceptual breakthroughs in economics is the idea that the most efficient economic solutions occur when what a consumer is willing to pay and the supply prices just match each other; the market is said to "clear." This concept, as originally formulated, was based on little economic theory; later, however, it was demonstrated that, for this to be the most efficient solution, all the assumptions made in Section 6 must also hold. Nevertheless, even in its simplest form it does provide planners and policymakers with a set of simple tools that refers to engineering, ecology, and physics (supply curves) and to observed behavior (demand curves) that give good indications of efficient economic solutions.

Using the examples given above, we can see that simply placing the supply curve over the demand curve will identify the price and the quantities at which the market would clear. This is shown in Figure 6–6, where both the supply curve of treatment at A and B are used. If we are forced to use the treatment processes available at B, then the market will clear with a 50% removal of the wastes; if we can use the function from A, then the market will clear with a 57.5% removal of the wastes. The level of treatment declines as the supply curve becomes steeper (i.e., the marginal costs of treatment increase).

This discussion highlights the role of prices in encouraging or discouraging excessive use of the environment. As is often the case, if the price of environmental resources—such as municipal wastewater treatment—is held unrealistically low, the demand grows to be very large. As consumption rises, the real costs of treatment become greater, necessitating an increase in the public subsidy. Such an increase often occurs because the utilities price their treatment on historical average costs that are much lower than the future marginal costs for expanding treatment.

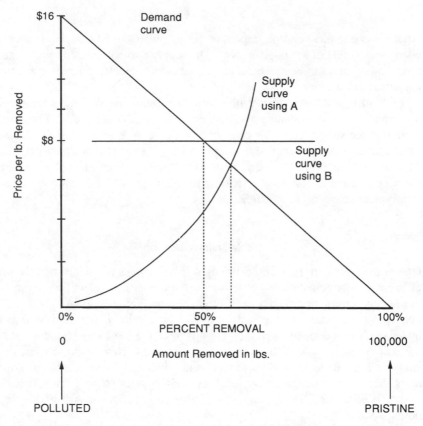

FIGURE 6–6.   Derived demand curve for water quality at B. This shows the environmental quality at B ranging from polluted at removal cost of $16 per pound to pristine if the cost were zero.

Due to restrictions on the transfer of rights to the amenities, such as water, it is possible to have multiple markets for the same commodity. In such cases, prices cease to give the correct rationing signals. Moreover, in heavily regulated markets, such as municipal water supply and wastewater utilities, the market will not clear where the supply curve intersects the demand curve because the price set by the regulators is either too high or too low. If the price is set below the marginal cost (shown in Figure 6–7), then the actual level of consumption will be at E' rather than at E. In order to maintain this consumption over and above the economically efficient level, consumers must be subsidized by the amount shaded in the figure; these are called "deadweight" losses. On the other hand, if the price is set above the marginal cost, then consumers will actually consume less than they would have under the efficient solution (E in Figure 6–8), and

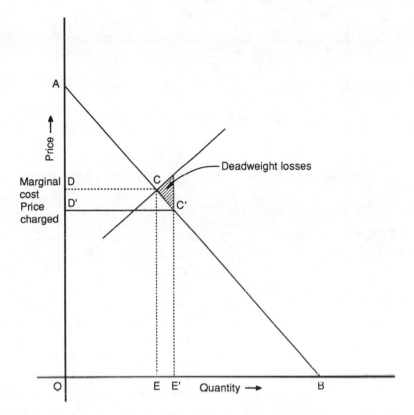

FIGURE 6–7.   Role of prices in encouraging the use or abuse of environmental amenities. In this case the price is set below marginal cost, leading to overuse of the resource and dead weight losses to be borne by society.

available resources will be underutilized. This less-than-optimal consumption means a "welfare loss" for society equivalent to the shaded area in Figure 6–8. Hence, marginal cost-pricing is the economic prescription for tariff setting.

4.4 Price and Income Elasticity

In the mid-nineteenth century, Ernst Engel was the first person to formulate the concept of elasticity as it is now used. Engel (not to be confused with Friederich Engels of Marx and Engels) was not a professional economist, but a medical doctor interested in nutrition. He noticed that persons in higher-income classes in Germany spent a smaller proportion of their income on food than people in the lower-income groups. He defined the income elasticity of food as the ratio of the percentage change in quantity consumed to the percentage change in income.

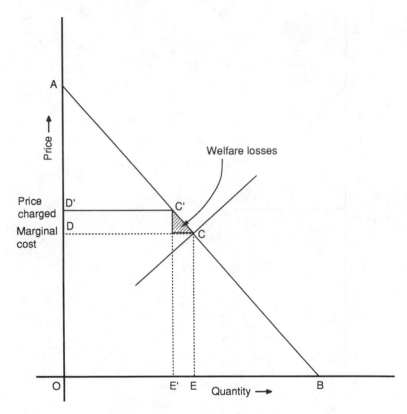

FIGURE 6–8.   In this case the price is set above the marginal cost, leading to welfare losses to be borne by society because of deviation from efficient prices.

Engel found that for food this ratio was less than 1; in other words, the relative amount of expenditures for food declines as income increases. If the elasticity is less than unity, the consumption is said to be "inelastic," meaning that a big change in income leads to a smaller increase in the quantity of food consumed; if it is above unity, it is said to be "elastic," meaning a small change in income leads to a larger change in the amount consumed.

Elasticities can be measured for almost any two sets of quantities that vary simultaneously, but the important ones from the point of view of water are those of price and income. A price elasticity for industrial wastewater treatment of −0.7 means that for a 10% price increase, demand for treatment would decrease by 7%. Even though this demand is said to be "price inelastic," it does not mean that pricing cannot be used as a rationing tool for industrial wastewater treatment. If waste production were "price elastic," the impact of pricing would be greater than when inelastic. Nonetheless, a 7% decline in waste production for a 10% price increase could have major implications for the future adequacy of a particular wastewater treatment system.

Municipal water supply is typically "income inelastic" (the demand grows with increases of income but less rapidly). The combination of price and income effects needs to be taken into account in making forecasts of future demand. For example, the Department of Commerce (1985) forecasts that the population by the year 2000 will be 267 million, that is about a 1% per annum growth from 1980. How large would the year 2000 demand for water be? If we simply assume water use proportional to the population growth rate, it would increase 22% above the 1980 level. If forecasters wanted to include the effects of increasing income levels estimated to be growing at 2% per annum over that period, they would need to know the income elasticity of water. This is typically inelastic, about 0.5. Incorporating this into the forecast would lead to a 49% increase of water demands by 2000.

So far this has assumed that price remains constant. What if forecasters allowed for a price increase at about 3.5% per annum and assumed a −0.5 price elasticity over this period? Then the demand would increase only 5% during this 20-year period. This projection would have tremendous implications for easing the water-quality management problems.

Which forecast should be used? The answer depends on whether a prescriptive or a descriptive stance is taken. According to our simple example, the United States could have a water crisis (the 49% increase) or just a modest increase in demand (the 5% increase). The choice is up to governmental policymakers. "Needs" forecasts do not reflect the restraining effects of price. If the regulators leave water sellers free to make water prices more nearly represent the marginal cost of supply and—in those cases where the supply has to be controlled by government—realistic pricing policies are pursued, then the crisis will never take place.

5 MEASUREMENT OF BENEFITS

5.1 Conceptual Issues

Saying that the "benefits must exceed the costs" is easy, but even when we use the GNP criterion of benefit-cost analysis the question still remains: "How do we measure benefits?" In a perfectly functioning market, *price* is a measure of *value*. Therefore, the total benefit of consumption can be measured simply by taking the sum of the price times the quantity of the commodity consumed. If we make the usual assumptions, this is a perfectly good way to estimate benefits for environmental-management decisions. But what about outputs for which there is no traditional market, such as health, air and water quality, and aesthetics? Or for which there is a market, but entry is constrained, or where there are large economies of scale, such as irrigation water, navigation, and hydroelectric power? Or cases where a policy or project creates a unique market, such as water-based recreation in an arid area? These are hard cases that have, nonetheless, been satisfactorily resolved conceptually by economists. In many cases, robust methods have been developed for operational measurement of the benefits.

5.2 Benefits of National Level Programs

Another, national, level of benefit estimation is also relevant to environmental decision making. Freeman (1982) discussed this for air- and water-pollution control and estimated the benefits of the Clean Air and the Clean Water Acts. Box 6–1 shows the categories of benefits that he included in his studies.

Using the above schema, Freeman culled the literature and summarized his results for air in Table 6–1 and for water in Table 6–2.

BOX 6–1

Assessing Benefits from Environmental Regulation.*

Effects on Living Systems (Involving Biological Mechanisms)
1. Human health (nonmarket)
   a. mortality
   b. morbidity
2. Economic productivity of ecological systems (market)
   a. agriculture
   b. commercial fisheries
   c. forestry
3. Other ecological-system effects impinging directly on human activities (nonmarket)
   a. sports fishing
   b. hunting
   c. wildlife
   d. water-based recreation
   e. home gardening and landscaping
   f. commercial, institutional, public landscaping

4. Ecological-system effects not directly impinging on humans
   a. species diversity
   b. ecosystem stability

Effects on Nonliving Systems
1. Producers (market)
   a. damages to materials, e.g., corrosion
   b. soiling
   c. reduction in product quality
2. Households (nonmarket)
   a. damage to materials
   b. soiling
3. Changes in weather and climate (nonmarket)
4. Other (nonmarket)
   a. visibility
   b. tranquility

*Source: From Freeman, A. Myrick III. 1982. *Air and Water Pollution Control: A Benefit-Cost Assessment*. New York: John Wiley & Sons. p. 9.

TABLE 6–1   Air Pollution Control Benefits Being Enjoyed in 1978 (in Billions of 1978 Dollars)

Category	Realized Benefit	
	Range	Most Reasonable Point Estimate
1. Health		
Stationary source		
Mortality	$2.8–27.8	$13.9
Morbidity	$0.3–12.4	$ 3.1
Total	$3.1–40.2	$17.0
Mobile source	$0.0– 0.4	$ 0.0
Total health	$3.1–40.6	$17.0
2. Soiling and cleaning	$1.0– 6.0	$ 3.0
3. Vegetation		
Stationary source	0	0
Mobile source	$0.1– 0.4	$ 0.3
Total vegetation	$0.1– 0.4	$ 0.3
4. Materials		
Stationary source	$0.4– 1.1	$ 0.7
Mobile source	$0.0– 0.3	$ 0.0
Total materials	$0.4– 1.4	$ 0.7
5.Property values		
Stationary source	$0.9– 6.9	$ 2.3
Mobile	$0.0– 2.0	$ 0.0
Total property value	**$0.9– 8.9**	**$ 2.3**
Total benefits	$4.9–51.1	$21.7*

*Estimated costs $16.6 × 10^9.
Source: From Freeman, A. Myrick III. 1982. *Air and Water Polution Control: A Benefit-Cost Assessment.* New York: John Wiley & Sons. p. 128.

These tables point to a major paradox which underlies the motivation for most environmental programs in the United States: public health is the main concern. Of the $21 billion in annual benefits that accrue from regulating air pollution, fully 78% is due to improved public health. For water-pollution control, however, only 10% of the benefits accrue because of improved public health; more than 50% are due to improved recreation possibilities. Politically, threats to the public health make it easier to motivate strong regulation. Getting the body politic exercised about providing more recreation facilities may be difficult.

TABLE 6–2   Benefits in 1985 From Removal of Conventional Water Pollutants
(in Billions of 1978 Dollars)

	Range	Most Likely Point Estimate
1. Recreation	$1.8– 8.7	$4.6
2. Nonuser benefits		
Aesthetics, ecology, and property value	$0.5– 4.0	$1.2
3. Commercial fisheries	$0.4– 1.2	$0.8
4. Diversionary uses		
Drinking water-health	$0.0– 2.0	$1.0
Municipal treatment	$0.6– 1.2	$0.9
Households	$0.1– 0.5	$0.3
Industrial supplies	$0.4– 0.8	$0.6
Total	**$3.8–18.4**	**$9.4***

*Estimated costs $15–20 billion.
Source: From Freeman, A. Myrick III. 1982. *Air and Water Pollution Control: A Benefit-Cost Assessment*. New York: John Wiley & Sons. pp. 15, 170.

5.3 User and Intrinsic Values

Recent work on benefit estimation has distinguished between user and nonuser (or intrinsic) values. All the benefits presented in Box 6–1 fall under the definition of "user benefits" (with the possible exception of category 4). Intrinsic values are associated with potential use by either oneself or someone else. A comprehensive review of the different types of benefits occasioned by environmental management is given by Desvouges and Smith (1983). In Table 6–3, examples from water development are given. In this table Desvouges and Smith split the benefits into two major categories of "current-user values" and "intrinsic or option values." The current-user values are split into two major categories of "direct" use and "indirect" use. Direct uses are in turn split into "withdrawal uses" and "in-stream uses." These represent the benefits of municipal, agricultural, industrial, and commercial uses, and of recreation and hydropower, that feature in the conventional analyses of water projects. The indirect uses that Desvouges and Smith categorize as "near-stream" uses include recreational, relaxation, and aesthetic benefits, not typically included in conventional studies.

Intrinsic values, the other major category Desvouges and Smith consider, almost never enter into project analysis. They are broken down into "potential use" and "no use." The potential use, often called "option value," is broken into the categories of near-term potential use and long-term potential use. In other words, some consumers of the project outputs would be potential consumers some time in the near or more distant future; not being current consumers does

TABLE 6–3   Types of Values Associated with Water-Resources Projects

Current User Values	Direct Use	In Stream	Navigation Recreational Commercial Hydropower
		Withdrawal	Municipal Agricultural Industrial/Commercial
	Indirect Use	Near Stream	Recreational Relaxation Aesthetic
Intrinsic Values	Potential Use	Option Value	Near-term potential use Long-term potential use
	No Use	Existence Value	Stewardship Vicarious consumption Pure existence value Bequest value

Source: From William H. Desvouges and N. Kerry Smith. 1983. *Benefit-Cost Assessment Handbook for Water Programs, Volume 1*, prepared for the U.S. E.P.A. Research Triangle Park, NC: Research Triangle Institute. p. 3–2.

not mean their benefits should be ignored. Finally, there are the "no-use" sets of benefits based on the existence value of the project itself or the resource base which it alters. These are based on the values associated with vicarious consumption by others, good stewardship of the Earth's resources, pure existence values associated simply with the knowledge that the project exists (or does not exist), and the idea of bequest value to future generations. The intrinsic-existence benefits are least well defined and distinguished from each other; nonetheless, they reflect real willingness to pay by the population at large and are, therefore, just as important and real as direct-use benefits.

Desvouges and Smith make the important point that individuals are willing to pay for all these types of benefits (or to avoid disbenefits in these areas) and, hence, they are just as important to evaluating a water-investment or -management decision as the more conventional benefits. Because most of the intrinsic—or option and existence—values tend to be preservationist or conservationist, they will show up as negative benefits for most water decisions that lead to significant changes in the environment. This means that they are not popular with proponents of water development. However, if people are indeed willing to pay for them, then—following strict economic logic—they must be considered in the analysis. To dismiss them because they are difficult to measure is not permissible; it behooves the analysts to attempt to measure the magnitudes of these benefits and incorporate them into the final decision calculus. In fact, incorporating them is all the more important because neglect of these benefits has generated much of the unhappiness about how current water policy has been implemented.

The approach advocated by Desvouges and Smith of estimating nonuser values has not been used extensively in other areas of environmental decision making, but there appear to be no insurmountable difficulties in making use of the concepts for nonwater impacts. Note that even though environmental values appear in economic analysis they still have to be articulated by some human's willingness to pay for preserving them. Using willingness-to-pay may be as close as possible to including environmental values in formal economic analysis.

5.4 Practical Approaches

When we estimate benefits for environmental uses, the easiest uses to deal with are those that have well-established markets and firm monetary valuations for the outputs. For example, evaluating benefits from hydropower and irrigation, and municipal, commercial, and industrial uses, is relatively straightforward compared to estimating benefits from recreation and aesthetics. Estimating the intrinsic values is expected to be significantly more difficult still. At the basic theoretical level, however, the approach to evaluating each of the benefits is more or less the same.

Details on how to estimate the intrinsic values of a wide variety of environmental amenities are given in Fisher and Raucher (1984), Stavins and Willey (1983), and Meta Systems (1985). What is beginning to emerge from these studies is that the intrinsic benefits are about the same order of magnitude as the current user benefits (ranging from 47% to more than 139% of the user benefits in Fisher and Raucher). It is clear that intrinsic benefits can no longer be dismissed out of hand by agencies promoting projects, even though most of the intrinsic values tend toward preservation and conservation and are, hence, likely to end up as "negative" benefits in the actual benefit-cost analysis.

The improvement of intrinsic-benefit measurement is an area of great importance for environmental decision making. From a purely philosophical point of view, incorporating these benefits makes the "rational" economic model of resource management much more acceptable in the policy arena. The difficulty in measuring these benefits with exactness in no way makes them any less real than the ones usually added up in the benefit-cost calculations. As Saunders (1986) shows, there can be great uncertainties and disagreements about conventional "user" benefits for water projects, but this has never implied that they should, therefore, be ignored. There is no reason to treat intrinsic benefits differently; the economics profession should insist that all the benefits be considered in the analysis.

6 ENVIRONMENTAL DECISION MAKING USING THE ECONOMIC PARADIGM

Among all environmental resources, water has received the greatest attention from the economics profession; hence, it is a good point of departure. Starting with the Flood Control Act of 1936, the "Green Book" in 1950, and in 1952 the Circular A-47 of the Bureau of the Budget, a series of studies led to the formulation of specific economic criteria to be applied to proposed federal water projects. These studies ensured that water was the area where federal concern with efficiency in government led the way, stimulated by the general perception that water projects were "pork barrel" and could not be justified otherwise.

Against this background two studies were carried out at Harvard University starting in the late 1950s. Eckstein (1958) and Maass et al. (1962) laid out the classic economic theory underlying the use of benefit-cost analysis for water-resource planning and analysis. These studies were the foundations for much of the later literature on environmental economics. The studies were notable for the fact that they were able to demonstrate that classic economic theory, as propounded by Alfred Marshall, could handle all the complexities of practical water problems. Implicit in the classical theory, however, is also a set of assumptions about the consumers of the project outputs, the producers of the outputs, and the structure of the market in which the project functions. Although the original context was for water, they apply to any other environmental amenity. These assumptions which have varying degrees of credibility are as follows.

Assumptions About Consumers

1. Rational consumers act consistently on preferences.
2. Successive units of a commodity add less and less to consumer satisfaction and hence add less and less to utility (diminishing marginal utility of consumption).
3. Preferences must be independent of purchases by others (no keeping up with the Joneses).

Assumptions About Producers

1. Producers pursue the principle of profit maximization rationally.
2. Production processes must not be such that successive units of production are cheaper (decreasing returns to scale).
3. There is no physical interdependence among production processes (no externalities).

Assumptions About the Structure of the Market

1. Markets must be "perfect."
   i. Producers and consumers have complete information about quality, prices, and availability of goods and services.
   ii. Both producers and consumers are small, relative to size of the market.
2. Resultant distribution of income is "appropriate."
3. Labor, capital, and other resources are relatively free to move from location to location.
4. There is full employment of labor and resources.

Many of the above assumptions appear reasonable enough (e.g., the assumptions about the consumers) or not reasonable, but there is little we can do about them (e.g., complete information about the market). A few assumptions, concerning producers and the structure of the market, however, particularly stand out as being too strong, or simply incorrect, for environmental resources. Let us look at five of them in turn.

1. Increasing returns to scale on the production side is prevalent in projects that have an impact on environmental amenities. Inland waterways and municipal water and wastewater services, for example, are natural monopolies because of the large economies of scale in the provision of the infrastructure. Most water-related investments tend to be very large to take advantage of these economies of scale.

2. Physical interdependence among production processes is inherent in many environmental activities. The externalities are experienced spatially in both water-quantity and water-quality differences between upstream and downstream users, and temporally between different seasonal releases of stored water, common pool effects on groundwater, and the export of pollution.

3. Producers are not small relative to the market. When the federal government is involved, it is often the *only* producer in the market. Moreover, the amenities supplied will make large changes in the local availability of the amenity, undermining the assumption of marginality inherent in the benefit measurements.

4. Concerning the income-distribution assumption: Many public projects are specifically aimed at changing the distribution of income.

5. The resources are not necessarily mobile. In the United States, capital resources are relatively mobile but labor resources are not. Pockets of poverty and unemployment still exist, and many water projects (like the TVA) were originally designed to address these problems. In addition, restricted water, land,

and air rights often impede the ease of transfer of resource from one use to another.

These violations of the basic assumptions are lumped under the title "market failures." In the early 1960s following the Harvard studies, Hirschleifer, Milliman and De Haven (1960) presented a "Chicago School" riposte to the Harvard studies, and a series of publications by Kneese and Bower (1972) and their colleagues from Resources for the Future started to deal with the above "problems of market failure." Hirschleifer, Milliman, and De Haven emphasized the use of market measures to assess benefits and the use of market rates of discount instead of the "social rate of discount" promoted by Harvard. Kneese and his colleagues researched pricing mechanisms for efficient allocation of water quality. The major improvements in the economic approach has come from development economics, where explicit consideration of market failure has been successively incorporated into the economics of resource management. Little and Mirrlees (1974), DasGupta, Marglin, and Sen (1972), Mishan (1976), and UNIDO (1978) showed in a practical way how to assess social rates of discount and shadow prices on constrained and underutilized resources.

Benefit-cost analysis based on the compensation principle as modified to correct for market failure is now a widely accepted practice, required by most federal agencies to decide whether a particular project should be carried out. It is often part of the environmental-impact analysis.

7 PRACTICAL PRICING PROBLEMS

"Market failure" is the legitimate concern of economists analyzing pollution and environmental amenities. In particular, the issue of how to internalize the externalities has received most of the attention. At the most obvious level, it would seem that if the pollutants emitted could be correctly priced, then industry and other polluters could be taxed by just this amount and the problem would disappear; the correct amount of pollution would be obtained, and if this were considered too large, then the price could be raised until the satisfactory lower level was achieved (as was the case in the introductory example). But as H. L. Menken once remarked, "for every problem economists have a solution— simple, neat, and wrong." Given the simplicity of the effluent-taxing suggestion, there must be something seriously wrong with it. It has never been seriously applied to solving pollution problems anywhere in the United States.

Pricing plays a twofold role in environmental policy. First, as discussed above, increasing prices tend to ration environmental amenities or discourage environmental deterioration by cutting uneconomical consumption. This lowers demand by moving up the demand curve, which is the effect most decision makers are looking for when pricing policy is advocated. The second aspect of pricing, the one most frequently overlooked, is that of increasing the supply of the commodity. When the price is higher, more expensive sources of supply become more economically available.

Policymakers should be careful to take the price response into account when they engage in setting prices. For example, Billings and Day (1983) showed that the Tucson Water Department estimated that the water rates would have to be increased by 17.6% in order to pay for the increasing cost of the city supply from the Central Arizona Project, but the authors pointed out that this would be too low by a factor of three when the price elasticity is taken into account. Billings and Day estimated a rate increase of 59% would be necessary to increase the total revenue by 17.6%.

The central proposition of price theory is marginal cost pricing. In other words, set the price at the point where demand and supply curves intersect. However, for investments that exhibit returns-to-scale, as most water infrastructure projects do, there are at least four equally plausible different ways of measuring marginal cost; each gives a different estimate of the marginal cost. An excellent summary of these approaches is given in Meier (1983). Unfortunately, Saunders and Warford (1976) showed that these four different approaches could give radically different estimates of marginal costs when applied to the analysis of the same project. This is cautionary advice to would-be "marginal cost pricers." It is disconcerting that the two most promising pricing schedules are not consistent with each other as the period of investment decreases. Even though there is an aspect of arbitrariness in the choice of any of the pricing schemes, it would be nice to have had some assurance that one or the other dominates over the entire range of potential use. The way it stands now, an agency must make an arbitrary choice and stick by it, come what may.

7.1 Regulated Monopoly Pricing

Even if the marginal costs could be unambiguously established, the pricing problem for most environmental uses is still not resolved because of the characteristics of environmental amenities that make them a natural monopoly. The existence of large economies of scale ensure that the first entry into the market will always be able to underprice and drive out any newcomers. Then they could decide on their desired profit level and set the prices accordingly. This has been recognized for a long time in the area of municipal water and wastewater treatment, and the suppliers have been regulated—typically by public-utility commissions. Unfortunately, most regulatory commissions have tended to take an accounting stance that allows such a pricing based only on average costs and the revenue needs to meet them. Such a stance is not appropriate in situations where the utilities face increasing marginal costs (all the best projects have been built; it now becomes increasingly difficult to supply the same amounts for their historical costs, or environmental mitigation costs must now be considered).

Under these conditions a forward-looking accounting stance, such as indicated in the section on marginal cost pricing, is indicated. The emphasis on revenue requirements of utilities could then be replaced by establishing adequate future investment funds.

If this approach were followed, however, another problem would be encountered. Take municipal water utilities. If the utilities charged a forward-looking rate for all the water they supply (as economic theory would dictate), they would raise substantially more revenue than needed to cover their operating costs and retire historical debt. Serious administrative and legal problems may arise because of this. It has been suggested that the prices be charged to motivate rational consumption behavior of the customers during the year, and that at the end of the year they receive a rebate from the water utility returning the surplus funds generated—but only after the consumption has taken place. Alternatively, the surpluses could be put directly into general revenue accounts of the municipality or placed in separate environmental-enhancement funds. Whichever approach is taken, dealing with these funds becomes an integral part in any recommendations for a move toward marginal cost pricing.

7.2 Effluent Pricing

Regulating environmental quality by pricing the effluents that individuals, municipalities, and corporations emit is one of the great debates that never took place in the United States. The economic literature is full of conceptual schemes for pricing or taxing effluents that would lead to internalizing the externalities of pollution. If this were done, environmental quality could be left entirely to the usual market forces. The Washington-based research institute, Resources for the Future, has led the campaign for fees on effluent discharges for more than 20 years with little success, for the most part opposed by those who think it improper to sell the right to pollute the environment.

Little actual contact between these opposing positions has occurred. This is probably because both positions are unrealistic; both ignore some basic imperatives of the environment. Even if it were possible to figure out optimal prices or taxes to impose, we would still have to monitor the actual performance of the polluters to make sure they were not cheating. Hence, we would still need large and intrusive bureaucracies to implement the market solution. Under these conditions would the "market" be quite as efficient as it is touted to be? The mainline environmentalist position, on the other hand, does not recognize that, under the current regulatory system, "permits to pollute" will still be issued— unless no emissions at all are permitted.

Despite all the nondebate, a substantial amount of effluent pricing has been going on in the United States. Hudson (1981) reports on the extent and mode of implementation of water-pollution pricing. He claims that by 1970 more than 90% of the municipalities with populations over 50,000 levied some form of sewerage charge on residences and industry, and that 40% of local expenditure on sewerage was derived from these charges. Residential charges are not particularly relevant here, since, once hooked up to a sewer, residences have few options to adjust their effluent quantities; the sewerage charge is typically set as a fixed proportion of the water bill, with the only option being to reduce water consumption.

Industry, however, can choose to pretreat its waste, decrease its water use, improve housekeeping, change either the production process or products—or pay the fee. The industrial charges are typically related to the quantity of water used and the "strength" of the effluent measured in terms of the oxygen-demanding organic waste load and total suspended solids. These charges can give an incentive to industries to change the amount and strength of their sewage effluents. Hudson's study of five cities [Atlanta, Chicago, Dallas, Salem (Oregon), and South San Francisco] and 101 industries found that effluent charges were overwhelmingly preferred to discharge limitations by the industrialists. There was a universal attempt by the industries in the sample to respond to the effluent fees despite their relatively small costs to the industries. Hudson concluded that

> . . . we are confident that economic incentives work well and can be effectively administered. (Hudson, 1981, p. 51)

Downing and Sessions (1985), studying water quality in streams, examined the innovative program of trading effluent permits on the Fox River in Wisconsin. They concluded that the method would be administratively feasible, but they could not judge its economic efficiency (since no trades actually took place). The state officials who were originally enthusiastic about the experimental program claimed that its lack of success was due to lack of support of the program in the Regional EPA office.

Effluent fees were proposed for the 1990 revisions of the Clean Air Act, but have run into serious opposition. Trading effluent permits for air pollution, however, has been undertaken for long periods of time in parts of the country. For example, California has well-developed markets for large point-source air pollutants. Industry can now figure air pollution costs directly into their plant-siting calculations.

8 AFTER ALL—WHY BOTHER WITH ECONOMICS?

This chapter could be read as an assertion of the futility of attempting economic analysis on a subject as complicated as environmental policy. We have great difficulty in measuring the benefits and disbenefits of development actions;

indeed, if you believe in the existence of the intrinsic benefits, then typically 50% of the benefits are completely ignored. Marginal cost-pricing is not strictly possible, and the plausible alternate methods for approximation give radically different policy implications. Cost-sharing for multiple-purpose projects is not even possible in principle, and again, plausible pragmatic alternatives give different answers. Finally, pricing of pollution externalities appears to be theoretically possible but an administrative nightmare that is never put into practice.

In sum, these problems appear to make economic approaches to water policy totally irrelevant. Why, then, has there been so much attention precisely upon the economic aspects of environmental decision making, particularly those relating to water? The answer is simply that economic thinking and conceptualization appear to be the only alternative to a chaotic political battle with no concepts of the public good, but only "log rolling" and "pork barreling."

Moreover, some very important economic phenomena are at work. First, as Saliba and Bush (1987) discovered, the market seems to work quite well in allocating scarce water in the West. In fact, it works better than most economists themselves would have predicted only 10 years ago. Second, consumption of environmental quality and the production of negative externalities are clearly price responsive. The problem is to find some reasonable "second or third best" (Hanke & Davis, 1973) pricing schemes.

We have seen, in sum, that although it by no means solves all the problems in the field, economic analysis and economic thinking on the part of environmental managers and consumers is essential if a coherent environmental policy is to emerge in the United States.

EXERCISES

1. Using the example given in Section 3, extend the analysis to include considerations of the ambient environment itself. What is the value of improved water quality in the stream? How could it be numerically estimated?

2. Protecting wetlands has now become a major issue. The costs of protection are straightforward to estimate. What are the benefits of protecting wetlands? How can they be estimated?

3. Present the economic case for reducing emissions of electric power plants in the vicinity of the Grand Canyon to restore haze-free vistas.

ADDITIONAL READING

For further information on environmental economics, see Baumol and Oates (1989), Dixon and Hufschmidt (1986), Kneese and Bower (1972), Kneese (1977, 1984), Kneese and Schulze (1985), Krutilla and Fisher (1985), Hufschmidt et al. (1983), Portney (1990) and Tietenberg (1988).

REFERENCES

Baumol, William J., and Wallace E. Oates. 1989. *The Theory of Environmental Policy* (2nd ed.). Cambridge, MA: Harvard University Press.

Billings, R.B. and W. M. Day. 1983. Elasticity of demand for water: policy implications for southern Arizona. *Arizona Review* 3:1–11.

Chechile, R. 1984. Logical foundations for a fair and rational method of voting. In *Group Decision Making,* ed. W. Swap. pp. 97–114. Beverly Hills, CA: Sage Publications.

Coase, R. 1960. The problem of social cost. *The Journal of Law and Economics*, 3 (October), pp. 1–44.

DasGupta, P., S. A. Marglin, and A. Sen. 1972. *Guidelines for Project Evaluation.* New York: United Nations Industrial Development Organization.

Desvouges, William H. and V. Kerry Smith. 1983. *Benefit-Cost Assessment Handbook for Water Programs, Volume I*. Prepared for the U.S. EPA. Research Triangle Park, NC: Research Triangle Institute.

Dixon, John A. and Maynard M. Hufschmidt, eds. 1986. *Economic Valuation Techniques for the Environment.* Baltimore, MD: Johns Hopkins University Press.

Dorfman, Robert and Nancy S. Dorfman, eds. 1972. *Economics of the Environment: Selected Readings* (2nd ed.). New York: Norton Books.

Downing, D. and S. Sessions. 1985. Innovative water quality-based permitting: a policy perspective. *Journal WPCF* 62:5.

Eckstein, O. 1958. *Water Resource Devlopment and the Economics of Project Evaluation.* Cambridge, MA: Harvard University Press.

Fisher, A. and R. Raucher. 1984. Intrinsic benefits of improved water quality. In *Advances in Applied Micro-Economics* (Volume 3), ed. V. Kerry Smith. Greenwich, CT: JAI Press.

Freeman, A. Myrick III. 1982. *Air and Water Pollution Control: A Benefit-Cost Assessment.* New York: John Wiley & Sons.

Hanke, S.H. and R. Davis. 1973. Potential for marginal cost pricing in water resources management. *Water Resources Research* 9(4):808–825.

Hirschleifer, J., J. W. Milliman, & J. C. De Haven. 1960. *Water Supply: Economics and Policy.* Chicago: University of Chicago Press.

Holmes, B. H. 1972. *A History of Federal Water Resources Programs, 1800–1960.* Washington, DC: U.S. Department of Agriculture, Economic Research Service.

Hudson, J. F. 1981. *Pollution Pricing: Industrial Responses to Wastewater Charges.* Lexington: Lexington Books.

Hufschmidt, Maynard M., et al. 1983. *Environment, Natural Systems, and Development: An Economic Valuation Guide.* Baltimore, MD: Johns Hopkins University Press.

Kneese, Allen V. 1977. *Economics and the Environment.* New York: Penguin Books.

Kneese, Allen V. 1984. *Measuring the Benefits of Clean Air and Water.* Washington, DC: Resources for the Future.

Kneese, Allen V. and Blair T. Bower, eds. 1972. *Environmental Quality Analysis: Theory and Method in the Social Sciences.* Baltimore, MD: Johns Hopkins University Press.

Kneese, Allen V. and W. D. Schulze. 1985. Ethics and environmental economics. In

Handbook of Natural Resources and Environmental Economics, Chapter 5. New York: Elsevier Science Publishing Co.

Krutilla, John V. and Anthony C. Fisher. 1985. *The Economics of Natural Environments: Studies in the Valuation of Commodity and Amenity Resources.* Washington, DC: Resources for the Future.

Little, M. D. and J. A. Mirrlees. 1974. *Project Appraisal and Planning for Developing Countries.* New York: Basic Books.

Maass, A, et al. 1962. *The Design of Water-Resource Systems: New Techniques for Relating Economic Objectives, Engineering Analysis, and Government Planning.* Cambridge, MA: Harvard University Press.

Meier, G. M. 1983. *Pricing Policy for Development Management.* Baltimore, MD: Johns Hopkins University Press.

Meta Systems, Inc. 1985. A methodological approach to an economic analysis of the beneficial outcomes of water quality improvement from sewage treatment and combined sewer overflow controls. Washington, DC: EPA, Office of Policy Analysis.

Mishan, E. J. 1976. *Cost-Benefit Analysis.* New York: Praeger.

Portney, Paul R., ed. 1990. *Public Policies for Environmental Protection.* Washington, DC.: Resources for the Future.

Saliba, B. C., and D. B. Bush. 1987. *Water Markets in Theory and Practice.* Fort Collins, CO: Westview Press.

Saunders, J. Owen, ed. 1986. *Managing Natural Resources in a Federation State: Essays from the Second Banff Conference on Natural Resource Law.* Toronto: Carswell.

Saunders, R. J. and J. J. Warford. 1976. *Village Water Supply: Economics and Policy in the Developing World.* Baltimore, MD: Johns Hopkins University Press.

Stavins, R. and Z. Willey. 1983. Trading water conservation investments for water. In *Regional and State Water Resources Planning and Management,* ed. R. J. Charbeneau. Bethesda, MD: American Water Resources Association. pp. 223–230.

Tietenberg, Thomas T. (1988). *Environmental and Natural Resource Economics* (2nd ed.). New York: HarperCollins.

UNIDO. 1978. *Guide to Practical Project Appraisal.* Vienna: United Nations Industrial Development Organization.

7

Resource Allocation

Richard M. Vogel

1 INTRODUCTION

Should a dam that saves human lives and reduces flood-damage costs by millions of dollars each year be built if it eliminates a fish species? Should the EPA introduce legislation to reduce stack emissions from industrial plants if the legislation will cause those same plants to lay off workers due to increased costs? Should a city in an arid environment limit growth when growth means pumping so much groundwater that the ground surface begins to depress? These are typical dilemmas that stem from our need to use environmental resources. They are social dilemmas (see discussion in Chapter 2) but—at the same time—they are resource-allocation problems, problems whose solutions require the balancing of competing and interacting resources.

Presumably, at some additional cost, the flood-control dam that puts at risk a fish species could provide an appropriate fish ladder (see the Fish Ladder Case in Chapter 4). The problem, then, reduces to balancing the benefits of flood control against the costs of protecting (or not protecting) a fish species. Similarly, when deriving an environmental policy to reduce stack emissions from industrial plants, the EPA needs to balance the benefits of improved air quality against the costs of achieving improved emissions. Finally, the benefits of increased growth of the city in the arid environment due to the pumping of groundwater should be balanced against the costs associated with measures to reduce depression of the land surface caused by groundwater pumping.

Environmental decision problems are usually fraught with such political, economic, social, and technological complexities that they often appear to defy rational analysis. The environment is a complex system comprised of a set of resources: air, water, land, energy, plants, and animals. Usually these resources

156

are not independent; rather, as in the need of animals for land and water, they interact. In many cases, some or all of these resources are in scarce supply; they may even be in competition with one another. As a result, most environmental decisions involve calculating the efficient allocation of these resources. Human resources such as labor, equipment, time, and money are often required for the sustainable development or preservation of the environmental resources; these, too, are often in scarce supply and subject to competing demands.

This chapter focuses on the presentation of a rational and systematic framework for structuring complex environmental decision problems. This framework, termed "systems analysis," was developed during World War II. The aim was to muster all available human and natural resources for the purpose of winning the war. Since World War II, the field of systems analysis has grown quickly, particularly after the advent of digital computers led to thousands of applications to complex business, political, economic, environmental, and other problems. Numerous texts now exist that formalize the systems approach to environmental decision problems (De Neufville & Stafford, 1974; Pantell, 1976; Loucks, Stedinger, & Haith, 1981; Haith, 1982; Ossenbruggen, 1984; De Neufville, 1990). Those texts include applications of systems analysis to resource allocation problems having to do with water, land, air, and energy.

As an introduction to the use of the systems approach in structuring a complex environmental decision problem, consider the simplified but realistic example shown in Figure 7–1. The industrial city depicted is situated near a reservoir. The

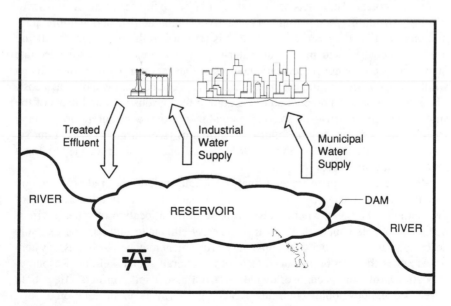

FIGURE 7–1.   Description of water resource-allocation problem.

city presently draws water from the reservoir for both its municipal drinking-water supply and its industrial-process–water supply. The water is then treated and returned to the reservoir as treated effluent. The reservoir serves as the only potential source of water, limiting the city's growth. Simultaneously, the reservoir serves as a recreational area, is host to an abundant fish and wildlife population, and protects the town against catastrophic flooding.

To what extent should future municipal and industrial growth of this city be limited by the environmental constraints posed by the reservoir and river? Which is more important—providing the city with an adequate supply of water for both municipal and industrial uses, preserving the fish and wildlife populations, maintaining recreational facilities, or controlling floods? Both the city and reservoir are artificial, yet both must act in harmony with the natural environment to assure the maintenance of fish and wildlife populations. Drawing too much water from the reservoir could result in water levels that are too low for swimming and boating, and too low to maintain fish and wildlife. The city also runs the risk of running out of drinking water and industrial-process water if the reservoir is drawn down too low. Water purveyors are reluctant to draw water from the bottom of a reservoir due to its typically poor quality. Yet if the reservoir is expected to prevent floods, then the water level must be kept relatively low, particularly during the flood season, to accommodate the storage of flood waters. In addition, adequate water must be released from the reservoir to satisfy the demand for water in downstream communities.

Further potential conflicts of interest exist between the use of the reservoir for boating, swimming, supplying water, and maintaining fish and wildlife populations. Ideally, the treated effluent that is returned to the reservoir after being used for industrial and municipal water-supply purposes must be of adequate quality so as not to prevent recreational uses of the reservoir, damage the fish and wildlife populations, or impact public health. This can be achieved only at a cost. The interactions and potential conflicts among the various uses and users of the single resource—water—are so complex that there exists a vast literature devoted solely to such water resource-allocation problems [see Burges (1979), Loucks, Stedinger, & Haith (1981), Yeh (1985), and Rogers & Fiering (1986) for a review of the literature].

Moreover, a complete systems analysis would include the trade-offs among all environmental resources; we focus on just water to simplify the discussion of the method. The potential conflicts that arise in the allocation of other environmental resources contain features that are very similar to those in the example described here. In all such problems, the environment may be viewed as a system of resources that can be managed to improve overall social welfare. Resource-allocation problems occur worldwide, and the associated conflicts affect both developed and developing countries. Reaching consensus on the solution of such problems can be particularly challenging when the resources are in scarce supply or are in competition with one another. In addition, resource-allocation problems tend to require the consideration of multiple, incommensurate, and often conflicting planning objectives.

Resource-allocation problems viewed in a systems-analysis framework generally contain two important features:

- The formulation of appropriate and relevant system objectives is a necessary prerequisite to the efficient management/allocation/exploitation of environmental resources (air, land, water, and energy).
- All pertinent environmental, economic, legal, political, ethical, technological, and other constraints must be evaluated together, as a system, in order to meet the desired system objectives.

For the example described in Figure 7–1, these two features may be summarized as follows:

- It is impossible to evaluate the trade-offs inherent in the allocation of water for the purposes of municipal drinking-water supply, industrial-water supply, flood control, boating, swimming, and the maintenance of fish and wildlife populations, without defining an objective or set of relevant objectives for the persons or sectors of society affected by the resulting environmental decisions.
- Once a suitable objective or set of objectives is formulated, all relevant conflicts and/or constraints regarding the allocation of the resource must be evaluated together, as a system, to meet the desired objectives.

The systems-analysis approach requires quantifying the system objectives in the form of an expression termed the "objective function." The systems approach then requires the optimization of that objective function in a fashion consistent with the constraints resulting from the finite availability of the various resources. An objective function is a measure of the effectiveness of a particular solution to the decision problem. In our example, one appropriate objective function measures the net social welfare of the neighboring region as well as of the town because the recreational and environmental benefits of the sound management of the reservoir extend beyond the boundaries of the town.

Net social welfare is difficult, at best, to estimate. Surrogate measures such as minimizing system cost to satisfy required demands, achieving equity among all system users, and enhancing overall environmental quality could be employed. The first of these measures is easily quantified, whereas the latter two are much more difficult. Many measures and objectives that first appear difficult to quantify are, in fact, amenable to quantification. At first, one may wonder how to quantify the utility or value associated with a scenic view. As shown in Chapter 4, Section 4.2, multiattribute utility can include dimensions of aesthetics. In addition, methods are available for quantification of some factors such as the land inundated by a lake, lake recreation, scenic vistas, or the loss of a wild and scenic river (James & Lee, 1971). Most system analysts attempt to satisfy what they perceive to be the dominant objective(s) and temper the analysis with subjective inclusion of other measures. Maknoon and Burges (1978) argue that this may not be the best way to proceed, but many environmental decisions have been implemented successfully, and many engineering projects have been constructed and maintained successfully, using such an approach.

In addition to a precise definition of the system objective(s), the constraints imposed upon the allocation of each resource must be quantified. "Feasible" solutions to a resource-allocation problem must satisfy all relevant constraints. For example, we might wish to maximize net social welfare, subject to the following constaints:

1. Town must have an ample quantity of high-quality drinking water.
2. Town must have ample industrial-water supply.
3. Reservoir must remain clean enough to support fish and wildlife populations.
4. Reservoir must remain low enough during flood season to accommodate flood waters.
5. Reservoir must remain high enough to supply ample municipal drinking water and industrial-water supply during periods of drought.
6. Reservoir levels must be stable enough to accommodate recreational functions.
7. Water release from the reservoir must be adequate for use by downstream communities.

Here a feasible solution would be one that satisfies all seven constraints. In most decision problems such as this one, there are an infinite number of feasible solutions. The optimal decision is to choose the feasible solution that best meets the desired objective(s).

Environmental decision problems such as this one usually contain features that are difficult to quantify. Hence, mathematical decision models are, at best, an approximation of actual systems. Nevertheless, systems analysis can lead to an increased understanding of a complex decision problem. When it does, it provides reliable input to the environmental decision-making process.

2 THE SYSTEMS APPROACH TO RESOURCE ALLOCATION

2.1 Optimal Resource Allocation Using Mathematical Programming

The field of systems analysis has come to mean different things to different people. Yet in the fields of engineering, applied mathematics, science, and even business, systems analysis is a well-defined and unified field that is synonymous with operations research or management science. Rogers and Fiering (1986) provide a description of the techniques of systems analysis. Hillier and Lieberman (1990a, 1990b) provide an excellent introduction to a variety of systems-analysis techniques for both stochastic and deterministic systems. The emphasis in this chapter—as was true in Ounjian (1979), Loucks, Stedinger, & Haith (1981), and Haith (1982)—will be on one of the most powerful of all systems-analysis techniques: mathematical programming.

Mathematical programming as a means of solving resource-allocation problems requires a set of precise statements regarding the overall objectives and constraints associated with an environmental decision problem. These statements must be precise enough to allow an analyst to convert each objective and constraint into mathematical terms.

For the moment, consider an abstract resource-allocation decision problem in which two resources x and y exist. Each of these resources is in scarce supply. In addition, there are certain physical, economic, political, legal, and ethical constraints or limitations associated with the separate and joint use of these two resources. Figure 7–2(A) depicts the feasible combinations of resources x and y given the physical, economic, political, legal, and ethical constraints associated

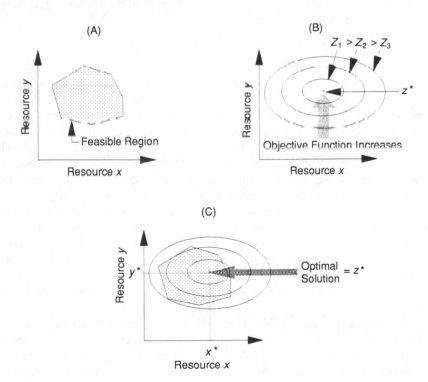

FIGURE 7–2.   A resource-allocation decision problem.

with their separate and joint uses. This region, known as the feasible region, corresponds to the shaded region in Figure 7–2(A). Essentially, the feasible region results from the simultaneous solution of the complete system of equations that describe the constraints or limitations associated with the separate and joint use of the resources. The feasible region contains an infinite number of possible combinations of resource x and resource y, all of which are potential solutions to this resource-allocation decision problem because they satisfy all the constraints. The decision problem reduces to determining which of these infinite possible feasible combinations of resource x and resource y is optimal in terms of the stated objective(s).

Suppose we define a set of objectives regarding the allocation of these two resources. Reaching consensus on objectives is often the most challenging task connected with the implementation of a mathematical program or any other systems-analysis method. Computer-aided exercises in negotiation are increasingly being used to help reach consensus regarding the complex economic, legal, political, and institutional issues that surround the allocation of scarce environmental resources, especially in times of crises (Sheer, Baeck, & Wright, 1989). For the moment, assume consensus is reached on the objectives having to do with the allocation of resources x and y. Suppose further that the objective is quantified in terms of a function

$$Z = f(x, y), \tag{7–1}$$

where Z is an agreed upon measure of utility or value of allocating an amount x and y of resources x and y, respectively. Essentially, x and y are decision variables whose optimal values we seek. For example, Z might be the net benefits, in economic terms, associated with the allocation of resource x and resource y. Figure 7–2(B) depicts values of the objective function Z as a function of the amount of resource x and y allocated. Here each ellipse represents a constant value of the objective function, and the objective-function value increases as we head toward the center of those ellipses. Figure 7–2(B) is like a mountain: As we climb to the peak (denoted by Z^*), the value of Z increases. If the objective function describes net benefits, then we seek a maximum; however, if the objective function describes net costs, then we seek a minimum. Figure 7–2(C) combines the feasible region with the objective function contours and shows that the solution Z^* is both feasible *and* optimal. Therefore, the optimal allocation of resources in this instance is to allocate x^* of resource x and y^* of resource y.

Other outcomes are possible. Often the largest (or smallest) value of an objective function is infeasible, in which case an inferior solution becomes optimal. In general, the optimal solution is the feasible solution that maximizes (or minimizes) the objective function. It is also possible, however, that the resource constraints are so conflicting that no feasible solution exists. Such cases may represent conflicts of interest among the participants in the decision-making process. In other instances, a poorly defined problem may lead to an unbounded solution in which it appears that the optimal solution is to allocate an infinite amount of one or more resources. While such situations are mathematically possible, they represent physically unrealizable cases.

When either the constraints on a problem or the objective function is non-linear, the problem is termed a nonlinear programming problem. Figure 7–2 is a representation of one such programming problem because the objective function is nonlinear (i.e., it is elliptical). In this instance, the feasible region is a convex polygon formed by the intersection of seven lines. Each of those lines represents a unique (linear, in this instance) constraint on resources x and y. In actual resource-allocation problems, there are often hundreds or even thousands of constraints and decision variables, in which case the feasible region becomes an n-dimensional polygon.

When both the objective function and constraints are linear, then the problem reduces to a linear program: Powerful algorithms have been developed to solve either class of problems [see Hillier & Lieberman (1990a) for an introduction]. Such algorithms are now available in the form of computer software for use on both mainframe and personal computers (Schrage, 1989).

2.2 A Linear Programming Example for Resource Allocation

In this section, a simple example of resource allocation is presented using a graphical approach to clarify the systems framework for formulating and solving an environmental resource-allocation problem. When several sources of water— such as groundwater aquifers and surface waters, each with different characteristics—are available, it is often possible to exploit their differences to improve the overall environmental quality of the water delivered to consumers. Use of surface water and groundwater supplies together in some systematic fashion is termed *conjunctive use* (Buras, 1963; Maknoon & Burges, 1978; Coe, 1990). The conjunctive operation of surface-water and groundwater resources can lead to increases in yield and reliability of the overall system. The idea is to manage and coordinate the resources in such a way that the total system-yield exceeds the sum of the yields of the separate components of the system when their operation is not coordinated.

Surface waters are available seasonally, yet often significant uncertainty exists as to when and how much water will be available in a particular year. Surface-water impoundments (storage reservoirs) can be constructed to store and regulate surface waters to reduce that uncertainty. Reservoirs are subject to evaporation and seepage losses in addition to all the potential conflicts of interest discussed in the problem in Section 1. For example, storing water for use during times of drought is in conflict with the need to keep surface-water storage reservoirs empty for flood protection.

Unlike the supply of surface waters, groundwater supply is much less variable over time and is already stored in large aquifers that are not subject to evaporation and seepage losses. Both surface and underground sources of water are subject to contamination from a variety of sources (landfills, dust and dirt accumulation on streets, agricultural wastes, industrial wastes, etc.), which in any given circumstance will cause either the ground- or surface-water reserves to be the cleaner source.

Figure 7–3 depicts a simple two-dimensional conjunctive-use problem in which a city seeks to allocate its groundwater (G) and surface water (S) supplies in an optimal fashion. Here we define S and G as the volumes of surface-water and groundwater resources to be delivered to the city on an annual basis. As in the example shown in Figure 7–2, each resource is subject to constraints or limitations. The hydrologic characteristics of each supply source dictate that only a finite amount of groundwater and surface water is available, hence $G \leq G_{max}$ and $S \leq S_{max}$, where G_{max} and S_{max} are the maximum sustainable groundwater and surface-water yields from each source. Estimates of these values would be obtained from detailed hydrologic investigations of the groundwater and surface-water supplies. The maximum sustainable yields correspond to the maximum

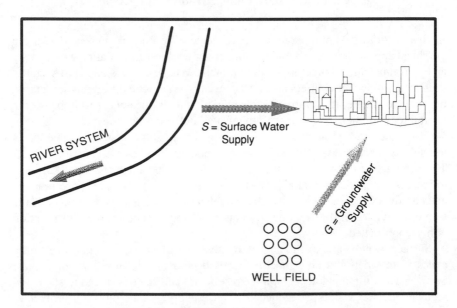

FIGURE 7–3.   Conjunctive-use example: problem description.

amount of groundwater and surface water that is available in a given year. Since groundwater reserves and surface-water reserves are physically connected at the stream-aquifer boundary, the determination of maximum sustainable yield poses a complex hydrological problem. In the case of surface water, delivery of an amount S may entail the construction of a reservoir. In the case of groundwater, delivery of an amount G will entail the construction of a well field. In both cases, a distribution system (possibly even a treatment plant) is required to assure adequate quality of the delivered water resource. In fact, the water supply will likely be contaminated by use; hence, a sewer system and associated wastewater treatment facility will be required. Furthermore, the yield of each system is subject to natural and artificially induced variability.

In planning for the growth of the city, it is necessary to provide an adequate conjunctive supply of both surface water and groundwater to meet the demand for water in the coming decades. Typically, water-use projections are obtained by predicting the increase (or decrease) in the demand for water on the basis of projections of population growth, industrial growth, and other demographic, economic, and political factors. For example, water-pricing strategies affect the demand for water [see Chapter 6, and Howe & Linaweaver (1967)] and hence should be included in water-use projections. Similarly, legislation that favors industrial growth can affect future demand for water. In addition, conservation programs that reduce per-capita water use will have an effect on the future demand for water. In short, all pertinent factors that influence future water use can be analyzed together to obtain a single water-use projection for planning purposes. Here we assume that such a comprehensive water-use projection leads to the conclusion that $G + S \geq K$, where $G + S$ represents the total conjunctive supply delivered, and K is the projected annual demand for water for the city at some future date.

In most situations, both the quality and the quantity of available groundwater and surface-water supplies will differ. Environmental legislation often dictates the allowable surface-water and groundwater withdrawals from a river basin on the basis of their impact on fish and wildlife populations, land subsidence due to drops in the groundwater level, or total basin yield. In this example, we assume that such considerations lead to the constraint that the groundwater allocation cannot be greater than the surface-water allocation or, mathematically, $G \leq S$. This constraint is mathematically simple—deceptively so. Arriving at such constraints in practice may involve very detailed engineering studies of the environmental consequences of various combinations of conjunctive use.

We have now summarized the environmental, legal, and hydrologic constraints on the allocation of ground and surface waters in this example. The optimal utilization of this natural resource is assumed to be essential for the establishment of a stable economic and social structure for the city in coming decades. The term "optimal" should always raise a number of important questions. Optimal for whom, to what end, and under what conditions? These questions amount to a quest to define objectives for the allocation of these two resources. In this example, we first assume that our objective is to maximize the net benefits corresponding to the allocation of groundwater and surface water. We define an objective function $Z = b_g G + b_s S$, where b_g and b_s denote the net benefits of one unit of groundwater and surface-water supplies, respectively. Then Z denotes the total net benefits that result from the decision to supply the amounts G and S. The total net benefits are defined as the total project benefits minus the total project costs corresponding to the allocation of resources G and S.

The project costs will include the construction costs (for the well field, reservoir, treatment plant, and distribution network associated with the conjunctive-use system) and operating and maintenance costs, all discounted over the life of the project to account for the time value of money [see Loucks, Stedinger, & Haith (1981, Chapter 2)].

The project benefits may include revenues from the sale of water, in addition to intangible and tangible benefits of the additional growth the city can now afford. For example, a portion of the benefits of increased growth can be measured in increased tax revenues that come with such expansions. It is likely that costs will accrue as well. For example, fish populations may suffer from lower instream-flows during the summer months. The coefficients b_g and b_s represent the aggregate net benefits associated with both resources. Note that it is entirely possible for b_g and/or b_s to be negative, denoting net costs from the allocation of these resources.

Most projects exhibit economies of scale, that is, the marginal cost of allocating an extra unit of each resource tends to decrease as the size of the project increases. Projects that exhibit economies of scale in their marginal or average costs do not necessarily also exhibit economies of scale in net project benefits. Nevertheless, when economy-of-scale effects are present, the objective function Z becomes a nonlinear function of the decision variables instead of the linear function assumed here.

This resource-allocation decision problem reduces to the mathematical problem of maximizing Z, where

$$Z = b_g G + b_s S, \tag{7-2}$$

subject to the following constraints:

$$G \leq G_{max}, \tag{7-3}$$

$$S \leq S_{max}, \tag{7-4}$$

$$G + S \geq K, \tag{7-5}$$

$$G - S \leq 0. \tag{7-6}$$

In addition, the constraints $G \geq 0$ and $S \geq 0$ are implied. This problem is a linear-programming problem because the objective function Z, and all constraints, are linear functions of the decision variables G and S. Figure 7–4 depicts the constraint Equations (7–3) through (7–6), using arrows to denote graphically the direction of each inequality. The shaded region satisfies all four constraints; hence, any combination of G and S that falls in that region is a feasible solution to the problem. Here feasibility is defined in terms of the issues that were considered in the development of each constraint equation.

Next, we consider which of the infinite number of feasible solutions is optimal with respect to our objective. Equation (7–2) can be rewritten as

$$G = (Z/b_g) - (b_s/b_g)\, S. \qquad (7\text{–}7)$$

Equation (7–7) is a straight line that intercepts the G axis at $G = Z/b_g$ and has a slope equal to $-b_s/b_g$. A variety of possible optimal solutions exist, depending on the magnitudes of the net benefits associated with one unit each of groundwater and surface water, b_g and b_s.

Below, two of these solutions are considered. Figure 7–5 plots the objective function [Equation (7–7)] by superimposing dashed lines over the feasible region. Figure 7–5 depicts the optimal solution to be $S^* = S_{max}$ and $G^* = K - S_{max}$ when the net unit benefits of surface water are positive ($b_s > 0$) and the

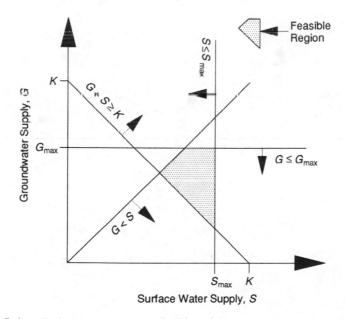

FIGURE 7–4.   Conjunctive-use example: feasible region.

net unit benefits of groundwater are negative ($b_g < 0$). This implies that the legal, economic, and environmental costs of construction and operation of the groundwater supply system are greater than their corresponding benefits, whereas the opposite is true for the surface-water supply system. The optimal solution is to provide as much surface water as is feasible—S_{max}—while limiting groundwater to its minimum feasible amount—which turns out to be $K - S_{max}$. In this instance, there is no incentive to increase groundwater supply to the point where the legal and environmental constraint ($G \le S$) becomes limiting. Hence the only constraints that have an effect on the problem are the demand-projection constraint $G + S \ge K$, and the hydrologic constraint on surface water $S \le S_{max}$.

Figure 7–6 plots the objective function again by superimposing dashed lines over the feasible region. In this instance, the net unit benefits of surface water are negative ($b_s < 0$) and the net benefits of groundwater are positive ($b_g > 0$). Now the optimal solution depends on the ratio b_s/b_g. As Figure 7–6 shows, the optimal solution is $S^* = K/2$ and $G^* = K/2$ when $|b_s| > b_g$. However, if $|b_s| < b_g$, then the optimal solution is $S^* = G_{max}$ and $G^* = G_{max}$. The solution to any linear programming problem is going to be one of the corners of the space associated with the region of feasible solutions. If the slope of the objective function is less than 45°, then the corner $S^* = K/2$ and $G^* = K/2$ is the optimal solution. If, however, the slope is greater than 45°, then the corner $G^* = G_{max}$ and $S^* = G_{max}$ is the optimal solution.

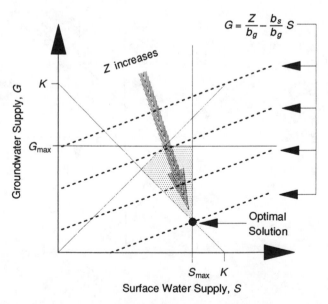

FIGURE 7–5.   Conjunctive-use example: optimal solution when $b_g < 0$ and $b_s > 0$.

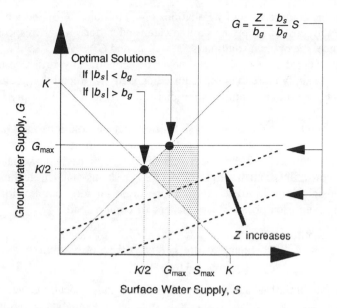

FIGURE 7–6.   Conjunctive-use example: optimal solution when $b_g > 0$ and $b_s < 0$.

Realistic cases of resource allocation usually involve so many constraints and such complex objective functions that our graphical approach needs to be replaced by mathematical programming methods. The two-dimensional example that we have been discussing demonstrates the principles of systems-analysis approach for resource allocation. Furthermore, the example demonstrates one of the most promising uses of systems analysis in practice, that is, to identify a range of nearly optimal solutions to a decision problem. An improved understanding of the variety of solutions—not necessarily optimal, yet in the neighborhood of the optimal solution—can provide important insight into the overall decision process.

2.3 Alternate Objectives Produce Alternate Solutions

This conjunctive-use example documents the way the optimal solution depends on both the feasible region (defined by the constraints) and the character of the objective function. Alternate objectives often lead to alternate optimal solutions. Suppose, for example, that our objective was to *minimize* the total cost associated with the conjunctive allocation of surface water and groundwater. Then the optimization problem becomes one of minimizing Z, where

$$Z = c_g G + c_s S, \tag{7-8}$$

subject to the constraints set by Equations (7–3) through (7–6) and where c_g and c_s are the unit cost of supplying groundwater and surface water, respectively. In this instance, the optimal solution is $S^* = S_{max}$ and $G^* = K - S_{max}$ if $c_s < c_g$ and $S^* = K/2 = G^*$ if $c_s > c_g$. It would never be economically attractive under this objective to supply more than the required capacity K. Recall that previously, in Figure 7–6, one of the optimal solutions did lead to a total supply $G + S$ in excess of K.

This example is perhaps so oversimplified that the solutions may be obvious without the application of systems analysis. Once again, in actual environmental decision problems, when there are often hundreds of decision variables, hundreds of constraints and multiple objectives, systems-analysis techniques can provide insight into the trade-offs that are often far too complex for any one analyst or even group of decision makers to comprehend.

2.4 Obstacles to the Effective Use of Systems Analysis

In fields like industrial engineering, business, and project management, the application of systems-analysis methods such as mathematical programming is routine and highly effective. For example, most airline companies could not survive without using mathematical programming to allocate their manpower, airplanes, and customers in an optimal fashion. Flight schedules are routinely obtained from mathematical-optimization programs. Most texts in project management contain chapters that describe the standard use of systems analysis to solve resource-allocation problems [see for example, Meredith & Mantel (1989)], where the resources are manpower, money, time, and equipment.

In environmental resource allocation, mathematical-programming approaches are in their relative infancy. Some investigators argue that systems analysis has had little practical value in solving complex water-resource–allocation problems, describing a host of obstacles to the effective use of mathematical programming in allocating water resources (Rogers & Fiering, 1986). Others have argued that the most important recent advance made in the field of water-resource allocation is the development and adoption of systems-analysis techniques to plan, design, and manage complex water-resource systems (Yeh, 1985). As with most engineering approaches, there are gaps between the theory and the application of systems analysis.

Perhaps the most significant obstacle to the successful and effective use of systems analysis is in reaching consensus on the relevant objectives and constraints in a particular decision problem. Usually, there are many participants and factors in an environmental decision problem (e.g., citizens, engineers, politicians, regulatory authorities, the environment, etc.), and reaching consensus on any issue—particularly the objectives—is not simple. (See Chapter 9 for a strong argument against the prospect of achieving a consensus.) Participants tend to have different objectives, which means multiple, incommensurate, and often conflicting objectives must be considered.

In most realistic environmental problems, constraint equations and objective functions are either mathematically intractable or difficult to quantify. In many instances, data are sparse or unavailable for the necessary mathematical formulation. Even in the best of situations, when the mathematics is tractable and the data are available, managers, politicians, and possibly even engineers are reluctant to attach much credibility to a mathematical interpretation of a problem that is fraught with nontechnical (e.g., political, legal, and social) complexities. Decision makers, resource specialists, and citizen groups often argue that their knowledge and experience are not properly incorporated into the systems models. The recent surge in research related to knowledge-based engineering (expert systems) has emerged as a potential approach for integrating general human expertise and some degree of intelligent judgment into what is often referred to as "decision support systems" (Simonovic & Savic, 1989).

3 SUMMARY

The approach introduced here, *systems analysis,* provides a useful framework for structuring the trade-offs inherent in the allocation of scarce and competing resources. Despite the obstacles discussed in Section 2.4, systems analysis is a powerful prescriptive tool of rational decision making. When consensus can be reached on a precise description of the objectives of a particular resource-allocation problem, combined with a precise description of the legal, ethical, economic, social, political, and environmental constraints, then systems analysis is likely to be an important aid in implementing the often difficult decisions required in environmental resource allocation.

Mathematical programming may appear mechanical, rational, and objective. Its sound application, however, requires substantial expertise in all facets of the decision problem including its environmental, political, legal, social, and ethical dimensions, in addition to a healthy dose of common sense and good judgment. In short, the analyst building the systems model should be a polymath! If systems analysis is to be an effective ingredient in the environmental decision-making process, then its associated model structure will have to include all relevant aspects of the problem. An effort should be made to quantify all measures or objectives that appear unquantifiable or "fuzzy."

A few important themes emerge from recent literature on the application of systems analysis to environmental resource-allocation problems. The obstacles to the effective use of systems analysis in actual resource allocation are substantial. Poor and limited data, nonquantifiable or fuzzy objectives and constraints, intractable mathematics, and the gaps inherent between the theory and practice of systems analysis are just a few of the obstacles mentioned. Even given these stumbling blocks, systems analysis still holds promise for clarifying the trade-offs among competing and conflicting environmental resources. At the very least, systems analysis can be used to identify a range of acceptable decision options. By examining a variety of "near optimal" solutions to a decision problem, systems-analysis methods hold great promise for improving our insight into environmental resource-allocation decisions.

EXERCISES

1. A regional authority has the responsibility of managing the use of water for all river basins under its jurisdiction. Environmental legislation dictates that the regional authority must issue permits to any industry or town that plans to withdraw water from the river basin. For example, the authority must issue permits for the withdrawal of water from a river basin for domestic purposes such as drinking water, lawn sprinkling, and car washing, and for industrial purposes such as cooling, manufacturing, treatment, and other commercial processes. On the one hand, the regional authority wishes to assure that, after all the necessary permits are issued, ample water to support fish and wildlife populations is left in the rivers. On the other hand, the regional authority does not want to prevent economic growth and prosperity in the region by restricting economic growth because of limited water resources. Use your knowledge of the systems approach to structure and formulate this problem. One of the most difficult tasks here is to define the decision variables. Carefully define in words each of the decision variables, objectives, and constraints. Once you have structured the problem, describe the information that must be collected to solve the problem faced by the agency. Discuss which characteristics of the problem are the most difficult to quantify.

2. A city is attempting to find the least-cost solution to allocating its water resources. Presently, the city has two reservoirs, numbered 1 and 2, with maximum yields of 10 and 5 million gallons per day (mgd), respectively. The city needs *at least* 10 mgd. Water from Reservoir 1 costs $1000 per mgd and water from Reservoir 2 costs $2000 per mgd. The quality of water in Reservoir 2 is higher than that in Reservoir 1; thus, to assure adequate quality of the delivered water, the water provided from Reservoir 2 must amount to at least half the quantity of water delivered from Reservoir 1. Formulate this problem as a linear program, and use the graphical approach (as applied in the discussion of Figures 7–4 through 7–6) to obtain the optimal allocation of water from these two reservoirs. If the city seeks to minimize its costs, how much water should it draw from Reservoir 1 and Reservoir 2?

3. Select an environmental decision problem that interests you. Attempt to formulate the decision problem, using the systems framework, in a manner similar to that used with the water-resource example in this chapter. First, carefully define in words the decision variables, the objective function(s), and the constraints. In resource-allocation problems, the decision variables are *usually* the resources that need to be managed, but that may not always be the case. Next, describe your model formulation in mathematical terms, as was done for the example in the text. If your problem contains only two decision variables, use the graphical approach described in the text to obtain the optimal solution. If you do not have sufficient information available to develop the mathematical formulation, describe what information you need and how you might obtain it.

4. Based on your own interests, select a case study from the list of additional readings in the next section. Evaluate the use of systems-analysis techniques for the case study you have chosen. Comment on the strengths and weaknesses of systems analysis for the case study in question.

ADDITIONAL READINGS

For further general information about systems analysis see Miser and Quade (1985) and Hillier and Lieberman (1990a, 1990b). For interesting case studies on resource allocation using systems analysis, see Moore (1973), De Neufville and Marks (1974), and Von Lanzenauer (1986). For allocation of land resources, see Williams and Massa (1983), Diamond and Wright (1989), and Alonso (1964); for allocation of energy resources, see Bruckner, Fabrycky, and Shamblin (1969), Cootner and Lof (1974), and Haith (1982). For more on the allocation of water resources, read Loucks, Stedinger, and Haith (1981), Biswas (1976), and Hall and Dracup (1970). Finally, see Davis (1973) and Gustafson and Kortanek (1976) for more information concerning allocation of air resources.

REFERENCES

Alonso, W. 1964. *Location and Land Use: Toward a General Theory of Land Rent.* Cambridge, MA: Harvard University Press.

Biswas, A. K. 1976. *Systems Approach to Water Management.* New York: McGraw-Hill.

Bruckner, A., W. J. Fabrycky, & J. E. Shamblin. 1969. Economic optimization of energy conversion with storage. *IEEE Spectrum* 5(4):101–107.

Buras, N. 1963. Conjunctive operation of dams and aquifers. *Journal of the Hydraulics Division, ASCE* 89(HY6):111–131.

Burges, S. J. 1979. Water resource systems planning in the USA: 1776–1976. *Journal of the Water Resources Planning and Management Division, ASCE,* 105(WR1): 91–111.

Coe, J. J. 1990. Conjunctive use—advantages, constraints, and examples. *Journal of Irrigation and Drainage Engineering ASCE,* 116(3):427–443.

Cootner, P. H. & G. O. G. Lof. 1974. Supply curve for thermal efficiency. In *Systems Planning and Design* (Chapter 7), eds. R. De Neufville & D. H. Marks. Englewood Cliffs, NJ: Prentice-Hall.

Davis, M. L. 1973. *Air Resource Management Primer.* New York: American Society of Civil Engineers.

De Neufville, R. & D. Marks, eds. 1974. *Systems Planning and Design—Case Studies in Modeling, Optimization and Evaluation*. Englewood Cliffs, NJ: Prentice-Hall.

De Neufville, R. & J. H. Stafford. 1974. *System Analysis for Engineering and Managers*. New York: McGraw-Hill.

De Neufville, R. 1990. *Applied Systems Analysis*. New York: McGraw-Hill.

Diamond, J.T. & J. R. Wright. 1989. Efficient land allocation. *Journal of Urban Planning and Development* 115(2):81–96.

Gustafson, S.A., & K. O. Kortanek. 1976. On the calculation of optimal long-term air pollution abatement strategies for multiple source areas. In *Mathematical Models for Environmental Problems*, ed. C. A. Brebbia, pp. 161–171. New York: John Wiley & Sons.

Haith, D. A. 1982. *Environmental Systems Optimization*. New York: John Wiley & Sons.

Hall, W. A. & J. A. Dracup. 1970. *Water Resources Systems Engineering*. New York: McGraw-Hill.

Hillier, F. S. & G. J. Lieberman. 1990a. *Introduction to Mathematical Programming*. New York: McGraw-Hill.

Hillier, F. S. & G. J. Lieberman. 1990b. *Introduction to Stochastic Models in Operations Research* (4th ed.). New York: McGraw-Hill.

Howe, C. W. & F. P. Linaweaver. Jr. 1967. The impact of price on residential water demand and its relation to system design and price structure. *Water Resources Research* 3(1):13–32.

James, L. D. & R. R. Lee. 1971. *Economics of Water Resources Planning*. New York: McGraw-Hill.

Loucks, D. P., J. R. Stedinger, & D. A. Haith. 1981. *Water Resource Systems Planning and Analysis*. Englewood Cliffs, NJ: Prentice-Hall.

Maknoon, R. & S. J. Burges. 1978. Conjunctive use of ground and surface water. *Journal of the American Water Works Association* 70:419–424.

Meredith, J. R. & S. J. Mantel, Jr. 1989. Resource allocation. In *Project Management* (2nd ed.), pp. 327–366. New York: John Wiley & Sons.

Miser, H. J. & E. S. Quade. (Eds.). 1985. *Handbook of Systems Analysis*. New York: Elsevier Science Publishers.

Moore, G. T. 1973. *Emerging Methods in Environmental Design and Planning*. Cambridge, MA: MIT Press.

Ossenbruggen, P. J. 1984. *Systems Analysis for Civil Engineers*. New York: John Wiley & Sons.

Ounjian, D. 1979. Linear Programming. In *Making Decisions: A Multidisciplinary Introduction*, ed. P. Hill, pp. 177–184. Lanham, MD: University Press of America.

Pantell, R. H. 1976. *Techniques of Environmental Systems Analysis*. New York: John Wiley & Sons.

Rogers, P. R. & M. B. Fiering. 1986. Use of systems analysis in water management. *Water Resources Research* 22(9):146S–158S.

Schrage, L. 1989. *Linear, Integer and Quadratic Programming with LINDO—Users Manual* (4th ed.). Palo Alto, CA: The Scientific Press.

Sheer, D. P., M. L. Baeck, & J. Wright. 1989. The computer as negotiator. *Journal of the American Water Works Association* 81 (February):68–73.

Simonovic, S. P. & D. A. Savic. 1989. Intelligent decision support and reservoir management and operations. *Journal of Computing in Civil Engineering, ASCE* 3(4): 367–385.

Von Lanzenauer, C. H. 1986. *Cases in Operations Research*. San Francisco, CA: Holden-Day.

Williams, E. & A. Massa. 1983. *Siting of Major Facilities*. New York: McGraw Hill.

Yeh, W. W-G. 1985. Reservoir management and operations models: A state-of-the-art review. *Water Resources Research* 21(12):1797–1818.

8

Ethical Aspects of Environmental Decision Making

Hugo Adam Bedau

1 INTRODUCTION

In environmental matters, it is easy to see how reasonable and informed persons might render ethical *judgments* about various events and the decision making that brought them about. For example, they might conclude that many decisions concerning hazardous-waste disposal have been negligent or reckless and in other ways threatening to innocent, uninformed, unconsenting human beings in the immediate vicinity of the disposal areas. Such judgments are obviously ethical judgments. We not only make such judgments, we can often agree in objecting on ethical grounds to a whole range of environmental practices and the decisions on which they rest. The accidental grounding of *Exxon Valdez* in Prince William Sound early in 1989, for example, is generally deplored because of (among other things) the extensive environmental damage inflicted on the waterway by the oil that flooded out of the ruptured tanker's hold. Exactly who is at fault—Exxon Corporation executives, the ship's crew, or various federal, state, and local officials—remains in dispute. But there is little disagreement that whoever is responsible and whatever their legal liability for the damage may be, grave harm was done to the environment and it ought not happen again.

It is equally easy to see that in rendering judgments of this type, we rely upon certain familiar ethical "principles." Quite apart from the contexts in which environmental decisions must be made, we have considerable experience using ethical norms—rules, principles, standards, and ideals—that prohibit (and, if violated, establish the immorality of) harm to the unconsenting, risk to the unwary, and negligence that poses grave dangers (Gert, 1988). Treating others unfairly, behaving in a manner contrary to the public interest, engaging in practices that impose unknown costs on those who have agreed to pay the bill,

176

preferring selfish advantage to the general welfare—all these are violations of ethical principles on which we constantly rely. Whatever the empirical facts may be in the minor premises of our ethical reasoning that yield ethical judgments of the sort mentioned in the previous paragraph, the major premises are very likely to be ethical principles of general repute and application rather than anything peculiar to environmental issues.

As soon as we leave retrospective applications of ethical principles and the judgments they enable us to make, however, and turn our attention to the forward-looking task of trying to improve our environmental decision making by introducing appropriate ethical principles, we encounter difficulties. The task can be conveniently divided into three general parts. One concerns the appropriate ethical principles on which to rely if we are to improve our environmental decision making case by case. The second concerns the method or methods of decision making by which the decision maker ought to use these principles in order to arrive at a judgment or decision. The third concerns how to get judgments and decisions that have been made with these principles implemented in actual practice, individual and social.

Of the three issues, the third is the easiest to address. Assume for the sake of argument that we have made a morally responsible environmental decision, thanks to proper employment of ethical principles. In most such cases, we can get it carried out—despite some backsliding, delay, and other forms of evasion—by enlisting the resources of the law. The threat of fines and other criminal or civil penalties, injunctions, and show-cause orders are standard ways of securing the compliance of those who will not wholeheartedly do what they ought to do. There is no more reason for leaving compliance with ethically defensible policies in the environmental arena entirely to uncoerced assent and purely moral motivation—such as a sense of justice or a concern for the welfare of others—than there is in other areas where individual or corporate conduct poses unwarranted hazard or harm to others. (See Chapter 10 for a general discussion of federal and state environmental regulations.)

Statutes and regulations ought to be enacted and enforced to give legal effect to whatever judgments result from applying the appropriate ethical principles to cases of environmental decision making. Examples of such principles are not hard to find: Siting decisions of hazardous-waste disposal dumps must not unfairly burden residents and businesses in the immediate vicinity; the cost of such disposal must be fairly distributed through the communities that create the waste or benefit from the commodities and services in whose production the waste is created. Such principles are no more absolute than other ethical principles. They reflect values of our society that ought to be enforced by law. We have a long history (starting with the definition of certain harms as criminal felonies) of tailoring our substantive law by reference to ethical rules and principles; the overlap between law and morals is, by any measure, considerable.

Thus, the challenge to implement our environmental decision making so that it conforms to the requirements of ethical evaluation does not pose any essential novelty, though daunting political problems must be solved before this goal can be achieved (they are addressed in Chapter 9). Whether new forms of law enforcment are needed, including transnational legal and political institutions peculiar to enforcement problems posed by environmental policies, is taken up in Chapter 12.

So much by way of answer to the third problem identified above. The second problem—what method or methods of ethical decision making ought to be used in environmental matters—can be disposed of with comparable brevity. Whatever methods can be used to make ethically responsible decisions in nonenvironmental contexts (Bedau, 1979, 1984, 1986) can be used in environmental contexts as well. Unfortunately, the practical reasoning that relies on weighing ethical *principles,* commonplace in daily life, has yet to receive much attention from the formal decision sciences. Instead, the overwhelming preoccupation has been with *values* that permit quantification (as used in the decision matrix or cost-benefit calculations familiar to every student of formal decision making). In this respect, ethically sensitive environmental decision making generally may be no worse off, but also no better off, than ethical decision making. In the discussion that follows, several examples of reasoning with principles in environmental contexts will be presented. Yet, together, these examples illustrate the kinds of problems that need to be faced and provide a variety of models on which to draw; none will meet the standards of rigor to be found in formal decision theory.

This leaves us with the first problem of the three mentioned above. What are the appropriate ethical principles for environmental decision making, and why, and what decisions would we reach if we relied on such principles?

2 TRADITIONAL WESTERN ETHICS

It is natural to begin to think about the ethical aspects of environmental decision making from the standpoint of the norms and the values they reflect that can be found in traditional Western ethics. These fundamental norms focus on *interpersonal* relations. We tend to assume, as a matter of definition, that there are no ethical decisions to be made by persons acting in total isolation from one another because all decision making in such nonsocial contexts is governed by nothing more than the principles of enlightened (long-run) self-interest, or prudence. Whatever may have been true in ancient times, the modern era in Western culture has been characterized by the belief that the physical environment is a morally indifferent repository of materials that *humans* may exploit and develop to satisfy their needs as they wish.

As a result, the basic concerns of traditional ethics have been twofold: first, to identify the appropriate *principles* to govern decision making in contexts of interpersonal interaction, where what one person decides to do has an impact on what others do; second, to decide under what conditions some portion of the material world becomes the *property* of a person (or group of persons), so that it may be used for whatever purposes its current owner sees fit. The setting for traditional ethics has always been a *plurality of persons* in relative conflict over a *scarcity of resources;* human desires (even human needs) commonly surpass the capacity of nature to satisfy them. The primary ethical problem, accordingly, has been one of *fair allocation*. The resulting tension between the claims of private-property ownership on the one hand, and fair distribution of natural and productive resources on the other, gives rise to much of the diversity in ethical thought from, say, Hobbes to Marx (Waldron, 1988).

Shaping and underlying these matters have been a number of traditional and usually unargued assumptions, three of which are of considerable importance. Until very recently, environmental decision making has proceeded under their shadow. First, nature itself—rivers, mountains, glaciers, waterfalls, forests, beaches—has no claims or rights. The point is not the trivial one that nature cannot *make* any claims, or claim any rights; rather it is that nature *has* no interests and that nothing counts as "good" for nature. How could it, since rivers, forests, and so on, have no "souls"? They are not animate creatures. Persons have interests, both in the sense that some things are in their interest and that they are interested in some things. Not so with nature. Nothing counts as "in the interest of nature," any more than anything counts as something in which "nature is interested." Without interests, there is no role for a right: A right is like a sword or a shield, advancing or protecting, respectively, the identifiable interests of something or someone that has interests. This is not all; it is also assumed that nature has no value in itself, and that such value as it has is purely instrumental, a means to satisfy human desires and purposes. Values are generated by interests, so of course inert nature cannot have any intrinsic value. Let us call this "the inert nature assumption."

Today, many of us will object that where the lower animate creatures are concerned, it is not so obvious they have no interests. Indeed, it appears they do have (in a manner of speaking) and that many things are in their interests. But traditional Western ethics has assumed that, unlike the interests of persons, the interests (if any) of infrahuman species are not and should not be protected by rights. For one thing, other species are not coequal with ours in rational capacity, potentially or actually. True, traditional ethics (at least in recent generations) has prohibited cruelty to animals; but it has rarely, if ever, required us to regard all of animate nature as a fit object of benevolent concern. The intentional killing of animals for the pleasures of hunting and for food and clothing, and in recent decades the use of animals in medical experimentation to benefit us (not them), has been widely practiced and—for the most part—accepted. In a phrase that

Peter Singer has made famous, traditional Western ethics suffers from a bad case of "speciesism" (Singer, 1975). Let us call this "the anthropocentric assumption."

Sharing the backseat of traditional ethical concern with the preservation of nature for its own sake and the welfare of infrahuman species is the welfare of future generations of our species (Partridge, 1981). Apart from special provisions made by individual persons for their heirs, future generations have usually been left to fend for themselves. In general, they have been viewed as having no claims—or at least no strong ones—on the conduct of the current generation. Just as we, prior to our birth, could not bargain with our predecessors over their legacy to us, so our successors, not yet being born, cannot bargain with us over our legacy to them. Each generation is thus at the mercy of its predecessors and lacks any ground for complaint over the size or nature of the legacy bequeathed to it. For one thing, the debt of the unborn to their parents is unquantifiably large. Without procreation and nurture by the parental generation, there is no next—and hence no future—generation at all. "First come, first served" and "Devil take the hindmost" are familiar maxims that characterize the conduct accepted by society and practiced by most of us, at least so far as our use of the physical environment is concerned. As a rationale for such generational self-centeredness, one cannot do better than the short answer implied by the rhetorical question: "What have future persons ever done for me?" Let us call this "the current generation assumption."

The consequences of these three assumptions need not be traced out here in detail; they can be seen at work in the extensive destruction of the natural world around us and in the long-term degradation and pollution of the physical environment. Continued acceptance of these assumptions constitutes a recipe for disaster. The predictable future within a few centuries [within merely four decades, according to Worldwatch Institute; see Shabecoff (1990)], if practices resting on these assumptions are not drastically revised, seems to be the death not only of our species but of virtually all life-forms as we know them on this planet. Any principles (including the assumptions on which they rest) whose outcome, if generally practiced, results in universal death are utterly self-defeating. Principles with such consequences can hardly be regarded as *ethical*.

Against this sobering background, the resources of traditional Western ethical reflection—such as self-interest, utilitarianism, Kantianism—are not very helpful:

1. An ethics of self-interest [popularized by the novelist Ayn Rand and politically triumphant in the 1980s; see Rand (1964)] cannot be relied on to avert long-run ecological disaster. Depending on what empirical assumptions are made, such an ethic could produce one or another form of planetary catas-

trophe no matter how mutual (universal) and "rational" the self-interest is.

2. Utilitarianism in any of its many forms is unlikely to suffice, for two reasons. First, it permits (even requires) trade-offs that have too high a price, sacrificing the good for the few wherever that is necessary and sufficient to advance the welfare of the many. Second, maximizing utility or welfare for all, if it includes the welfare of future generations and of all sentient creatures, requires calculations of consequences among possible alternatives that simply cannot be carried out. Negative utilitarianism, whose counsels to avoid the worst often seem to be within our reach, underdetermines the choices that remain.

3. Kantianism is insufficient as well, even if its central counsels ("What if everyone were to do that whenever similar circumstances occur?" and "Would you knowingly and freely consent to others acting as you propose to do?") suffice to rule out much immorality and folly in environmental decision making (O'Neil, 1985). Yet the Kantian constraints on ethical decision making are confined to what is in the rational interest of other rational autonomous creatures like us. Preservation of the environment, insofar as that is a necessary condition of satisfying human needs, may well emerge from such an ethic. But the needs and interests of other living creatures not necessary to ours cannot be taken into account.

For more than a generation, Western thinkers have been aware of the limitations of traditional ethics and have tried to develop an ethical outlook with new norms of behavior to supplement or supersede the norms handed down to us by our tradition. The pioneering example is provided by Aldo Leopold's "land ethic" (Leopold, 1949). Perhaps the most influential current version is the doctrine of nature's rights advocated by Christopher Stone (Stone, 1987). But it is still too soon to speak with any precision about exactly what ethic of this sort, if any, will prove persuasive.

Large-scale ethical theorizing, whether of the traditional or nontraditional variety, of course, deserves closer attention than can be provided in the space available here. A more feasible strategy, for expository purposes as well as actual practice, may be found in the piecemeal examination of particular cases, suspending if not rejecting the idea that some grand theory or single overriding norm alone must be used for ethical purposes in all cases. An advantage of such an approach is that it easily accommodates the plurality of ethical and other norms which we actually use. After all, day-to-day ethical decision making has usually taken this form. In this way, perhaps the casuistry of ethical decision making traditionally used in daily life (Jonsen & Toulmin, 1988; Bedau, 1991) can be extended to environmental decision making as well. At worst, it is a second-best approach until such time as something better becomes available.

3 TOXIC WASTE DISPOSAL AND
SELF-INTEREST

It may prove useful to start with a very simple case in which the limits of an ethics of self-interest, as it affects environmental decision making, can be tested. Consider a decision to dispose of toxic waste, such as paints, used motor oil, solvents, and other chemicals found around the house. Here is how self-interest reasons:

"Why should I bother to dispose of this stuff except in the manner most convenient to me? Perhaps I ought to bury it at the back edge of my property because the cans and rags are an unsightly mess (not that the neighbors will complain; it's just that I don't like seeing the stuff around). If I drew my water from a shallow well on my property, it would be contrary to my self-interest to bury the waste near the well because of the risk of contamination. But I don't draw my water from such a well; it is piped in from the town supply. So I might as well bury the stuff wherever it's handy to do so. The likelihood that this waste eventually might contaminate the immediate area is of no concern to me. I don't intend to use that area of my property for anything anyway, and if the contamination takes several decades to develop I'll be long gone before it shows. Obviously, spending my money and time to dispose of this waste 'properly' (whatever that means) is not in my self-interest, short-run or long-run. Another possibility is to gather the stuff up, shove it in the trunk of the car, and dump it along the roadside (when no one's looking), and get it off my land once and for all. But that's more of a nuisance to me than putting it into the wheelbarrow and burying it in the back of the yard."

From the standpoint of self-interest, is it possible to criticize such reasoning and the decision that it yields? I don't think so. Such decision making, if universalized (or even if merely widely practiced), might very well produce an environmental nightmare in the long run, and is a special case of the more general problem famously described as the "Tragedy of the Commons" (Hardin, 1968; see Chapter 2)—but that is a separate matter. Of course, *your* action in your self-interest might well produce a situation in the short (or long) run contrary to *my* self-interest. This would give me a self-interested reason for objecting to your self-interested action. But unless I am in a position to impose a cost on your selfish behavior (e.g., to retaliate) or to reward you for your unselfish behavior, the fact that your action creates a risk of harm to me doesn't give you a self-interested reason to alter your ways. The fact that it is not in each person's interest for everyone else to act in a self-interested way does not entail that it is not in my interest to act in a self-interested way. This would change, of course, if I knew I would risk suffering some penalty for acting in my self-interest when that interest flouts yours; or if there were some other incentive for me to consider your interest, for instance, a guarantee that my self-restraint will be generally reciprocated. Only under such conditions have I a self-interested reason for doing what otherwise would not be in my self-interest.

How much preservation of the environment for future users can we hope to secure by appeals to nothing more than the self-interest of current users? Not much. I can afford to be completely indifferent to any adverse effects of my actions that do not accrue and impinge on me during my lifetime because my self-interest cannot reach any further.

If we think of current users as members of families or corporations that outlive any of their current members, then we may get a different answer. (This is but a special case of persons who take an interest in the welfare of others, including those who pursue goals in the belief that achieving them will benefit others whether or not it also benefits themselves. I will return to this point below.) Thus, it is not in the interest of Exxon as a corporation to be indifferent to the consequences of the oil spill in Prince William Sound, even if these consequences are not severely contrary to the interest of current Exxon employees, officers, or stockholders: Exxon as a corporation is legally and logically independent of the persons currently involved in managing and owning it. But not all actual or potential polluters and exploiters include within their interests the welfare of some larger unit such as the family of which each is a member, the corporation of which each is (partial) owner or manager, or even the community in which one lives. Nor would it be reasonable to try to argue on grounds of self-interest that everyone ought to take such broader (family, corporate, community) interests into account. (One thinks of the classic argument from self-interest of the childless against higher property taxes to fund public schools for other people's children.) Not even the long-range self-interests of families and corporations will suffice to supply a motive for everyone to use restraint and caution in their interactions with the physical environment.

We must be careful to notice that the self that has a given interest need not be the self benefited by acting on that interest: Not all interests of a self are interests in that self, that is, selfish interests. Thus, a person might be interested in the welfare of her grandchildren and therefore go to some trouble to avoid polluting the physical environment she expects them to inherit. As a result, she acts contrary to her selfish advantage (self-interest) by imposing costs on her conduct (in this case, avoiding pollution) for which she can expect no direct compensating benefit. The trivial point that when one tries to benefit another, one is acting out of an interest that one has (viz., in that other person's welfare), and thus acting out of interests that are genuinely one's interests, must not be allowed to obscure the important point that the person whose welfare is being advanced is another's, not one's own, and that one's success in this endeavor may indeed reduce one's own welfare.

It is, in fact, typical of people to have interests in the interests and welfare of other selves as well as of themselves. Thus, it is possible to motivate people to act without regard to (and even contrary to) what they take to be their own self-interest. This raises the question of how much we might hope to have people today acquire interests in the welfare of others. One route to the acquisition of such interests is the hope of reciprocity, that is, the hope that the beneficiaries of my initiatives will in turn take an interest in my welfare. But no such route is open to us where it is the interests of *future* people (or current plants and animals) that concern us: Future persons cannot do anything for current persons, unless their lives overlap in time and space.

The impossibility of straightforward reciprocity need not blind us to the appropriateness of a somewhat indirect version of the same thing. Each member of the present generation is the beneficiary of the savings and future-oriented patterns of conservation practiced by our predecessors, most of whom acted without any hope of reward from their temporally remote progeny. (Part of the legacy from our predecessors typically burdens rather than benefits us today. We will have to ignore this complication here.) So the current generation—indeed, any given generation—might be persuaded to see itself in a comparable position with respect to the next generation. One might argue that it is wrong for the current generation to squander all or even most of what it inherited from its predecessors and then leave no comparable beneficial legacy to its successors. The idea is vividly expressed in the Kenyan proverb, "Treat the earth well. It was not given to you by your parents. It was loaned to you by your children." Better yet is to think of it as on loan from one's great-grandchildren, whom one is most unlikely ever to meet. A vision of intergenerational ethics from the standpoint of self-interest alone can at best endorse only a fragmentary version of such a picture.

4 THE PROBLEM OF PROLONGING LANDFILL USE

The public landfill in the typical suburban Boston town, if used more or less at the current rate (with some allowance for slight population growth), will be completely filled by the year 2000. Another decade of use could be added, however (i.e., the current lifetime of the landfill doubled), if metal, glass, paper, and plastic trash were no longer dumped and buried, but instead were scrapped or recycled. Is there a requirement on ethical grounds for local government to institute such measures that would require recycling, for example, in order to extend the life of the landfill? Is there an objection on ethical grounds if such measures are not introduced?

It may be helpful in answering these questions to see them against the background of two earlier decisions affecting landfill use. The town landfill would have lasted far longer than is currently predicted if certain practices had not already been curtailed. The first is open burning. Until about 1970, all inflammable trash was burned at the landfill site. Open burning at the dump ensured a relatively long period of use for the dump. However, open burning was stopped (by statute) in order to reduce local air pollution. Ethically speaking, it was banned on the principle that no town had the right to dispose of its trash by methods that adversely affected the air quality of the towns downwind—even if those towns consented to a continuation of burning (as they might well have, so that they, too, could continue to use this method of waste disposal). Public-health officers knew that it was not in the interests of current breathers to breathe the ash-laden air produced by open burning. Ethically speaking, this is equivalent to invoking a principle of fairness: It is unfair for some to dispose of their waste in a manner that prejudices the interests of others who have not freely consented to such a method of disposal.

The second important decision affecting use of the landfill involved protecting the groundwater. During the 1970s, another important state law was enacted, requiring landfill sites to be sealed at their bottoms and sides with a layer of thick and relatively impermeable clay in order to prevent rainwater seepage through the soil-covered trash into the groundwater. This, too, reduced the available space for trash, thus further shortening the life span of the dump. Ethically speaking, one can view preventing such seepage as arising out of a concern for fairness akin to that which ended open burning: It is unfair to future residents for current residents to dispose of their trash by methods that jeopardize the town's water supply (and perhaps that of neighboring towns as well).

Both these environmental decisions also reflect the application of a principle of paternalism: the liberty of current residents to dispose of waste as they desire must be regulated for their own future good. Whether they realize it or not, clean air and potable water are more important for their good than is further use of less expensive forms of waste disposal.

These policies of seepage prevention and ash reduction can also be seen as results of utilitarian reasoning because they can be defended as necessary to protect the town residents' collective long-run welfare: it is not in the best interest of all the town's residents (including all present and all future residents) for current residents to dispose of their solid waste in a manner that pollutes the water supply or makes the air hazardous to breathe. From the point of view of collective self-interest, avoiding such pollution also probably has a higher priority than prolonging the life of the dump (though this is a factual question, not an ethical one). Of course, individual town residents might have found it in their self-interest to protest both the cessation of open burning and the requirement of seepage control—especially if they were affluent enough to afford the costs of air conditioning and of bottled water (or private well water), and they preferred to pay other costs.

Thus, the role of several different principles—fairness, paternalism, collective self-interest (but not of individual self-interest)—is quite evident in the town's use of its landfill over the past two decades. What role do these principles have to play in resolving the current problem, described above, of whether the town should require recycling to extend the life of the landfill? At least three lines of argument must be considered.

Some might claim that we ought not waste reusable materials ("Waste not, want not," Mother Wit used to say), and that this principle is clearly violated by past and current landfill practices. Compliance would have the beneficial side effect of adding a decade to the useful life of the landfill.

Others might agree with the desirability of not burying reusable waste, but argue that the best reason for doing so is the long-run collective self-interest of current residents. After all, "Waste not, want not," is only a prudential counsel, not a fundamental ethical principle.

Still others might agree that recyclable materials should not be buried in the landfill, but base this on self-interested economic grounds. It is arguably in the self-interest of all but a few current residents to extend landfill use as long as possible. Every alternative method of disposing of the town's nonreusable and nonrecylable trash, they argue, is going to be far more expensive per unit volume of trash than the current method.

Perhaps a fourth group might argue that it is essentially trivial whether recycling is introduced. The volume of reusable material is not impressively large and the added life span of the landfill is not great, they point out, whereas the nuisance of sorting and recycling waste is so great that most residents would be better off by delaying such measures as long as possible. Perhaps this position is too cynical to deserve serious consideration.

What this discussion shows, I suggest, is that consideration of the general welfare, defined broadly by reference to the good of all (and not only current) town residents, in conjunction with plausible beliefs about the relevant empirical facts, recommends an environmentally sound decision: Recycle reusable materials rather than bury them in the town dump, and gain the benefit of another decade of use of the landfill. The cessation of open burning and protection of the groundwater benefit current and future neighbors in other towns and unborn future town residents to the relative disadvantage of current town residents, thus requiring the invocation of considerations beyond self-interest, individual or collective, as well as beyond collective interest among current residents. Nothing so demanding is involved in the question of recycling to extend landfill use, however. The fundamental ethical considerations governing landfill use were those involved in the decisions two decades ago, to stop open burning and to start protecting the groundwater. Those decisions did involve considerations of fairness to the interests of others, and paternalistic interference with the liberty of everyone to protect everyone's welfare. But those considerations are essentially irrelevant to the current problem of whether to recycle in order to extend the life of the landfill by a decade or so.

5 THE INTERNATIONAL SEWAGE
PROBLEM

In the San Diego area there is a stream originating south of the Mexican border and running northward that is used to carry off waste from Tijuana. In effect, the stream had become an open sewer, with all the attendant noxious consequences and hazards to public health. Population growth in the Tijuana area naturally exacerbated the problem; what a generation ago was merely a nuisance has now become a matter for bitter resentment. Officials on both sides of the border agree that a proper sewer system and sewage treatment plant for Tijuana could restore the stream to its previous condition in fairly short order. They agree that there is no way to reduce, much less eliminate, the waste that produces the pollution, short of evacuating the entire Tijuana region; and they also agree that the situation is rapidly growing worse. Until recently, they disagreed over whether such a system should be built because they disagreed over who should pay for it.

The Mexicans argued that they could not pay for the necessary capital improvements. At least, they could not put such investments very high on their agenda of public expenditures, given other, more pressing problems. Besides, their benefit from the system would not be commensurate with the costs such a system would impose on them. In any case, they were not deeply troubled by the pollution they generate because it was carried away daily from their region by the stream. "Out of sight, out of mind" (and out of nose, too) explained their relative complacency.

The Americans probably could afford to pay for the required system (with some combination of local, state, and federal financing). But they objected to doing so on two grounds: First, since the Mexicans caused the problem, the Mexicans should remedy it. Second, it was the Mexicans, not the Americans, who benefited from the cheap sewage disposal that the north-flowing stream provides.

What does ethical reflection tell us about how to resolve this problem? First, it tells us that appeals to short-run local or national self-interest probably cannot provide an acceptable solution. From the standpoint of Mexican self-interest, nothing should be done about the pollution until such time as retaliation (or threat thereof) from north of the border comes into play and poses perceived costs in excess of the perceived benefits that come from preserving the status quo. Likewise, from the standpoint of American self-interest, the growing menace of the polluted stream will have to be tolerated until the point is reached where paying the costs for a new Mexican sewage system is preferable to enduring further pollution, or where American threats have made it in the self-interest of the Mexican government to assume the costs of building the sewage system rather than risk further American displeasure.

But if the problem is looked at from an ethical point of view, with each side recognizing that the interests and concerns of the other must be accommodated, the general framework of a solution is reasonably evident. The underlying considerations must be a bilateral recognition of a nonethical fact: The unpolluted stream is an important natural asset to the whole region, and its further destruction ought to be averted. Neither local government, in Tijuana or in San Diego, ought to attempt to solve this problem alone. Because an international border is involved, the federal government of each nation ought to take some economic responsibility for solving the problem. Neither Mexicans nor Americans alone ought to pay the costs, since neither the causes of the problem nor the benefits from its solution are confined to one country. Instead, the construction of the sewage system should be a joint venture involving resources from both countries. Because the ability to pay and the benefits from the new construction are not equally distributed between the two parties, the allocation of costs to the parties should take this into account; those north of the border must expect to contribute a considerably larger share of the capital costs than those south of the border. The stream's having become a free sewer for the poorer community through which it flows (San Diegoans already have an adequate sewer system) was just an accident of local geography.

Guiding such ethical reflections is a conception of justice between nations that starts with a recognition that societies sharing a common (permeable) border must cooperate, that national isolation is politically and geographically impossible, and that costs and benefits must be allocated so that neither party has reason to believe the other has taken unfair advantage of it. These reflections are not, of course, peculiar to environmental decision making; they are most plausibly seen by John Rawls (1971) as an application of the general theory of social justice as fairness developed over the past generation. Although environmental decision making plays no explicit role in that theory, it is possible to profit from its counsels in environmental contexts, as the foregoing discussion illustrates.

We have not solved the Tijuana sewage-disposal problem, of course, until we know exactly how the portion of economic costs of the sewer system for each party should be allocated. We need to know, for example, whether the U. S. contribution should involve a mix of outright cash grants plus long-term interest-free loans. Ethical principles by themselves cannot settle such questions. Nor do these principles dictate the method of dispute settlement. Direct negotiation between the parties acting in good faith and in full knowledge of all the relevant facts is obviously one such method. Were that to fail, one could resort to mediation or arbitration, involving third parties. Fortunately, as recent events have shown, an acceptable solution to the problem did not require the intervention of third parties (Mydans, 1990).

6 THE PROBLEM OF DRIFTNET FISHING

Beginning in the 1970s, deep-sea trawlers of several nations bordering the Pacific Ocean began to fish for red squid by using nylon filament driftnets that hang several fathoms below the water's surface and stretch out for many miles. With a thousand trawlers using such efficient nets in 1990, the haul of squid for commercial use has increased several-fold. So has the rate of depletion of the squid stock. So has the destruction of myriad unintended victims: marine mammals, birds, turtles, sharks, and many species of fish not normally sold for human consumption. Forecasts indicate that, in vast regions of the Pacific within a few years, many of the species currently being caught in these nets may be eradicated (Nobbe, 1990). What is an ethically defensible response to this problem?

The problem is obviously another example of "the Tragedy of the Commons"; its solution cannot be left to private agreements unenforced except by moral sanctions. The challenge to the interests of future generations of human beings is clear. The most obvious solution, one that borrows from practices developed in forestry management and widely used with other renewable resources, is to apply the principle of Maximum Sustainable Yield: harvest no more of the resource than is sufficient to permit it to replenish itself naturally. Using this principle as the criterion defining the upper limit of deep-sea fishing, driftnets would be immediately and permanently suspended from use in the areas currently being depleted (and probably prohibited everywhere, lest new problems of marine-life depletion arise). All other forms of fishing in the endangered area would either be temporarily suspended or allowed to continue only at a much lower rate using other, traditional methods. This would severely limit the catch, and it might be several years or more before the edible species were caught in quantities remotely sufficient to feed those (mostly Asians) who currently rely on a regular diet of squid.

There are empirical obstacles to the effective employment of such a criterion: do marine scientists have adequate knowledge to specify the volume of fish to be left in the ocean in order to permit natural replenishment? Can the limit, once specified, be effectively enforced, or is it likely that for some time to come the best that could be done is to punish violators (those who persist in using driftnets, and those who overfish their quota by conventional methods)? From the ethical standpoint, these are not serious worries because any alternative criterion to that of Maximum Sustainable Yield will also have its empirical uncertainties. Besides, until one or more alternative criteria are proposed, it is unclear whether the empirical difficulties in application and enforcement tip the balance in favor of one criterion rather than another.

From the standpoint of conventional Western ethics, the criterion of Maximum Sustainable Yield is defensible and probably preferable to any alternative. True, this criterion in conjunction with plausible empirical considerations (such as increased cost per fish to the consumer, owing to abandoning the highly effective and inexpensive driftnets, plus the increased population desiring to consume fish) is very likely to leave future consumers relatively worse off than recent and current ones. Nevertheless, it would leave them better off than any other alternative criterion probably acceptable to current consumers. To that extent, the criterion of Maximum Sustainable Yield is probably preferable to any alternative on grounds of intergenerational fairness. At least, it probably provides the best first approximation that we can achieve to whatever intergenerational fairness requires. A utilitarian planner probably would find this criterion acceptable as well. Strict application of the criterion would, of course, do nothing to remedy the recent overfishing of the ocean and the historically cheap cost to the consumer for fish already harvested by the driftnets.

But the anthropocentric assumption that underlies adopting a criterion such as Maximum Sustainable Yield is all too obvious. To see an environmental problem that puts this assumption in doubt, we need to consider a different kind of example altogether.

7 THE PROBLEM OF THE SPOTTED OWL

Some years ago, the snail darter—an obscure species of freshwater fish—was threatened by the planned damming of a river in the TVA system. During 1990, the spotted owl, whose habitat is first-growth forest in the Pacific Northwest, was threatened with extinction by inadequately regulated timbering. The extinction of any life-form in the United States is now prohibited by the Endangered Species Act of 1973. Does such a law rest on sound ethical principles, or does it rest on something else altogether?

In each case, this legislation mounts an argument against harmful human intervention (damming, timbering) where that would destroy a species of plant or animal life. But on what principles does such an argument rest? There are various alternative possibilities. One line of argument relies on showing that current and future generations of humans should impose costs on themselves in order to prevent the extinction of some infrahuman species, whether or not the species is of any current commercial value, or aesthetic or scientific interest. Insofar as the argument relies on the idea that the current generation should not prejudice future generations by judging for them—that is, by acting on its own ideas about what is and is not commercially valuable, or aesthetically or scientifically interesting—it is best understood as another instance where the principle of intergenerational fairness is being applied. On this view, the value of the endangered species, in any sense not relevant to human concerns, is of no importance. What is of primary concern is guaranteeing to our successors the right to judge the matter for themselves; it is not within our rights to moot their choice by destroying the species first.

Perhaps the one line of reasoning that can clearly be ruled out in this example is a cost-benefit approach. It really is not plausible to think that if the value of jobs in the timber and lumber industries were weighed against the value of the spotted owl, the latter would win out. Although it may well be possible to measure the *preferences* of some designated decision makers for one rather than the other of these alternatives, this is not enough to yield a measure of the *value* of preserving, endangering, or extinguishing the spotted owl. But without a measure of that value, the costs and benefits of the two alternatives cannot be calculated.

Let us agree that the loss of a species owing to deliberate human intervention (as in the case more than a century ago with the carrier pigeon) impoverishes the planet, in some nontrivial sense of the phrase. But if one believes only that the loss, by way of human destruction, of an entire species merely depletes the richness and variety of nature, then the complaint against such destruction is not an *ethical* objection. Rather, it is mainly *aesthetic*. Not only that; the judgment against destruction is surely made from the familiar anthropocentric viewpoint. It is as if we were to say that when we contemplate nature, and realize that with the spotted owl (carrier pigeon, snail darter) extinct, something hitherto part of the rich fabric of nature on this the planet is gone forever, we sense that the natural world—of which, of course, our species is a part—is impoverished. It is as if a small but noticeable element in the picture is suddenly missing and irreplaceable, thereby forever marring the remaining whole. Yet it is *our* discomfort in contemplating such a flawed picture that provides the incentive for avoiding the flaw. Indeed, the language of the Endangered Species Act itself, stressing as it does the "esthetic, ecological, educational, historical, recreational, and scientific value to the Nation and its people" of all species, is formulated in just this way.

However interesting and plausible such a line of reasoning may be, it does not seem to result in an ethical judgment. Nevertheless, our environmental decision making may well want to take such nonethical considerations into account; no one reasonably believes that the only considerations relevant to environmental or any other decision making are ethical. But that is a separate matter we need not consider here.

Nor is it a judgment from the point of view of the endangered species itself. It is increasingly common for environmentalists today to argue that all living and inert matter is interdependent, so that destruction of any species may jeopardize in the long run the prospects of other species, including our own. If this is the argument against destroying the spotted owl, then the objection is again clearly made from the anthropocentric standpoint. Furthermore, it seems to be a judgment reflecting only collective human self-interest. Thus, arguing against species destruction on the ground that it depletes genetic diversity, which might be important to our survival in the future, is but another form of the "speciesism" noticed in an earlier context. Since the beneficiaries of such conservation would not be any current human generation, but only future generations, this argument does not rest on a principle of self-interest confined to the present generations. Instead, it represents, once again, a consideration of intergenerational fairness: it is unfair for any current generation to deplete the genetic diversity on the planet, given the likely adverse effects such depletion may have on future generations.

What it does not represent is an attempt to reject the destruction of any infrahuman species on the ground that the species has a *right* to survive—perhaps as much of a right to survival as our species does. This way of viewing the matter does abandon the anthropocentric assumption. It is tantamount to viewing the issue of species survival without catering to *any* particularly human desire, interest, or need. Instead, it places humans on the same moral level as owls. Thus, we are required, as it were, to think through the issue of the survival of life-forms on this planet from the point of view of any representative life-form.

But can we effectively think in this way? What is the criterion for successfully thinking through decision making from an infrahuman point of view? Is it some particular *outcome,* such as preservation of the current status quo? Or survival of currently living creatures until after propagation of their species? Or is some *procedural stance* necessary, such as the capacity to take an interest in whatever is in the creature's interest—a criterion under which the interests (if any) of the spotted owl and snail darter would not be further considered, and which would protect the interests of the members of very few species?

What this discussion shows is that familiar principles (moral, aesthetic) can be formulated and introduced into environmental decision making to show why it would be wrong to extinguish other living species on the planet. But whether any principle can be formulated and applied outside an anthropocentric standpoint—from the point of view of all species whether or not currently at risk, or from the point of view of the planetary biosphere (if there is such a point of view), and if so, whether such a principle is best viewed as an *ethical* principle—remains uncertain. Partly, the problem is one of drawing the contours of the concept of the ethical. Partly, it is a problem of trying to apply criteria that seem to require us to do the impossible—thinking like a fish or a bird.

Philosophers during the past decade or so have at last begun to worry about the appropriate norms and argumentation needed to take the welfare, interests, and rights of future generations into account lest they be victimized (wittingly or not) by their progenitors. They have also begun to explore, but so far without conspicuous agreement or success, the nature of norms that reject the anthropocentric assumption and the inert nature assumption. The discussion has barely gotten underway; there is no cause for alarm in the fact that no resolution is currently in sight.

EXERCISES

1. Using the index to the *New York Times,* look up the story of the discovery of environmental harm from toxic wastes buried in the Love Canal area of upstate New York during the 1970s and 1980s. Describe the nature and extent of the harms involved. Identify the ethical norms, if any, that were violated by those who improperly disposed of the waste. Were these harms, in your judgment, eventually adequately remedied?

2. Examine the writings of Aldo Leopold and Baird Callicott (see the References Section), and write out in 500 words your account of their "land ethic." What difficulties do you find in using such an ethic in envionmental decision making?

3. In the chapter you have just read, three different environmental problems were discussed—the Tijuana/San Diego stream, the Pacific Ocean driftnets, and the spotted owl in the Northwest. Do further research in the library on one of these problems, outline the factual situation, and indicate the ethical norms that seem to you relevant to the problem. [You might want to check the language of the Endangered Species Act of 1973 (see the References Section).] Does your research lead you to disagree with any of the comments on the problem made in the discussion of it in the text? What solution to the problem would you recommend? How does that solution vary from what is or was actually done about the problem?

ADDITIONAL READINGS

Several anthologies of ethically relevant readings contain essays that shed light on problems of environmental decision making: Barbour (1973), Regan (1984), Scherer & Attig (1983), Schrader-Frechette (1981), and VanDeVeer & Pierce (1986).

Four recent books undertake to spell out in a more systematic manner the requirements of an environmentally sensitive ethic: Callicott (1989), Nash (1990), Rolston II (1989), and Taylor (1986).

REFERENCES

Barbour, I. G. 1973. *Western Man and Environmental Ethics*. Reading, MA: Addison-Wesley.

Bedau, H. A. 1979. Ethical decision making. In *Making Decisions,* ed. P. H. Hill. pp. 27–55. Reading, MA: Addison-Wesley Publishing Co.

Bedau, H. A. 1984. Ethical aspects of group decision making. In *Group Decision Making,* ed. W. Swap. pp. 115–150. Beverly Hills, CA: Sage Publications.

Bedau, H. A. 1986. Ethical decision making and a primitive model of rules. *Philosophical Topics* 14:117–129.

Bedau, H. A. 1991. Casuistry. In *Encyclopedia of Ethics,* eds. C. Becker & L. Becker. New York: Garland, to appear.

Callicott, J. B. 1989. *In Defense of the Land Ethic: Essays in Environmental Philosophy*. Albany, NY: State University of New York Press.

Endangered Species Act of 1973. Public Law 93-205, enacted December 28, 1973. Printed in U.S. Statutes at Large 87:884ff.

Gert, B. 1988. *Morality*. New York: Oxford University Press.

Hardin, G. 1968. The tragedy of the commons. *Science* 162:1243–1248.

Jonsen, A. R. & S. Toulmin. 1988. *The Abuse of Casuistry: A History of Moral Reasoning*. Berkeley, CA: University of California Press.

Leopold, A. 1949. *A Sand County Almanac*. Oxford: Oxford University Press.

Mydans, S. 1990. U.S. and Mexico agree on border sewage plant. *New York Times*, August 22:A18.

Nash, R. F. 1990. *The Rights of Nature: A History of Environmental Ethics*. Madison, WI: University of Wisconsin Press.

Nobbe, G. 1990. The driftnet menace: walls of destruction. *Wildlife Conservation* 95(5): 90–91.

O'Neil, O. 1985. *The Faces of Hunger*. London: Allan & Unwin.

Partridge, E. 1981. *Responsibilities to Future Generations: Environmental Ethics*. Buffalo, NY: Prometheus Books.

Rand, A. 1964. *The Virtue of Selfishness: A New Concept of Egoism*. New York: New American Library.

Rawls, J. 1971. *A Theory of Justice*. Cambridge, MA: Harvard University Press.

Regan, T. 1984. *Earthbound: New Introductory Essays in Environmental Ethics*. New York: Random House.

Rolston II, H. 1989. *Environmental Ethics: Duties to and Values in the Natural World*. Philadelphia, PA: Temple University Press.

Scherer D. & T. Attig. 1983. *Ethics and the Environment*. Englewood Cliffs, NJ: Prentice-Hall.

Schrader-Frechette, K. S. 1981. *Enviromental Ethics*. Pacific Grove, CA: Boxwood Press.

Shabecoff, P. 1990. 40-year countdown is seen for environment. *New York Times*, February 11:48.

Singer, P. 1975. *Animal Liberation: A New Ethics for Our Treatment of Animals*. New York: New York Review Press.

Stone, C. 1987. *Earth and Other Ethics: The Case for Moral Pluralism*. New York: Harper & Row.

Taylor, P. 1986. *Respect for Nature: A Theory of Environmental Ethics*. Princeton, NJ: Princeton University Press.

VanDeVeer, D. & C. Pierce. 1986. *People, Penguins, and Plastic Trees: Basic Issues in Environmental Ethics*. Belmont, CA: Wadsworth.

Waldron, J. 1988. *The Right to Private Property*. Oxford: Clarendon Press.

9

Public Environmental Policy Decision Making: Citizen Roles

Kent E. Portney

1 INTRODUCTION

The traditional "rational" methods of environmental decision making constitute flawed ways of approaching public problems. Before we begin directly to make the argument that citizen involvement in public environmental decision making is not only desirable, but unavoidable and even necessary in contemporary America, we will take a look at the context of public environmental-policy decisions. We will see that there are at least two major approaches to making public decisions about the environment, and that the role one sees for citizens in these decisions depends in large part on which of these major approaches one subscribes to. We will also see that disagreements about the roles for citizens in environmental decision making reflect the tension between the expert assessment of environmental risk and the public's perception of environmental risk.

2 WHO MAKES PUBLIC ENVIRONMENTAL DECISIONS?

First, we need to be clear about who makes environmental decisions. Ultimately, of course, public decisions are made by our public officials. These include, at the federal level, the president and members of Congress. At the state level, governors and state legislators play this role. To say, however, that these people make the decisions is to ignore the dynamics of what really occurs in forming public policies. Public decisions are made by many different people, often representing a variety of sometimes competing interests.

One of the more prominent roles in many public decisions is played by people in the executive branch of government, through the federal agencies that decide

195

environmental issues. Not the least of these are the federal Environmental Protection Agency (EPA), the Occupational Safety and Health Administration (OSHA), and the Food and Drug Administration (FDA). Every state in the nation has a counterpart to the federal EPA, that is, an agency given some responsibility for administering environmental regulations. These administrative agencies often have authorization to make major decisions that affect the environment. In the process of making decisions, these administrative agencies use a variety of approaches or techniques (National Research Council, 1983).

Other actors, too, are involved in making environmental decisions. We will take a closer look at who influences environmental decisions when we examine the policy-making process as applied to the environment. For now, however, let us just note that the president, Congress, governors, or state legislators are not alone charged with making public environmental decisions. Indeed, decision-making authority and responsibility are spread throughout the government.

It is a common error for new students of government to assume that decision-making authority and responsibility is always vested in individual people. For example, some people assume that the Administrator of the EPA makes the decisions concerning federal policies toward the environment—or at least those decisions delegated to the EPA by Congress. While this may be accurate in a legal sense, to attribute actual decision making to this official is to misunderstand the dynamics of how decisions are made.

3 THE PRINCIPAL APPROACHES TO PUBLIC ENVIRONMENTAL DECISION MAKING

Many ways of examining any major social or political problem exist; undoubtedly students of the environment develop clear ideas of what they believe are the best ways to make public environmental decisions. When public decision makers examine an environmental problem with an eye toward improving or protecting the environment, they, too, can choose from among several ways of looking at the problem at hand.

3.1 "Positivist" Orientation

Increasingly common today are two different but related ways of approaching environmental decisions that might be termed "positivist" orientations; the term comes from the "logical positivist" description of the foundations of empirical social analysis. In both of the positivist orientations the focus is on the individual analyst—the researcher charged with using analytical techniques to derive factual and value-neutral answers to the question "How should we improve or protect the environment?"

The first of the two positivist orientations has been called the "cause and consequence" approach (Portney, 1988). In this way of looking at environmental decisions, the analyst uses quantitative analysis to try to determine from past experience what "caused" the environmental problem in the first place, or what "consequences" earlier environmental policy decisions have had. As an example, when we discovered that air pollution was rapidly becoming a serious health problem in the mid- and late-1960s, analysts set out to discover what caused the pollution problem to begin with. Research tried to understand the sources of pollution with the idea that, once the causes were known, we simply needed to decide to eliminate these causes. Much of this type of research focused on emissions from automobiles and from heavy manufacturing industries as the main culprits. The solution was to change the nature of emissions from these sources.

The second of the positivist orientations is what has been called the "prescriptive" approach—very much like the cause and consequence approach, but with at least one major distinction. The prescriptive approach uses very sophisticated analytic methods, such as simulation models or probabilistic risk assessment. For example, one often hears media reports about what will happen to our air quality by the year 2000 if action is not taken today. One hears similar discussions of the ozone layer, global warming, the greenhouse effect, and so on. Many of these predictions are made with the benefit of sophisticated environmental simulation models. Probabilistic risk assessments are often used to project into the future the likelihood of events that will have serious environmental impact. Sometimes these events apply to individual people (as in the probability of a person getting cancer after being exposed to a specific chemical) or to groups of people (as with the probability of a nuclear-plant meltdown). In many governmental agencies, such risk assessments are extended to weigh systematically the risks against the costs of eliminating those risks (see Chapter 5 for a review of this approach). In this type of analysis, if the costs of eliminating or reducing a risk are greater than the anticipated benefits, the decision would be not to eliminate the risk (Peskin & Seskin, 1975). Under this prescriptive approach, analysts try to determine in objective and rigorous fashion what would happen in the future if specific decisions were or were not made.

These two "positivist" approaches to environmental decision making have a common thread: They share a view of the role analysis plays in making decisions. Both approaches are built on the implicit assumption that there is a single or small number of correct decisions to be made, and that analytical methods can discover them. They both start with the assumption that the analyst can and will discover the facts about the environment. They also assume that once these facts are known, the decision will be almost automatic. At a minimum, they suggest that the techniques of analysis will succeed in delineating several different alternatives that can be pursued to achieve the same desirable results. Both these approaches assume that, at a minimum, the range of decision options can and will be narrowed to the point where the actual decision is anticlimactic.

Characteristically, positivist analysts perceive their role as one of simply discovering and presenting information—objective knowledge for the benefit of final decision makers. Analysts who rely on positivist approaches rarely admit that their analysis advocates any one alternative over another. Yet when one reads such analyses, they often do seem to advocate specific policy or program alternatives. The message that comes across is something like this: "If this decision is made intelligently, alternative one will be pursued rather than alternative two." Because both approaches ultimately seek to subordinate decisions to analytical techniques, they are often referred to as "rational" approaches to decision making.

People who take a positivist orientation toward environmental decision making come from many disciplines. Sometimes they are trained in one of the so-called hard sciences, such as biology, biochemistry, biostatistics, or physics. Sometimes they are trained in a branch of engineering, such as civil engineering or operations research. Sometimes they come from health sciences, such as epidemiology, medicine, or public health. Sometimes they come from social sciences, such as economics or urban planning. Sometimes they come from multidisciplinary backgrounds, such as the decision sciences, environmental studies, or policy sciences. Despite the very different foundations these disciplines bring to bear on environmental decision making, there is a strong tendency for them to share a positivist's values about the role of experts.

3.2 Public Policymaking Process

The two approaches discussed above are so dominant in thinking about environmental problems that it may come as a surprise to some that there is any other way to approach decisions. However, there is at least one other approach to examining public environmental decisions, often referred to as the "public policymaking-process" approach.

The policymaking-process approach does not assume that there is a single best answer, or even a small number of correct alternatives, to be found. Nor does it assume that public decisions are made by individuals, per se. Instead, it suggests that the range of answers to a specific environmental problem can be wide, and that it is rather the process our public decision makers go through that will ultimately determine the kind of decision made. Public decision making is seen as inherently a group decision, sometimes involving large numbers of diverse interests.

In order to understand this approach more fully, we need to present the policymaking process in its general outline. After we present this general outline, we will present some examples and applications of it to environmental problems.

The policymaking-process approach toward environmental decisions tends to be much more descriptive than prescriptive. Rather than prescribing the best ways to make policy, it simply seeks to describe how policies have been made in the past and how they are likely to be made in the future. The policymaking process is usually described in terms of multiple stages, where many decisions have to be made involving many different decision makers. Each stage of the process is itself thought of as consisting of a series of processes.The first stage in the process is often referred to as the "problem-formation" or "problem-recognition" stage. For example, it may well be that we are at the earliest stages of recognizing the issue of global warming.

Once a problem has been recognized as important enough to warrant public-policy response, decisions have to be made about what alternatives could be pursued. This stage is often called the "policy-formulation" stage of the policymaking process. In essence, the formulation process consists of decision makers sorting through the specific possible decisions in order to delineate a few alternatives. Once alternatives are agreed upon, a decision has to be made concerning which one or combination will be pursued as a matter of public policy. This is often called the "policy-adoption" stage. Usually we think of this stage as consisting of the process that Congress or a state legislature goes through in enacting a law. When Congress enacts a new environmental law, for instance, Congress' actions involve the process of policy adoption. But policy adoptions can take other forms as well. When the president makes a decision by executive order, as was the case with the initial creation of the EPA by President Nixon, this was also an action that adopted a policy. The process Nixon went through in making this decision is an example of a nonlegislative policy-adoption process.

After a decision is made to adopt a policy, whether by a legislature or executive order, it generally becomes the responsibility of an administrative agency to put the policy into effect. This process is called the "implementation" stage. (See Chapter 10 for a more detailed description of this process.)

In the environmental policymaking process, responsibility for implementation usually falls to the EPA, although other agencies might also be involved. The EPA and these other agencies need to make numerous decisions. For example, often the EPA is given responsibility for establishing the acceptable level of pollution that will be allowed. When the EPA makes this type of decision, it is making decisions about the establishment of "environmental regulations." Before administrative agencies can issue final regulations, they are required to go through a rather lengthy process which includes public participation and commentary. As we will see later, it is at this stage that the tension between the positivist and policymaking approaches becomes most pronounced.

Even after regulations are established, there are numerous other decisions to be made, such as whether and to what degree to enforce these regulations. Although it might seem only rational for any regulatory agency to take actions against noncompliance, in practical terms action is not always possible. Largely because virtually no regulatory agency possesses enough resources to take actions against every party engaged in noncompliance, decisions must be made about how to allocate scarce enforcement resources. In other words, decisions have to be made about which parties will and which will not be required to comply.

Finally, after decisions are implemented, there may be a process of evaluating how well the decision to pursue one course of action seemed to work, that is, to what extent the desired result was actually produced. This is usually referred to as the "policy-evaluation" stage of the process.The results obtained from the evaluation process are then fed back into the formulation stage in order to inform "policy reformulations." Policymaking continues in a circular process.

3.3 Are the Two Approaches Mutually Exclusive or Contradictory?

Now that we have briefly described the two approaches to public environmental decision making, we can directly confront the question of whether these approaches are mutually exclusive, or merely semantic variations of processes with considerable overlap. It should have become clear that these approaches represent very different ideas about the best way to make public environmental-policy decisions. As we argued earlier, the positivist approaches suggest that analytical methods used by the value-neutral researcher will yield the best decisions, that is, the methods are capable of producing research that will point toward the best decision. They are, therefore, considered "rational" approaches to policy decisions. The implication is that if public decision makers do not choose to pursue the course(s) of action set forth by rational analysis, they are being irrational.

There is a clear contrast to be drawn between the rational approaches and the view of decisions as a policymaking process. The process conception of making policy decisions accepts as inevitable that "politics," or interpersonal value-based interactions, will determine which decisions are made. Underlying the policymaking-process conception is the notion that, in a democracy, we accept that reasonable people can disagree about what the best course of action is or should be. Therefore, we need a procedure—a *process,* if you will—to resolve these disagreements. The fundamental premise of the policymaking-process approach is that no analytical technique will necessarily produce the best course of action. Indeed, there is no best course of action to be found; there are only courses of action that can be agreed upon, courses of action that are politically acceptable, and these are the correct decisions.

There is certainly no dearth of attempts by positivists to subordinate policy decisions to analysis, and such thinkers have even attempted to discover ways of systematically incorporating differences of opinion into the analytical process. For example, many analysts go off in search of what they call "utility functions" for society or groups in society in an attempt to record people's preferences in quantifiable terms. Although such attempts are laudable, to date no one has been able to derive utility functions that everyone can agree on.

This characterization of the positivist approach versus the policymaking-process approach suggests that they are, indeed, mutually exclusive. In other words, it is difficult to imagine an approach that gives the ultimate decision-making prerogative to expert analysts and at the same time accepts the idea that no analytical method will produce the single best answer. To be sure, many rational studies of environmental problems assert that their purpose is to lay out the facts without making value judgments, to elaborate the alternatives open to policymakers, without committing to any one alternative (Wilson & Crouch, 1987; Morone & Woodhouse, 1986). But implicit in almost all such studies—as noted above—is a conclusion that one or another of the alternatives is better on some criterion or criteria. The idea that analysts can lay bear the facts in a totally value-neutral way is incompatible with the idea that no analytical method is capable of determining the best course of action (Wynne, 1982). We can see how this incompatibility plays out in the way either approach considers the issue of citizen roles in decision making.

4 CITIZEN ROLES IN PUBLIC ENVIRONMENTAL DECISIONS

Now that we have reviewed the context of public environmental decision making, we can examine the potential and actual involvement of citizens in making some of these decisions. Each of the two major approaches we described earlier, the positivist and the policymaking process, carries with it implications about the extent to which citizens can and should be involved in environmental decision making. These implications are more obvious, perhaps, with respect to the positivist approach, but they exist in each of the approaches.

From the positivist's perspective, expert roles are of paramount importance. Decisions at all stages of the policymaking process are to be made by the people who know the most about the technical side of the environment. Expert-based rational analysis should identify which problems in society are severe enough to warrant government intervention; analysis should lay out the alternatives that can be pursued to alleviate these problems; and once the "best" alternative is selected, expert analysis should prescribe how the alternative would be implemented. The decisions affecting the environment are thought of as necessarily very technical, requiring substantial investment in scientific training and knowledge. Ensuring that policy decisions do not suffer from seriously flawed scientific conclusions requires that the policy decision be made by such experts. In this sense, positivism is quite elitist, prescribing that relatively few people—the experts who conduct analysis—need to be involved.

To the pure positivist, no role is anticipated for the general public in decision making. The idea that, for example, the public might be charged with making the decision about whether to allow the use or banning of a particular pesticide, or where to site a hazardous-waste treatment facility, is anathema to the positivist environmental scientist. The positivist believes that private citizens do not have the background, knowledge, or expertise to make sound and well-informed decisions. Consequently, to the positivist, environmental decisions made by the general public are likely to be bad ones. One might even argue that a positivist orientation toward environmental decision making is antidemocratic.

The pragmatic positivist generally does not take such a hard line; the desire to subordinate politics to analysis runs head-on into the political reality that some role for citizens must be defined. Begrudgingly, the pragmatic positivist acknowledges the political reality that citizens have to be "consulted." Sometimes this takes the form of a search for ways of "managing" public involvement; sometimes it takes the form of assessing the "political feasibility" of specific alternatives. As often as not, such efforts are motivated by an implicit attempt to limit and control public participation in order to minimize the effect of participation on the decision under consideration. In these cases, the efforts become symbolic exercises channeled toward deflating rather than incorporating public views into the decision process (Arnstein, 1969; Checkoway & Van Til, 1978). These efforts are sometimes seen by positivists as a means of educating the uninformed public (Krimsky & Plough, 1988; Fischhoff, 1985) about why the expert's decision or proposed decision is the best one.

From the policymaking-process perspective, citizen roles are paramount. The policymaking-process advocate starts with the recognition that we live under a democratic, albeit representative, political system. Because the policymaking-process approach is largely a descriptive rather than a prescriptive one, much of its analysis does not assert that citizens should be involved so much as it accepts the fact that citizen involvement is inevitable. It suggests that whether or not it is sound science for the general public to make decisions, the general public or some segment of the general public is, in fact, charged, either directly or indirectly, with the authority to influence such decisions. In other words, citizens are legitimate actors in any public-policy decisions in which they choose to participate.

To some people, there is a clear value-based prescription that emerges from the policymaking-process perspective: Democratically derived decisions, decisions that are the result of the democratic process, are superior to others. Since purely rational analytic methods will in any case never give us indisputably best answers, the only legitimate answers are those derived through a process that incorporates the public will. As Charles Lindblom has stated it:

. . . if we imagine a situation without politics, one wholly dependent on analysis, we must assume that for any given problem analysts will come to the same conclusion. (If not, only some kind of political action—voting, for example, could resolve their differences.) They could arrive at agreement only if none of them made any mistake of fact or logic, for if they made mistakes they would diverge in their policy conclusions. . . . In short, analytical policy [decision] making is inevitably limited—and must allow room for politics. . . . (Lindblom, 1980, pp. 18–19)

Lindblom's purpose in making this argument is to prescribe ways that expert opinion can be incorporated into policymaking without the expectation that analysis will be determinative. Indeed, it is difficult to escape the impression that Lindblom's prescriptions seek to subordinate analysis to politics. This brings us full circle, demonstrating how the two approaches to policy decision making—the positivist and the policymaking process—can be considered mutually exclusive.

There are three general ways that citizens affect, directly or indirectly, public decisions about the environment. One of these is through voting. A vote for a particular political candidate may carry with it some element of policy preference. It is, in fact, common for candidates to read their elections as policy "mandates" to pursue all kinds of policies, but research has demonstrated quite clearly that knowing how people vote reveals extremely little about their policy preferences (Erikson & Luttbeg, 1973; Mitchell, 1984). It reveals even less about public preferences in individual decisions. What can one infer from the election of George Bush in 1988 about public preferences on the decision concerning whether to permit offshore oil drilling near the Florida Keys or off the coast of California? The answer is, virtually nothing. Electoral participation provides little role for citizens in public environmental decision making. This is the most indirect channel of public access, since votes for a particular candidate tell that candidate virtually nothing about the specific policy preferences of the electorate.

Voting provides another role for citizens, through initiatives and referenda—available to citizens in many, but not all, states. Referenda are often placed on electoral ballots to provide a means for citizens to express their views on specific issues. Sometimes referenda are binding, that is, they require some state or local action; frequently they are nonbinding, providing a forum for expression of the electorate's views without requiring any action. States that permit initiatives allow citizens to place proposed laws on electoral ballots, laws that, if adopted, carry the weight of statutes. Many states have adopted "bottle bills" requiring deposits and return of beverage containers through just such mechanisms (Geiser, 1990).

Even though ballot-based techniques provide one means for citizen access to decisions, no such provisions exist at the federal level. More frequently, parties wishing to gain access to federal policy decisions do so through the operation of interest groups (Rosenbaum, 1977, 1985). Of course, interest groups may be said to "represent" a variety of interests, public and private. Although private interest groups—those that represent the interests of business or industry—can also be said to represent the interests of citizens, individual citizen's interests are thought to be more frequently represented by citizen-based, or "public," interest groups. Public environmental interest groups are distinguishable from other types of interest groups by the extent to which they advocate policy decisions based on pure self-interest (Berry, 1977). Unlike private interest groups, public environmental interest groups advocate decisions for reasons other than the financial gain of their members.

Public environmental interest groups, like their private counterparts, seek to gain access to decision making by various means, including trying to set the public agenda, proposing solutions to problems in the form of new legislation or regulations, lobbying legislators and administrators, and mobilizing the general public. Agenda-setting consists of trying to get policymakers to recognize that there is a problem that should be dealt with, that is, affecting the problem-formation stage of the process. Sometimes this is attempted by trying to change legislators' minds, and sometimes by trying to get more favorably disposed candidates elected to office. Public environmental interest groups sometimes offer their own policy proposals, often in the form of legislation or regulations that they would like to see adopted. Groups frequently lobby legislators to vote in favor of, or against, legislation with an environmental impact. But lobbying also occurs in administrative agencies. For example, when Congress delegates authority for establishing environmental regulations to the EPA, many interest groups lobby EPA decision makers to write (or, in agency jargon, to promulgate) regulations in a way they approve.

While fairly large citizen-based environmental interest groups are very active in trying to influence federal decisions, there are other types of citizen groups that seek to influence decisions in state and local government. Local citizen groups are often very active in trying to block the location of facilities they think would have a detrimental effect on their communities. We will discuss more clearly the activities of such groups shortly.

Still another way that citizens affect public environmental decisions is through direct participation; individual citizens may be offered the opportunity to take part in the decision-making process of government agencies. Sometimes this occurs in the form of the operation of public-participation programs (Kraft & Kraut, 1988; Ragan, 1978; Mazmanian, 1976). While such participation programs for federal agencies were largely terminated by the Reagan administration, similar programs still exist in many states. Sometimes direct citizen participation occurs through the operation of citizen boards, where an elected official may appoint citizens to a board with narrowly defined jurisdiction. For example, many states have citizen boards that review proposals to site various kinds of facilities with an environmental impact. There are many other ways that citizens affect or try to affect public environmental decisions. What all of them have in common is that they represent ways in which citizens can subordinate analysis to politics.

5 THE CASE OF SITING HAZARDOUS-WASTE TREATMENT FACILITIES

There are many specific examples we could give of the tension between positivist and policymaking-process conceptions of environmental decision making. One of the clearest examples comes from efforts to site hazardous-waste treatment facilities. Before we look at this tension, let us take a brief look at the general idea and context of facility siting.

One of the most serious and emerging areas of environmental concern in the United States is the issue of hazardous wastes. In recent years, the federal government and most state governments have taken numerous actions to attack the hazardous-waste problem on several fronts (Cohen, 1984). First, much attention has been focused on trying to clean up, or remediate, existing hazardous-waste sites around the country. For example, in 1980, Congress passed the Comprehensive Environmental Response, Compensation, and Liability Act (CERCLA). This act established the Superfund program, aimed at identifying and cleaning dangerous waste sites. The act was modified and renewed in 1988.

Second, efforts have been made to reduce the amount of hazardous waste being produced so that new hazardous-waste sites are not created. This source-reduction strategy has helped to moderate the potential hazard created by the dual problem of increasing amounts of hazardous wastes and dwindling safe places to dispose of them. Yet it seems widely agreed that there is still a considerable need for ways to dispose safely of hazardous wastes produced today and in the future.

This has led to a third set of actions, mostly at the state and local level, to site new, relatively safe ways to dispose of, treat, or process, hazardous wastes. Some of these siting efforts involve building new facilities to incinerate hazardous wastes, to subject wastes to some chemical process so they will be less hazardous, or to extract some recyclable element from the wastes. It is the siting of these types of treatment facilities that bears closer scrutiny.

There are very clear differences of opinion about the best way to site hazardous-waste treatment facilities. These differences are often reflected in the state laws that govern how siting is to take place, and they are almost always reflected in actual attempts to build facilities in specific locations. Below, we will take a look at a "typical" way in which such attempts are played out, to find the differences between positivist and policymaking-process conceptions of environmental decisions.

The typical siting process begins with decisions made in the private sector. Commonly, a private company from the waste-disposal industry will decide that it wants to build a waste-treatment facility in a particular state or region. The decision to build a facility usually results from some internal corporate-decision process that has established the potential market for the service.

Once the decision is made within a corporation to build a facility, the next decision is where the facility should be built. Usually this decision takes into consideration a variety of factors not unlike those any business contemplating a facility expansion would consider. They include:

• The cost of, and access to, routes of transportation (such as highways and railroads)
• The cost of available land
• Earning potential due to proximity to local markets
• The cost of facility construction
• The suitability of given sites in terms of potential environmental impact (making sure, for example, that such a facility is not going to be built on top of a heavily used drinking water aquifer)
• The cost of complying with state or local regulations (including environmental regulations such as bans on hazardous-materials transport, and nonenvironmental regulations such as building codes)

Once all the factors have been considered, the company will probably decide to propose building the facility in a spot that optimizes earning potential at a minimal cost.

The company's formal proposal to build the facility must be made in compliance with state and local laws. The process may require submitting the proposal to a state siting board or authority, a local zoning board, or some other entity with legal authority for deciding the proposal's fate. It almost always requires as part of formal application the preparation of an environmental-impact report, a type of analysis designed to determine objectively whether and to what extent the proposed facility would threaten the environment. Often included in the initial analysis are probabilistic risk assessments that try to estimate the likelihood and impact of accidents if the facility is built.

All these initial decisions on the siting of hazardous-waste treatment facilities are dominated by the positivist approach to decision making. In every specific decision, the idea is that rational analysis will lead to the correct conclusion. The problem is, however, that these "correct" decisions always run headlong into citizens who do not want the facility in their community, an attitude we have come to know as the NIMBY, or not-in-my-back-yard, syndrome. This opposition generally stimulates a variety of citizen efforts to alter the decision. Frequently citizens organize—they start or join local citizen groups—to affect the decision. They contact their local officials to express opposition.

Commonly, residents of a community where a treatment-facility site is proposed view the company's analysis as flawed; the conclusion that their community is the one best site must be, they maintain, mistaken. Often, residents will try to cloak their opposition in similarly objective or positivist terms, commissioning an independent analysis to show that their community is precisely the wrong place to build a facility. In doing this, residents rarely are able to establish a compelling argument that the initial analysis was wrong; at best, they establish as plausible the idea that rational analysis itself is incapable of yielding a single best decision. In so doing, they make use of the political process to resolve the conflict.

In practice, once subjected to a political process, the decision is nearly always made in favor of the local residents (Morell & Magorian, 1980). The legal entity given authority for making the public decision about whether to accept the proposed site is by its very nature a political body. Sometimes members are elected, as often is the case with a zoning board. Sometimes the members are appointed by an elected official, such as a governor, as is the case with many statewide facility siting boards. Whatever type of public authority is involved, the rational analysis is subjected to political scrutiny. This in turn has become a source of considerable frustration and irritation for parties wishing to site facilities, mainly because processes involving such scrutiny tend to take time and cost developers money. To them, the problem is "too much democracy" at the expense of rational decision making, while to the local public it looks as if the siting party is trying to impose its will on an unwilling populace.

One common response by the adherents to positivist approaches has been to propose limiting local authority for, and participation in, siting decisions. The idea is that a state legislature, for example, could preempt local decision making and thereby force local residents to accept the conclusions derived from the positivist's analysis. As a case in point, the North Carolina state legislature established a statewide siting board and gave it the responsibility for making the decision about where and whether to permit hazardous-waste treatment facilities. This board consisted of representatives from a variety of backgrounds, including members of the "lay public." The idea, however, was for the board to assess rational analyses objectively, and if the analyses seemed correct, to permit the facility to be built even if local residents opposed it. What happened in practice, however, was that after the board accepted corporate analysis and approved a local site, the local community was able to generate such political opposition that ultimately the legislature abolished the board. Rational analysis was again subordinated to politics.

The positivist will undoubtedly go on searching for ways to eliminate politics from siting decisions, seeking ways to subordinate politics to analysis. People viewing such efforts from the policymaking-process perspective will continue to observe that these efforts are futile, and some will continue to argue that they should be futile. But the case of the siting of facilities is not alone in capturing the tension between these two perspectives.

6 THE RECURRING PROBLEM
OF ENVIRONMENTAL-RISK ASSESSMENT
IN PUBLIC DECISIONS

Perhaps the next logical question about the tension between positivist and policymaking-process perspectives on environmental decision making is whether there is some generalizable reason for it. We have seen from our example of siting a hazardous-waste treatment facility that decision analyses pointing to the objective correctness of a given site are rarely accepted by the people potentially most affected by the facility. This resistance probably is a reflection of a systemic problem that recurs in different forms around different issues.

During the past decade or so, we have come to recognize a pattern in which people who conduct risk assessments, that is, analysts who attempt to determine objectively how much risk a certain event or action will incur, often come to conclusions quite different from those reached by the general citizenry. This discrepancy has found its way into a wide range of environmental decisions. Among them are whether or where to site and license nuclear-power plants; license or ban specific pesticides, fertilizers, other agricultural chemicals, food additives, industrial chemicals, and pharmaceutical products; shut solid-waste landfills; regulate emissions to the air and water from industrial plants and automobiles; clean up existing hazardous-waste sites; and many others. The recurring pattern is of a positivist analysis that demonstrates the risks from some action are quite low—and of the public disagreeing.

It would be quite easy to attribute this discrepancy simply to flawed decision analysis or to an uneducated or insufficiently trained populace. Yet such explanations would not take us very far in understanding how and why positivist decision analysis seems consistently to yield publicly unacceptable decisions. In recent years, much research has gone into examining the elements of risk perception, at least partly with an eye to understanding this discrepancy (Fischhoff, Slovic, & Lichtenstein, 1983; Fischhoff et al., 1978).

Analyses of risk perception have been made in an effort to determine why some risks are more acceptable to people than others. The results suggest there are perhaps nine related dimensions to the issue of how risky people perceive some action or event to be and whether the event or action is acceptable (Litai, Lanning, & Rasmussen, 1983; Rowe, 1977). As discussed in Chapter 5, these dimensions include whether the action or event is perceived to be:

- Of one's own volition
- Of incremental or catastrophic severity
- Of natural or human-made origin
- With delayed or immediate effects on people
- With a sporadic or continuous exposure pattern
- Controllable or uncontrollable
- Old/familiar or new/unfamiliar
- Having clear or unclear personal benefit
- A matter or necessity or luxury

Acceptable risks tend to be those that are perceived to be:

- Faced voluntarily
- Of incremental severity
- Of natural origin
- Delayed in their effect from sporadic exposure
- Controllable
- Old and familiar
- Of clear personal benefit
- Associated with or producing some necessity

Risks perceived to be unacceptable tend to be those from actions or events that have the opposite characteristics. Table 9–1 summarizes these characteristics of risk acceptance.

The important point about these dimensions is that they are not invariant characteristics of events or actions themselves. Rather, people can and often do perceive events and actions in various ways. In other words, the same event can often be perceived as being "new" or "old" to different people, and whether a person is willing to accept the risk from this event is determined in part by

TABLE 9-1   The Nine Dimensions of Risk Acceptance

Dimension of Risk Acceptance	Features That Enhance Acceptability	Features That Diminish Acceptability
1. Volition	Voluntary	Involuntary
2. Severity	Ordinary or incremental	Catastrophic
3. Origin	Natural	Human-made
4. Effect manifestation	Delayed effect	Immediate effect
5. Exposure pattern	Occasional or sporadic exposure	Continuous exposure
6. Controllability	Uncontrollable	Controllable
7. Familiarity	Old/familiar	New/unfamiliar
8. Personal benefit	Clear benefit in return	Unclear benefit
9. Necessity	Necessary	Luxury

precisely this perception. The risks people associate with events or actions that are perceived as having multiple high-risk characteristics are likely to be over-estimated—which is why in these situations the public is most likely to disagree with positivist analysis.

In the case of siting hazardous-waste treatment facilities, people tend to perceive the risks to be much higher than those assessed by the experts because of several characteristics the proposed facility is often perceived as having. Most people consider the risk unfamiliar or "new"; they see it as "uncontrollable," especially since they see no way they can affect operation of the facility once it is built; they perceive it as posing both long-term and short-term health risks (there might be some kind of chemical spill, or the facility might blow up—and even if none of this transpires, it might still give off noxious emissions). In short, people tend to perceive treatment facilities as having many properties of unacceptable risks.

If the inability of positivist analysis to site treatment facilities is due to problems of risk perception, especially the overestimate of risks by the general public, then would this not simply point to a search for ways of changing peoples' perceptions? Though many people have drawn this conclusion, public perceptions are not easily changed. The effort to find ways of integrating citizen and expert conceptions of risk analysis has, however, barely begun.

The lesson for the decision analyst from the case study of siting hazardous-waste treatment facilities, especially in the context of the risk-perception studies, is that there may be a direct clash of values over what analysis can and should do. As analysts begin to understand that decisions are and must be at least partly the results of the processes used to reach them, specific decisions will be better informed by incorporating nonpositivist values. How this is to be done, however, remains to be determined.

7 INTEGRATING CITIZEN AND EXPERT PERCEPTIONS INTO DECISION PROCESSES

As we suggested earlier, positivists have frequently attempted to find ways to incorporate differences of opinion into objective analysis. Despite the fact that positivist analysis has led to substantial improvements in our understanding of the reasons for such differences, it has not discovered ways of resolving them or systematically incorporating them into generally successful decision processes. The effort continues to find decision processes that can integrate citizen and expert perceptions.

There are perhaps three predominant methods or types of processes used today in the attempt to integrate "expert" and "lay" perceptions of risk associated with specific government actions or events. These are public-participation requirements; risk-communication methods; and negotiation and mediation methods. Each of these consists of prescriptions about what kinds of processes might work to integrate expert and lay perceptions of risk. In most cases, the idea is to define a process that will enable the public to understand why the experts are right and they are wrong.

As we discussed earlier, many federal, state, and local agencies require some form and amount of public participation in environmental decision making (Kraft & Kraut, 1988). When federal agencies make decisions about whether to regu- late pesticides, for instance, they are often required to provide the opportunity for public participation and comment. The idea is for the process to provide an opportunity for the experts proposing a regulation to be confronted by conflicting points of view. Participation programs may also be seen as providing the opportunity for experts to educate participants.

While public participation might seem like a reasonable way to incorporate citizen perceptions into environmental decisions, it is fraught with problems. First, the people who participate in the process are not always representative of the general public. Indeed, the Reagan administration consistently argued that federal public-participation requirements simply gave special interests—by defi- nition an unrepresentative lot—the ammunition to get their way at the expense of what was good for the public in general. Second, administrative officials often feel threatened by the prospect of having to respond to participants' views by making decisions that disagree with their own views (Kweit & Kweit, 1980, 1981). Third, such a process brings into direct focus disagreements between expert and lay perceptions of risk without providing any mechanism for resolving the disagreements.

In the case of siting hazardous-waste treatment facilities, public participation has not been very successful. As we noted earlier, people who want to site facilities typically feel that providing citizen participation constitutes "too much democracy"—while the citizens who participate are those for whom the facility is unacceptable. The participation process becomes simply a political mechanism for opponents to block the facility's construction (Matheny & Williams, 1988; Portney, 1990).

Another method of attempting to integrate expert and public perceptions is through some risk-communication process (Krimsky & Plough, 1988). Risk communication consists mainly of the search for processes that provide optimum settings for the experts to communicate to the general public what the "real" risks are. Much of the emphasis on risk communication is motivated by a belief that experts have done a poor job of teaching the general public how and why they reach the risk conclusions they do, and that they need to learn more about how to communicate with people. When risk communication is defined this way, as a one-way process, it appears not to have the intended result. Often, the public does not easily acquiesce to the risk conclusions derived by experts.

More recently, however, risk communication has been investigated as a two-way process, where citizens and experts exchange views and ideas to reach a mutually acceptable understanding of the risks that a particular set of decisions poses. Seen this way, risk communication results in much greater public acceptance.

Another method of reaching consensus on risks is found in mediation and negotiation (Elliott, 1984). In these processes, opportunities are created for the parties in dispute over a siting to sit down, often with a neutral mediator, to identify the conditions under which they would change. What would it take to get members of the general public to accept a hazardous-waste treatment facility? What can the siting party do to change peoples' minds? How can the siting proposal be changed to make it more acceptable? These are questions that need to be answered in ways specific to each siting situation. Perhaps because mediation and negotiation processes are silent with respect to substantive content, such processes have not been especially effective in achieving successful siting.

Efforts to integrate expert and citizen perceptions of risk must confront the tension between positivist and policymaking conceptions of the best way to make environmental decisions. As long as environmental policy decision making is believed to lie solely within the domain of the expert analyst, conflicts with the general public are inevitable. Because it is unrealistic to prescribe processes that would help expand the legitimate domain of expert analysts in a democratic society, there is no reason to believe that such conflicts generally will be resolved. Although there may be alternative solutions to siting hazardous-waste treatment facilities, such as using analysis to help identify places where risk perceptions would permit facility construction, integrative decision processes remain elusive.

EXERCISES

1. We presented a case study of siting hazardous-waste treatment facilities as an example of the tension between positivist approaches and policymaking-process approaches to environmental decision making. Is this a special case, or is this type of tension present in most major environmental decisions? Choose an environmental policy decision that has been made and about which you know something or in which you have some specific interest. Then find out as much as you can about who was involved in the decision, what interest groups played a role in trying to influence the decision, and the extent to which competing interest groups relied on expert analysis to advocate their positions. As you answer these questions, you should be able to begin painting a picture of the extent of the tension between analysis and politics in making public environmental decisions.

2. We have argued that citizen participation in the decision-making process is a desirable and usually even a necessary feature of environmental decision making in the public sector, at least in a democratic society. Experts and policymakers themselves sometimes argue that public participation is undesirable because it causes delays in the decision-making process, and because citizens usually do not know enough to make informed decisions. Yet the dilemma is that very often if citizens are not intimately involved in decisions, the decision-making process becomes gridlocked—the decisions do not have enough public support to gain approval. Use your imagination to think of some ways that citizen participation can occur in an environmental decision-making process without causing delays or creating a serious burden on the process. Start by choosing a specific environmental decision that is to be made. Prescribe how, in your view, citizens can participate most effectively in environmental decisions. As you describe the elements of this participation process, make sure the participation addresses the following issues:

a. How are the citizen participants to be selected? Who does the selecting?
b. How many different identifiable "interests" or sides to any debate or potential debate are represented? Is there any interest that you have omitted or would not want to see represented among citizen participants?
c. What specific roles or activities would the citizen participants play in the decision-making process? How would these citizen participants interact with experts and public officials involved in the decision-making process?
d. Put yourself in the place of one of the citizen participations as you have described them. Given the roles, interactions, and types of participants, how effectively do you think you would be able to influence the decision-making process? To what extent do you think your presence would be welcomed by the experts and by the public officials? Why might these people not want you to be involved? Why might these people not want you to have any influence on the final decisions?
e. Now consider how citizen participation could be improved to avoid the problems you identified earlier. Is it possible to prescribe a way that citizens can participate without omitting important interests, without creating tensions with experts and public officials, and without guaranteeing failure to make decisions?

3. The need to site hazardous-waste treatment facilities presented in this chapter was motivated by the growing concern about what to do with the increasing amounts of these materials being produced in industry and in homes. Yet because of local opposition to siting, such facilities have not turned out to be truly viable ways of reducing the dangers from hazardous wastes. Think of a way that technology can be used to diminish the dangers from hazardous waste without having to confront issues of local opposition. If you were able to prescribe a way that technology can do this, to what extent do you think the public and major interests would welcome your idea? Would this technology actually create risks or dangers for anyone in the population? Who in the population do you think would oppose the use of that technology?

ADDITIONAL READING

If you would like to read more about the politics and political issues surrounding hazardous-waste policy in the United States, Davis and Lester (1988) present a number of well-written articles from a variety of perspectives. For greater detail on the variety of approaches and efforts that have been made in siting hazardous-waste treatment facilities, Portney (1991) presents a broad description of why none of these approaches has worked very well. He also explains some reasons why citizen participation in facility siting does not necessarily make the decision-making process more effective. For a look at some of the tensions between experts and nonexperts in a variety of other environmental policy areas, see Kamieniecki, O'Brien, and Clarke (1986). The volume presents a number of articles, many of which document this type of tension. As was the case in our example, many environmental decisions must confront issues of risk and risk perception from technologies with an environmental impact. If you would like to read more about how experts and nonexperts approach the issues of risk, especially perceptions of risk and danger, Covello et al. (1983) present what is still a very important set of discussions. In their work we can see many examples of ways that experts disagree with the general public, and some possible reasons why they disagree. We can also see some explicit examples of the near contempt that many experts hold for nonexpert evaluations of risk.

If you believe that the best possible course of action to diminish the discrepancy between expert and nonexpert evaluations of risk is through some sort of education, then Krimsky and Plough (1988) is "must" reading. Here the authors focus on the risk-communication process—normally thought of as a mechanism expert analysts can use to educate and explain to nonexperts why their evaluations of risk are superior. Krimsky and Plough make perfectly clear that risk-communication processes do not, and perhaps cannot, perform this function.

Finally, if you want to read in more detail about the politics of environmental decision making in another area (pesticides), Bosso's (1987) work documents how federal environmental decisions on pesticides have been made. This should provide you with a very detailed understanding of the complexity of national environmental decision making; it provides a glimpse into the inner workings of several federal agencies charged with making such decisions. For a more general discussion of problems in implementing environmental legislation, Mann (1982) provides a good overview.

REFERENCES

Arnstein, Sherry. 1969. A ladder of citizen participation. *Journal of the American Institute of Planners* 35:216–224.

Berry, Jeffrey M. 1977. *Lobbying for the People*. Princeton, NJ: Princeton University Press.

Bosso, Christopher J. 1987. *Pesticides and Politics: The Life Cycle of a Public Issue*. Pittsburgh, PA: University of Pittsburgh Press.

Checkoway, Barry & Jon Van Til. 1978. What do we know about citizen participation? A selective review of research. In *Citizen Participation in America*, ed. Stuart Langton. pp. 25–42. Lexington, MA: Lexington Books.

Cohen, Steven. 1984. Defusing the toxic time bomb: Federal hazardous waste programs. In *Environmental Policy in the 1980s: Reagan's New Agenda*, eds. Norman J. Vig & Michael E. Kraft. pp. 273–291. Washington, DC: Congressional Quarterly Press.

Covello, Vincent T., W. Gary Flamm, Joseph V. Rodricks, & Robert G. Tardiff. (Eds.). 1983. *The Analysis of Actual Versus Perceived Risks*. New York: Plenum Press.

Davis, Charles E. & James P. Lester. (Eds.). 1988. *Dimensions of Hazardous Waste Politics and Policy*. Westport, CT: Greenwood Press.

Elliott, Michael, L. P. 1984. Improving community acceptance of hazardous waste facilities through alternative systems for mitigating and managing risk. *Hazardous Wastes and Hazardous Materials* 1:397–410.

Erikson, Robert S. & Norman R. Luttbeg. 1973. *American Public Opinion: Its Origins, Content, and Impact*. New York: John Wiley & Sons.

Fischhoff, Baruch. 1985. Managing risk perceptions. *Issues in Science and Technology* 2: 83–96.

Fischhoff, Baruch, Paul Slovic, & Sarah Lichtenstein. 1983. "The public" vs. "the experts": Perceived vs. actual disagreements about the risks of nuclear power. In *The Analysis of Actual Versus Perceived Risks*, eds. Vincent T. Covello, W. Gary Flamm, Joseph V. Rodricks, & Robert G. Tardiff. pp. 235–249. New York: Plenum Press.

Fischhoff, Baruch, Paul Slovic, Sarah Lichtenstein, S. Read, & B. Combs. 1978. How safe is safe enough? A psychometric study of attitudes towards technological risks and benefits. *Policy Sciences* 9:127–152.

Geiser, Kenneth. 1990. *Environmental Ballot Initiatives*. Medford, MA: Center for Environmental Management, Tufts University.

Kamieniecki, Sheldon, Robert O'Brien, & Michael Clarke. (Eds.). 1986. *Controversies in Environmental Policy*. Albany, NY: SUNY Press.

Kraft, Michael E. & Ruth Kraut. 1988. Citizen participation and hazardous waste policy implementation. In *Dimensions of Hazardous Waste Politics and Policy*, eds. Charles E. Davis & James P. Lester. pp. 63–80. Westport, CT: Greenwood Press.

Krimsky, Sheldon & Alonzo Plough. 1988. *Environmental Hazards: Communicating Risks as a Social Process*. Dover, MA: Auburn House.

Kweit, Robert W. & Mary Grisez Kweit. 1980. Bureaucratic decision-making: Impediments to citizen participation. *Polity* 12:646–666.

Kweit, Mary Grisez & Robert W. Kweit. 1981. *Implementing Citizen Participation in a Bureaucratic Society*. New York: Praeger.

Lindblom, Charles E. 1980. *The Policy Making Process* (2nd ed.). Englewood Cliffs, NJ: Prentice-Hall.

Litai, D., D. D. Lanning, & N. C. Rasmussen. 1983. The public perception of risk. In *The Analysis of Actual Versus Perceived Risks*, eds. Vincent T. Covello, W. Gary Flamm, Joseph V. Rodricks, & Robert G. Tardiff. pp. 213–224. New York: Plenum Press.

Mann, Dean E. (Ed.). 1982. *Environmental Policy Implementation*. Lexington, MA: Lexington Books.

Matheny, Albert R. & Bruce A. Williams. 1988. Rethinking participation: Assessing Florida's strategy for siting hazardous waste disposal facilities. In *Dimensions of Hazardous Waste Politics and Policy*, eds. Charles E. Davis & James P. Lester. pp. 37–52. Westport, CT: Greenwood Press.

Mazmanian, Daniel. 1976. Participatory democracy in a federal agency. In *Water Politics and Public Involvement*, eds. John Pierce & Harvey Doerksen. Ann Arbor, MI: Science Publishers.

Mitchell, Robert Cameron. 1984. Public opinion and environmental politics in the 1970s and 1980s. In *Environmental Policy in the 1980s: Reagan's New Agenda*, eds. Norman J. Vig & Michael E. Kraft. pp. 51–74. Washington, DC: Congressional Quarterly Press.

Morrell, David & Christopher Magorian. 1980. *Siting Hazardous Waste Facilities: Local Opposition and the Myth of Preemption*. Cambridge, MA: Ballinger.

Morone, Joseph G. & Edward J. Woodhouse. 1986. *Averting Catastrophe: Strategies for Regulating Risky Technologies*. Berkeley, CA: University of California Press.

National Research Council. 1983. *Risk Assessment in the Federal Government: Managing the Process*. Washington, DC: National Academy Press.

Peskin, Henry M. & Eugene P. Seskin. (Eds.). 1975. *Cost Benefit Analysis and Water Pollution Policy*. Washington, DC: The Urban Institute.

Portney, Kent E. 1988. *Approaching Public Policy Analysis*. Englewood Cliffs, NJ: Prentice-Hall.

Portney, Kent E. 1990. The dilemma of democracy in local hazardous waste treatment facility siting. In *Mass Communications, Democratization, and the Political Process*, ed. John Havick. Westport, CT: Greenwood Press.

Portney, Kent E. 1991. *Hazardous Waste Treatment Facility Siting: The NIMBY Syndrome*. Dover, MA: Auburn House.

Ragan, James. 1978. *The Nuts and Bolts of Public Participation in Water Quality Planning*. Pacific Palisades, CA: James Ragan Associates.

Rosenbaum, Walter A. 1977. *The Politics of Environmental Concern*. New York: Praeger.

Rosenbaum, Walter A. 1985. *Environmental Politics and Policy*. Washington, DC: Congressional Quarterly Press.

Rowe, William D. 1977. *The Anatomy of Risk*. New York: John Wiley & Sons.

Wilson, Richard & E. A. C. Crouch. 1987. Risk assessment and comparisons: An introduction. *Science* 236:267–270.

Wynne, Brian. 1982. Institutional mythologies and dual societies in the management of risk. In *The Risk Analysis Controversy: An Institutional Perspective*, eds. H. Kunreuther & E. V. Ley. pp. 127–143. Berlin: Springer-Verlag.

10

Regulatory Environmental Decisions

David M. Gute

1 INTRODUCTION

This chapter will explore the special province of environmental decision making (EDM) which falls largely to governmental agencies, namely: the conceptualization, implementation, and enforcement of environmental statutes and regulations. The role of the structure of these agencies, for both the benefit and detriment of the actions they take, is also described.

April 22, 1990 marked the twentieth anniversary of Earth Day. This 20-year period makes a useful and instructive span to view the effects of the passage of time in the conducting of regulatory EDM. Earth Day 20 years ago burst upon the national consciousness full of political and human energy which was largely directed at the presence of bulk pollutants (particulates in air, direct discharge of effluent into waterways) and concerned environmental degradation and its attendant effects upon flora and fauna (the befouled river and the endangered species). The theme for this environmental movement, following, interestingly, in the path of the civil-rights movement, was found in such writings as *Silent Spring* by Rachel Carson. This work, which bears rereading, eloquently drew the nation's attention to the harmful, unintended effects of DDT and other substances on living organisms (Carson, 1962). The linkage of such human-made or anthropomorphic activities with the demonstrated persistence and ubiquitousness of these compounds and other substances—virtually all U.S. adults have measurable levels of DDT, PCBs, DDE, and heptachlor epoxide (Mack & Mohadier, 1985)—engendered governmental and popular concern in the ensuing decades.

Implementation of regulatory environmental programs achieved some noteworthy successes; for example, from 1975 to 1982 ambient levels of certain air pollutants decreased: particulates, 15% (less than half of the 1950 estimate);

sulfur dioxide, 33%; ozone, 18%; carbon monoxide, 31% (Conservation Foundation, 1984). For surface water, improvements were of similar orders of magnitude. Over the time period 1972 to 1982, the U.S. Environmental Protection Agency (EPA) estimated that pollutants from industrial sources dropped by the following percents: total suspended solids, 80%; oil and grease, 71%; phosphate, 74%; and heavy metals, 75% (U.S. Environmental Protection Agency, 1984).

Such demonstrated success pales before the array of problems confronting attendees at the 20th observation of Earth Day. Three structural differences are immediately apparent in the tenor of the debate now, as compared to that of 20 years ago. The first difference concerns the shifting of emphasis for the protection of human health from acute to chronic exposures that are generated from sources that are increasingly numerous, subtle, and interconnected. The seeking of possible effects on human health, though frustrating due to the difficulty of establishing causality for increasingly complex, multifactorial processes, is now an ever-present reality in any regulatory EDM. The search for the etiology of environmental disease is conducted in the presence of an enhanced capability to measure contaminants in human biologics (blood, urine, etc.) or in environmental media (air, water, soil) at the part per trillion (ppt) level in the reference laboratories of today as compared to the part per million (ppm) standards of 20 years ago. Such sensitivity offers advantages in ascertaining a variety of exposures, but also complicates the acceptance of trace levels of contaminants by the public and regulators alike. In many instances the visualization of these trace amounts is owed solely to the vast improvements in the level of detection afforded by the new laboratory procedures and methods.

The second difference is the increasing realization of the interrelatedness and complexity of the Earth's environment and its inherent fragility and susceptibility to human perturbations. This realization, backed by the scientific data concerning global climate change, acid deposition, and ozone depletion (see Chapters 11 and 12) leads to the unmistakable realization that the pursuit of regulatory EDM policy by a set of isolated, uncoordinated, subnational policymakers is not only parochial and shortsighted, but potentially counterproductive and even harmful. Clearly, the locus of meaningful environmental change continues to be the local political unit; however, the objectives of this local entity must be consistent with regional, national, and international efforts—if control measures are to be successful. Such a relationship provides added credence for the oft-repeated bumper-sticker slogan, "Think globally, act locally."

The third and most significant difference is a subtle change in the need for action in the abatement and prevention of environmental problems. The call for action, although articulated for a number of years, has increased in urgency as we approach the twenty-first century. Indeed, many observers posit that time is at a premium, perhaps even past, for the amelioration of certain environmental problems. Other analysts believe that even if the 1990s are not the last chance for reversing national and global environmental problems, it is a decade of crucial importance (National Geographic Society, 1988; Brown, 1989). Such concern has extended into the realm of geopolitics and has catapulted the issue into the lexicon of individuals concerned with global-security issues (Mathews, 1989).

The consideration of current environmental decision making is thus infused with concerns regarding human health effects, a growing awareness of the interrelatedness of action or inaction, and an increasing necessity for meaningful action. Each of these forces further complicates the taking of action within the regulatory arena, but in no way diminishes the need for such action.

Although this volume addresses environmental issues largely attributable to the effects from ambient contaminants, it is increasingly understood that environmental exposures should be considered alongside occupational exposures and seen as a continuum. In reality, most ambient environmental contaminants with human-made sources stem from occupational antecedents. For this reason relevant developments in the field of occupational regulatory decision making will be touched on in this chapter.

2 GOVERNMENTAL INTERVENTIONS

The review of factors associated with human health effects comprises, not in the unique sense, but certainly as a primary activity, the domain of public health. Public health embodies an activist perspective which highlights the identification of health problems and the prevention or lessening of the harmful effects of these factors. Given the range of factors that influence the health of humans (ranging from personal risk factors such as cigarette smoking, uncontrolled hypertension, etc., to environmental problems), the range of public-health activities is broad and based on powerful tenets of legal authority. This oversight, in the United States, is transmitted through government at a variety of levels: local, state, and federal. It is important to keep the level of government in mind because the legal authority for each level differs. We shall begin our consideration of the levels of government with state government.

3 HIERARCHY OF GOVERNMENT

State government's ability to enact public-health measures flows from the "police power" of any sovereign government. Police power simply describes the special authority of government to provide for the health, welfare, and safety of citizens. State government's claim to the sweep of the police power is found in the existence of this power prior to the creation of a federal structure within the United States (Grad, 1965). With the state as the locus of legal authority, delegated police power has flowed to local municipalities. This delegation has taken place to promote efficiency and monitoring for issues ranging from sanitary codes to environmental quality.

Federal government, although a principal seat of environmental regulatory oversight, derives its legal authority not from plenary powers, but rather from authority delegated to it by the states through the federal constitution. In general, federal authority within the sphere of public health rests on the specific powers of Congress to regulate interstate commerce. Such a construct is visible in federal authority ranging from the Food and Drug Administration, which governs the distribution and safety of food and pharmaceuticals, to the production and sale of toxic substances under the Toxic Substances Control Act. Federal authority has extended to other spheres such as governing the health and safety of workers under the Occupational Health and Safety Act.

The principal governmental vehicles for exercising this authority are statutes and regulations. A statute is a law passed by Congress or, at the state or local level, by the legislature, which becomes the law of the relevant political subdivision. The authority to enforce such statutes is generally delegated to administrative agencies which possess specialized expertise used in the promulgation of regulations that set forth an administrative structure through which enforcement activities may be carried out. Such regulations, given the delegated authority from the Congress or legislature, possess the force of law. In general, statutes create a broad framework or mandate for agencies to operate within and interpret via the enactment of regulations.

Other applications of federal authority are made through other avenues under federal jurisdiction: for example, the right to tax and spend for the welfare of citizens. Such a method of extension of federal oversight can be seen in grant-in-aid programs which depend on the intimate involvement of the other layers of government, both state and local. The grant-in-aid vehicle has been particularly important in terms of providing capital for the development of environmental infrastructure (e.g., water-treatment facilities, environmental sanitation). The control is exercised as a result of a state or a municipality complying with federal regulations pertaining to the construction of the facility in exchange for full or partial funding of the project. [For a full discussion of this phenomenon, see *Fragile Foundations* (National Council on Public Works Improvement, 1988).]

4 FEDERAL PREEMPTION

Given the amount of involvement of all three levels of government in environmental problems, agreement between levels (interlevel) and cooperation on the same level (intralevel) become significant issues. This tension will be discussed in Section 5; it is especially apparent in the recent increase in environmental policy development and program implementation at the local and state level in the United States during the past decade (Armstrong, 1990). This surge of activity has been occasioned either by federal quiescence and by the belief of environmental groups that new and innovative approaches to environmental problems can find a more favorable hearing in state capitols than in the halls of Congress (see Chapter 9 for a fuller discussion of citizen participation). Innovation, as well as a diversity of standards and regulations, can be found at the state and local level. Such diversity is perceived as a bane for private-sector firms with national markets because of difficulties of complying with different state requirements. Witness the furor over state authority to regulate such substances as ethylene dibromide (EDB) and daminozide (alar) appearing in the food chain at lower levels than provided for by the appropriate federal authority (Krimsky & Plough, 1988; Koshland, 1989). See Chapter 5 for a summary of the EDB case.

Such difficulty underscores the issue of federal preemption, that is, the right of the federal government to set national standards for a given environmental contaminant or, as in the cited examples, residues in food. When viewed in a hierarchical context, such a provision for federal preeminence rests on the Constitutional provision that statutes of the federal government are the supreme law of the land (U.S. Constitution, Art. VI2). This preemptive power can be enacted by Congress; a good example is the national standards for operation of nuclear-power plants. In many instances state and local jurisdictions are permitted to regulate down to lower levels or ban given contaminants, as in the case of Vermont's recent action which provides for the phased ban of chloroflurocarbons (also see Chapter 11), in contrast to the position of federal authorities.

The role of the federal government vis-à-vis other levels of government depends on the environmental problem in question. A useful comparison can be made between two problems of growing national significance: hazardous waste and solid waste. Hazardous waste can be a solid, a liquid, or a gas. The defining characteristic is that it "may cause, or significantly contribute to, an increase in mortality or an increase in serious irreversible illness or pose a substantial present potential threat to human health or the environment. "Within the area of hazardous waste, the federal presence is strong, flowing from the Resource Conservation and Recovery Act of 1976 (RCRA), amended in 1984, which sets out everything from defining what constitutes "hazardous waste" to enacting a broad regulatory framework including provisions for the documentation, storage, transportation, and disposal of such wastes. Enforcement and monitoring of these statutory requirements are delegated to state authorities, both for efficiency and because of the scale of the problem; a sobering statistic is that annually approximately one ton of hazardous waste is generated per capita in the United States (Wentz, 1989). Currently, 41 states have exercised the option of administering their own programs in accord with federal standards.

The management of solid waste, in contrast to hazardous waste, is almost exclusively in the province of state and local authorities. For instance, there are currently no federal requirements pertaining to municipal solid-waste landfills.

Guidelines that appeared in the original version of RCRA, not standards, are currently being revised at the federal level. The guidelines, in contrast with standards, will serve only as recommendations to state authorities on siting and operating of municipal solid-waste landfills. State authorities will receive no financial incentive to adopt these guidelines nor suffer any penalty for noncompliance (Barbeau, 1989).

5 STRUCTURE OF THE FEDERAL-LEVEL REGULATORY ENVIRONMENT

The thrust and direction of the governmental regulatory presence is shaped to a certain extent by the structure of the agencies carrying out these activities. Regulation for environmental issues is no exception. Each governmental entity brings to the task a specific mandate and set of perceived responsibilities. In the environmental sphere, there are a number of significant agencies with oversight and policymaking responsibility. Starting with the federal level of government, we should begin with the Environmental Protection Agency (EPA) which was formed in 1970 and acquired regulatory responsibility, under the Clean Air Act Amendments of 1970 and the Clean Water Act of 1972, to set national air and water standards for selected contaminants. For a complete list of the major statutes that comprise the mandate of EPA, see Box 10–1.

It is significant that EPA's creation represented an initial consolidation of activities that previously had been carried out by units of the U.S. Public Health Service. President Bush has proposed the elevation of the Administrator of EPA to the level of a Cabinet Secretary. Such action, if enacted, will only further increase the prominence and visibility of EPA. This model, of creating a separate regulatory entity for environmental issues through the reassignment of these activities from health agencies to the new environmental agency, served as a template for the reorganization of many state-level environmental activities. This genesis is significant because it can account for some of the existing confusion between the mandates of both federal and state health and environmental agencies, a situation that has only intensified with the increasing complexity and interrelatedness of environmental health issues. EPA retains an active involvement in the carrying out of applied and theoretical research into environmental issues as well as providing national leadership in the promulgation of standards and the setting of priorities.

As EPA has matured, it has placed greater reliance on the activity of its regional offices scattered throughout the country to maintain oversight as a result of the added burdens imposed on the agency by the passage of the Toxic Substances Control Act of 1976, and the Comprehensive Environmental Response, Compensation, and Liability Act of 1980 (and its subsequent set of amendments—Superfund Amendments and Reauthorization Act of 1986—

BOX 10-1

Major Environmental Legislation Administered by the EPA

Clean Air Act (CAA):
The Administrator is given broad authority to conduct research relating to the "causes, effects, extent, prevention, and control of air pollution." Special emphasis should be given to research on the short- and long-term effects of air pollutants on public health research to "improve our knowledge of the contribution of air pollutants to the occurrence of adverse effects on health, including, but not limited to, behavioral, physiological, toxicological, and biochemical effects." (Title I, part A, sec. 103)

The Administrator is given authority to conduct studies on "biomedical, or other research and monitoring . . . to ascertain any direct or indirect effects upon the public health and welfare of changes in the stratosphere, especially ozone. . . ." (Part B, sec. 153)

Safe Drinking Water Act (SDWA):
"The Administrator may conduct research . . . of physical and mental diseases and other impairments of man resulting directly or indirectly from contaminants in water, or to . . . improve methods to identify and measure the health effects of contaminants in drinking water." (Part E, sec. 1442)

Clean Water Act (CWA):
". . . the Administrator shall conduct research on the harmful effects on the health and welfare of persons caused by pollutants in water. . . ." (Part 1254, sec. 104)

Toxic Substances Control Act (TSCA):
". . . research undertaken by the Administrator and directed toward the development of rapid, reliable, and economical screening techniques for carcinogenic, mutagenic, teratogenic, and ecological effects of chemical substances and mixtures. . . ." (Sec. 10)

Federal Insecticide, Fungicide, and Rodenticide Act (FIFRA):
"The Administrator shall undertake research . . . to carry out the purposes of this Act. . . ." (Sec. 20)

Resource Conservation and Recovery Act (RCRA):
"The Administrator shall conduct . . . research, investigations, experiments . . . and studies relating to any adverse health and welfare effects of the release into the environment of material present in solid waste." (Subtitle H, sec. 8001[A])

Comprehensive Environmental Response, Compensation, and Liability Act (CERCLA or Superfund):
"The Administrator may conduct and support . . . research with respect to the detection, assessment, and the evaluation of the effects on and risks to human health of hazardous substances. . . ." (Sec. 311[c])

Superfund Amendments Reauthorization Act:
"The purposes of this section are to establish a comprehensive and coordinated Federal (SARA) Program of research . . . to improve the scientific capability to assess, detect and evaluate the effects on and risks to human health from hazardous substances." (Sec. 209)

". . . The Administrator of the EPA shall establish a research program with respect to radon gas and indoor air quality . . . The research program required under this section shall include . . . research related to the effects of indoor air pollution and radon on human health. . . ." (Sec. 403) commonly known as "Superfund" or CERCLA). Superfund is grappling with the exigencies imposed by the estimated 23,000 potential hazardous-waste sites in the United States. The EPA has weathered severe criticism for a perceived lack of speed and responsiveness to the identification, control, and abatement of these sites. EPA put in place a system of ranking hazardous-waste sites for inclusion on the National Priority List (NPL) which takes such factors as level of hazard, routes of possible exposure, and magnitude of the affected population into account in the selection of specific sites for inclusion under the Superfund program. The NPL is reviewed to establish priorities for Agency action.

Critics of the Agency point to the grudging progress evidenced in cleanup activities. As of February 1986, 12 of the 541 NPL sites had been completely abated or cleaned up. The number of NPL sites has currently grown to 1,175. Such review of Agency activities can be useful in spurring further efforts aimed at further progress, but also can be an overly simplistic assessment of abatement activities which are complex, involving extensive engineering, health and community-outreach components, and expensive—averaging approximately $8 million per site (Office of Disease Prevention and Health Promotion, 1988). The potential for human exposure from these sites is clearly present. The Agency for Toxic Substances and Disease Registry (ATSDR) estimates that as many as 80% of the Superfund sites already investigated could contain human pathways of exposure (Bureau of National Affairs, 1989).

The EPA, as has been mentioned, is not the only player of significance in the environmental sphere at the federal level. See Figure 10–1 for the structure of the key federal agencies with environmental responsibilities. There is a multiplicity of agencies with specific sets of responsibilities. These include the already-mentioned ATSDR, formed largely to respond to the difficult investigatory and control functions associated with both acute and chronic exposure to toxic substances; the Department of Agriculture, with responsibility for safeguarding the nation's food supply; and the National Institute for Environmental Health Sciences (NIEHS), a largely research-based entity located within the National Institutes of Health structure within the U.S. Public Health Service.

In the occupational setting, the preeminent occupational-health agencies are the Occupational Safety and Health Administration (OSHA), administratively placed in the jurisdiction of the Department of Labor, and the National Institute for Occupational Safety and Health (NIOSH), an entity operating within the sphere of the Centers of Disease Control (CDC). This model diverges from the previously reviewed EPA construct in that OSHA is solely responsible for enforcement of existing federal occupational-health standards, either directly or in concert with state agencies acting under OSHA's oversight. OSHA, in contrast to EPA, does not have significant research responsibilities. Such functions are entrusted to NIOSH, operating from its health-based location within the federal structure.

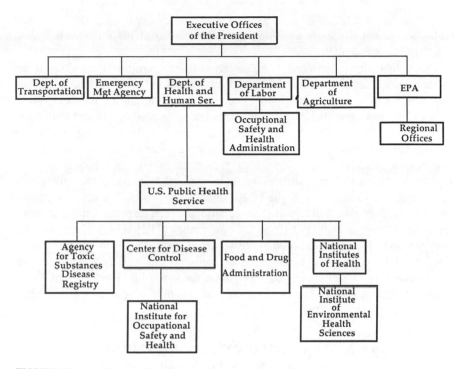

FIGURE 10–1.   Selected U.S. federal agencies engaged in environmental activities.

The theory behind this positioning held that the development of new scientific information regarding the effects of occupational toxins on human health should be separate from ultimate enforcement decisions. The supposition was that a more purely science-based entity, freed from the regulatory responsibilities carried out by OSHA, could operate with greater independence and objectivity. But this model has suffered in implementation in that NIOSH may recommend new, more protective, standards to OSHA which can, at its discretion, adopt them as revisions to existing regulations or not.

The effect of a number of federal agencies with different areas of environmental oversight can be visualized in a simple example. If a substance within the walls of a factory makes people sick, it is the responsibility of OSHA. If this same substance leaves the stack of the factory or enters an abutting stream as effluent, the locus of federal concern shifts to EPA. If the same substance is en route to the plant and a mishap occurs (ruptured railroad tank car, overturned tractor-trailer truck), ATSDR may become involved in providing technical assistance in support of local cleanup efforts. Such complexity and overlap can create great frustration on the part of legislators, citizens, local officials, and other interested parties in assessing the performance of these agencies and in ensuring accountability.

This difficulty is mirrored in the structure of environmental activities at the state and local level. A similar mix of agencies exists at the state level. In fact, an added level of confusion is present because not only might the interlevel problems be present, but also the intralevel problems of coordination and collaboration can exist among federal, state, and local agencies. Partly in response to the coordination difficulties and problems in the dissemination of information, a major new initiative for providing local communities with information concerning toxic chemicals has been launched at the federal level under the Emergency Planning and Community Right-To-Know Act of 1986. This act, commonly known as Community Right-To-Know, among other responsibilities, requires EPA to prepare an annual Toxic Release Inventory (TRI). The TRI represents a compilation of information on the release of toxic substances by manufacturing facility. These data are available in an annual report as well as by accessing an EPA data base via microcomputer telephone modem (U.S. Environmental Protection Agency, 1989). The provision of this information presents both a challenge and an opportunity.

6 CRITERIA USED BY ENVIRONMENTAL DECISION MAKERS

Environmental decision makers usually begin without enough information on the substances being evaluated. For example, of the approximately 67,000 chemicals currently in use in the U.S. commercial market, fully 70% lack *any* human health-effects data. Adequate amounts and kinds of data are available to quantify human health effects for only 2% of these substances (Conservation Foundation, 1984). This information deficit is unyielding, particularly in the absolute necessity for regulatory action even in the face of such uncertainty. The picture does not improve with the realization of the possible effects of scores of new compounds being introduced annually or for the even more vexing problem of estimating the health effects of mixtures of substances. The overwhelming majority of studies performed (either in animals or humans) are conducted on single discrete substances, thus contributing only partial information on how these substances may interact as encountered in ambient or workplace settings. The existence of such complex mixtures can be imagined when even cursory reviews of hazardous-waste facilities are performed and literally hundreds of different substances may be handled in a given enterprise (Ozonoff et al., 1987).

However, this lack of a sufficient information base does not preclude the necessity for decisions to be reached. Environmental decision makers generally view data on health effects in totality, no matter what the source. These sources include (expressed in rough order of utility) human data, animal test data, *in vitro* tests such as those that assess mutagenicity, and information on the structure and physical characteristics of the substance. One of the first tasks of the environmental decision maker is to define the problem. This is usually not a simple task, for it assumes arriving at answers to the following questions:

* What is the magnitude of the problem?
* What is the level of hazard?
* What is the number of people affected?
* What are the possible routes of exposure (respiration, skin contact, ingestion, etc.)?
* What is the source of exposure?
* Is an intervention feasible?

All these questions must be pursued rigorously by the environmental decision maker. Problem definition provides a substratum for conducting risk and exposure assessments. In particular, environmental decision makers must remain cognizant of differences in susceptibility between occupational and community populations. For instance, a community-based, environmentally exposed population would potentially include infants, the elderly, and the chronically ill, all of whom would not be present in the occupational population. Each of these groups could conceivably exhibit greater susceptibility to the agents in question.

Often it is not possible in human occupational studies to find data that are consistent with the expected exposure levels encountered in ambient studies. Occupational studies tend to present higher-dose, acute-exposure levels, whereas the general model for ambient exposures tends to be more of the chronic, low-dose variety. This complicates the role of the environmental decision maker.

7 RISK MANAGEMENT

Once a risk-assessment decision has been made, other decision makers must devise interventions to achieve certain goals. This is the domain of risk management, formally defined as the process of applying a decision concerning environmental risk to the conditions that exist in society, so as to balance exposure to toxic agents against the need for products and processes that may be inherently hazardous (Williams & Burson, 1985). For example, a risk manager within the area of pesticides would choose from a range of possible actions including the following:

* Acceptance of the status quo
* Substitution of a less toxic alternative
* Restriction of use of the existing formulation either along geographic or temporal parameters

- Withdrawal of certification of the pesticide
- Restriction of use depending on the training applicators would have to possess
- Setting of quantitative standards regulating allowed levels either in food or in the environment

Consideration of these alternative actions is affected by considerations such as the level of hazard (lethality, reversibility of possible health effect), magnitude of the effect, and economic, social, and logistical constraints. Logistical constraints, from a regulatory perspective, would include the possession of sufficient resources to enforce proposed risk-management decisions. Such resources would extend to the laboratory capability to test accurately for the presence of the regulated contaminant at the level of the standard as set by regulation.

Current debate swirls around the risk-management options presented to policymakers about two well-known environmental threats to human health: lead and asbestos. Recent analyses have prompted reconsideration of risk-management strategies for both of these agents. Lead is a human toxin which serves no salutary biological purpose. Its detrimental, acute effects on humans have been known for centuries. Two recent studies have added to the knowledge base about the chronic effects of lead exposure as well as the threshold for biologic damage. Investigators looking at the long-term (11 years' postinitial, documented exposure) noted disturbing developmental- and educational-attainment deficits in lead-exposed children as compared to nonexposed children of similar socioeconomic status (Needleman et al., 1990). The persistence of the effect was striking in that it was previously assumed that prompt treatment of lead-exposed children would limit pernicious effects. Of equal importance to risk managers is another recent finding which suggests that the present level for blood lead exposure (25 μg/dl) does not afford adequate protection against reduced levels of hematocrit (Schwartz et al., 1990). Risk managers must thus decide whether to lower the threshold for lead exposure and must reconsider the long-term health effects of such exposure. Both of these factors could have profound implications for lead-screening programs (which attempt to identify children with elevated blood lead levels) as well as for abatement programs (the deleading of housing units).

Even as risk managers consider toughening standards for lead exposure, they may be relaxing their position on asbestos. Recent discussions concerning asbestos have focused on adapting existing procedures so as to place less emphasis on the removal of asbestos from such indoor environments as public buildings. At present, $9 billion are expended for asbestos removal (Koshland, 1989). Such expenditures have come under increasing scrutiny, mainly occasioned by the publication of a set of proceedings emanating from a conference entitled "Symposium on Health Aspects of Exposure to Asbestos in Buildings" held December 14–16, 1988, under the joint auspices of Harvard University, the National Association of Realtors, the Institute of Real Estate Management

Foundation, the Urban Land Institute, and the Safe Buildings Alliance (Harvard University, 1988). The conference attempted to answer the following questions: What is the extent of health risk posed by asbestos in buildings? Who in the population is being exposed? How do we measure the level of exposure? How do we communicate the extent of the associated risk?

8 CASE STUDY: REEVALUATING LEAD AND ASBESTOS

The specific role of regulatory environmental decisions can be understood better with the help of a case study. In this case study, we will contrast the regulatory and scientific responses to these two well-known environmental agents: lead and asbestos.

Both lead and asbestos are hazards to human health, well known to the practitioners of occupational and environmental medicine. In fact, reports of lead exposure and the resulting negative effects on human health extend back to antiquity. One interesting source of exposure was the glazes used to cover the nobility's drinking goblets in ancient Rome. Reports of asbestos being used for commercial purposes extend back about 100 years with references to the way German and British navies packed steam engines (Murray, 1990). Early uses of asbestos included weaving the mineral into cloth to produce the "miracle fabric," a fire-resistant cloth. It began to be associated with the expression of disease in the early part of the twentieth century

8.1 Health Effects

Health effects attributable to both lead and asbestos are relatively well characterized. In lead exposure, several organ systems may be affected, including the gastrointestinal, nervous, hemopoietic (bloodforming), reproductive, and renal systems (Rempel, 1989). A classic feature of human sickness caused by lead exposure is a well-documented variation in susceptibility to lead intoxication. That is, the same concentration (dose) of lead translates into frank disease in one individual, but not in another similarly exposed individual. This variation in susceptibility raises a vexing question for regulators, whether at the local, state, or federal level. How do you set health-based standards that offer protection (even protection for special populations of highly susceptible individuals) without being unnecessarily complicated with regard to compliance?

Health effects attributable to asbestos exposure include lung cancer, mesothelioma (a cancer of the pleura, or lining of the lung), cancers of the gastrointestinal tract and larynx, asbestosis (a pulmonary fibrosis induced by asbestos particles), and a group of benign pleural disorders (Mossman & Gee, 1989). A cardinal feature of asbestos exposure is that the disease interacts synergistically with other personal-risk factors, resulting in effects greater than additivity. This characteristic emerged in a study published by Hammond et al. (1979), which compared the risk of lung cancer in several populations to the risk for a nonsmoker with no occupational exposure to asbestos. The risk of lung cancer in nonsmoking asbestos workers is greater than five times the risk in the baseline group. The risk for smokers not working with asbestos is more than ten times the risk in the baseline group. The impact of synergy is best understood when one inspects the expression of lung cancer in the population of smokers that is asbestos-exposed. The risk in this group is 53 times that in the baseline group, thus outstripping the additive influence of smoking or asbestos exposure independently.

8.2 Routes of Exposure

In approaching the control of lead- and asbestos-induced disease, regulators must concern themselves with some basic attributes of the agents.

- What are the sources of exposure?
- Where are the agents used and by whom?
- Do safe alternatives exist?
- How many people are potentially exposed?
- If human exposure is occurring, how is this happening?
- What is the pathway?
- If the pathway can be identified, how can it be blocked and the individual be protected?

Before assigning risk to a given agent, researchers need detailed knowledge about how the agent is metabolized and whether the toxic effect of the agent is immediate or delayed, acute or chronic, in terms of its manifestation in illness. Can the agent be accumulated in the body or is it metabolized and excreted?

Once human health risks are assessed, the regulatory community can turn its attention to their management. Risk management entails the identification of steps that can lead to reductions in potential exposure and perhaps even to the prevention of exposure or the elimination of the agent by substituting less toxic materials. Examples include substituting electronically welded cans for cans formed by using leaded solder, and using fiberglass instead of asbestos. Of continuing concern to the regulator is ascertaining that the supposedly less toxic alternative does not, in fact, have more harmful health effects; vigilance must be exercised to guarantee that the remedy is not worse than the status quo.

8.3 Abatement of Lead and Asbestos

Abatement of both lead and asbestos has been encouraged by a plethora of federal and state health regulations, the intent being to remove the harmful agent from contact with susceptible populations and to dispose of the removed material in a safe manner. Health-based standards for lead are under intense scrutiny, but there is little disagreement among experts as to which direction revision should take. The effects of low-level lead exposure seem to be even greater than previously imagined, and the persistence of these effects is substantial (Needleman et al., 1990; Schwartz et al., 1990).

Currently, controversy swirls around a federal statute, the Asbestos Hazard Emergency Response Act (AHERA), which requires that all public and private schools in the United States be inspected for asbestos-containing materials. The statute does not require removal, but much removal has, in fact, taken place; it is estimated that, in 1989, approximately $9 billion was spent for asbestos removal in the United States. These expenditures have been projected to grow to $100–$150 billion for the 1990s. Not everyone agrees that this level of activity is necessary.

The positions of the opposing camps in this debate are taken up by the occupational-health community on the one hand (led by scientists such as Irving Selikoff and Philip Landirgan, who were involved in the early identification of increased risks for working populations) and prominent reevaluations of the risks imposed by asbestos-containing materials in public buildings and schools on the other hand (Mossman et al., 1990). The argument turns on the physical characteristics of the agent and the relationship between dose and human health response. Regulators who are trying to set standards that protect human health need highly quantitative data on human health response.

8.4 Standards for Lead

Health investigators as well as regulators have long been aware of the pernicious effects of lead even in acute, short periods of exposure to high doses of lead. Evidence confirms that more common, chronic, low-level exposures such as those found in the classic example of children exposed by consuming lead-containing paint or mouthing lead-containing dust can also have real and continuing health consequences. This finding has led to a rich panoply of state and federal regulations concerning lead exposures, as well as to aggressive outreach programs in some states to identify lead-exposed children. These programs culminate in health-screening studies and mandatory abatement activities.

Greater vigilance, both in program implementation and in the actual levels of the health-based standards, has occurred because levels once thought to be safe are now associated with a variety of adverse health consequences. These consequences include delayed cognitive development, reduced IQ scores, growth deficits and impaired social development. The United States Centers for Disease Control (CDC), which maintain a current standard of 25 micrograms per deciliter of blood (μg/dl), are currently entertaining the notion of lowering the standard.

This level is used by CDC in making referral judgments from screening programs, but it is not meant to imply a risk-free state. In fact, both the World Health Organization (WHO) and the Clean Air Scientific Advisory Committee to the United States Environmental Protection Agency have advocated blood levels lower than 25 μg/dl as acceptable upper limits.

The lead standard takes on added significance the better the metabolic and toxicologic properties of lead are understood. In contrast to certain compounds such as water-soluble vitamin C that are excreted once certain tolerances are met, lead is bioconcentrated. Only about 10%–15% of biologically available lead passes through the body. The rest is preferentially stored in long bones and, without subsequent reexposure, is released into the circulating blood in a balanced state. This release can take quite a bit of time and provides the explanation of the manner in which measured lead levels in blood serve as indicators of the total amount of lead in the body.

8.5 Standards for Asbestos

The standards for asbestos require a consideration of what asbestos has been used for and what uses have been previously banned by government action. Currently asbestos is used in a variety of products including cement pipes, brake linings, thermal and electrical insulation, flooring and roofing products, and textiles. Some past practices, such as spraying asbestos onto building surfaces as an insulator and fire retardant, have been banned.

Historically, regulatory standards have been driven by the number of asbestos fibers of certain lengths in air. For example, the current occupational standard is 0.2 asbestos fibers greater than 5 μm in length per cubic centimeter of air collected over an 8-hour period. This standard applies only to work settings and not to settings covered by the AHERA statute. The new variable in the regulatory debate over standards and abatement practices for asbestos has to do with the characteristics of the agent itself. That is, asbestos is not a single substance, but rather a family of six minerals that possess different physical and chemical properties. These six types of asbestos are chrysotile, crocidolite, amosite, anthophyllite, tremolite, and actinolite. Two distinct classes of asbestos fibers are commonly used: the amphiboles and chrysotile. Chrysotile, estimated to represent 95% of the asbestos in the United States, consists of pliable curly fibrils that occur in bundles. Amphiboles, on the other hand, are generally needle-like in physical appearance and quite complex in their chemical characteristics, with an ability to combine with a variety of metals. Some researchers think that both the potentially increased reactivity of amphibole asbestos and its physical shape (more conducive to deep penetration into lung tissue) may account for possibly greater harm to human health. Chrysotile asbestos, because of its curly, bundled aspect, is more easily obstructed from deeper penetration into the lung by the architecture of the bronchi and other anatomical structures.

The asbestos debate encourages regulatory agencies to consider fiber type when setting health standards and when issuing guidelines for abatement. Whatever the fiber type, a key concern of anyone attempting to make a risk-management decision for an asbestos-containing structure is the condition of the asbestos in the building. Is it intact? flaking? friable? Additionally, an assessment must be made as to the relative exposure to this asbestos among occupants or users of the structure. For instance, is the asbestos in an exposed situation in the building, within the reach of schoolchildren? Or is it contained in locations outside normal traffic flows? Potentially, the consolidation of asbestos in such relatively out-of-the-way areas such as boiler rooms might cause more concentrated exposure in custodians, for example, than in schoolchildren.

Another current concern of regulators is whether the abatement activities produce a better environmental result than the status quo. Any material removed from a structure, be it lead-paint dust or asbestos, will have to be disposed of safely (according to the dictates of hazardous-waste regulations). In addition, care will have to be exercised to ensure that the abatement workers do not suffer occupationally induced illness in fulfilling their responsibilities and that their efforts do not present additional risks to abutters or occupants upon reentry.

The quality of the evidence about the differential of risk between fiber types concerns regulators and is a matter of contention among interested scientists. This debate coalesced at a conference held at Harvard University's Energy and Environmental Policy Center, summarized in a report released on August 9, 1989. The report held that differences in fiber types and dimensions can be significant in determining health risks. Existing EPA policies, which make no distinction between fiber types, came under attack. The conference report went on to assert that the federal government should establish an "asbestos risk-management policy consistent with the latest risk assessment evidence." Otherwise, the report noted that there would be a "mismatch" between expenditures and actual environmental health risks. Critics of the findings of the conference report include representatives of the asbestos-abatement equipment industry and health researchers (led most prominently by Irving Selikoff). They contend that the Safe Buildings Alliance (SBA) underwrote the meeting, and that this financial support could amount to an orchestrated campaign on the behalf of the interests of former manufacturers of asbestos (see Air/Water Pollution Report, 1990).

The economic and political realities should not obscure the scientific points: the possible differential effect on health of fiber types and the possible health effects of very low levels of exposure seen in public buildings and schools covered under the AHERA statute. Estimating lower levels of exposures usually engenders considerable controversy. It is difficult to apply the results of human populations exposed to higher levels of an agent to populations exposed to much lower levels. For example, the epidemiological studies of asbestos pioneer Irving Selikoff note high risk in miners, shipbuilders, and other trade occupations.

These effects are real and substantial. The question remains as to what happens when we must extrapolate from high-dose to low-dose scenarios.

9 CONCLUSION

Both lead and asbestos are, undeniably, major sources of human misery and disease. The question before the regulatory community is whether the reconsideration of scientific evidence can lead to managing these risks in new ways. The control of lead in the human environment appears to be following a trend of even more stringent regulation, with more rigorous standards for protecting health spurring greater abatement and screening activity. Asbestos, although a well-known occupational hazard, is currently being reevaluated as a risk in public buildings and schools. The struggle to revise attendant policies will not be an easy one. In fact, a special study group of nationally known experts has recently been empaneled, supported by both public and private monies, to evaluate the evidence and to provide an objective assessment of the current situation. This entity is called the Health Effects Institute–Asbestos Research (HEI-AR) and will produce a report in mid-1992. Tracking the development of further regulatory action for both lead and asbestos over time will be of great interest.

The need for governmental action in the control of environmental hazards can be immediate and pressing. Action must be taken in the face of uncertainty, using risk assessment and other tools available to decision makers to try to increase the likelihood that beneficial results can be achieved. The use of these techniques is subject to controversy, evidenced in such disparate situations as estimating the effect of dioxin exposure suffered as result of military service in Vietnam (Gough, 1987) and estimating the potential health effects of hazardous-waste sites (Anderson, 1985).

The openness of the private sector to progressive environmental action is increasing. This phenomenon is prompted in part by top management's greater sensitivity to the environmental consequences of its corporate operations, and in part by concerns about controlling both costs of production and exposure to liability. But if the previous record of environmental and occupational health is of any use in predicting the future, firm governmental supervision will still be needed to ensure compliance with existing statutes and regulations. Such supervision is a critical ingredient in moving the system toward a future of greater environmental integrity. Government regulatory policies and the other incentives available to government must shift from the previous focus on dealing with pollutants after they are produced, popularly known as "end-of-the-pipe" controls, to more progressive stances that seek to promote prevention through source reduction, redesign of manufacturing processes, and product substitution. Corporate initiatives and well-integrated, well-conceived governmental programs will both be required to lead toward an environmental result that is achievable and acceptable.

EXERCISES

1. State-of-the-art laboratories of 20 years ago could quantify biologic or environmental substances in the parts-per-million order of magnitude. Recent advances in measurement capability can now produce results, at selected laboratories, in the parts-per-trillion range for both environmental (air, water, soil) and biologic (blood, fat tissue, hair) media. Discuss what advantages are offered to the environmental decision maker by these advances. What disadvantages or complications may be produced?

2. How does the expanding scale of environmental problems and solutions, from regional to national and even to global parameters, enhance or complicate such generic activities as problem definition, the enforcement of international agreements, and choosing risk-management options?

3. Compare and contrast society's seeming acceptance of greater potential health risks being posed to workers as a result of workplace hazards with the lower threshold of acceptance for environmental risk borne in the community? What accounts for these differences? Are they justified? How should environmental decision makers confront the differences?

ADDITIONAL READING

For a general review of governmental activity internationally and in the United States, see Brown (1990) and Lave and Upton (1987). For current computerized data bases, see *Some Publicly Available Sources of Computerized Information on Environmental Health and Toxicology* (1988), and the EPA Toxics-Release Inventory (1989). For up-to-date information on a variety of the topics discussed in this chapter, there are three interesting newsletters: *HEI-AR* (Health Effects Institute–Asbestos Research) *Newsletter, Health and Environmental Digest,* and the *Occupational and Environmental Medicine Report.*

REFERENCES

Air/Water Pollution Report. 1990. Silver Spring, MD: Business Publishers, Inc.

Anderson, H. A. 1985. Evolution of environmental epidemiologic risk assessment. *Environmental Health Perspectives* 62:389–392.

Armstrong, S. 1990. States, towns fill environmental void. *The Christian Science Monitor* 82(47):1–2.

Barbeau, B. 1989. Issues in solid waste management: A background paper for state and local policy makers. Prepared for: Sources and Uses of Environmental Health Policy Information—A Workshop for Senior State and Local Policymakers, held December 4–6, Durham, NH.

Brown, Lester. (Ed.). 1989. *State of the World 1989*. New York: W. W. Norton.

Brown, Lester. (Ed.). 1990. *State of the World 1990*. New York: W. W. Norton.

Bureau of National Affairs. 1989. *Environment Reporter*. Washington, DC: Bureau of National Affairs. October 6, 1989.

Carson, Rachel. 1962. *Silent Spring*. Greenwich, CT: Fawcett.

Centers for Disease Control. 1988. *Some Publicly Available Sources of Computerized Information on Environmental Health and Toxicology*. Atlanta: Centers for Disease Control.

Conservation Foundation. 1984. *State of the Environment and Assessment at Mid-Decade*. Washington, DC: Conservation Foundation. pp. xxiii and 89.

Gough, M. 1987. Environmental epidemiology: separating politics and science. *Issues in Science and Technology* 3(4):20–31.

Grad, F. 1965. *Public Health Law Manual*. Washington, DC: American Public Health Association.

Hammond, E. C., I. J. Selikoff, H. Seidman. 1979. Asbestos exposure, cigarette smoking and death rates. *Annals of the New York Academy of Sciences* 330:473–490.

Harvard University. 1988. Symposium on health aspects of exposure to asbestos in buildings. *Proceedings*. December 14–16, 1988. p.1.

Koshland, D. E. 1989. Scare of the week [editorial]. *Science* 244:9.

Krimsky, Sheldon & Alonzo. Plough. 1988. *Environmental Hazards—Communicating Risks as a Social Process*. Dover, MA: Auburn House.

Lave, Lester B. & Arthur C. Upton. 1987. *Toxic Chemicals, Health, and the Environment*. Baltimore: The Johns Hopkins University Press.

Mack, G. A. & L. Mohadier. 1985. Baseline estimates and time trends for BBHC, HCB and PCBs in human adipose tissues. *Report for the Office of Pesticides and Toxic Substances*. Washington, DC: Environmental Protection Agency.

Mathews, J. T. 1989. Redefining security. *Foreign Affairs* 70 (Spring):162–177.

Mossman, Brooke T. & J. Bernard Gee. 1989. EPA Asbestos-related disease. *New England Journal of Medicine* 320:1721–1730.

Mossman, B. T., J. Bignon, M. Corn, A. Seaton, & J. B. L. Gee. 1990. Asbestos: scientific developments and implications for public policy. *Science* 247:294–301.

Murray, R. 1990. Asbestos: a chronology of its origins and health effects. *British Journal of Industrial Medicine* 47:361–365.

National Council on Public Works Improvement. 1988. *Fragile Foundations: A Report on America's Public Works*. Washington, DC: National Council on Public Works Improvement.

National Geographic Society. 1988. *Earth 88: Changing Geographic Perspectives*. Washington, DC: National Geographic Society.

Needleman, H., A. Schell, D. Bellinger, A. Leviton, & E. N. Allred. 1990. The long-term effects of exposure to low doses of lead in childhood: An 11-year follow-up report. *New England Journal of Medicine* 322:83–88.

Office of Disease Prevention and Health Promotion—U.S. Public Health Service. 1988. *Disease Prevention/Health Promotion: The Facts*. Palo Alto, CA: Bull Publishing Company.

Ozonoff, David, Mary Ellen Colten, Adrienne Cupples, Timothy Heeren, Arthur Schatzkin, Thomas Mangione, Miriam Dresner, & Theodore Colton. 1987. Health problems reported by residents of a neighborhood contaminated by a hazardous waste facility. *American Journal of Industrial Medicine* 11:581–597.

Rempel, David. 1989. The lead-exposed worker. *Journal of American Medical Association* 262:532–534.

Schwartz, J., P. J. Landrigan, E. L. Baker, W. A. Orenstein, & I. H. Von Lindern. 1990. Lead-induced anemia: dose-response relationships and evidence for a threshold. *American Journal of Public Health* 80:165–168.

U.S. Environmental Protection Agency. 1984. *Environmental Progress and Challenges: An EPA Perspective.* p. 45. Washington, DC: U.S. Government Printing Office.

U.S. Environmental Protection Agency. 1989. *The Toxics-Release Inventory: A National Perspective.* EPA 560/4-89-005. Washington, DC: U.S. Government Printing Office.

Wentz, C. A. 1989. *Hazardous Waste Management.* New York: McGraw-Hill.

Williams, Phillip L. & James L. Burson. 1985. *Industrial Toxicology: Safety and Health Applications in the Workplace.* New York: Van Nostrand Reinhold.

11

Private-Sector Environmental Decision Making

Ann Rappaport and Patricia Dillon

1 INTRODUCTION

People in the private sector routinely make many decisions that can affect environmental quality, either positively or negatively: for example, the decision to develop and market certain products, the choice of technology, and the methods of waste management.[*] The private sector controls extensive resources and the types of decisions made can have significant effects on the environment. Even though several aspects of environmental decisions are influenced by government regulation, a large number of decisions are made at the discretion of private-sector decision makers. Because prevention of environmental problems is widely recognized as a preferred alternative to mitigating or controlling environmental hazards after occurrence, the private sector through its decision-making processes can play a major role in preventing or limiting environmental risk.

Private-sector decision making does not occur in isolation. Company decisions are influenced by a variety of factors, including market demand, government regulation, public opinion, liability issues, and competition. Companies are in business in order to provide goods and services and, in so doing, to make profits; they therefore respond to customer demand for certain products and seek cost-effective manufacturing strategies. Since the early 1970s, a growing recognition of the threats to public health and environmental contamination, arising from past and present industrial activity, has given rise to public pressure for more stringent control of industry. As a result, a large volume of environmental legislation, which ultimately affects company decisions, now exists.

The interactions between government and companies have become in-

---

[*]In this chapter, the term "private sector" refers to companies and private institutions, not private individuals in their capacities as consumers, activists, and homeowners.

creasingly complex as government has exercised a more directive impact on corporate and institutional environmental decision making. Many companies have responded by developing management systems to address regulatory as well as other environmental liabilities: for example, incorporating the consideration of environmental impacts at several points in decision-making processes and adding environmental professionals to corporate, division, and plant staffs.

Much has been written about creating optimal policies for government to better regulate the private sector. However, relatively little attention has been paid to how companies make environmental decisions and how, aside from traditional "command-and-control" or a variety of "taxation" schemes, company decisions can be altered in favor of the environment. Given the potential impact of private-sector decisions on the environment and the potential for the private sector to incorporate environmental considerations in decision making, this neglect is surprising.

Private-sector environmental decision making is an exciting field because it is currently in a phase of rapidly increasing sophistication. New decision-making tools are being developed, new alliances are being formed, and new ways of looking at old problems are emerging. One constant remains: Companies are in business to make money. Society as a whole benefits when environmental issues and solutions can be framed in such a way that this fundamental objective of companies is not compromised.

This chapter explores the types of decisions made by companies; the factors influencing private-sector decision making; companies' responses to environmental challenges; the incorporation of environmental considerations in the decision-making process; and the role of companies in the further reduction of environmental risk.

2 TYPES OF ENVIRONMENTAL DECISIONS MADE BY THE PRIVATE SECTOR

The popular press, and to some extent the government as well, have tended to focus on the by-products or wastes produced by industry and the impact of their disposal on air, water, and land, and on unintentional releases to the environment. In the course of its day-to-day business activities, however, the private sector makes a wide variety of decisions that can have either a positive or negative impact on the environment. This section briefly indicates the range of decisions made by industry in order to illustrate the multiplicity of opportunities for the environment to be affected by private-sector decisions.

2.1 What Products Should the Company Offer?

A range of environmental impacts, both positive and negative, may result from the use of products manufactured by the private sector. Some popular products may cause disposal problems: for example, disposable diapers increase the volume and perhaps the pathogenicity of solid waste. The use of other products may harm the environment: for example, pesticides may leave long-lasting residues with undesirable health and ecological effects and are implicated in the contamination of drinking-water supplies. Other products may contribute to environmental problems in sensitive areas: for example, off-road recreational vehicles may exacerbate erosion.

Alternatively, products may contribute to environmental solutions. Some companies have developed environmentally friendly or "green" products such as phosphate-free detergents, energy-efficient lighting systems, pollution-control equipment, and environmental monitoring systems. Nonetheless, recent press reports suggest that consumer demand has outstripped company response (Elkington, 1989).

2.2 What Materials Should Be Used in the Manufacturing Process?

In manufacturing, the private sector uses numerous materials which vary in their degree of hazard. Depending on the nature of the product and the process being used, it may be possible to substitute raw materials that are less toxic to dispose of and pose reduced risk of accidental release.

> One example of reformulating a product comes from Cleo Wrap, a printer that has developed water-based inks to avoid disposing of hazardous solvents. A six-year conversion project has allowed the company to virtually eliminate hazardous waste and save $35,000 in waste-disposal costs annually. The project has made underground storage tanks and other materials to comply with new regulations unnecessary, and it has lowered fire insurance premiums. (Hirschhorn, 1988, p. 57)

Substitutions of this sort sometimes reduce worker exposure to toxic materials as well.

2.3 How Should Natural Resources be Used?

Companies that use natural resources often have a range of options that are more or less environmentally sensitive. In harvesting timber to make wood pulp for paper manufacture, some companies simply clear-cut forests, allowing valuable topsoil to wash away while ground cover regenerates. Others clear-cut, but replant with "genetically improved" tree strains. Still others harvest selectively, so that the remaining trees can reseed themselves. The implications for the affected ecosystem vary accordingly.

2.4 What Technology Should be Selected to Produce the Product?

Decisions on manufacturing processes can have a major impact on the amount of resources used and the amount and type of waste produced. New waste-reduction technologies, many of which involve recycling intermediate waste streams and recovering material for use in other manufacturing processes, can reduce the amounts of process water used, energy consumed, raw material used, and waste produced.

2.5 How Should By-products Be Handled?

The range of appropriate treatment and disposal-technology choices is highly dependent on the type of waste produced. In addition, federal and state regulations, resulting from past improper disposal of waste both by the private sector and by government installations, constrain and influence the choice of technology.

Materials such as solvents can be recycled either by the original user or by a commercial recycler. In some cases, wastes from one process or firm may be used directly, either in making a product or as a fuel. Disposal options such as incineration or landfilling may also be selected by a company generating waste. In making decisions on how to handle an individual waste stream, many companies not only consider the cost today of disposing of the material, but also take into account whether an option (such as landfilling) might result in long-term environmental damage or public-health problems for which the corporation could be held liable in the future. The increasing scrutiny of government regulators and the resulting cost increases for waste handling have motivated many firms to modify their processes in order to produce less waste.

2.6 Where Should the Company be Located?

The geographical location of a facility is a business decision that may have significant environmental implications. For example, construction of a new facility or office park may destroy ecologically sensitive wetlands. During operations, a manufacturing facility might degrade groundwater or air quality. A manufacturing facility might be sited near a source of raw material but relatively far from its customers, or vice versa, which might require long-distance transport of hazardous substances. In some cases, design and policy measures can be implemented to overcome adverse effects of less-than-ideal locations. For example, the private sector can work with local and state government during the planning phase to ensure minimum impact on wetlands, use of adequate pollution controls, an adequate buffer zone around the facility to minimize damage to neighbors if an accident were to occur, and easy access to public transportation.

Even if a facility performs no manufacturing, it can have an impact on air quality. An insurance company might be located in a suburban area where virtually all employees commute to work by car. If the local road system is at capacity before the company opens its doors, then the additional traffic from the insurance company will cause traffic back-ups. Depending on meteorological conditions, back-ups in turn could cause locally severe air pollution. Company policies, such as offering flexible work hours and providing incentives like priority parking for employees who carpool, can help reduce local air pollution and thereby improve the environment.

2.7 Is Concern for Environment Reflected in the Facility Design?

Decisions concerning the facility design can have profound implications, not only for effectiveness and cost of pollution control, but also with respect to a wider range of environmental concerns. Aesthetics of the community, the possibility of industrial pollution, and demand on energy supplies are all environmental concerns related to facility design. Has every effort been made to create energy-efficient structures and production processes? Are energy sources renewable or nonrenewable? Have efforts been made to include active and passive solar features? Two other design features important for environmental protection include building dikes around areas where hazardous materials are transferred and stored so that spills do not seep into the ground, and draining rainwater from diked areas into a wastewater-treatment system so that trace quantities of toxics do not enter the local ecosystem.

2.8 What Accounting Methods Should the Company Use?

Use of methods that discount future environmental liability or that require rapid payback to show profitability will prevent a company from investing in process changes that reduce waste at the source. Some companies, such as General Electric, have begun to factor costs of future liability into decisions in an effort to encourage waste reduction (full-cost accounting is discussed further in Section 4.4). Such an approach makes sense because large corporations are currently incurring huge costs for the cleanup of past land-disposal of toxic wastes under the joint and several liability provisions of Superfund. (The issue of liability is discussed further in Section 3.2.)

2.9 What Should the Company's Position Be Regarding Regulatory Compliance?

One option for companies is to weigh the costs of compliance with regulations against the likelihood and magnitude of penalties for noncompliance. They may then decide to operate at or near the compliance level, or well above or below minimum legal requirements. In addition, companies can act in anticipation of future requirements or in reaction to specific government requirements and deadlines. For example, with respect to programs such as Superfund that address environmental problems from the past, the company can wait to be ordered to clean up, or it can take initiatives without government intervention.

The CFC case study described in the next section illustrates a number of the features of private-sector decision making regarding environmental issues. The case illustrates some of the decisions that are made by Du Pont in regard to scientific and regulatory developments. For further details on the history and background of the CFC case, see the Appendix of this chapter.

2.10 Illustrative Case: Du Pont's CFC Decision

Du Pont is the single largest producer of CFCs, manufacturing about 25% of the 2 billion pounds generated annually worldwide (Browne, 1989). In 1987, sales of CFCs were worth $600 million to Du Pont and represented approximately 2% of the company's revenues (Shea, 1988).

On March 24, 1988, Du Pont announced its decision to phase out manufacture of CFCs over a 10-year period. This was the result of a 1974 pledge to stop manufacturing the chemicals if they were shown to be harmful to public health (Shea, 1988). The announcement came within one week of the report from the Ozone Trend Panel, which provided strong evidence linking CFCs to ozone depletion. The decision had to transcend the powerful economic incentive for the continued production of CFCs given the lucrative global market for these substances. Du Pont decided to phase out production of CFCs prior to an international agreement.

Du Pont monitored scientific and political events closely, and in the mid-1970s began a program to develop CFC substitutes. Over the years, Du Pont's investment in substitutes has fluctuated, along with the increased and decreased scientific concern about ozone depletion and the possibility of regulatory restrictions that would increase demand for the more expensive substitutes (National Wildlife Federation, 1989). Expenditures on Du Pont's research program totalled over $30 million at the time of their announcement; 1987 expenditures on CFC alternatives were in excess of $10 million. Du Pont led industry support for the Montreal Protocol, but as recently as the fall of 1987, it objected to production cuts beyond the target of 50% by 1999 (Shea, 1988).

Although the company's actions had been anticipatory from the time the ozone depletion theory was announced, J. R. Cooper, Director of Environmental Affairs at Du Pont, attributes the Spring 1988 decision to step out in front with a 10-year phase-out to having the right person in the right place at the right time (1989). A Du Pont researcher from the Freon Product Division had been invited to join one of the Antarctic expeditions; he departed a skeptic and returned convinced of the ozone-depletion problem and of its urgency. Shortly after returning from the expedition, the scientist met with the Executive Committee of the Board of Directors and presented his conclusions, and, according to Cooper, management acted. In Cooper's view, hearing the evidence from a credible industry scientist was critical to the prompt response.

Since Du Pont's decision to cut production of CFCs on an accelerated schedule, there have been several announcements by individual companies to restrict production and use of CFCs beyond the requirements of the international accord. In addition, industry groups have been addressing the CFC issue from several perspectives. For example, Du Pont, Allied-Signal, and 12 other chemical companies have pooled resources to expedite toxicology testing for CFC substitutes. Industry efforts have also been coordinated to examine the environmental effects of ozone-layer depletion (Cooper, 1989; Kurtzman, 1988).

2.11 Summary

In many cases, actions that benefit the environment also benefit worker health and safety. This is particularly true in situations where a company makes a decision to substitute less hazardous materials or reduce the amount of waste it produces. For example, process changes that capture volatile compounds or substitute water-based dyes for solvent-based dyes will expose workers to far fewer potentially harmful chemicals—though there is some question in the case of CFCs. Most of the likely CFC substitutes are expected to pose greater risks to workers and to equipment than the compounds that cause damage to the ozone layer (Browne, 1989).

Changed values, as reflected in laws, regulations, and the media, are one factor in currently acceptable decisions becoming unacceptable in the future. Another factor is increased understanding brought about by scientific research and use of increasingly sophisticated monitoring devices. Precisely this has happened in the case of industrial waste disposal. Companies are now investing enormous resources, under Superfund, in hazardous-waste cleanup of disposal sites now considered dangerous as a result of practices considered acceptable at the time disposal occurred. CFCs are another good example of environmental decisions becoming unacceptable over time. At the time CFCs were developed, they were far superior in most respects to the materials they replaced. Subsequent evidence has shown, however, that the positive attributes of CFCs in industrial applications are outweighed by the negative impact of CFCs on the upper atmosphere.

3 KEY FACTORS IN PRIVATE-SECTOR ENVIRONMENTAL DECISION MAKING

Researchers have identified several factors that may influence contemporary environmental decision making in the private sector. However, much additional work is needed before we can know with certainty which are causes, which are effects, and how to link them in an explanatory theory.

Kasperson et al. (1988) examined the field of corporate management of health and safety hazards and identified a set of variables that contribute to successful corporate hazard management. Exogenous variables, or factors external to the corporation, are regulation by government, liability and insurance costs, and public scrutiny. Endogenous variables, or factors internal to the corporation, are profitability, commitment of high-level management to the issues, and the degree of hazard associated with the product. These factors are generally presumed to be important in private-sector environmental decision making as well, but we do not know how the factors compare in importance relative to one another, nor do we know how endogenous factors compare in importance to exogenous factors. The remaining discussion in this section is a brief examination of these factors.

3.1 Government Regulation

Government regulation can influence private-sector environmental decision making by constraining the choices available, affecting the cost of various alternatives, and providing incentives for the development of environmental protection technology. For example, the Resource Conservation and Recovery Act (RCRA) resulted in performance and design standards (for the treatment and disposal of hazardous waste) that forced environmentally unsound disposal facilities out of business. The result was a shortfall in adequate treatment and disposal capacity, which in turn escalated costs for legal disposal. The federal Superfund legislation and its state counterparts increased costs to the private sector by holding companies responsible for the full cost of correcting problems that resulted from past disposal practices.

Some U.S. environmental regulatory efforts have made explicit attempts to "force" the development of new pollution-control technology. However, Novick et al. (1988) observe that the deadlines set by government in the Clean Air Act were too short for the private sector to respond with new developments; most companies faced a choice of using available technology or closing their operations.

3.2 Liability

Liability, responsibility—in this context—for environmental damage or public health consequences, is often cited by the private sector as having a profound impact on environmental decision making. The concept of liability has undergone an important transformation in the United States as a result of environmental legislation (particularly the Comprehensive Environmental Response,

Compensation, and Liability Act—also known as Superfund) and its state counterparts; and new case laws evolving in the U.S. courts.

The objective of Superfund and its state counterparts is to ensure that contributors to the creation of an environmental problem are held responsible for the
cost of cleanup and for damages. Superfund established retroactive liability,
holding companies responsible for past actions, and "joint and several liability."
Under joint and several liability, a party can be held accountable for any or all of
the cleanup costs regardless of the size of the original contribution to the
problem. For example, even if a company's waste accounted for only 10% of the
wastes disposed of at a site, the company could be required to pay up to 100% of
the cleanup costs. Provision of joint and several liability in Superfund threatens
large companies with "deep pockets," making them targets for government
agencies seeking to establish financial responsibility for waste sites.

U.S. courts also have changed the rules governing tort liability in a way that
brings potentially higher costs to industry. [In simple terms, tort liability is the
failure to act in a reasonable manner (usually with negligence that results in
personal injury) but without the intention to harm.] New tort-liability rules tend
to favor persons claiming personal injury and property damage due to company
activities over the companies themselves; the courts have replaced negligence
theory—which requires proof of unreasonable corporate behavior—with strict
liability, which does not require proving negligence. They have also eased
requirements for proving causation. In addition, juries have made very high
awards for compensatory and punitive damages (Baram, 1988).

In the past, the private sector successfully used the corporate structure to limit
liability by creating separate entities whose assets could be protected, and by
shielding the personal assets of the key corporate decision makers. One noteworthy example of this approach was the restructuring of Johns-Manville Corporation in order to deflect asbestos-related liabilities. However, increasingly,
enforcement actions by the federal government seek to hold individuals within
the company personally liable for wrongdoing (Seymour, 1989).

3.3 Insurance

Insurance became a critical issue in corporate environmental management in the
1980s. During that decade, insurance policies were interpreted more broadly
than insurers had intended when the policies were issued. This resulted in greater
exposure to insurers. For example, courts were awarding compensation for
environmental damage caused to natural resources by gradual release of pollutants even though the insurance policies were written at a time when environmental damage meant sudden, accidental releases. In addition, insurers had to share
the costs incurred by companies due to changes in liability, as discussed above.

Insurance companies were unprepared for the magnitude and increasing
frequency of environmental claims; initially, they responded by severely limiting

the kinds of insurance they were willing to sell. For a time, many firms stopped offering insurance for gradual environmental pollution. Subsequently, the insurance industry responded to market demand and began offering this type of coverage once again. However, costs to manufacturers are very high.

3.4 Public Scrutiny

Public scrutiny affects companies both indirectly and directly. First, heightened public concern about environmental degradation historically has led to the passage of legislation that tightens government oversight and control of companies' activities. In this way, public scrutiny indirectly leads to corporate action, through compliance with regulations.

Second, some companies may seek to respond directly to public scrutiny as a means of allaying public concerns and warding off or lessening the impact of future legislation. A recent study by Baram, Dillon, and Ruffle (1990) documented the initiatives of companies precipitated by the Emergency Planning and Community Right-to-Know Act of 1986 (SARA Title III), which requires companies to report annually their routine chemical emissions. The annual emissions inventories of manufacturing establishments are then made available to the public on a facility-by-facility basis and in aggregate form (e.g., by chemical and industrial sector). SARA Title III does not directly require corporate action. The Baram study found, however, that companies are taking voluntary steps to reduce routine chemical emissions because the availability of chemical-release information makes companies and their operations open to increased public scrutiny. The annual emissions inventory provides the public, as well as government officials, with a yardstick to evaluate industrial contributions to environmental degradation and to measure progress in achieving societal goals of environmental quality.

Following the passage of SARA Title III, for the first time, companies like Du Pont, Monsanto, 3M, and Polaroid are publicly announcing numerical goals for emissions reduction. For example, Polaroid Corporation, known for its instant photography products, has made a commitment to reduce toxic use and waste by 10% per year for 5 years (Polaroid Corporation, 1989). The goal at 3M Corporation is to reduce its hazardous emissions by 90% by the year 2000 (Bureau of National Affairs, 1989). Du Pont had a goal of 35% reduction of hazardous waste at the source by 1990 (Woolard, 1989). Comparing these numbers without additional data, incidentally, is not possible, because compounds, volumes, and current emissions vary across companies.

3.5 Profitability

Profitability may be an important factor in private-sector environmental decision making; however, work in progress at Tufts University's Center for Environmental Management (CEM) suggests it is profitability of the unit or facility that influences environmental decisions, not profitability of the corporation as a whole. The trend in many large corporations is to decentralize decision making, which results in variability in environmental practice across organizations. The assumption is that profitable units will do more to protect the environment, though CEM case studies have not found this universally true (Rappaport et al., 1990).

3.6 Top Management Commitment

Top management commitment means involvement and support of top corporate decision makers in environmental matters. Following the Bhopal tragedy and passage of SARA Title III, Baram, Dillon, and Ruffle (1990) found an increased commitment to environmental and facility safety issues at the highest levels within the eight companies studied. This commitment provided leadership and direction for company initiatives through such mechanisms as new corporate policies and goals for emission reduction, as noted above, and an increased availability of resources, both financial and personnel, to achieve company goals.

3.7 Degree of Hazard

Degree of hazard—not only of the product, but of the raw materials, by-products, and manufacturing processes—is yet another factor influencing private-sector environmental decision making. It is assumed that more hazardous materials will be handled more responsibly, with protection of personnel and property as important motivators. Isolated evidence exists that this is true, but a more systematic evaluation is needed to test the assumption.

3.8 Other Factors

Other factors may be important in influencing private-sector environmental decision making: for example, a legacy of serious environmental problems—either in the corporation or in the industrial sector—and corporate peer pressure.

In one study, companies consistently cited environmental incidents—internal and external—as influencing their environmental management practices (Dillon & Fischer, 1991). Following the Bhopal incident, Baram, Dillon, and Ruffle (1990) document a variety of accident-prevention initiatives undertaken by companies. These include conducting special safety evaluations of facilities and reducing chemical inventories. In another case, shortly after the *Exxon Valdez* oil spill, the oil industry announced it was forming an industry collaborative to respond to future spills (Shabecoff, 1989a). Companies respond to environmental incidents to avoid associated costs and liabilities, and to create an image of responsibility in an attempt to preclude intrusive regulation by government. In addition to tangible costs, companies are concerned with damage to the corporate image arising when such incidents as Bhopal and Love Canal become household words, symbolic of inadequate corporate environmental performance.

As part of the response to government regulations, public concern, and increased insurance and liability costs, the private sector increasingly appears to be searching for management systems and approaches that will improve environmental decision making and help avoid future problems. The anticipatory actions of corporate peers have become the subject of discussion in the private sector, and the behavior of leading companies is a factor in shaping private-sector environmental decision making. In the case of CFCs as well as emission-reduction goals following passage of SARA Title III, the decision of one company provided the catalyst for other companies to initiate similar activities.

4 CORPORATE ENVIRONMENTAL DECISION MAKING

Companies have responded to heightened public concern for environmental quality and government regulation by developing internal management systems and tools designed to guide and influence decisions that have the potential to impact the environment. In a study of 15 corporations, Dillon and Fischer (1991) found that the increase in environmental regulations in the United States was paralleled by the creation of environmental departments within companies, the elevation of the senior-most corporate environmental managers within the companies' organizational structures, and the development of corporate environmental policies.

While many advances in the structure and process for environmental decision making within companies appear promising, our research indicates that there are wide variations in the extent and quality of companies' practices. In addition, the decision-making processes and practices of seemingly progressive companies could be improved. The remainder of this section highlights progressive corporate practices. These practices could serve as a prescription for the direction in which companies should move if their activities are to benefit (or minimize the impact on) the environment and public health.

4.1 Formal and Informal Organizational Structure

Decisions with potential environmental impact are made throughout the company—by different hierarchical levels (from the facility to the boardroom) and by different functions within the company (such as production on the one hand, and research and development on the other). (See Figure 11–1 for an illustration of corporate structure.) While companies often have corporate, division, or facility

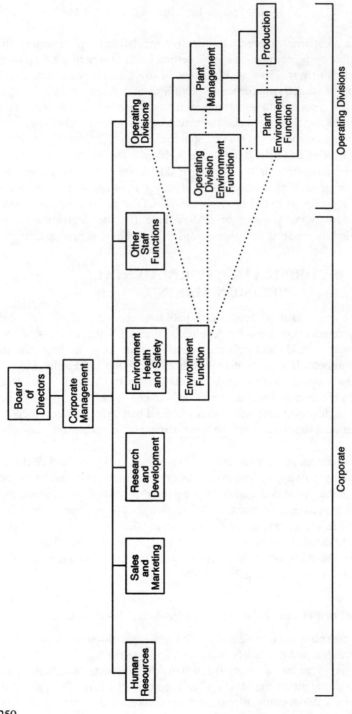

FIGURE 11-1. Organizational chart depicting the environmental functions and reporting relationships.

—— formal reporting relationship

········ staff relationship

250

environmental staff, many "environmental" decision makers are business and production managers with varying degrees of training in environmental issues. For example, decisions regarding what products to develop, what raw materials to use, and what manufacturing technology to use are made by such groups as research and development or engineering, whereas routine production decisions are made by manufacturing personnel. As seen in the CFC case, the initial recommendation that Du Pont stop manufacturing CFCs came from the business manager of the product division (National Wildlife Federation, 1989).

Increasingly, U.S. companies of all sizes have positions within corporate headquarters, divisions, and/or facilities wholly or partly dedicated to environmental management. Corporate environmental staff often develop corporation-wide environmental policies and strategies, ensure that the company's various activities are meeting internal and external environmental standards, and advise senior, business, and production management of environmental issues of interest to the company and its operations. At the facility level, the environmental manager usually provides assistance to production management in meeting internal and external environmental requirements and provides oversight of operational areas of environmental significance. The study by Baram, Dillon, and Ruffle (1990), documenting the voluntary initiatives of eight firms in response to SARA Title III, found that leadership from corporate headquarters most often provided the driving force for environmental-management initiatives at facilities.

One organizational feature of companies, the staff-line relationship, is vital to understanding environmental decision making. Since companies are in the business of providing goods and services, the chain of command, or line of authority, is from the board of directors down through the hierarchy of the organization to the units that are delivering the company's goods or services (see Figure 11–1). The role of the environmental-management function is to provide support to other units within the company; as a staff function, environmental managers do not necessarily have direct control over activities or decisions that affect the environment. In actuality, primary responsibility for compliance with environmental regulations and the costs of environmentally related expenditures (e.g., hazardous-waste disposal, pollution-control equipment) generally rests with production management because these activities are an integral part of the production operation.

Because the environmental manager lacks direct authority over other units within the company, managing through influence and enlisting the support of those who have authority and control of company activities and decisions are important (Dillon & Fischer, 1991). While gaining support for environmental decisions may occur through formal organizational mechanisms such as reporting relationships and multifunctional committees, Dillon and Fischer's study, as well as that of Petulla (1987), found that the formal organizational structure of the environmental function within the company (i.e., the functional and hierarchical level) seemed to have little bearing on the performance and quality of environmental management. Rather, the environmental managers interviewed by Dillon and Fischer cited individuals, their informal relationships, and their political and communication skills, as critical to successful environmental management. Who the environmental manager is may be more important than where this individual is located within the organization.

4.2 Environmental Policies: Setting the Stage for Decision Making

Environmental policies provide the foundation or guiding principles for environmental decision making throughout a company's operations. While companies of all sizes might have environmental policies, written environmental-policy statements are found predominantly in large companies and are developed by or in conjunction with corporate environmental staff (Lund, 1974; Dillon & Fischer, 1991).

According to a study by Little (1988), with the increased recognition of environmental hazards and the subsequent increase in laws and regulations for environmental control, environmental-policy statements of companies have evolved over the past two decades from social-responsibility statements to explicit statements of compliance with laws and regulations. More recently, some companies have gone a step further to adopt policies covering all significant environmental, health, and safety risks, whether regulated or not. It is now common for environmental-policy statements to contain implementing requirements or management directives in addition to expressing corporate intentions.

A case study of Du Pont's decision to stop manufacturing CFCs illustrates the company's environmental principles, as defined in its policy, provided the company with a firm direction for its decision-making process (National Wildlife Federation, 1989). Du Pont's company-wide policy (1985) states that the company "will determine that each product can be made, used, handled, and disposed of safely and consistent with appropriate safety, health, and environmental quality criteria." Immediately following the release of a National Aeronautics and Space Administration report that provided strong evidence linking CFCs to the destruction of the ozone layer, Du Pont implemented their policy with regard to CFCs.

Other espoused principles found in companies' environmental policies include:

- Complying with environmental, health-and-safety, and product-safety laws and regulations
- Protecting the health and safety of employees and the community
- Conserving natural resources

- Minimizing or controlling environmental pollution through proper management of wastes, design of manufacturing processes, and development of internal standards designed to protect the environment
- Going beyond compliance to reduce environmental, health, and safety risks
- Communicating about safety and health hazards to employees, customers, the public, and government bodies

In addition, policies may specifically delineate requirements for conducting environmental reviews of business decisions such as new products, capital expenditures, and manufacturing processes. Companies may also issue written policies covering specific issues such as hazardous-waste management, waste reduction, and groundwater protection.

There is a danger in assuming a company's environmental policy statements translate into its actual environmental conduct for two reasons. First, environmental policies are a reflection of a variety of company characteristics and the individuals who developed the policy; the comprehensiveness and level of specificity does not always accurately reflect the environmental record of the company (Dillon & Fischer, 1991). Second, in some companies the environmental policy may be primarily a public-relations tool, whereas in others the company may fall short of its intentions.

4.3 Management Controls

The structure and constraints of private-sector environmental decision making, as discussed above, raise an important issue: the gap between policy and implementation. The problem for companies, particularly large companies with geographic and product diversity, is how to ensure that the intentions of corporate management, as reflected in policies and programs, are implemented consistently by decision makers, given the reality that different units within an organization have different priorities. In addition, within a company some units or decision makers might perceive environmental activities as a drain on resources at the expense of profits, whereas others might see financial benefits. The following sections discuss some of the management tools and controls developed to ensure that the intentions and goals of the company as a whole are achieved.

4.3.1 Measurement of Performance Against Goals and Standards

The establishment of goals and standards, followed by the evaluation of operating units against these criteria, sends a message to decision makers that the environment is a priority; provides corporate headquarters with some control over company operations; makes operating units more accountable for their environmental actions; and helps to keep top management informed of company activities so environmental issues can be dealt with as they arise. Three types of evaluations are discussed below: environmental audits, environmental performance criteria, and numerical waste-reduction goals.

Environmental audits are periodic, systematic, and objective reviews of facility operations and practices, performed either by internal staff or by outside consultants. At a minimum, environmental audits usually evaluate and verify compliance with federal, state, and local environmental requirements as well as company requirements; they are usually followed by recommendations and actions to correct any deficiencies uncovered during the audit process. Environmental audits have grown in popularity recently. According to the U.S. Environmental Protection Agency's Environmental Auditing Policy Statement, several hundred major firms in diverse industries have environmental-auditing programs (U.S. Environmental Protection Agency, 1986). Unlike financial audits, the results of environmental audits are not made public. Rather, they are used for internal purposes.

As the Department of Defense recently acknowledged, the conflict between production goals and environmental management will be less if environmental performance is a criterion in the evaluation of business managers. According to Anshen:

> When managers see that their execution of socially responsible policies and programs is evaluated in promotion and compensation decisions, along with performance in meeting familiar profit, cost, and productivity goals, they will believe and they will be motivated. For obvious and valid reasons middle managers concentrate their attention and skill on the accomplishment of performance objectives for which they know they are held responsible. They appraise responsibility in terms of two familiar criteria. The first is what is measured, and the second is what is rewarded. (Anshen, 1980, p. 23)

The incorporation of environmental performance (e.g., 100% complying with environmental regulations; reducing the generation of waste or toxic-air emissions to achieve a company-specified goal) into the company's overall performance appraisal system reveals a tangible commitment by top management to environmental issues. Although it is not known how common this practice is, it appears to be gaining in popularity. For example, in May 1989, E. S. Woolard, the Chairman of the Board of Du Pont, announced that—as part of its corporate agenda for environmental leadership in the next decade—the company would formally incorporate environmental-performance criteria in the determination of compensation for company managers from middle management through senior officers of the company. While this is a seemingly effective mechanism, many companies are probably not willing to take such a drastic step as putting environmental performance on a par with production criteria because doing that alters the companies' priorities in very real terms.

As we mentioned earlier, in response to growing public concern over industrial emissions, companies are publicly announcing their goals to reduce waste generation and emissions. In order to achieve such goals, companies might hold individual manufacturing units responsible for a specified portion of the reduction goal. For example, if the company wants to reduce emissions by 10% over one year, it might require each manufacturing location to achieve a 10% reduction. The environmental performance of individual manufacturing units can then be measured against progress toward meeting the goal.

4.3.2 Environmental Reviews

Companies may have requirements for the environmental review of such business decisions as those concerning capital expenditures, new products, new chemicals, new processes or modification to processes, property acquisitions, or operating budgets. Dillon and Fischer (1991) found that within the 15 companies they studied, environmental considerations were most often taken into account in the capital investment decision-making process.

Capital investments include such things as building construction or modifications, equipment, new products, or property. Incorporating environmental considerations into capital-investment decisions, therefore, can cover a wide range of business activities. The environmental review of capital-investment requests can ensure that proposed projects identify environmental risks and potential financial liabilities, address environmental impact, be compatible with internal and external environmental requirements and concerns, and allot adequate funding to achieve regulatory and internal compliance.

Dillon and Fischer (1991) found that it was most common for business managers to be responsible for assessing and documenting the environmental impact of business decisions with guidance provided through checklists or manuals developed by the corporate environmental department. While many environmental managers interviewed felt that their opinions were voluntarily solicited for important matters by other departments or functions within the company, timeliness was often a problem. That is, the advice of the environmental manager might have been solicited, but only after some irreversible, perhaps costly, decisions had been made. One hypothetical example would be in the selection of a manufacturing technology. In this case, the engineering department might decide on and invest in the development of a new technology, and then consult with the environmental manager on how to handle the by-products of the process. The timing of the consultation might result in the use of pollution-control technology rather than in process recycling, an environmentally preferred alternative. Finally, Dillon and Fischer (1991) discovered that environmental managers from both large and small companies would like to see more formal procedures instituted within their companies to include environmental professionals in the review of business decisions, particularly those involving new products, new processes, and real-estate transactions.

4.4 Decision-Making Tools

In a survey of 95 companies, Nikolai, Bazley, and Brummet (1976) found that the cost of environmental activities—concentrated in traditional areas such as the cost of equipment and research and development—weighed heavily in company decision making, whereas the benefits accrued or costs avoided were largely not considered. Cost measurement also relied mostly on monetary values. The researchers stated that companies viewed the possibility of shutdown of their operations as critical, overshadowing any need to measure possible benefits. In addition, when environmental projects went into operation, the associated costs were generally integrated with typical production expenditures.

As costs of environmental management and long-term liabilities (e.g., those associated with hazardous-waste disposal and cleanup activities) have escalated, some companies are reevaluating and developing new methods and tools for economic and information analysis. New decision-making tools are necessary because environmental projects often have long-term benefits that cannot compete in a short-term, profit-oriented production environment. Furthermore, the benefits associated with environmental expenditures cannot always be measured in tangible, monetary terms (e.g., the benefits of good community and public relations).

Some large companies (such as General Electric), as well as the U.S. Environmental Protection Agency, have developed full-cost accounting methods that analyze the total cost of waste-management options, that is, both current and future costs, to help production facilities select the most cost-efficient option (General Electric Company, 1987). In addition to considering the direct cost of disposal (e.g., price per barrel to dispose of waste), full-cost accounting incorporates such factors as the cost of cleanup of a hazardous-waste site under RCRA or Superfund and claims of personal injury resulting from company actions. Through a systematic analysis of all costs, short- and long-term, these methods help decision makers realize the true cost versus benefits of environmental-management activities. They also provide a powerful tool for those trying to influence decision making.

Another example of an environmental decision tool is found at Polaroid Corporation (1989). This company developed the Environmental Accounting and Reporting System (EARS) to provide support and identify opportunities for the company's Toxic Use and Waste Reduction Program (TUWR), which began in 1988. EARS categorizes all raw materials and waste according to an assigned level of environmental risk. These categories are then used to prioritize and guide the toxic use and waste-reduction efforts at the facilities. For example, the company's TUWR Program urges the replacement of materials that pose the greatest environmental risk (Categories I and II) with less-hazardous materials, while recycling is encouraged for the three remaining categories of materials. EARS tracks toxic use and waste reduction per unit of production, providing an assessment of the company's progress toward meeting its goals.

One a more general level, Baram, Dillon, and Ruffle (1990) found that many corporate headquarters are developing new or expanding computerized information systems for environmental affairs to accomplish several objectives. These include:

Assuring regulatory compliance
Better tracking of chemical use and waste generation
Improving communication within the company and between headquarters and their facilities to ensure consistent approaches to environmental problem solving
Increasing the efficiency of data collection and regulatory reporting

4.5 Sources of Information Used by Companies

The private sector draws on information from many sources in making environmental decisions. The information sources fall into five broad categories:

- In-house expertise
- Industry trade groups and environmental organizations
- Government
- Consultants
- Universities

Each of these sources performs a mix of original research, literature review, policy analysis, and networking.

4.5.1 In-House Expertise

Depending on the size of the organization and its staffing, in-house expertise may prove to be the most valuable single source of environmental information for a company. For example, the 3M Corporation has relied extensively on its own staff to examine its manufacturing processes and identify opportunities for reducing the amount of toxicity of its waste stream. Du Pont is another example of a company whose in-house expertise is sufficiently deep that its scientists reformulate products, develop alternatives, and help modify processes to achieve environmental objectives. Corporate expertise in environmental policy and regulation is often enhanced by strategic hiring of former state and federal environmental professionals.

4.5.2 Industry Trade Groups and Environmental Organizations

Industry trade groups serve as an important mechanism for information exchange on a wide variety of technical and political issues of interest to their constituents. Groups such as the American Paper Council, the American Petroleum Institute, and the Chemical Manufacturers Association have evolved in recent years as important sources of information for their constituents on environmental matters. In the case of the Chemical Manufacturers Association (CMA), the organization has developed a set of recommended practices for members, many of which relate to the environment and anticipate state and federal regulatory programs. In some instances, trade groups can stimulate the advancement of their memberships' practices. Responsible Care, a CMA program implemented in 1989, goes beyond current regulatory requirements in many jurisdictions and its implementation is required for membership in the organization.

Industry environmental organizations also have been formed to address the challenges of helping industry meet societal goals for environmental quality and for industrial development, a concept that is called "sustainable development." Examples of industry environmental organizations include the International Chamber of Commerce's International Environment Bureau and the World Environment Center.

4.5.3 Government

Government is a rich source of information for private-sector decision making. Laws and regulations are generally the end products of a long process of information exchange among a variety of interest groups, including academics, scientists, environmentalists, other concerned citizens, various levels of government, and the private sector. The information exchanges precipitated by government action may occur in a variety of forums, including Congressional testimony, Advisory Committee meetings, public hearings, and media debates. Laws and regulations are an important source of information for the private sector, in that they articulate the goals of society with respect to environmental management, the range of acceptable practice, and the penalties for failing to perform.

4.5.4 Consultants

Consultants are used in private-sector decision making in many capacities, depending on the nature of the client company and the in-house resources available. Consultant activities cover a range that includes providing assistance in preparing environmental-impact statements for the construction of a new facility; developing corporate-management systems for very large, diverse corporations; developing and helping to implement audit programs; examining production processes; recommending changes to reduce the amount of waste produced; and preparing strategies for addressing public concerns and media questions if environmental problems occur.

4.5.5 Universities

The results of university research have always been available to the private sector through the open or unclassified literature. However, this has not historically been a very effective vehicle for provoking environmental action. Government programs through the U.S. Environmental Protection Agency, as well as the initiatives of some states, have sought to channel resources to universities. As the programs encourage research in areas such as incineration technology, waste reduction, and air-pollution control, benefits accrue to the private sector. In addition, the private sector is increasingly forming more direct relationships with universities through support of research centers and individual projects on topics related to the environment.

5 TRENDS IN CORPORATE ENVIRONMENTAL DECISION MAKING

Private-sector decisions have been affecting the environment since the beginning of the industrial revolution, though recognition of this phenomenon is recent. Responding to public concern, government regulatory actions, increased liability, and escalating costs of doing business, corporate environmental management has undergone a complete transformation in the past 20 years.

Often housed within a "facilities-management" group, private-sector environmental decision makers in the late 1960s included the person who stood on the loading dock and made arrangements for disposal of solid industrial process waste; the design engineer who made decisions about process controls and pollution-abatement technology; and the person who explained to neighbors why the effluent being discharged to the nearby river occasionally smelled bad, killed fish, or had vivid colors. Now, the key environmental decision maker in many Fortune 500 companies holds the title of Vice President, and, in some cases, a corporate Board of Directors has a separate committee on environmental matters. In the corporate world, these are strong indicators that environmental decision making is being treated seriously and is becoming an important part of doing business.

Resources in some companies are devoted primarily to reacting to environmental problems of the past, such as Superfund sites, or simply to complying with the complex and growing body of government regulations. Other companies, such as Du Pont, have positioned themselves so that they can anticipate changes in the political and regulatory climate. There are no reliable indices for predicting which companies will exhibit anticipatory behavior. In fact, in the large, highly diversified companies that dominate U.S. business, different business groups or divisions within a company may have vastly different environmental performance records. In these cases, the key challenge for the top corporate environmental decision maker is to resolve discrepancies in practice that occur among decentralized units.

In a field that is young and changing rapidly, it is risky to take the slim body of data and draw conclusions about trends in the making. This chapter concludes by raising key questions about the directions that private-sector environmental decision making might take in the near future.

5.1 Are Companies Increasingly Taking Responsible Environmental Actions Even in the Absence of Clear Regulatory Pressure?

Du Pont's decision to phase out manufacture of CFCs over a 10-year period beginning in 1988 is one example of a company's taking responsible environmental actions in the absense of regulatory pressure. There are others. Recently, the American Telephone and Telegraph Company (AT&T) announced it would end the use of CFCs on a schedule considerably faster than that required by international treaty. AT&T plans to cut consumption of CFCs 50% by 1991, and eliminate consumption by 1994; international accords call for a 50% reduction in production and use by 2000. Both Northern Telecom of Canada and Seiko Epson of Japan have set 1991 as the dates by which they will eliminate use of CFCs (Shabecoff, 1989b). In addition, several companies (including Monsanto, Polaroid, and 3M) have voluntarily made public commitments to reduce dramatically emissions of a wide variety of toxic compounds. These actions are laudable and responsible; but it would be hasty to conclude from these few examples that industry collectively has turned a corner and is uniformly ahead of government on environmental issues.

Press accounts of the 1989 *Exxon Valdez* oil spill in Prince William Sound, Alaska, suggest that Exxon's response was slow, inept, and legalistic even in a situation where corporate visibility and public concern were high. With this dramatic evidence that there is room for improvement, one must assume that government action will continue to play an important role in private-sector environmental decision making.

5.2 What Private-Sector Changes are Needed for Sustainable Development?

The World Commission on Environment and Development describes sustainable development as development that

> . . . meets the needs of the present without compromising the ability of future generations to meet their own needs. the concept of sustainable development does imply limits—not absolute limits but limitations imposed by the present state of technology and social organization on environmental resources and by the ability of the biosphere to absorb the effects of human activities (World Commission on Environment and Development, 1987, p. 8).

The Commission itself, the United Nations Environment Programme, and the United Nations Center for Transnational Corporations have all suggested industry actions that they believe would contribute to sustainable development. Included among them are conducting environmental audits and sharing data with host-country governments, implementing low-waste and nonwaste technology in production processes, and supporting educational programs to build capacity for environmental regulators in developing countries. There is broad support for some of these activities, and qualified support or divergence of opinion on others.

At a fundamental level, however, the key change required of industry to support sustainable development and improve environmental management is a shift from short- to long-term planning horizons. Interestingly, the same shift to the long term is a key prescription of Dertouzos, Lester, and Solow (1989) for the MIT Commission on Industrial Productivity, which studied ways to improve the United State's competitive position. With the same message coming from a variety of directions, it is possible that changes in private-sector planning horizons will occur. Whether these changes produce significant improvements in private-sector environmental decision making remains to be seen.

6 APPENDIX. A CASE STUDY: GLOBAL CFC REDUCTION

When chlorofluorocarbons (CFCs) were developed in the 1930s, they were considered "wonder chemicals" by industrial and chemical engineers. Because they are nontoxic, nonflammable, and chemically stable, CFCs became widely used as refrigerants, replacing toxic and explosive or flammable materials such as methylene chloride, ammonia, and sulfur dioxide (Rand Corporation, 1986). Since their invention, CFCs have been used in an increasing number of residential, commercial, and industrial applications.

In 1974, approximately 40 years after CFCs were invented, two scientists at the University of California at Irvine published a theory linking CFCs to stratospheric ozone loss (Molina & Rowland, 1974). The scientists hypothesized that CFCs were so chemically stable that they did not break down in the lower atmosphere, but migrated to the upper atmosphere where they served as catalysts for the destruction of the ozone. One CFC molecule, the scientists argued, could destroy thousands of ozone molecules. This theory shocked the world, not only because ozone loss has extremely serious health and environmental implications, but because CFCs were so widely used. The same year that the CFC/ozone theory was first published, United States production of CFCs topped 1 billion pounds (ICF, Inc., 1986); more than 3 billion aerosol spray cans containing CFC propellants were manufactured and sold in the United States alone (Houk, 1988).

The scientific evidence is accumulating that stratospheric ozone is decreasing and that CFCs are a major cause of this loss. Recent research has also implicated CFCs in the global-warming phenomenon, another human-made effect with potentially dire health and environmental consequences. This case briefly examines issues relating to CFCs and ozone-layer destruction with respect to the scientific environment, government response to the scientific data, and responses by industry—particularly Du Pont, a key manufacturer of CFCs.

6.1 Background and Uses of CFCs

Chlorofluorocarbons are synthetic chemicals. Chemical engineers have developed hundreds of compounds that fall under the CFC classification and these compounds have been put to scores of uses. Five CFC compounds are considered to be the msot significant causes of ozone depletion: CFCs-11, -12, -113, -114, and -115. These five chemical constitute more than 90% of the CFCs manufactured in the United States (Browne, 1989).

CFCs are used as refrigerants in many systems, including refrigerators and freezers, cooling systems for buildings, and automobile air conditioners. Another major use of CFCs is as blowing agents for rigid and flexible foams. (Rigid foams are used for insulation in building construction; residential and commercial refrigerators, and refrigerated trucks and railroad cars; and for packaging material such as egg cartons, meat trays, plates, and food containers. Flexible foams are widely used in furniture, bedding, carpet underlay, automobile seats and dashboards, and packaging.) One CFC compound is used extensively as a solvent, primarily in the electronics industry and to a lesser extent in dry cleaning and other applications, because it is compatible with virtually all materials. The five most ozone-depleting CFCs are also used in sterilizing, with hospital and industry applications, and in a rapid food-freezing process developed by Du Pont (Rand Corporation, 1986).

Because CFCs are nontoxic, engineers and designers have not developed controls to prevent or limit CFC emissions into the environment. Aerosol cans that use CFC propellants emit the compounds directly into the environment. When flexible foams are manufactured, CFCs escape from the product within a matter of hours or days (Rand Corporation, 1986). CFCs are also released into the environment from refrigerators, cooling systems, and automobile air conditioners when these pieces of equipment leak, are repaired, and disposed of. Environmental releases also occur when CFCs are used as solvents in industrial and commercial applications.

The current annual dollar value of the CFC market in the United States is $750 million. Although "nonessential" uses of CFC aerosol propellants were banned in the United States in 1978, expanded nonaerosol uses of CFCs have boosted CFC production 5% a year since 1983 (Chlorofluorocarbons, 1988). Chemical-industry production data published by *Chemical and Engineering News* (1989) noted that CFC production "soared" in 1988.

Use of CFCs is not uniform throughout the world (see Table 11–1). In fact, when use is expressed on a per-capita basis, it becomes apparent that Americans consume six times the world average. Such disparities in use and implied benefit complicate efforts at negotiating global production decreases. In the absence of limitations, CFC use is expected to grow dramatically as developing nations increase their demand for products enjoyed for so many years in the West.

6.2 Scientific Issues

Simply put, ozone in the upper reaches of the atmosphere (the stratosphere) benefits living things by preventing harmful solar ultraviolet radiation from reaching the surface of the Earth; an abundance of the same ozone in the lower atmosphere (the troposphere) can lead to smog-induced eye irritation, impaired lung function, and damage to trees and crops. As with any atmospheric system, the levels of both stratospheric and tropospheric ozone seem to be in flux. What is clear is that levels of ozone near the surface of the Earth are rising, largely due to human activities (including the production of oxides of nitrogen and hydrocarbons from motor-vehicle exhaust). Raised levels of ozone (four to ten times higher than background levels) are routinely recorded in many industrialized areas. Ozone in other less-industrialized areas of the world is typically liberated through the open burning of grasslands.

The change in upper-level or stratospheric ozone is still under intense scrutiny, but recent evidence shows that the most dramatic depletion has occurred over Antarctica, as indicated by the celebrated "ozone hole." In the past 20 years depletion of from 2% to 10% have occurred in the middle-to-high latitudes of the Northern Hemisphere, with the greatest declines in the higher latitudes (Graedel & Crutzen, 1989). Reductions in the stratospheric ozone could have far-reaching implications, including increased incidence of skin cancer and cataracts in humans (Leaf, 1989).

The very properties that allow CFCs to have many industrial applications and

TABLE 11–1   Global CFC Use, by Region, 1986

Region	Share of Total
United States	29%
Other industrial countries[a]	41%
Soviet Union, Eastern Bloc	14%
Other developing countries	14%
China and India	2%

[a]European Community accounts for more than half, followed by Japan, Canada, Australia, and others.

Source: Shea, Cynthia Pollack. 1989. Protecting the ozone layer. In *State of the World 1989*, ed. L. Brown. p. 87. New York: W. W. Norton.

uses also provide them with tenacious environmental properties; they can reach the stratosphere unchanged. Here they may enter into a process of transformation fueled by the abundant stores of solar ultraviolet radiation available in the thin atmosphere. Chlorine atoms, liberated from the CFCs, act as a catalyst with ozone to form molecular oxygen. Since catalysts cause chemical reactions to accelerate without being consumed themselves, each chlorine atom available in the stratosphere can eliminate many thousands of ozone molecules.

The level of stratospheric ozone over Antarctica has been studied by the British Antarctic Survey since 1957. Researchers finally noted decreases in ozone, beginning in 1982 (Farman, 1987). Successive sampling studies were conducted in 1987 by an array of governmental agencies including the British Meteorological Office, the United States National Oceanic and Atmospheric Administration (NOAA), and the National Science Foundation (NSF), and by companies producing CFCs, under the auspices of the U.S. Chemical Manufacturers Association.

The Ozone Trends Panel, an interagency body formed by the U.S. National Aeronautics and Space Administration (NASA) in conjunction with the Federal Aeronautics Administration (FAA), the World Meteorological Organization (WMO), and the United Nations Environmental Programme (UNEP), attempted to provide explanations for some of these disquieting trends. In March 1988, the Panel concluded in its report that protective stratospheric ozone has decreased and that the evidence strongly indicates that CFCs are primarily responsible (Kerr, 1988). The Panel's finding was consistent with speculation voiced by Molina and Rowland as early as 1974 about the role of CFCs; it was further buttressed when experiments conducted in the upper atmosphere revealed highly elevated levels of chlorine monoxide. Many researchers consider discovery of chlorine monoxide a "smoking gun" in the case, as they endeavor to show that the CFCs are the cause of ozone depletion (Zurer, 1988).

6.3 Government Response

Regulatory responses to CFCs began on an application-specific basis. Spurred on by the suggestive data linking CFCs to ozone destruction, the United States in 1976 banned nonessential aerosol propellants made of CFCs. A variety of regulatory agencies (Food and Drug Administration, Environmental Protection Agency, and the Consumer Product Safety Commission) cooperated in this regulatory activity.

Partially as a result of the growing body of scientific data, international attention focused on control strategies directed at CFCs. The Montreal Protocol on Substances that Deplete the Ozone Layer has 24 signatories, including the European Economic Community. This protocol froze CFCs at 1986 levels on July 1, 1989. Later cuts will reduce CFC consumption, first by 20% in mid-

1993, and then by an additional 30% in mid-1999. [Consumption of halons (bromine containing fluorocarbons implicated in ozone destruction), carbon tetrachloride, methyl chloroform, and other ozone depleters will also be restricted.] Frank concerns exist about whether the management interventions taken in the Montreal Protocol go far enough. As of the summer of 1990, there is a general agreement to phase out all CFCs in industrial countries by the year 2000, and a fund has been developed to help developing countries make the transition.

Unanimity regarding the ozone-trend data did not exist until recently. The Chemical Manufacturers Association, represented by 19 CFC producers undertook an independent review of the raw-trend data. Du Pont participated directly in some of the data gathering. This participation served as a stimulus for the company's decision to cease production of CFCs by the year 2000.

EXERCISES

1. In June 1989, Uniroyal, the producer of daminozide (trade name: alar), a chemical used on apples, announced that it would halt U.S. sales even though the chemical is safe. What were the important elements underlying this corporate decision? Do you agree with the decision? Examine contemporary newspaper accounts of the events leading up to Uniroyal's announcement, and determine which agencies and public-interest groups had a stake in the decision, and indicate which you think had the greatest influence on the company, and why.

2. With growing interest among consumers in environmentally friendly products, and increasing expenditures by government and corporations to clean up various forms of pollution, the environment is a potential money-maker. If you were a consultant in industry, what priorities would you identify for environmental programs? What basic guidance would you give to companies in order to have environmentally sound operations?

3. Proposals have been made to include environmentalists on the boards of directors of corporations. In your view, will this enhance corporate environmental performance? If you were an environmentalist placed on the board of directors, what types of decisions would you try to influence? If you were a corporate business manager, what would you see as the positive and negative aspects of having an environmentalist on the board?

ADDITIONAL READING

For a detailed analysis of accident prevention, emission reduction, emergency response, and public outreach and risk communication, see Baram, Dillon, and Ruffle (1990). This report examines the voluntary initiatives of eight companies in response to Bhopal and the information-disclosure requirements of the Superfund Amendments and Reauthorization Act of 1986.

For some useful context for corporate environmental decision making and a presentation of Occidental Petroleum's management system, see Friedman (1988). For information on the issues surrounding environmental performance of multinational corporations in the various countries in which they operate, see UNCTC (1985). This document also contains extensive references.

For papers and case studies on diverse topics, including natural-resource management, pollution havens, hazardous exports, workplace health, and Bhopal, see Pearson (1987). For background information on multinational corporations and the environment and an examination of the practices of five U.S.-based multinational corporations in Mexico, Brazil, Canada, and France, see Rappaport et al. (1990).

REFERENCES

Anshen, M. 1980. *Corporate Strategies for Social Performance*. New York: Macmillan.

Authur D. Little. 1988. *Environmental Health and Safety Policies: Current Practices and Future Trends*, Cambridge, MA: Authur D. Little.

Baram, M. 1988. *Corporate Risk Management: Industrial Responsibility for Risk Communication in the European Community and the United States*. Brussels-Luxembourg: Commission of European Communities, EUR 11555EN.

Baram, M., P. Dillon, & B. Ruffle. 1990. *Managing Chemical Risks: Corporate Response to SARA Title III*. Medford, MA: Center for Environmental Management, Tufts University.

Browne, M. W. 1989. In protecting the atmosphere, choices are costly and complex. *New York Times,* March 7.

Bureau of National Affairs. 1989. Focus on industry. *Right-to-Know Planning Guide* 2(22):3.

Chlorofluorocarbons: a valuable chemical threatens the environment. 1988. *Health and Environment Digest* 2(4):1–6.

Cooper, J. R. 1989. CFCs—Du Pont's research and implications for the future. Lecture delivered at Tufts University, April 21.

Dertouzos, M. L., R. K. Lester, R. M. Solow. 1989. *Made in America: Regaining the Productive Edge*. Cambridge, MA: MIT Press.

Dillon, P. & K. Fischer. 1991. *Environmental Management in Corporations: Methods and Motivations*. Medford, MA: Center for Environmental Management, Tufts University.

Elkington, J. 1989. New boom area predicted. *Financial Times* April 21.

Facts and figures for the chemical industry. 1989. *Chemical and Engineering News* 67(25):36–90.

Farman, J. 1987. What hope for the ozone layer now? *New Scientist,* November 12: 50–54.

Friedman, F. B. 1988. *Practical Guide to Environmental Management*. Washington, DC: Environmental Law Institute.

General Electric Company. 1987. *Financial Analyses of Waste Management Alternatives*. Fairfield, CT: GE Corporate Environmental Programs.

Graedel, T. E. & P. J. Crutzen. 1989. The changing atmosphere. *Scientific American* 261(3):58–68.

Hirschhorn, J. S. 1988. Cutting production of hazardous waste. *Technology Review* 91(3):52.

Houk, Vernon N. 1988. The sky—or at least part of it—is falling. *Health and Environment Digest* 2(4):6–7.

ICF, Inc. 1987. Scenarios of CFC use: 1985–2075. In U.S. EPA, Office of Air and Radiation, December. *Projecting Production of Ozone Depleting Substances: Volume VI of Technical Support Documentation for Assessing the Risks of Trace Gases That Can Modify the Stratosphere*. Washington, DC: U.S. EPA.

Kasperson, R., et al. 1988. *Corporate Management of Health and Safety Hazards: A Comparison of Current Practice*. Boulder, CO: Westview Press.

Kerr, R. A. 1988. Stratospheric ozone is decreasing. *Science* 239:1489–1491.

Kurtzman, J. 1988. The race to commercialize substitutes. *New York Times*, April 10.

Leaf, A. 1989. Potential health effects of global climatic and environmental changes. *New England Journal of Medicine* 321(23):1577–1583.

Lund, L. 1974. *Corporate Organization for Environmental Policymaking*. Report No. 618. New York: The Conference Board, Inc.

Molina, M. J. & F. S. Rowland. 1974. Stratospheric sink for chlorofluoromethanes: chlorine atom catalyzed destruction of ozone. *Nature* 249:810–812.

National Wildlife Federation. 1989. *Du Pont Freon Products Division*. Washington, DC: National Wildlife Federation.

Nikolai, L. A., J. Bazley, & R. L. Brummet. 1976. *The Measurement of Corporate Environmental Activity*. New York: National Association of Accountants.

Novick, S. M., D. W. Stever, & M. G. Mellon. (Eds.). 1988. *Law of Environmental Protection*. New York: Clark Boardman.

Pearson, C. S. (Ed.). 1987. *Multinational Corporations, Environment, and the Third World: Business Matters*. Durham, NC: Duke University Press.

Petulla, J. 1987. Environmental management in industry. *Journal of Professional Issues in Engineering* 113:167–183.

Polaroid Corporation. 1989. *A Report on the Environment*. Cambridge, MA: Polaroid Corporation.

Rand Corporation. 1987. Product uses and market trends for potential ozone depleting substances. In U.S. EPA, Office of Air and Radiation, December. *Projecting Production of Ozone Depleting Substances: Volume VI of Technical Support Documentation for Assessing the Risks of Trace Gases That Can Modify the Stratosphere*. Washington, DC: U.S. EPA.

Rappaport et al. 1990. *Global Corporate Environmental, Health and Safety Programs: Management Principles and Practices*. Draft. Medford, MA: Center for Environmental Management, Tufts University.

Seymour, J. F. 1989. Civil and criminal liability of corporate officers under federal environmental laws. *Environment Reporter* 20(6):337–348.

Shabecoff, P. 1989a. Oil companies create program to fight spills. *New York Times*, June 21.

Shabecoff, P. 1989b. AT&T barring chemicals depleting the earth's ozone. *New York Times*, August 12.

Shea, C. P. 1988. The chlorofluorocarbon dispute: Why Du Pont gave up $600 million. *New York Times*, April 10.

Shea, C. P. 1989. Protecting the ozone layer. In *State of the World 1989*, ed. L. Brown. New York: W. W. Norton.

UNCTC. (United Nations Center on Transnational Corporations). 1985. *Environmental Aspects of the Activities of Transnational Corporations: A Survey*. ST/CTC/55 UN Pub. Sales No. E.85.II.A.11.

U.S. Environmental Protection Agency. 1983. *Report to Congress on the Progress of Regulation to Protect Stratosphere Ozone*, April.

U.S. Environmental Protection Agency. 1986. Environmental auditing policy statement. *Federal Register* 51(196):25004–25010.

Woolard, E. S. 1989. Corporate environmentalism. Remarks before the American Chamber of Commerce, London.

World Commission on Environment and Development. 1987. *Our Common Future*. New York: Oxford University Press.

Zurer, P. S. 1988. Studies on ozone destruction expand beyond Antarctic. *Chemical and Engineering News* 66(22):16–25.

12

International Environmental Decision Making: Challenges and Changes for the Old Order

William R. Moomaw and Judith T. Kildow

1 INTRODUCTION

For the past several decades, we have witnessed a series of events that result from systemic failures in our society. The failures represent incremental breakdowns over long periods of time that went unnoticed until they reached thresholds that triggered massive dislocations as they became visible. These catastrophic events represent the synergistic consequences of many poor decisions made in isolation throughout complex organizations so that no one person could perceive the potential risks of the sum of these decisions. The list of these events is long and includes the spectacular shipping accidents of the *Torrey Canyon* and the *Exxon Valdez,* the nuclear accidents at Three Mile Island and Chernobyl, and the chemical-plant accident at Bhopal. It also includes the Minamata Bay mercury poisoning, Love Canal, and many more failures that resulted in catastrophes for human health and ecological systems. These systemic breakdowns have the common element mentioned above: the inability of people to understand the complexities of the systems in operation.

Current problems evolved gradually, with still inadequate evidence to meet the standards set by our policy machinery. These standards demand that we know something with certainty, and they therefore press us to respond to crises instead of anticipating or preventing them. In the ozone-depletion and global-warming cases, such standards could push us to a precipice that leaves little room for response and creates massive dislocations by the time we have the certainty required by the policymaking mechanisms. While earlier incidents had major, but local and limited, consequences, these two evolving problems have global consequences and potentially devastating impacts on some regions of the planet.

Until recently, we in the Western industrialized societies have lived in a world

269

where the traditional framework within which we perceive and act has become out of phase with contemporary life. The pace and intensity of change in our society has shifted the parameters within which we must make our decisions, although the assumptions and perceptions upon which decisions are made remain much the same as in the past. The consequence of using antiquated political machinery is a painful, controversial, conflict-ridden international political system that is almost unable to respond effectively to international environmental problems.

The qualities, characteristics, and institutional infrastructure—the machinery of the system that generates international decisions—have begun to shift during the past several decades, particularly in response to the above-mentioned global environmental challenges. The system continues to change as scientific evidence of ecological and economic linkages demonstrates the expanding interdependencies among the peoples of the planet. Furthermore, fundamental assumptions and institutional infrastructures are now being questioned because of the perceived need to make more timely decisions. Meanwhile, the issues are becoming increasingly complex and include more nations and peoples all the time. Uncertainties abound.

There are two main purposes of this chapter. The first is to outline the conditions dictating and the qualities inherent in the international decision-making paradigm as it was before enormous, new, environmental problems confronted the system. The second is to sketch out the emerging paradigm under which we are attempting to meet these new challenges. We will compare the old paradigm with the new in terms of the key factors that represent the changes underway. Moreover, we will incorporate some fundamental influences on the dynamics and policy outcomes of the international system for decision making into a multitiered model of filters to demonstrate where the changes are taking place. We will describe some of the specific institutional changes that have been brought about by the demands of the issues (like ozone depletion and greenhouse gases), including the increase in the numbers of actors and their ever-greater influences on the outcomes of the decision process. These new actors, such as nongovernmental public-interest groups and multinational corporations, play dominating roles previously played by nation-states. For, confounded by limitations of the old paradigm, nation-states—crippled by inertia and risk aversion—are unable to maintain their role as lead agents. New organizations are, in fact, filling the void.

2 THE OLD PARADIGM AND THE NEW

Several characteristics of the new environmental challenges compel changes from traditional coping mechanisms to new ones. We will explore six of them.

2.1 High Degrees of Uncertainty
for Long Periods of Time

The political system has attempted to force standards of evidence that may be inappropriate for emerging problems. If, for example, high certainty is required for taking action, it may take too long for us to act effectively. Sometimes problems intensify quickly, forcing quick fixes that are likely to cause dislocations—economically, ecologically, and politically. This, then, precludes broad systemic changes over longer periods of adjustment time. It should be pointed out that the same high standards of evidence regarding the probability of an event's occurring in the environmental arena have not been applied to defense issues, where governments have made decisions to spend enormous amounts of money on weapons for an occurrence that actually had very low probability (like a Soviet or American nuclear attack). This insurance policy has been called a deterrent and was believed to be necessary for survival. Could not the same relaxed evidence standards be used in environmental issues? The debate about how much we need to know before we act has become a heated one in environmental decision making.

2.2 Complex Interrelationships of Numerous
Variables

Interrelationships are so numerous that they confound the decision-making system, paralyzing its movement toward a resolution. The old system did not require knowledge of all linkages; simpler, segmented problems were handled more easily. Human systems and natural systems were considered separately, and decisions were focused on satisfying the needs of humans, disregarding the impacts of anthropomorphic activities on natural systems. Integrating the two systems requires major ideological shifts. It also requires a far more sophisticated mode of analysis for decision making than we have used in the past.

2.3 Time Constraints

Time has become of the essence in some instances, as, for example, in the case of ozone depletion. Old procedures included convening meetings over long time periods to negotiate treaties. For example, the Third United Nations Law of the Sea negotiations lasted for 10 years, for a law that was meant to be valid for many more years. Such procedures are no longer relevant for two reasons. First, the numbers of nations (160+) have multiplied threefold since 1950 and present an enormous obstacle to completing a concrete, inflexible type of agreement. Second, data and situations change so rapidly now that agreements are quickly outdated; they must have flexibility built into them to accommodate the changes. The Montreal Protocol (discussed below) is a good example of an emerging process that should facilitate progress toward ever better solutions.

2.4 Shrinking Distances

Impacts of laws used to be national; now they are global. Nations have to consider the external effects of their behavior. Also, both information (thanks to modern communications) and people (thanks to modern transportation) flow more rapidly across large distances. This "shrinking" of distances permits new procedures for reaching agreement.

2.5 Scope

In the past, environmental challenges had boundaries and limits. In the case of present challenges, the breadth and depth of potential impacts and the numbers of people affected are profound and all-encompassing. We are now dealing with problems that truly have global environmental impact.

2.6 Cultural Relativity

Once it becomes apparent that the global community is responsible for and harmed by detrimental activities, the perspectives of many nations with different cultural traditions, economic standards, and political ideologies come into play. Industrial societies and developing societies may have different values, but all need to be considered, because all are affected.

3 EMERGING NEEDS FOR CHANGE

Other types of interdependencies and international networks have emerged to influence the international decision-making system. Science, during the past several decades, has produced evidence that the actions of peoples in one part of the world can affect people far away. The expansion in time, space, and intensity of the effects of human activities on natural systems beyond national boundaries has challenged the old coping methods. Discoveries about the effects of acid rain, greenhouse gases, and ozone-depleting substances have compelled shifts in international decision making. In the old paradigm, nations could behave without regard for external effects in other parts of the world. In general, fragmented and reductionist thinking has traditionally impeded the capacity of industrialized nations to see relations between components of the system.

The traditional system of diplomacy is not suitable for handling contemporary international environmental problems. Rapid population growth, coupled with increasing consumptive habits, the growing intensity of human impact on the environment, and heightened technological capacity to identify environmental consequences of human actions (such as remote sensing from space and laser-beam technology under the oceans) has forced nations to cooperate in crafting a new, international environmental decision-making model.

4 THE NEW INTERNATIONAL MODEL

The international environmental decision-making system can be depicted as a many-tiered process. Future generations and cultures distant from major power centers are among the losers in this process. Each tier, or filter, through which decisions pass entails discounting of value at each level. Options are narrowed as the devaluation continues, until the process is complete.

Cultural influences like religion, national traditions (customs), and proper interpersonal behavior (mores), which contribute to the cultural biases that influence decisions of peoples and nations, constitute one tier. Economic factors representing a range of economic conditions, which influence perspectives of what should be, make up a second. For example, the need to calculate monetary value in order to apply cost/benefit assessments often overwhelms less quantifiable quality-of-life elements; the decision system under the old paradigm always preferred the certain, the concrete, the predictable, the quantifiable.

Technological limitations that might preclude certain options because of lack of expertise, or because of time constraints, are the third tier. Technology is a very political phenomenon; investments in it reflect values and ideologies, interests, and power balances. For example, the dependence on burning fossil fuels that threatens the warming of our planet has, in large part, been determined by decisions of powerful nations not to invest in alternative-fuel technologies. These investment decisions often reflect the problems inherent in the old paradigm, where investments were made only when an impending crisis forced them or the opportunity to make large profits from an identified market encouraged them. Except in the case of military spending, as mentioned previously, investments in technology, as an insurance policy, are rare.

A further narrowing takes place through what might be considered a fourth filter: an understanding that some things are intractable and not open for discussion and negotiation. For example, it is not reasonable to expect Indian authorities to change their policy in order to reduce the number of cows in an effort to reduce methane produced by the animals through flatulence. The automobile as a form of transportation, particularly in the industrialized world, is probably not negotiable either. However, the use of noncarbon fuels for autos is open for discussion. Thus, we must recognize, and realistically proceed in accordance with, which options are tractable and which are not.

A final filter in this process might occur when strong military, economic, and political forces further control which issues are discussed. In recent years, new units of power have been playing more important roles. Multinational corporations (MNCs), through their economic strength (some have higher revenues than some nations), and nongovernmental organizations (NGOs), such as the many public-interest groups that influence the dissemination of information, now exercise unprecedented power in pushing nations toward international environmental-policy responses. As the inertia characterizing nation-state decision making prevails, these growing forces in the international system are filling the void.

5 FOUNDATIONS FOR THE NEW MODEL

The global ecosystem is now understood to operate through the complex interaction of many different species with their abiotic environment. As human beings, through their activities, appropriate a larger share of the Earth's resources for their own use, first local, and now global, ecosystems are being altered in unprecedented ways.

It is now reasonable to ask whether human actions, amplified by a rapidly growing population and ever-more-powerful technologies, are jeopardizing the natural processes that provide us and other species with the essential goods and services that have evolved over millions of years. It is equally important to determine whether existing institutions are capable of integrating the complexities of natural ecosystems into the decision-making process, as society tries to respond to regional and global threats such as transboundary air pollution, stratospheric ozone depletion, and the greenhouse effect. The process is analogous to the successive stages that occur when a natural ecosystem is altered and new species, with differing relationships, move in to fill specific needs no longer being met in the altered environment. We refer to this altered-policy development process as the "new ecology" of environmental decision making.

The old system of decision making no longer matches the new reality of transboundary and global environmental problems. What has arisen in response to this situation is a plethora of official and unofficial intergovernmental mechanisms and a new set of nongovernmental actors who have not previously played important roles. Active participation by NGOs, MNCs, and private volunteer organizations (PVOs), along with independent scientists and grass-roots action groups, represents a whole new strategy. The goal is a remedy for the inability of traditional mechanisms to respond. How rich the ecology of international environmental decision making is may be appreciated by even a superficial look at the many niches, ranging from scientific and economic analysis to direct implementation, filled by NGOs and PVOs. There is an interesting correspondence between the role played by the grass-roots movement in international environmental decision making and the role played by the primary producers of the natural ecosystem in feeding the system.

While the new method of operation is a good deal less tidy and controllable than the system it is replacing, it does provide for greater flexibility and responsiveness. As in natural ecosystems, there is less overt coordination of the process, but more suppleness. At least in the initial phases of addressing issues of global change, it has been possible to innovate and test various response strategies in a manner that is often not permitted by the more rigid prescriptions of agreements negotiated by nation-states. At some point, however, nation-states and international structures must play a role in order to ensure worldwide political compliance. How that process will unfold remains to be seen, but at this point it is clear that the successive processes now under way are leading to new procedures for addressing transboundary and global issues.

6 ENVIRONMENTAL ISSUES THAT CHALLENGE THE OLD ORDER

As indicated earlier, human activity has expanded to the point that resource use and pollution problems are no longer merely national or bilateral issues. The increased use of oceans, seas, underground repositories, and the atmosphere as a sink for the effluents of industrialized societies has created problems for everyone. The issues of the so-called commons, in which a critical natural resource or service is available to each nation, but is the direct responsibility of no one, pose an unprecedented challenge to the old diplomatic order. First, these issues by their very nature require agreement among a large number of nations (sometimes the entire family of nations), yet traditional power relationships based on military or economic concerns may be significantly different in the global environmental context. Global environmental issues tend to emphasize dramatically differing concerns and agendas between groups of nations, for example, between industrializing and industrialized countries. Second, there is an unprecedented amount of scientific content to these issues that often conflicts with the perceived economic and political interests of individual nations or blocks of nations. Third, just as the issues themselves may be global in nature, there are global organizations and institutions whose interests transcend traditional national interests. In the following case, we describe several of the environmental issues that have created the need for new instruments for international environmental decision making.

Perhaps the first attempt to address a truly global environmental and resource issue was made at the Third United Nations Law of the Sea (LOS) conference, which convened in December 1972. This meeting took place shortly after the 1972 World Conference on the Human Environment in Stockholm, which was largely responsible for the creation of the United Nations Environment Programme (UNEP). Called originally to address the problems of increased competition for the fishery and seabed resources of the world's oceans, the LOS conference provided the opportunity for nations to incorporate mutually agreeable elements of traditional navigation issues—national commercial zones and environmental protection of the ocean and its resources from pollution—into their national codes and behavior. While the proceedings began with the notion that the oceans and their resources were the "common heritage of mankind," the formal treaty text represented more of an accommodation to the economic interests of coastal nations. The approach was largely within the multilateral diplomatic tradition and was driven primarily by a desire to address the issues surrounding commercial marine resources. However, for the first time, NGOs played a facilitating role, and technical assistance from university researchers was explicitly utilized.

The final treaty text was to be a comprehensive document, a fixed set of agreements with specific rules covering every topic considered by the signatory nations. In the end, only seabed mining of metal-rich nodules remained within the realm of the "common heritage" notion, and even that proved to be too controversial for the United States (and other nations with major investments in mining technologies) to deal with. The majority of nations has never ratified the treaty, which has, therefore, never officially gone into effect. Despite the formal failure of this negotiating process, many of the issues addressed in the LOS were handled according with customary international practice, and several of the unresolved issues that arose then are likely to resurface in future discussions of issues like global climate change.

More immediately threatened than the oceans have been regional seas such as the Mediterranean and Baltic, surrounded by several nations, each of which has been polluting the common resource. Learning from the Law of the Sea problems, negotiators developed more flexible instruments that were capable of evolving as additional scientific information became available. Incorporating new scientific data became an important precedent because the practice recognized the continuing role of science in technical environmental issues and regularized the participation of a whole new class of actors in the international diplomatic process. Similarly, the agreements to address transboundary air pollution by sulfur and nitrogen oxides, developed by the Economic Commission for Europe (ECE), were based on computer models developed by the International Institute for Applied Systems Analysis (IIASA). These models, and the expertise of their developers, were used throughout the negotiations to determine the origins of pollutants and their consequences for other nations, as well as to generate a least-cost strategy for reducing the damage. Similar agreements in North America are still pending between the United States and Canada, who were both participants in the ECE proceedings (although the United States failed to join in the sulfur-dioxide agreement).

Two global atmospheric issues—depletion of the stratospheric ozone layer and global climate change—represent a new level of attempted international cooperation to protect a global commons. The ozone layer protects all life from ultraviolet radiation, which has been shown to cause severe skin damage, skin cancer, eye cataracts, immune-system suppression, decreased productivity by plants, and increased mortality in the larvae of some important fisheries species. In 1974, a paper was published (see the Appendix to Chapter 11) describing the implications of research into the light-induced dissociation of industrial chemicals, the chlorofluorocarbons (CFCs). The investigators, Rowland and Molina, suggested that these chemicals, which were being released by the hundreds of thousands of tons annually into the atmosphere, were sufficiently stable to diffuse to the stratosphere. In the stratosphere, the molecules were broken apart (by the ultraviolet light normally screened out by ozone at lower altitudes), producing individual chlorine atoms, each of which was capable of destroying approximately 10,000 ozone molecules.

As a result of the Rowland and Molina study, Congressional hearings were held in the United States, an interagency Executive branch task force was formed, and industry began a major research effort that included both in-house studies and peer-reviewed, sponsored research. Led by Oregon, several states enacted CFC bans for aerosols. By 1976, Congress had passed legislation banning the use of CFCs in aerosol products with nonessential uses. Canada and several Scandinavian countries instituted similar national bans. The combination of declining consumer acceptance of CFC-containing aerosols (as a result of the widespread publicity) environmental-group pressure, and the ban, produced a rapid worldwide reduction in CFC production (by nearly 25%). UNEP also began a process during the late 1970s that eventually led to the Vienna Convention, which set a framework for considering worldwide agreements to reduce the production of CFCs. That framework was used effectively to produce the Montreal Protocol, which called for industrialized nations to reduce CFC production by 50% by the end of the 1990s and permitted increases in the use of these substances by developing nations to a fixed per-capita level. Most importantly, the agreement built on the lessons (learned in previous negotiations) that permitted the continuous revision of the reductions depending upon new scientific information. The dramatic appearance of the massive ozone deficit over Antarctica each October (and proof that it is caused by CFCs), the finding of similar— but less severe—chemistry in the Arctic stratosphere, and the confirmation of significant ozone depletion at mid-latitudes, have all led to revised agreements to eliminate CFCs and other ozone-depleting chemicals entirely by the year 2000. The process of developing the framework, the Montreal Protocol, and subsequent agreements to eliminate totally the use of ozone-depleting commercial chemicals is notable for the direct participation by NGOs, corporations, and scientists, and for the high degree of public awareness of the issue. (The corporate decision-making role is discussed more fully in Chapter 11.)

As important as the previous examples are, each is, in some sense, only a preliminary test of the evolving international diplomatic process for what will be the most overarching environmental issue of all: human-induced global climate change. Following a more detailed examination of the new mechanisms of international environmental decision making, and how they are perceived by an increasingly large cast of characters, we will return to the problem of global climate change to see how these mechanisms might respond.

7 THE NEW INITIATORS OF INTERNATIONAL ENVIRONMENTAL DECISION MAKING

New agents of international change are emerging from new quarters. An array of nongovernmental organizations, ranging from local public-interest groups to formal international organizations, are forcing issues onto the public agenda. The greater role of the UNEP, lending legitimacy to the activities of these organizations and filling a void left by the failure of national governments to make timely decisions, provides a dynamic force in the international system. The international-media focus on international environmental problems informs the public, which continues its push from below while international organizations act from above.

Finally, the multinational corporation, a key link in the international economic system, but also a perpetrator of many of the environmental assaults and economic development problems, is responding to changing conditions as well. Consumer pressures and liability fears, as well as a heightened sense that their business survival will depend on environmental sensitivities, is driving corporations to environmentally responsible decisions. They are beginning to help fill the void and be part of the solution.

The traditional pattern—one or more nations identify an issue of international significance and a negotiation process is set in motion to address it—has been drastically altered in the case of transboundary environmental problems. More often than not, independent scientists (often at universities) are the first to raise the possibility that human activity is altering the function of some planetary process. In many cases, the problem's existence may be discovered only through technical measurements or model predictions by the scientific community itself. This is certainly the case with stratospheric ozone depletion and global warming. As Richard Benedick (1988), the United States negotiator at the Montreal Protocol, has noted, for the first time in history a multibillion-dollar industry is being shut down for releasing invisible gases (CFCs) that are producing an invisible hole in an invisible ozone layer that permits invisible ultraviolet radiation to reach the Earth's surface. Likewise, nations are being asked—on the basis of experimental measurements and theoretical models that have been developed by the scientific community and about which uncertainty still exists—to take major actions to prevent global climate change that will substantially alter their economics.

Following the identification of a global issue, nation-states are goaded into action by subnational and supernational entities and a host of NGOs that have become increasingly sophisticated at influencing governmental policy. Indeed, while NGOs have a century-long tradition in the United States, especially in wilderness and civil-liberties protection, their appearance in other nations and in international decision making is a phenomenon of the past decade. NGOs have been able to influence international environmental decision making, both directly and indirectly, through their interaction with the political process. They have often played the role of publicist by informing and engaging the public through the media. It is difficult to find an article or television program today in which a prominent environmentalist is not quoted as counterpoint to an official governmental spokesperson.

Second, NGOs have developed their own capabilities for independent analysis with their own staff, scientists, economists, and policy analysts providing alternative interpretations and strategies to those of governments reluctant to alter the status quo. Utilizing their own expertise, NGOs have drawn additional attention to issues like climate change by participating in international conferences organized by official international organizations, such as the United Nations; they have also organized such meetings on their own. NGOs have effectively used the meetings in Villach and Bellagio in 1985 and 1987, and in Toronto in 1988, to legitimize concern for global climate change. The series of NGO-sponsored meetings in New Delhi, Cairo, Nairobi, and Sao Paulo during 1989 and 1990 have been important in shaping developing countries' views. Finally, NGO members increasingly have direct access to legislators and individual officials within their own governments and in the multinational organizations. Indeed, beginning with the Law of the Sea negotiations, NGOs, as well as representatives of interested corporations, were given official observer status. That role was expanded during the Montreal Protocol.

In addition to working to influence the more traditional national and international decision-making process, NGOs have increasingly begun to take direct actions. Perhaps the best known are the much-publicized activities of Greenpeace and its attempts to halt nuclear-weapons testing in the Pacific and to protect whales by directly confronting the military and whalers. The major consequence of this activity has been to make the selected issue into a newsworthy event.

An important example of an NGO taking direct action in the face of governmental unwillingness to do so is the nuclear-testing and environmental-monitoring programs initiated in the Soviet Union by the American-based group, the Natural Resources Defense Council (NRDC). When the United States government refused to agree to an on-site monitoring program of underground testing with the Soviet Union, the NRDC negotiated an agreement, set up its own equipment near the Soviet test site, and convincingly refuted the United States' claim that it was impossible to distinguish low-level tests from earthquakes. This agreement has been expanded so that members of the NRDC are now working with the Soviets on board warships to develop methods for verifying the presence of nuclear warheads. The NRDC is also working with the Soviets to carry out direct monitoring of a variety of environmental problems. The result is an unprecedented openness on the part of the Soviets to on-site inspection of their sovereign territory by outsiders who monitor both military and environmental activities.

A final example of an NGO initiative in response to a failure of governments to act has been the implementation of Thomas Lovejoy's Debt-for-Nature swaps. Through an ingenious scheme, this mechanism allows direct purchase and protection of ecologically important lands in developing countries. Organizations outside the country purchase debt instruments at a substantial discount (because of the unlikelihood that a financially overburdened developing country will be able to repay its creditors). These instruments are then made available to indigenous NGOs, who negotiate the land purchase with their government in exchange for relieving some level of debt. The scheme has been highly success-ful in nations like Costa Rica that are strongly committed to land protection; it is only now being considered by nations like Brazil which has viewed this approach as an imperialistic infringement on its sovereignty.

The traditional role of governments in international negotiations has been to defend their national interest and protect their sovereignty. NGOs and MNCs, on the other hand, have interests not limited by political boundaries. In fact, such boundaries, while important for political jurisdiction, have little relevance to global issues such as climate change or stratospheric ozone depletion. As a consequence, the participation of NGOs and MNCs, even as part of national delegations to international environmental negotiations, tends to "soften" sovereignty by reducing hard-edged, nationalistic positions. NGOs such as the World Resources Institute, Worldwatch, the Woods Hole Research Center, the World Wildlife Fund, the NRDC, the Environmental Defense Fund, and the Beijer Institute (now the Stockholm Institute) have played a disproportionately important role in developing new strategies to address global environmental problems compared to national governments. The latter have been more con-cerned with defending perceived national interests.

Traditionally, MNCs have seen most international environmental-protection proposals as threats to their commercial interests; they have tended to work with governments to protect those interests in the face of proposed international agreements. More recently, though, a small number of MNCs have begun to transform the international environmental decision-making process by their pro-active positions. Pressed by a public whose awareness of global issues has grown as a result of publicity by environmental NGOs and the press, corporations have begun to take action in advance of national and international legislation. In some cases, corporate response has been directly tied to marketplace factors. As mentioned earlier, CFC production in the United States peaked in 1974, the year in which the theory of ozone depletion was first announced. A law was enacted in 1976 to ban the use of CFCs in aerosols, but regulations were not put in place nationally until 1979. Nevertheless, U.S. aerosol sales dropped significantly during the period prior to regulation as many customers shifted to alternative products. The cosmetic industry produced substitutes and mounted an aggressive advertising campaign to promote the use of substitutes. The result was that the bulk of the decline in CFC use occurred before regulation, not afterwards.

More recently, corporations have begun to take even more aggressive, and often unilateral, actions. Following the release of the finding that high chlorine concentrations were strongly associated with the appearance of the Antarctic ozone hole, Dupont Corporation announced in early 1989 that it would go beyond the requirements of a 50% reduction in CFCs and cease production entirely as soon as appropriate alternatives could be developed (see Chapter 11). Other large manufacturers such as Allied-Signal, Pennwalt, and ICI soon followed suit. The decision of the international-protocol process during 1990 to phase out CFCs totally and other ozone-depleting chemicals by the year 2000 was substantially accelerated by the actions of the major producers.

During 1989 and 1990, individual corporate action to address international and global environmental issues reached major proportions. Digital Corporation announced that it had developed a water-based technique for cleaning computer chips and circuit boards, thereby eliminating what until then had been an "essential use" of CFCs. More remarkable was that Digital offered to license the technology free of charge to anyone who wished to use it. This single development has the potential for eliminating 10% of CFC use in the United States within the next 5 years. In 1989 the manufacturers of CFC-blown styrofoam containers for the fast-food industry concluded an agreement with a group of NGOs to replace the ozone-depleting foaming agents with a substance that has only one-twentieth the ozone-depleting potential. Moreover, the manufacturers further agreed to phase out the use of the most damaging CFCs within 6 months and to replace the substitute chemical within 1 year of the time a totally nondepleting alternative became available.

H. J. Heinz announced that it would cease to purchase tuna that had been caught either in driftnets or purse-seign nets (which kill dolphins). They were quickly joined by their two largest competitors. The fast-food restaurant giant, McDonalds Corporation, has announced that it will create a market for recycled materials by committing itself to purchasing $100 million worth of recycled products, recycle as much of its own waste as possible, and become the major educator of the public about environmental matters by providing environmental information at all of its restaurants. During late 1990, McDonalds, which is responsible for one-tenth of U.S. styròfoam use, went further and halted its use of this material altogether. More recently, Conoco announced that the next three oil tankers it purchases would be double-hulled in order to reduce the probability of a major oil spill such as occurred in Alaska in 1989.

What is motivating corporations to anticipate environmental regulation or to exceed existing requirements? The answer is quite clear. Corporations have correctly concluded that a significant fraction of consumers really want to purchase two products from them. The first is the traditional functional item and the second is a clean environment, or at least a clear conscience that the item they have purchased does not contribute significantly to environmental damage. Corporations are responding to a kind of consumer democracy; they are attempting to give a significant plurality of people the cleaner environment they want. In some cases corporations are forced to respond with "greener" alternatives when customers walk away from products, as happened with aerosol personal products. In other instances they are responding to threatened or organized boycotts such as were encountered by Exxon after the massive oil spill at Prince William Sound, or by the tuna industry when consumers realized dolphins were being killed. The Chief Executive Officer of Du Pont, Edgar S. Woolard (1989), stated recently that "Industrial companies will ignore the environment only at their peril. Corporations that think they can drag their heels indefinitely on genuine environmental problems should be advised: society won't tolerate it, and Du Pont and other companies with real sensitivity and environmental commitment will be there to supply your customers after you're gone."

What has clearly changed in recent international environmental decision making is that the nation-state has ceased to be the exclusive initiator and implementor of responses to environmental threats. It has become difficult to develop consensus at the national level because of the ease with which affected interests are able to block effective action. This has been particularly evident in the United States in the much-stalled, but finally passed, Clean Air Act, which must address transboundary air pollution and acid rain with Canada. The problem also surfaces within the European Community as it attempts to respond to air-pollution problems. Within the United States, this difficulty leads to individual states, and even cities, enacting their own more restrictive laws governing CFCs and greenhouse gases. This strategy, which displaces traditional decision making, is influencing the national debate. It is having an even more significant effect on manufacturers who, as demonstrated above, are increasingly opting to alter their product rather than to battle a divergent, and sometimes conflicting, collection of state laws.

International governmental organizations (IGOs) such as UNEP, the World Bank, and other international lending institutions, are also playing an increasingly important role in environmental decision making. Although nominally the creation of nation-states, IGOs have taken on more independent roles. UNEP surprised almost everyone by successfully developing the Montreal Protocol to protect the stratospheric ozone layer. Along with the World Meteorological Organization, it is directing the Intergovernmental Panel on Climate Change (IPCC), which is evaluating the scientific basis of global warming, the likely consequences of human-caused climate change, and possible responses to it.

Running parallel to this official IGO process has been a series of government-sponsored meetings to address global-change issues: the seven major industrialized nations in Paris, a gathering of more than 60 environmental ministers in the Netherlands and another of 100 high-ranking government officials in London, and a conference called by President Bush to examine research options. The 1992 UNEP Conference on Environment and Development in Brazil is increasingly being seen as an opportunity for concluding at least a global climate-change framework convention and perhaps some specific protocols. As indicated earlier, in addition to official meetings, many other conferences initiated by NGOs, but sanctioned by international organizations, have kept pressure on governments to address global-change issues.

International funding agencies, such as the World Bank and the several regional development banks, have come under more pressure to shift funding priorities to less environmentally destructive development projects. National foreign-aid programs are facing similar pressures; Sweden, Norway, Canada, and the Netherlands, in particular, have responded with sustainable development programs. At this point, the influence of the major development banks has been modest. They are still attempting to determine how they can incorporate concerns about such matters as the greenhouse effect, ozone depletion, and species loss into development-funding decisions, and shift their traditional emphasis away from large-scale projects. The potential for assisting developing countries by simultaneously meeting their development needs and protecting the global commons is enormous if these lending institutions can devise effective strategies for doing so.

Thus, the old role of the nation-state as the agent for international decision making has changed. A new, complex set of international environmental and economic groups is setting the policy agenda and forcing decisions and actions to meet emerging environmental challenges. The nation-state appears to be moving into a response mode. International decisions will influence national leaders to carry out local mandates that will work toward some of the solutions. Instead of setting the agenda from within, nations will respond to pressures from without.

8 ADDRESSING GLOBAL CLIMATE CHANGE: A CASE STUDY

Human-induced global climate change, more than any of the issues examined thus far, poses the most direct challenge to the traditional approach to international decision making. Because so much of modern and traditional economic activity produces gases that can contribute to the heat-trapping capacity of the atmosphere, the matter of climate change poses a fundamental challenge to generally accepted views of economic development. Not surprisingly, few of the traditional decision makers and policy influencers are interested in raising the issue. It has been brought to the fore largely by some of the other actors discussed earlier.

There exist in the atmosphere trace gases such as water vapor, carbon dioxide, methane, nitrous oxide, and components of smog that permit sunlight to reach the Earth's surface and warm it, but then act to trap much of the radiant heat that would otherwise escape back into the cold of outer space. This basic mechanism has been understood since the early nineteenth century, when it was first proposed and called the greenhouse effect by the French physicist Fourier (1827). By the end of the nineteenth century, not only had the greenhouse gases been identified, but calculations of their effectiveness in trapping heat had been made as well. Scientists estimate that the Earth would be frozen and uninhabitable, with a temperature some 59°F colder than at present, were these gases missing. Of concern is that humans are raising carbon dioxide levels at a rate in excess of 0.4% per year by burning fossil fuels such as coal, oil, and natural gas; by making cement; and by burning forests and grasslands. Fossil-fuel combustion and extraction also contribute to increases in several of the other greenhouse gases. Agriculture raises the level of both nitrous oxide and methane. The net result is that carbon dioxide is now 25% higher and methane is 250% higher than at any time in the past 160,000 years (Barnola et al., 1987), and all these gases are increasing. In addition, our industrial activities are adding totally new heat-trapping gases, such as CFCs, which, of course, also destroy the ozone layer. While these and other trends suggest that there should be additional heat trapping by the atmosphere, there is no way to prove beyond any doubt that the currently observed global warming is linked to rising concentrations of greenhouse gases. Some policymakers and scientists are demanding a higher level of proof before they implement any climate-protection policies.

Global climate change is an issue that, until very recently, was entirely outside the policy community. Except for a few claims of the link between carbon dioxide and climate, which were largely greeted with skepticism, even the scientific community ignored the problem until the late 1950s. Based on findings about the uptake of carbon dioxide in the ocean, Roger Revell persuaded Charles David Keeling to begin a systematic study of the buildup of that gas in the atmosphere. The resulting 32-year record shows unequivocally that concentrations continue to increase, and that they are influenced by forest communities on land and by regional events in the ocean (Keeling et al., 1989). During the discussions of the stratospheric ozone-depletion issue, Ramanathan noted that CFCs were also greenhouse gases. His work with Ralph Cicerone et al. in the mid-1980s revealed that these, and other trace gases, doubled the heat-trapping capacity of the atmosphere compared to carbon dioxide acting alone (Ramanathan et al., 1985). These findings have inspired additional studies of other greenhouse trace gases in the atmosphere. Despite the efforts of some members of the scientific community and a few political leaders to move the climate-change issue into the policy arena, little interest was shown by the policy community.

Most politicians were unwilling to address, or in some cases acknowledge, the greenhouse problem because of the enormous threat it poses to the status quo. Virtually every aspect of economic activity contributes to the release of greenhouse gases, and, to many politicians, the prevention of their release is a cure worse than the problem. Yet the threat of drastically altered rainfall patterns leading to possible massive droughts, the rapid decline of forests and other ecosystems unable to migrate or adapt to climate change, and the potential coastal damage from rising sea levels, have convinced others that the consequences are too severe to ignore. The largely irreversible nature of these gas additions, many of which have an average lifetime of a century or more, has added to the concern. Should these events take place, enormous inequities would occur. The poorer, less technologically advanced nations, which are living close to the margin now, would suffer the most from climate change to which they had contributed relatively little. There is also a major ethical issue that currently is being debated concerning intergenerational equity (see Chapter 8). People today are enjoying the benefits of greenhouse-gas-producing technologies, yet the most severe consequences of climate change will be felt by those living in the second half of the twenty-first century. The "polluter pays" principle argues that the burden of the cost for responding to the greenhouse-warming problem should lie with those industrial nations that, in the past and the present, have contributed the most to the problem.

Critics of the notion that we should begin addressing the greenhouse problem often cite the uncertainties in our knowledge and the lack of definitive proof that global warming is occurring as a result of intensified atmospheric concentrations of greenhouse gases. They point to the proven adaptive capacities of many plants and animals. They also argue that it would be unethical to divert economic resources from conventional economic development to address the greenhouse problem. This assumes that the current development path is the only one possible, and that all others are more expensive to achieve. The whole question of the international obligation of wealthier nations to assist those less affluent countries in developing either prevention or response strategies has been particularly contentious.

While most national governments largely ignored the greenhouse issue until recently, other actors worked to build the momentum for its sudden appearance to the public and the larger body of policymakers in 1988. First, a number of the scientists who were working on the problem gradually became increasingly alarmed at the implications of their findings. Meetings organized by international organizations such as the World Meterological Organization (WMO) and United Nations Environmental Programme (UNEP) provided an officially sanctioned forum within which these scientists could develop their arguments and present their views (UNEP/WMO, 1987). A number of NGOs and individuals began to see climate change as the ultimate environmental issue, one that incorporated a whole host of other high-priority environmental concerns. As part of a wider "green" political movement in Europe, they began to influence governments there, whereas in the United States, they made certain that the issue received media attention. The NGO-organized conferences in developing countries from 1989 to 1991 helped to give the issue visibility within the developing nations. Corporations tended to be cautionary in their approach, but everyone from the nuclear-power industry to solar-energy specialists touted the advantage of their particular technology to address the greenhouse problem.

Several of the warmest years ever recorded occurred during the 1980s; 1988 produced an unusually hot and dry summer. Major droughts, crop failures, forest fires, and loss of both navigation and hydroelectric capacity on major rivers coincided with a congressional hearing chaired by Senator Wirth of Colorado. One of the witnesses testifying on that especially hot day was Dr. James Hansen of NASA, a prominent climate modeler and student of planetary atmospheres. His testimony that there was a 99% certainty that the warm years being observed were related to the greenhouse effect made front-page news, and propelled the issue from obscurity into the policy debate. Although Hansen, along with others, was careful to point out that it was not possible to correlate the hot summer causally to the greenhouse effect, that nuance was lost on the press and the public. The Toronto Conference, sponsored jointly in 1988 by the Canadian government, the WMO, and UNEP, added a tone of international legitimacy to calls for action. Shortly thereafter, the two international organizations sponsored the IPCC to evaluate the science of climate change, assess the seriousness of the consequences, and recommend policy options. Beginning in January 1989, the three working-groups met, and in October 1990 they presented their findings at the World Climate Conference in Geneva. Their assessment that the problem presented a real threat (although the recommendations were far more equivocal) reinforced calls for a global climate-framework convention similar to the Vienna Convention for CFCs. The majority of nations at Geneva favored the stabilization of carbon dioxide, and several European nations have announced unilateral actions to reduce greenhouse-gas emissions; Germany leads the way with a proposed 25% decrease by the year 2005. The United States, by way of contrast, continues to oppose goal-setting or action, arguing that the evidence is still not strong enough. Many developing nations fear that they will be the victims of climate change, but they still want assurances that the wealthy nations will assist them in their economic development.

While there has been much discussion about global climate change and what might be done about it, the only concrete action that has occurred to date is the unilateral response of Applied Energy Services (AES). This company is an independent power producer that builds relatively small-scale, coal-burning electric power plants and sells the electricity to utilities. The plants exceed all pollution-control requirements as a matter of policy, but CEO Roger Sant has become concerned about coal burning's contribution to the greenhouse effect. Since scrubbing of carbon dioxide from the stack is impractical, Sant proposed planting enough trees to absorb the carbon emissions from each generating facility over its lifetime. An NGO, the World Resources Institute, carried out an analysis and concluded that, to be effective, 52 million trees would need to be planted in the tropics or twice that number in the United States. World Resources Institute announced the project and selected a volunteer organization—CARE Guatemala—from among eight applicants to carry out an elaborate, 10-year, sustainable-development project that would achieve the carbon-sequestering goals for the power plant. The cost of the tree-planting project is being borne by AES with the help of additional leveraged money (Trexler, Faeth, & Kramer, 1989).

An important question to raise about individual corporate action is whether it is effective in responding to global environmental problems. The answer here must be more qualified. The principal advantage of corporate action is that it can occur far more quickly than responses by governments or intergovernmental bodies. This is particularly striking in the case of the CFC manufactures or the development of an alternative to CFCs by Digital. But these companies were, in effect, responding to the imminent tightening of an international agreement. The more complex action taken by AES to offset its carbon-dioxide emissions is noteworthy in that it completely anticipates any requirements or agreements and was initiated by a for-profit corporation in one country, with a PVO in a second country, through the intervention of an NGO. The government of the country in which the project will occur was brought into the process as a willing participant, but only at a later stage. A possible disadvantage of the project itself is that it might be seen not as an interim strategy to slow the rate of buildup of greenhouse gases in the atmosphere, but as a solution that would permit a continued use of fossil fuels into the indefinite future.

Global climate change incorporates all the complex dimensions of international environmental decision making along with a complete cast of participating players. Politicians, highly influenced by the attention that the issue has received in the press, have begun building political careers on it. Nation-states, locked into defending traditional economic interests and worried about a loss of sovereignty, have been relatively late arrivals on the issue, but many have now committed themselves to unilateral action. Eventually they will be called upon to decide whether and how much sovereignty they are willing to relinquish to address it. Meanwhile, IGOs, PVOs, NGOs, and MNCs continue to expand their roles as initiators and implementors of decisions that may gradually mitigate the global greenhouse effect.

EXERCISES

1. What major events or changes in the past 20 years have caused changes in the international decision-making system?

2. Describe the most significant changes that have occurred in the international decision-making system over the past 20 years. Are these changes adequate to address the new global problems? What additional changes do you believe are needed to respond effectively to issues like global climate change?

3. Identify several specific actors in international environmental decision making. Identify the factors that determine their role. What is the basis for their participation? In traditional terms, what is their power base?

4. Predict or outline the mechanism by which global environmental decisions are going to be made in the next decade.

ADDITIONAL READINGS

For further general information on the topic of international environmental decision making, see MacDonald (1988), Moomaw (1990), World Commission on Environment and Development (1988), World Resources Institute (1990), White (1990), Schneider (1989), and Solow and Broadus (1990).

REFERENCES

Barnola, J. M., D. Raynaud, Y. S. Korotkevich, & C. Lorius. 1987. Vostok ice core provides 160,000 year record of atmospheric CO_2. *Nature* 329:408–414.

Benedick, Richard. 1988. Speech made at the International Conference on Global Warming and Climate Change: Perspectives from Developing Countries. New Dehli, India, February 21–23.

Fourier, J. 1827. Mémoire sur les températures du globe terrestre et des espaces planétaires. *Mem. de l'Académie Royal des Sciences de l'Institut de France* 7: 569–604.

Keeling, C. David, R. B. Bacastow, A. F. Carter, S. C. Piper & T. P. Whorf. 1989. A three-dimensional model of atmospheric CO_2. In *Aspects of Climate Variability in the Pacific and the Western Americas,* Geophysical Monograph 55, American Geophysical Union, Appendix A.

MacDonald, Gordon J. 1988. Scientific basis for the greenhouse effect. *Journal of Policy Analysis and Management* 7(3):425–444.

Moomaw, William R. 1990. Scientific and international policy responses to global climate change. *The Fletcher Forum of World Affairs* 14(2):249–261.

Ramanathan, V., R. J. Cicerone, H. B. Singh, & J. T. Kiehl. 1985. Trace gas trends and their potential role in climate change. *Journal of Geophysical Research* 90:5547–5566.

Schneider, Stephen H. 1989. The greenhouse effect: Science and policy. *Science* 243: 771–82.

Solow, Andrew R. & James M. Broadus. 1990. Global warming: Quo vadis. *The Fletcher Forum of World Affairs* 14(2):262–269.

Trexler, Mark C., Paul C. Faeth & John M. Kramer. 1989. *Forestry as a Response to Global Warming: An Analysis of the Guatemala Agroforestry and Carbon Sequestration Project*. Washington, DC: World Resources Institute.

UNEP/WMO. 1987. Priorities for policy management—a new policy agenda. A Report of the Developing Policies for Responding to Climatic Change Policy Issues Workshop, Sponsored by the UNEP and the WMO, Bellagio, Italy.

White, Robert. 1990. The great climate debate. *Scientific American* 263(1):36–43.

Woolard, Edgar S. 1989. Corporate environmentalism. Speech delivered before the U.S. Chamber of Commerce, London, April. Available from the Du Pont Corporation.

World Commission on Environment and Development. 1987. *Our Common Future*. Oxford: Oxford University Press.

World Resources Institute. 1990. *World Resources 1990–91*. A Report in collaboration with UNEP and UNDP. pp. 11–31; 345–56. Oxford: Oxford University Press.

Index

291